Maritime Counterproliferation Operations and the Rule of Law

Maritime Counterproliferation Operations and the Rule of Law

Craig H. Allen

Foreword by Slade Gorton

PSI Reports

PRAEGER SECURITY INTERNATIONAL
Westport, Connecticut · London

Library of Congress Cataloging-in-Publication Data

Allen, Craig H., 1951–
Maritime counterproliferation operations and the rule of law / Craig H. Allen ; foreword by Slade Gorton.
p. cm.
Includes bibliographical references and index.
ISBN 978–0–275–99698–7 (alk. paper)
1. Nuclear nonproliferation. 2. Nuclear arms control. 3. Maritime law. 4. Searches and seizures. 5. Security, International. I. Title.
KZ5675.A45 2007
341.7'35—dc22 2007014261

British Library Cataloguing in Publication Data is available.

Library of Congress Catalog Card Number: 2007014261
ISBN-13: 978–0–275–99698–7
ISBN-10: 0–275–99698–0

First published in 2007

Praeger Security International, 88 Post Road West, Westport, CT 06881
An imprint of Greenwood Publishing Group, Inc.
www.praeger.com

Printed in the United States of America

The paper used in this book complies with the Permanent Paper Standard issued by the National Information Standards Organization (Z39.48–1984).

10 9 8 7 6 5 4 3 2 1

To the Sailors, Coastguardsmen and Marines who make the layered defense on which our security depends a reality.

Contents

Foreword

The members of the National Commission on Terrorist Attacks upon the United States were gravely concerned about the potentially devastating synergy between terrorism and weapons of mass destruction. In our final report we concluded that the "greatest danger of another catastrophic attack in the United States will materialize if the world's most dangerous terrorists acquire the world's most dangerous weapons." We therefore recommended that the coalition strategies we set out for combating Islamist terrorism should be combined with parallel efforts to prevent and counter the proliferation of weapons of mass destruction.

More specifically, the bipartisan Commission unanimously recommended that the United States act to strengthen counterproliferation efforts, support the Cooperative Threat Reduction Program, and expand the Proliferation Security Initiative (PSI). We encouraged the government to expand the PSI by opening it to non-NATO countries, including Russia and China, and by more effectively utilizing the intelligence and planning resources of the NATO alliance. I am pleased to see that those recommendations have been acted on.

The number of states supporting the PSI has grown to more than 70 and now includes the Russian Federation. Even though China has so far declined to join the PSI, it voted in favor of U.N. Security Council measures targeting the proliferation threats posed by North Korea and Iran and by non-state actors, such as the A.Q. Kahn network we identified in our final report. In addition, the PSI Statement of Interdiction Principles and the G-8 Intelligence Sharing Agreement clearly set us on the path toward the kind of intelligence-sharing approach that will replace the myopic need-to-know mentality with a proactive need-to-share outlook.

The fate of multilateral counterproliferation initiatives such as the PSI will be determined in no small measure by perceptions regarding their legitimacy. If the alliance's or coalition's actions are seen as necessary, fair, and consistent with existing international law, the kind of friction that deters other states from joining or cooperating with the coalition or otherwise impedes the coalition's operations can be minimized.

Craig Allen has written a thorough and timely analysis of the legal issues surrounding maritime counterproliferation operations. Focusing on the announced Statement of Interdiction Principles agreed to by all of the states participating in the PSI, he examines each of its planned "specific action" categories to assess their consistency with international law. His analysis demonstrates that the PSI offers a potentially winning combination of capability and legitimacy. Its capability derives from its formula for marshalling resources and authorities from all of the participating states to respond to proliferation threats while the window of opportunity is still open. Its legitimacy finds its source in the participating states' pledge to carry out their activities in accordance with international law.

Professor Allen, a renowned scholar on the law of the sea who now holds the prestigious Charles H. Stockton Chair in International Law at the U.S. Naval War College, has shown us that there is no irreconcilable tension between our capability to effectively mount a multilateral counterproliferation effort and the legitimacy of that effort.

Now, more than five years after the September 11, 2001, attacks on the United States, there are those who argue that some exaggerated the threat posed by transnational terrorism and that as a nation we overreacted. They urge that we return to "normal." Such complacency demonstrates a culpable underestimation of the threat. The Commission sought to convey the extraordinary magnitude of that threat in this way: a nuclear device constructed around a core of plutonium no larger than an orange or a grapefruit and placed in a van like the one Ramzi Yousef parked in the garage of the World Trade Center for his 1993 attack would, when detonated, level Lower Manhattan. We are, of course, all thankful that we have been spared this, or any similar horror, for more than five years, but we cannot let this period of relative domestic calm blind us to our enemies' announced threats. The PSI provides a pragmatic framework for keeping weapons of mass destruction out of the hands of terrorists like Ramzi Yousef. That we can carry out those operations consistently with international law helps ensure the program's legitimacy, thereby enhancing its odds for success.

Professor Allen has carefully laid out an analysis that enables readers to decide for themselves whether we can realistically hope for a program that is both effective and legitimate. He has taken pains to ensure the book is accessible to both lawyers and non-lawyers, and to those who might not be familiar with the intelligence and operational aspects of maritime interdiction. I am confident that his book will be widely read and appreciated by those concerned with this vital component of our national and homeland security strategies.

Slade Gorton
Former United States Senator and
Member, National Commission on
Terrorist Attacks on the United States

Preface

We could have other missile crises in the future—different kinds, no doubt, and under different circumstances. But if we are to be successful then, if we are going to preserve our own national security, we will need friends, we will need supporters, we will need countries that believe and respect us and will follow our leadership.

Robert F. Kennedy, *Thirteen Days: A Memoir of the Cuban Missile Crisis* (1969)

The proliferation challenge has taken an ominous turn in the 45 years since the 1962 "Missiles of October" crisis confronted President John F. Kennedy and Premier Nikita Khrushchev. The Cold War standoff, which was predicated on concepts regarding rational state actors and deterrence, has been replaced by a world of rogue regimes and non-state actors, neither of which conforms to global nonproliferation norms or fits the rational actor profile. As a result, many states have concluded that the arms limitation and nonproliferation regimes for weapons of mass destruction and their delivery systems no longer provide a sufficient basis for national or collective security. The reluctant answer for those states is an enhanced counterproliferation initiative, which seeks to keep the world's most destructive weapons away from the world's most dangerous actors.

What has not changed in the intervening years is what Senator Robert F. Kennedy referred to as the need for supporters who "respect us and will follow our leadership." Today, more than ever, success in containing proliferation requires a creative and adaptive multilateral effort. Most recently, that leadership has taken the form of the Proliferation Security Initiative, launched in 2003 with 11 states, and now numbering well over 70 supporters. Despite its growing support among states and even the

United Nations, the initiative raises questions for some. This book seeks to address the legal questions surrounding maritime counterproliferation operations.

The impetus for this book was my reaction to the sharply contrasting positions taken in testimony provided to the Senate Foreign Relations Committee during its 2003–2004 consideration of the question whether or not the United States should accede to the 1982 U.N. Convention on the Law of the Sea. Some of the convention's opponents argued that acceding to the convention would undermine the Proliferation Security Initiative. The clear implication of their position was that by remaining a non-party to the convention, the United States would enjoy greater freedom of action to interdict weapons of mass destruction at sea. By contrast, those directly involved in maritime counterproliferation operations argued that the initiative's success would in no way be impaired, and might even be enhanced, if the United States joined the vast majority of states—including all of the PSI partner states—by becoming a party to the convention. This book seeks to evaluate the positions taken in that debate. It does so by providing a thorough analysis of the Proliferation Security Initiative's Statement of Interdiction Principles and an assessment of the extent to which the measures contemplated by the PSI interdiction principles conform to existing international law.

I am grateful to Dr. Frank Wiswall for the red-line version of the 2005 Protocol to the SUA Convention reproduced in Appendix E. I would also like to thank the *Naval War College Review* and the *Naval Law Review* for granting permission to republish parts of Chapters 3 and 5. A special thanks to the professional librarians and staff of the Marian Gould Gallagher Law Library of the University of Washington, who guided me through our library's vast collection of international and maritime law resources, and to Jeri Miles, my assistant at the university, whose meticulous attention to detail in proofreading the final manuscript proved to be indispensable. Lastly, I would like to thank Hilary Claggett and the editorial staff at Praeger Security International for their vision in adding a book that brings a rule of law analysis to their collection and for their patience and understanding in working through the numerous legal formatting issues.

Craig H. Allen
December 2006
Newport, Rhode Island

1

Introduction: Deadly Cargoes

The threats posed by weapons of mass destruction (WMD) have menaced the human race for nearly a century. The use of chemical weapons in World War I contributes to its reputation as one of the most gruesome armed conflicts in modern history. The visual images documenting the consequences of President Truman's decision to order atomic bomb attacks on Hiroshima and Nagasaki left an indelible impression that continues to haunt us six decades later. Since their introduction in 1945, nuclear weapons have become the most feared armaments in human history, both because of their planetary-scale destructive potential and the massive and multigenerational injuries caused by their unseen radiation. A sinister new front has now emerged, manned by extremists with an apocalyptic world view. A widely circulated *fatwa* sanctioning the use of weapons of mass destruction against infidels "even if you kill them without exception"[1] and complementary pronouncements by international terrorist organizations have put the world on notice that the threat from nuclear and radiological weapons now comes from radical and ruthless non-state actors as well.

To the demonstrated destructive power of nuclear and chemical weapons we must now add biological and toxin weapons. Experts warn, for example, that a single airplane dispersing anthrax over a large city could wreak devastation on its inhabitants. Any description of the progressive and usually fatal effects of anthrax exposure is sure to send shudders through the reader. Public health officials are now girding for newly

---

[1]The sheik's *fatwa*, issued in the wake of al Qaeda's February 1998 declaration that it is the duty of all Muslims to kill U.S. citizens, military or civilian, and their allies wherever they are found, declares:

> Everyone knows what has been published in the media about al-Qa'ida's intention to strike America with weapons of mass destruction. Perhaps the so-called weapons of mass destruction are calamities of modern times. . . If the Infidels can be repelled from Muslims only by using such weapons, their use is permissible, even if you kill them without exception and destroy their tillage and stock.

Nasir Bin Hamid Al-Fahd, *A Treatise on the Legal Status of Using Weapons of Mass Destruction Against Infidels,* Rabi'I 1424, May 2003, *available at* http://www.carnegieendowment.org/static/npp/fatwa.pdf.

engineered anthrax strains that are immune to presently known countermeasures. The world has awakened to the bioterrorism threat and its long-term implications. The risk led Greece to request that the Czech Republic provide a biological warfare detection battalion to assist Greek security forces during the 2004 Summer Olympics, leading some to conclude that such precautionary measures have become a necessary planning requirement for any event likely to attract large crowds and the media attention so essential to the terrorists' strategy.

For the first half-century of the nuclear era, the Cold War policy of deterrence and its ominous strategy of mutually assured destruction arguably prevented either of the two Cold War alliances from unleashing weapons of mass destruction.[2] But with the end of the Cold War it has become apparent that among the world's nearly 200 states, a few are immune from the stabilizing influence of deterrence. Sometimes referred to as "rogue states" or "rogue regimes,"[3] it is said that these states understand that they could not win a "symmetric" war against a major power's military forces. However, they have learned through experience that they might well be able to improve their strategic bargaining position, or even gain immunity from retaliation for acts of aggression, by inflicting, or threatening to inflict, an unacceptable level of damage through carefully calculated asymmetric strikes, particularly on nonmilitary targets. Proliferators stand ready to help. In early 2004 the world learned that for more than 15 years, Dr. Abdul Qadeer Kahn, the chief architect of Pakistan's nuclear weapons program, and his global network had been selling nuclear weapons technology and equipment on the black market to North Korea, Libya, and Iran,[4] using components obtained or assembled in Europe, Dubai, and Malaysia.[5] The revelation by Dr. Kahn that he was motivated not just by the lure of the astronomical profits, but also by a desire to put nuclear weapons in the hands of Muslims in order to lessen the threat of U.S. hegemony,[6] will lead some to ask who else and what other materials Dr. Kahn supplied, and how likely will those buyers be to use WMD against their perceived enemies.[7] There is good reason to believe that Iran, a country known to have provided

---

[2]*See* John Lewis Gaddis, *The Long Peace: Elements of Stability in the Postwar International System,* 10 INT'L SECURITY 92–142 (1986); JOHN KEEGAN, A HISTORY OF WARFARE 48–49 (1993).

[3]The term "rogue state" entered into common usage when former National Security Adviser Anthony Lake chose the term in a 1994 article. *See* Anthony Lake, *Confronting Backlash States,* 73 FOREIGN AFF. 45 (1994). Secretary of Defense Les Aspin had used the term in a speech given in 1993.

[4]Paul Reynolds, *Pakistan Leaks Prompt Western Resolve,* BBC NEWS.COM, Feb. 5, 2004, *available at* http://news.bbc.co.uk/1/hi/world/south_asia/3461855.stm.

[5]William J. Broad & David E. Sanger, *The Bomb Merchant: Chasing Dr. Kahn's Network,* N.Y. TIMES, Dec. 26, 2004, at A1.

[6]Craig S. Smith, *Roots of Pakistan Atomic Scandal Traced to Europe,* N.Y. TIMES, Feb. 19, 2004. *See also* Congressional Research Service, *Weapons of Mass Destruction: Trade Between North Korea and Pakistan,* CRS Report RL31900 (updated Mar. 11, 2004).

[7]After describing Iran's progress in developing nuclear weapons, one source reports "Saudi Arabia and Egypt would feel threatened by Iran's bomb and would start their own search for nuclear technology." Fareed Zakaria, *Iran: The Next Crisis,* WASH. POST, Aug. 10, 2004, at A19. He goes on to observe that "we don't really know all of the buyers who patronized Pakistani scientist Abdul Qadeer Kahn's nuclear supermarket. It's quite possible Saudi Arabia already has a few elements of such a program." *Ibid.*

sophisticated arms to Hezbollah, is well on its way to developing an indigenous nuclear weapons capability. In 2006, North Korea tested both intermediate-range ballistic missiles and a nuclear device. Some believe that once Pyongyang has successfully proven its technology and stockpiled enough nuclear weapons to meet its own military needs, it might enter the export market, to ameliorate its dire economic condition.[8] Others worry about evidence of direct cooperation between North Korea and Iran, perhaps accelerating Iran's quest for a nuclear weapons capability.

The threat does not stop with irresponsible or failed states. It has become manifest that nation states no longer have a monopoly on the large-scale use of force. Sub-national groups, including terrorist organizations and crime syndicates, have demonstrated all too often their capability and willingness to unleash ruthless attacks on civilian and military targets.[9] When the capability of those malevolent non-state actors[10] is enhanced a thousandfold by the addition of WMD to their arsenal, the prospects for international security are grim.[11] One need not rely on Hollywood for examples. The Aum Shinri Kyo (Aum Supreme Truth) terrorist group released sarin nerve gas in a Tokyo subway in 1995, killing 11 and injuring more than 5,000.[12] In April 2004 Jordanian police disrupted a plot by al Qaeda terrorists who later confessed to making preparations to release a deadly chemical cloud over Amman.[13] On August 3, 2004, British authorities arrested eight men, including at least one senior al Qaeda operative, on charges of conspiring to launch attacks on financial centers in the United States and to use radioactive materials, toxic gases, chemicals and explosives against unspecified targets.[14] One particularly gloomy report claims that al Qaeda is putting together the final pieces for an "American Hiroshima" scenario that will include up to 40 nuclear devices, to be detonated simultaneously by members of sleeper cells deployed across the country.[15]

---

[8]Scott Stossel, *North Korea: The War Game,* ATLANTIC MONTHLY 97, 98 (July/Aug. 2005) (observing that North Korea's "weak economy owes its continued functioning in part to the income from vast smuggling networks, primarily for drugs and counterfeit foreign currencies and sales of missiles").

[9]*Report of the Interagency Commission on Crime and Security in U.S. Seaports* 57 (2000).

[10]As used herein, "non-state" and "sub-national" actors and organizations refer to identifiable entities that do not meet the legal test for statehood. The terms include terrorist organizations and crime syndicates.

[11]*See* Lewis A. Dunn, *Can Al Qaeda Be Deterred from Using Nuclear Weapons?,* Center for the Study of Weapons of Mass Destruction, Jul, 2005, *available at* http://www.ndu.edu/WMDCenter/.

[12]The incident is described in D.W. BRACKETT, HOLY TERROR: ARMAGEDDON IN TOKYO (1996). The group's activities were not limited to making and using sarin nerve gas. Aum members also attempted to manufacture other deadly gasses, such as VX and hydrogen cyanide, and attempted to produce biological toxins.

[13]*Jordan Says Major al Qaeda Plot Disrupted,* CNN.COM NEWS, Apr. 26, 2004, *available at* http://www.cnn.com/2004/WORLD/meast/04/26/jordan.terror/index.html. According to two of the cell members arrested, the attack was to involve 71 chemicals, which would be mixed to produce blister, nerve and choking agents.

[14]Patrick Tyler, *British Charge 8 Tied to Terror Plot with Murder Conspiracy,* N.Y. TIMES, Aug. 17, 2004 (electronic edition). The targets of the murder conspiracy were to include the World Bank and International Monetary Fund in Washington, DC, the Citigroup Tower in New York, the New York Stock Exchange and the Prudential Building in New Jersey.

[15]PAUL L. WILLIAMS, AL QAEDA CONNECTION: INTERNATIONAL TERRORISM, ORGANIZED CRIME, AND THE COMING APOCALYPSE (2005).

There is evidence that terrorist organizations are also exploring bioterrorism options. According to one estimate, a release of 100 kilograms of anthrax spores by a low-flying airplane over a large city like Washington, DC, on a clear, calm night could kill one to three million people.[16] It is known that shortly before the September 11 attacks al Qaeda cell members in the United States were inquiring about obtaining access to crop dusting airplanes. It is also known that anthrax was released on a small scale following the 9/11 attacks. Reports of efforts to develop or deploy "dirty bombs" and "suitcase bombs" are common. The Russian government is reportedly unable to account for some 80 small atomic demolition munitions (suitcase-size bombs), which were manufactured in the USSR during the Cold War,[17] and the governments of Ukraine and several other former Soviet republics are reportedly unable to effectively secure the more than 80 so-called "Antiplague Station" labs containing highly lethal strains of viruses and bacteria, along with research equipment and technical expertise, left over from the Soviet biowarfare research program.[18]

This battle to contain and eventually eliminate WMD is not one mankind can afford to lose. However, controlling access to WMD while also pursuing their eventual abolition and disposal will be a daunting geopolitical challenge. Risk management strategies must include nonproliferation measures and eventual disarmament, layered counterproliferation activities and consequence management. The existing nonproliferation regime will never, by itself, provide an adequate level of security because even a one percent failure rate is unacceptable. Speaking on the subject of nonproliferation, U.N. Under-Secretary-General for Disarmament Affairs Nobuyasu Abe observed that violations by even a few states can have profound effects on international peace and security.[19] If only two of the nearly 200 states in the world refuse to comply with the nonproliferation regime, other states may reasonably conclude the threat is too great. While *necessary* to international peace and security, nonproliferation measures are not *sufficient.* Counterproliferation measures, which may include maritime interdictions, fill some of the gaps in the nonproliferation regime, while simultaneously providing additional deterrents to proliferation. A new cooperative undertaking provides a framework for those interdictions, thereby adding a layer to the homeland security protective blanket.

The urgency of the threat to the United States and its allies from the proliferation of weapons of mass destruction has galvanized a coalition of like-minded states to develop responses proportional to the risk. In 2003, President George W. Bush launched the Proliferation Security Initiative (PSI) to counter the proliferation of

---

[16]U.S. Congress, Office of Technology Assessment, *Proliferation of Weapons of Mass Destruction: Assessing the Risks,* Report No. OTA-ISC-559 (1993), at 53. *See also* COMBATING WEAPONS OF MASS DESTRUCTION: AVOIDING THE ABYSS ch. 2 (Barry R. Schneider & Jim A. Davis, eds. 2006).

[17]Statement by former Russian Federation Security Council Secretary Aleksandr Lebed, Monterey Institute of International Studies, *Are Suitcase Nukes on the Loose? The Story Behind the Controversy,* CNS REPORTS, Nov. 1997, *available at* http://cns.miis.edu/pubs/reports/lebedlg.htm.

[18]Joby Warrick, *Soviet Germ Factories Pose New Threat,* WASH. POST, Aug. 20, 2005, at A1.

[19]United Nations, Statement by Nobuyasu Abe, U.N. Under-Secretary-General for Disarmament Affairs, Sept. 18, 2003, *available at* http://disarmament.un.org:8080/speech/19sept2003.htm.

WMD and prevent them from falling into the hands of rogue regimes and terrorist organizations.[20] In the following year, the United States, together with eight NATO allies[21] and Australia, Japan, and Singapore, participated in a series of PSI planning sessions, experts' meetings, exercises and operations to develop and refine the initiative. Contrary to the predictions of critics and skeptics alike, by the time of the first anniversary meeting in Krakow on May 31, 2004, 62 states had signaled their support for the PSI, the Russian Federation had joined the original group of core participants, a number of states asked to participate in PSI exercises and experts' meetings throughout the world, and six significant flag states had entered into treaties to facilitate PSI boardings of their vessels. By the third anniversary in 2006, the number of supporting states had grown to 77.

As the PSI matures and intersects the antiproliferation resolutions handed down by the U.N. Security Council, maritime boardings under the counterproliferation framework may present a number of practical and legal issues. The first, an important but nonlegal issue, is the safety of the boarding teams, who will be exposed not only to the risks associated with boarding potentially noncompliant vessels at sea (rather than in the comparative safety of a port), but might now also face the risk of exposure to radiological, biological, or chemical materials and explosive devices.[22] The second issue, which is related to the first, concerns the adequacy of boarding platforms, equipment and trained personnel to conduct the necessary detection, surveillance, screening, boarding, searching, and seizure of vessels, cargoes, and crews, while also carrying out the multitudinous other missions already imposed on armed forces and maritime law enforcement agencies. The third issue that could be presented in some cases concerns the scope of a state's authority to board and search foreign vessels in its ports and coastal waters, or to permit other states to conduct boardings in their coastal waters, and the authority of states other than the flag state to intercept, interrogate, board, and seize vessels on the high seas, with or without consent of the flag state or master of the vessel or the authority of a Security Council resolution. The fourth area requiring examination will arise in cases where illicit WMD or missile delivery materials are discovered during a boarding, and concerns the handling and disposition of those materials and the possible actions to be taken against the vessel and the owner and crew found to be involved in transporting WMD. The final issues concern the legal limits on the use of force in carrying out WMD interception operations and state responsibility and liability for operations that violate international

[20] *See* United Nations, 2004 Report of the Secretary-General, Oceans and the Law of the Sea, at 40–41, para. 162, U.N. Doc. A/59/62 (2004).

[21] NATO members participating in the PSI since its inception include France, Germany, Italy, the Netherlands, Poland, Portugal, Spain, and the United Kingdom. Canada and Norway joined several months later.

[22] The danger may be inherent in the WMD materials themselves or posed by devices installed to kill or injure anyone tampering with them. Depending on the location of the vessel at the time of the boarding, an explosion of a chemical, biological, or radiological (CBR) agent release might also threaten the crew of the boarded vessel, who might be unaware of the nature of their cargo, and nearby vessels and coastal communities.

law. Analysis of some of these questions has taken on added urgency in light of the fact that some U.S. critics of the 1982 U.N. Convention on the Law of the Sea (LOS Convention)[23] have urged the U.S. Senate not to give its consent to accession to the treaty, in part because in the critics' opinion, the terms of the treaty would undermine the PSI.[24]

The threat posed by proliferation of WMD and the grave risk that such weapons will find their way into the possession of rogue regimes or terrorists has united much of the world. Chapter 2 begins with an assessment of the threat posed by WMD. Chapter 3 then surveys the global nonproliferation regime. Chapter 4 introduces the evolving Proliferation Security Initiative in the context of multilateral counter-proliferation strategies. Intelligence collection, assessment and distribution are indispensable in any counterproliferation operation. Chapter 5, therefore, highlights the importance of intelligence and examines the effect on uncertainty in WMD risk management decisions, particularly decisions regarding possible at-sea interdictions. Chapter 6 presents a description of the various modalities of counterproliferation operations at sea, to provide context for application of the international law principles outlined in Chapter 7 and application of those legal principles to the issues raised by maritime counterproliferation activities in Chapter 8. State responsibility and liability for unwarranted enforcement actions or other violations of international law is the subject of Chapter 9.

---

[23]U.N. Convention on the Law of the Sea, Dec. 10, 1982, U.N. Doc. A/CONF.62/122 (1982), 1833 U.N.T.S. 3; S. Treaty Doc. 103–39 (1994), *reprinted in* 21 I.L.M. 1261 (1982) [hereinafter "LOS Convention"].

[24]*See, e.g.*, Frank Gaffney Jr. *John Kerry's Treaty*, Nat'l Rev. Online, Feb. 26, 2004 (asserting that "the sorts of at-sea interdiction efforts central to President Bush's new Proliferation Security Initiative (PSI) would be prohibited. Communist China has already taken to citing the treaty to object to PSI maritime interdiction and the boarding of suspect vessels"), *available at* http://www.nationalreview.com/gaffney/gaffney200402261356.asp. For testimony rebutting those claims, see Senate Foreign Relations Committee, Report on the United Nations Convention on the Law of the Sea, S. Exec. Rep. No. 108–10 (Mar. 11, 2004), at 49, 64, 97, 103 & 111–12.

2

Empowered Malefactors: Weapons of Mass Destruction and the Undeterrable or Irrational Enemy

Accurate threat assessments serve as the indispensable building blocks for security and safety planning. Technology empowers without regard to the identity, legitimacy, motive, or intent of the one in possession. Technology can eradicate disease, dramatically increase agricultural production, and harness the power of the atom to light our cities. But technology also can and occasionally does empower the irrational and the malevolent. And there is good reason to believe such actors have every incentive to put that technology to use:

> The time, effort, and expense required to develop a first-class conventional military capability provide tremendous incentives for non-Western states to pursue other ways of countering Western conventional military power. The perceived shortcut is the acquisition of weapons of mass destruction and the means to deliver them.... If Saddam Hussein had delayed his invasion of Kuwait for two or three years until Iraq had nuclear weapons, he very likely would be in possession of Kuwait and quite possibly the Saudi oil fields also.[1]

Before turning to the present and planned measures to halt and eventually reverse the proliferation of WMD, their delivery systems, and associated materials, it is important to understand the nature of the threat this technology poses and to distinguish the present threat environment from the threats that characterized the Cold War era.

---

[1] Samuel P. Huntington, The Clash of Civilizations and the Remaking of World Order 186 (1996).

NATURE OF THE THREAT

In any risk management strategy it is critical to identify the full range of the threat and its source before selecting and prioritizing measures to reduce or eliminate its causes and consequences. Risk management measures seek to reduce the probability that an event will occur and if, despite the prevention efforts, it does occur, the consequences of the realized risk. In evaluating the effectiveness or wisdom of a proliferation security strategy, it is important to understand that the threat the world faces is not global terrorism or weapons of mass destruction. Those are merely the modalities and means that one class of enemy uses to visit death and destruction on those with whom they are "at war." The true risk comes from a handful of states and non-state actors, including seemingly implacable terrorists acting alone or as part of a larger organization, and organized syndicates that engage in a variety of crimes of violence and trafficking.[2]

There is good reason to believe that the post–September 11, 2001, era is one in which the destructive force of WMD is or may soon be available to states and non-state actors, some of whom are prepared to use them without warning, without distinction between military and civilian targets, and without concern for reprisal. The risk posed by WMD must be seen as a function of the existing stockpiles of WMD, the capacity to produce more, the availability of suitable delivery systems or methods, the forces that drive and restrain proliferation, the willingness of those in possession of WMD and appropriate delivery systems to use them, and the vulnerability of potential targets to such attacks. The first three factors determine the capability for use; the last two determine the ability and willingness of the actors to put them to use.[3] Nonproliferation strategies, which target the first set of factors, include a range of measures, from eliminating production of fissionable materials, to safeguarding materials already produced and strictly controlling their transfer.

The threat of a WMD attack is sometimes classified as a low-probability/high-damage risk. But many now believe terrorists will increasingly take the path of least resistance and highest yield, selecting those weapons that are most readily available and consistent with their destructive goals. A lethal synergy is therefore created when those terrorist organizations combine with hostile or greedy states who are willing to provide the terrorists with WMD and delivery systems, or who look the other way when networks operating in the state seek to do so. Most security strategists have concluded that the best response to such a threat is to construct a layered defense that addresses threats from their inception. For example, the threat that a nuclear device hidden in a shipping container coming into the Port of Miami could certainly be addressed in part by a thorough container inspection program in the port of entry, but for many that measure by itself is unsatisfactory. A layered approach reaches back

---

[2]Terrorism may actually facilitate the syndicates' narcotics, weapons and human trafficking operations, providing an incentive for the syndicates to encourage and finance terrorist groups.

[3]For example, throughout the Cold War the USSR had the capability to use nuclear weapons, but not the intent (or was deterred from acting on any such intent). By contrast, al Qaeda has expressed the intent to use WMD, but so far lacks the capability to do so.

at least to the port where the container was loaded for shipment. Counterproliferation strategies might look for intervention opportunities even earlier in the timeline, perhaps intercepting the fissile material essential to make such a device as it is being transferred or shipped from the material supplier to the weapon assembler. Serious students of antiproliferation strategies understand that the challenge cannot be taken lightly. Between 1993 and 2003 the International Atomic Energy Agency (IAEA) recorded 540 confirmed incidents (roughly 50 per year) involving illicit trafficking in nuclear and radioactive materials. An additional 344 incidents were reported to the IAEA, but have not yet been confirmed.[4] No estimate was available for the number of unreported incidents. The majority of the incidents confirmed by the IAEA involved a deliberate attempt to illegally acquire, smuggle, or sell nuclear material or other radioactive materials.

Threats Posed by State Actors

The threat of WMD proliferation and eventual use comes from two sectors, both of which must be addressed by any strategy that aspires to address the problem comprehensively. The first sector of concern is the states and non-state actors who seek to acquire and use WMD. The second group of concern is the proliferators: the states and non-state actors that ignore nonproliferation norms or fail adequately to enforce them, thus permitting such weapons to fall in the hands of rogue actors.

Few would argue that all states in possession of WMD or their delivery systems pose the same risk. The vast majority of states adhere to international law limits on the use of armed force, particularly WMD. A few states that might be tempted to push those limits are effectively deterred from doing so by the threat of sanctions and individual or collective self-defense responses. However, a handful of states operate outside, or at least on the worrisome fringe, of the boundaries of international norms, and appear to be relatively immune from conventional deterrence approaches. Prominent among them are two states that have so far ignored U.N. Security Council resolutions directed at their nuclear programs: North Korea, which is also known to engage in drug trafficking and foreign currency counterfeiting to finance its nuclear ambitions,[5] and Iran. Both states are also believed to have chemical and biological-toxin weapons programs. The threat might migrate to the Western Hemisphere in the near future. In May 2005, Venezuelan President Hugo Chavez announced that the government of his oil-rich state is also interested in developing a nuclear energy program and may soon initiate talks with Iran to obtain the necessary materials and technology.[6] President Chavez had earlier announced that Iran could count on

---

[4]Vladimir A. Orlov, *Illicit Nuclear Trafficking and the New Agency,* IAEA BULLETIN 46/1, at 55 (June 2004).
[5]Larry M. Wortzell, *North Korea's Connection to International Trade in Drugs, Counterfeiting, and Arms,* Testimony before the Senate Governmental Affairs Subcommittee on Financial Management, Budget and International Security, May 20, 2003.
[6]*Venezuela to Seek Nuclear Power with Iran's Help, Chavez Says,* BLOOMBERG NEWS.COM, May 22, 2005 (electronic edition).

Venezuela's support in any confrontation with the United States over Iran's nuclear program.[7]

Rogue regimes may attempt to acquire WMD for any of several reasons, including a desire to intimidate their neighbors or deter outside intervention.[8] Such states are likely to view a credible nuclear weapons capability as insurance against outside intervention while they pursue their regional or global strategic objectives.[9] The U.S. *National Security Strategy* warns that: "Rogue states and terrorists do not seek to attack us using conventional means. They know such attacks would fail. Instead, they rely on acts of terror and, potentially, the use of weapons of mass destruction—weapons that can be easily concealed, delivered covertly, and used without warning."[10] Rogue regimes pose a unique danger and are often insatiable or intractable negotiators. The difficulties are likely to increase if and when such a state comes into possession of deliverable WMD.

Some states pose a less direct, but no less urgent, threat through their unwillingness or inability to meet their international responsibilities to control access to WMD materials or to police terrorist activities. A handful of states go so far as to actively sponsor such activities. Over the years, the U.S. State Department has designated a number of nations as states that sponsor terrorism, including Cuba, Iran, Libya, North Korea, Sudan, and Syria.[11] Iran, for example, has been listed based in part on its support of terrorists at least as far back as the 1983–1984 bombings of the U.S. embassy and Marine barracks in Beirut by Hezbollah terrorists.[12] Designation as a state that sponsors terrorism carries with it a number of consequences. Arms-related exports and sales to the listed states are banned under U.S. law, and exports of dual-use items[13] to those states are strictly controlled. Designated states are not eligible for economic assistance from the United States, are subject to a number of financial restrictions, and will likely find their representatives are banned from travel to the United States. The United States will also vote against any aid measures for such states presented to the International Monetary Fund or the World Bank. Finally, under a 1996 amendment to the Foreign Sovereign Immunities Act, states that sponsor terrorism lose their sovereign immunity to private tort claims in U.S. courts.[14]

---

[7] *Ibid.*

[8] HENRY M. KISSINGER, DOES AMERICA NEED A FOREIGN POLICY? TOWARD A DIPLOMACY FOR THE 21ST CENTURY 159 (rev. 2002 ed.).

[9] *See, e.g.*, Scott Stossel, *North Korea: The War Game,* ATLANTIC MONTHLY (July/Aug. 2005), at 97; James Fallows, *Will Iran be Next?,* ATLANTIC MONTHLY (Dec. 2004) (describing "war games" staged by the magazine's staff involving Iran and North Korea).

[10] White House, *The National Security Strategy of the United States of America* 15 (2002) [hereinafter "2002 NSS"].

[11] *See* U.S. Dep't of State, *Country Reports on Terrorism 2004,* pp. 88–91 (Apr. 2005). *See also* Derek Jinks, *State Responsibility for Sponsorship of Terrorist and Insurgent Groups,* 4 CHI. J. INT'L L. 83 (2003) (arguing that state support of terrorism should be viewed as a breach of a "primary" legal obligation).

[12] HARRY HENDERSON, GLOBAL TERRORISM 47–48 (2001).

[13] Dual-use materials are those that have both legitimate (peaceful) and illegitimate (weapons) application.

[14] *See* 28 U.S.C.A. § 1605(a)(7) (West 2005).

Threats Posed by Non-State Actors and States that Support Them

More than a decade ago, Martin van Creveld concluded that the age of conventional warfare described by the often-cited military strategist Carl von Clausewitz[15] is coming to an end, as states lose their monopoly on the use of force (acting within the international law of armed conflict) to terrorists, guerrillas, warlords, and other non-state actors.[16] The effectiveness of non-state actors is enhanced by the dramatic leaps in technology—much of which is readily available in the public domain—and by rapid and efficient global communication and transportation networks, creative financing and banking arrangements, and progressive legal systems that sometimes compromise security to maintain or enhance privacy and civil liberties. The new threat has prompted most of the international community to reexamine the fundamental architecture of national and global security.

After analyzing responses by 85 nonproliferation and national security experts from around the world, Senator Richard Lugar reported in his June 2005 *Lugar Survey on Proliferation Threats and Responses* that the "average" response concluded that there was a 16.4-percent probability of a nuclear attack somewhere in the world in the next five years.[17] When the timeline was extended to 10 years, the average probability rose to 29 percent. The experts concluded, on average, that should such an attack occur, the likelihood that it would be carried out by terrorists was 79 percent.[18] In *The Four Faces of Nuclear Terrorism,* the authors conclude that terrorists have four "mechanisms by which they can exploit military and civilian nuclear assets around the globe to serve their destructive ends."[19] The four mechanisms, listed in order from least probable to most probable, are:

- The theft and detonation of an intact nuclear weapon.
- The theft or purchase of fissile material leading to the fabrication and detonation of a crude nuclear weapon (an "improvised nuclear device," or IND).
- Attacks against, or sabotage of, nuclear facilities, in particular nuclear power plants, causing the release of large amounts of radioactivity.
- The unauthorized acquisition of radioactive materials contributing to the fabrication and detonation of a radiological dispersion device (RDD)—a "dirty bomb"—or a radiation emission device (RED).

---

[15]CARL VON CLAUSEWITZ, ON WAR (Michael Howard & Peter Paret, transl. & eds., 1976, rev. 1984).

[16]*See* MARTIN VAN CREVELD, THE RISE AND DECLINE OF THE STATE 394–408 (1999). The states' historical monopoly on the legitimate use of physical force was a political concept formalized by the sociologist Max Weber in his 1918 speech *Politik als Beruf* (*Politics as a Vocation*).

[17]Richard G. Lugar, *The Lugar Survey on Proliferation Threats and Responses* (June 2005), at 13, *available at:* http://lugar.senate.gov/reports/NPSurvey.pdf. The average probabilities of other CBRN attacks by terrorists in the next five years were: radiological attack 27.1%, biological attack 19.7% and chemical attack 20.1%. *Ibid.* at 18, 20, 22.

[18]*Ibid.* at 15. The vast majority of the experts believed that the most likely method by which the terrorists would obtain a nuclear weapon was through black market purchase. *Ibid.* at 16

[19]CHARLES D. FERGUSON & WILLIAM C. POTTER, THE FOUR FACES OF NUCLEAR TERRORISM 3 (2004).

The authors go on to point out that any risk analysis must consider not only the probability of the event, but also the magnitude of its consequences. Presumably, any assessment of consequences would consider the vulnerability of potential targets. Although the first listed mechanism—detonation of an intact nuclear weapon—carries the lowest probability (because it is the most difficult to accomplish), it would lead to the gravest consequences.[20] The authors conclude that any risk reduction strategy should strive to reduce the probability of the nuclear terror threats with the highest probability and to mitigate the consequences of those acts that are the most probable.[21]

Well before the September 11 attacks, the United States was aware of the dangers to national and homeland security posed by domestic and international terrorism and organized crime.[22] The threat continues to evolve. For example, there is now evidence that some terrorist groups are studying scuba diving, while others are "learning to drive a ship,"[23] much as the September 11 terrorists learned to fly large commercial jets. One group is experimenting with stealth craft, minisubmarines and antiship mines. A commonly discussed scenario involves the use of a ship with flammable or toxic cargo as a weapon against a strategic port. Recent opposition to liquefied gas ships and reception terminals provides convincing evidence that many are taking the threat seriously.[24] In the post–September 11 era, former Secretary of State Colin Powell warned that the war on terrorism "has become the United States' number one foreign policy priority. It will remain so for as long as necessary, because terrorism—potentially linked to the weapons of mass destruction (WMD)—now represents the greatest threat to American lives."[25]

Noted terrorism analyst Jessica Stern observed that after most of al Qaeda was driven from Afghanistan, the organization became even more decentralized and recruited more young people, including women and converts to Islam, who adopted an even more menacing attitude than their predecessors.[26] Formerly independent terrorist organizations who espouse radically different ideologies are nevertheless cooperating now in training and the use of common facilities,

---

[20] *Ibid.* at 5.

[21] *Ibid.* at 7.

[22] *See* Interagency Commission on Crime and Security in U.S. Seaports, *Report of the Interagency Commission on Crime and Security in U.S. Seaports* (Fall 2000).

[23] *See Perils on the Sea,* THE ECONOMIST, Oct. 2, 2003 (reporting the temporary hijacking of the *Dewi Madrim,* and likening the conduct of the hijackers to the al Qaeda terrorists "going to flying school in Florida").

[24] *See* John J. Fialka & Russell Gold, *Fears of Terrorism Crush Plans for Liquefied Gas Terminals,* WALL ST. J., May 14, 2004.

[25] Colin L. Powell, *A Strategy of Partnerships,* 83 FOREIGN AFF. 22, 22 (2004). *See also* National Commission on Terrorist Attacks Upon the United States, *Final Report of the National Commission on Terrorist Attacks Upon the United States* 16–17 (2004).

[26] Jessica Stern, *The Protean Enemy,* 82 FOREIGN AFF. 27 (2003).

while also reaching out to organized crime syndicates.[27] The network's growth in Southeast Asia, where the maritime domain is characterized by large numbers of small craft and myriad, complex waterways adjacent to well-traveled international straits, is particularly troubling. The terrorists' goal is to continuously expand their numbers and influence and to wear the enemy down through a campaign of attrition made up of a combination of destruction, disruption, and demoralization aimed at the enemies' centers of gravity. WMD technologies fit conveniently into all three methods.

Much of the current debate over the legitimate and/or optimal approach to terrorism and terrorist organizations focuses on the so-called paradigm choice: the choice between treating terrorism as a crime or an act of war. Both paradigms are grounded in the responsibility of the state to provide for the security of its nationals, but they seek to provide that security by alternative paths. The terrorism-as-crime approach to non-state actors calls for steps to identify, prosecute, and punish those who commit acts of terrorism. The fact that the terrorist organization is transnational, potentially even global in its reach and ambition, merely requires an enhanced multilateral and cooperative approach. The terrorism-as-war approach treats global terrorism as a threat that is different in kind than ordinary criminal activities, and therefore calls for steps by specially trained and equipped members of the armed forces to detect, disrupt, and ultimately destroy terrorist organizations—hopefully before they can commit further acts of terrorism.[28] It recognizes that transnational terrorist organizations often operate under the sponsorship of states or are given sanctuary by states that refuse to cooperate in transnational law enforcement efforts. The terrorism-as-war approach employs the nation's military forces and specialized intelligence agencies to safeguard the nation.[29] The war paradigm depends less on deterrence for its success than does a law enforcement approach. Most would agree the optimal strategy will, like current measures to interdict the well-financed and organized transnational criminal syndicates engaged in narcotics trafficking, include elements of both approaches, particularly when the target organization is sponsored or shielded by one or more states, with the balance between the two shifting in response to risk assessment findings.[30] One of the key issues in striking a prudent balance of the two will be the role and potential

---

[27] *Ibid.*

[28] Former U.S. Department of State Legal Adviser Abraham Sofaer advocated more than fifteen years ago that "[t]o deal effectively with state-sponsored terrorism requires treating its proponents not merely as criminals but as a threat to our national security." Abraham D. Sofaer, *Terrorism, The Law, and The National Defense,* Sixth Annual Waldemar A. Solf Lecture in International Law, *reprinted in* 126 Mil. L. Rev. 89 (1989).

[29] Those acts will most likely be carried out subject to limits on the use of armed force, including the U.N. Charter and the international law of armed conflict. The activities may constitute unilateral self-defense, multilateral or collective self-defense or "universal" enforcement obligations, pursuant to U.N. Security Council resolution or established international law. *See* Chapter 8.

[30] National security and homeland security are both part of the larger state security construct. Law enforcement and military means are therefore not mutually exclusive.

efficacy of deterrence as a means of reducing the threat of terrorist attacks to "acceptable" levels.

Deterrence analysts often divide the concept into specific deterrence and general deterrence. Specific deterrence refers to the practice, usually through imposition of sanctions such as imprisonment, of deterring a particular actor from committing future crimes. General deterrence refers to the "public example" effect of such punishment in deterring others from committing crimes. General deterrence presumes a rational actor will refrain from criminal behavior if the potential cost, as discounted by the probability of apprehension, is too high. To the extent a deterrence approach to criminal justice relies on the "choice theory" of criminal behavior,[31] which views the decision to engage in criminal activity as a rational choice based on the perceived consequences of engaging or not engaging in such conduct, the deterrence approach often breaks down with respect to terrorists.[32] Indeed, some terrorist organizations intentionally seek to provoke a state to overreact in its use of force, in the hope that the global media will portray the terrorists as the ultimate victims. Typically, the rational person would weigh consequences by calculating the probability that his criminal act will be detected and he will then be apprehended, prosecuted, and punished. The rational person will also consider approbation by peers and disapprobation by others. However, the terrorist calculus, particularly the homicide-suicide bomber, sometimes leads to an outcome many would label irrational. The terrorist's peer group may treat the killing of innocents not as morally wrong, but rather as righteous. "Homicide-suicide" bombers are accorded martyr status, providing reinforcement and incentives for similar conduct in the future while simultaneously breaking down any societal aversion to conduct involving extreme violence against civilians.

Robust interdiction by maritime interception or law enforcement agencies can be an effective, if not wholly sufficient, deterrent to rational proliferators. Interdiction actions can expose states that are complicit or lax, and may lead to international censure and sanctions. Private entities that supply, finance, transport, or seek to obtain WMD may face criminal prosecution and confiscation of their property for violations of national laws. But deterrence approaches to conduct by nation-states similarly assume that state leaders will behave rationally, and will not risk destruction or massive injuries by initiating a conflict that is sure to trigger a violent response. Where the regime in power does not value the safety of its people, or has reason to believe that the international legal regime will effectively bar other states from interfering with its course of conduct, ordinary deterrence approaches are less likely to be effective.

---

[31] James Q. Wilson & Richard J. Herrnstein, Crime and Human Nature, ch. 2 & 19 (1986).

[32] Rational choice theory assumes a rational decision maker whose preferences about outcomes are consistent, complete and transitive. There is good reason to question whether rational choice theory is an appropriate model for describing or predicting the behavior of extremist groups or so-called rogue regimes.

Role of Arms Producers, Dealers and Transporters

In assessing the risk and formulating an appropriate global, regional, and national response, the role of those who produce, sell, transfer, and ship those arms must be understood. Weapons of all kinds, including WMD, have now become commodities, traded and transported through a network of clandestine state and private participants. Nonproliferation and counterproliferation strategies must acknowledge that arms producers and sellers—both state and private—are players in a competitive and wildly lucrative global market in which the unscrupulous player stands to reap a fortune. Black market arms dealers like the A.Q. Kahn syndicate have a strong incentive to circumvent or ignore the nonproliferation and export control regimes[33] or to exploit any loopholes or gaps in them.[34] Shipowners operating on ever-thinner profit margins, while perhaps declining to become "knowing participants," may nevertheless be willing to turn a blind eye to a dubious bill of lading if the price is high enough.

The sea-based front in proliferation security must also bear in mind that the threat will rarely come from the sale or transport of fully assembled WMD or delivery systems. Interdiction efforts must be tailored to intercept and interdict the components, materials, and even technology required to produce WMD or delivery systems, much of which may have dual-use characteristics. One commentator estimated that 95 percent of the components for WMD are dual-use in nature; that is, they have both legitimate and illegitimate applications.[35] Measures adopted must therefore be able to distinguish legitimate transactions from black market and gray market transfers.[36] They must recognize the dual-use nature of much of the materials and equipment employed in producing WMD. A "research" reactor can provide a steady supply of plutonium, and a pharmaceutical or pesticide plant may be turned into a biological warfare agent production facility by reprogramming computers that control the process.

WEAPONS OF MASS DESTRUCTION

The threat posed by weapons of mass destruction has become one of the most urgent foreign policy and national security issues for the nations and peoples of the world. Traditional international usage defines weapons of mass destruction

---

[33]Methods used include falsification of end-user documentation or cargo manifests, or simply hiding the illicit cargo within the massive volume of legitimate commercial trade. Illicit suppliers and shippers are also likely to collude and use transport routes and transshipment points in states that lack strong controls and enforcement measures. *See* U.S. Dep't of State, *United States Initiatives to Prevent Proliferation,* DOS Pub. No. 11,254 (2005).

[34]The A.Q. Kahn network operating out of Pakistan was reportedly exposed when Libya provided information to U.S. and UK intelligence agencies, which then used that information to pose as a buyer for Kahn's nuclear technologies.

[35]Michael E. Beck, *The Promise and Limits of the PSI,* THE MONITOR 16–17 (2004), at 10.

[36]Admittedly, the terms take on a variety of meanings, depending on the context. *See* Chapter 3.

as nuclear, chemical, and biological weapons capable of enormous destructive power. Some definitions also include radiological weapons. However, international usage typically does not include extremely explosive conventional devices. For example, the bomb used to destroy the federal building in Oklahoma City, which was responsible for massive destruction and falls within the U.S. federal definition for WMD, would not be considered a WMD under common international usage.[37]

The threat posed by WMD is not merely an idiosyncratic concern of the United States. The European Security Strategy lists terrorism and proliferation of WMD as "key threats" to European security.[38] More emphatically, it concludes that proliferation of WMD is potentially *the greatest threat* to European security. It posits that the "most frightening scenario is one in which terrorist groups acquire weapons of mass destruction. In this event, a small group would be able to inflict damage on a scale previously permissible only for States and armies."[39] At their 2003 summit in Evian France, members of the Group of Eight (G-8) declared that the proliferation of weapons of mass destruction and their delivery systems, together with international terrorism, constitute the preeminent threat to international peace and security.[40] The G-8 reaffirmed their commitment at the 2006 summit in St. Petersburg, Russia.[41] More than a decade ago, the president of the U.N. Security Council declared that "The proliferation of all weapons of mass destruction constitutes a threat to international peace and security. The members of the Council commit themselves to working to prevent the spread of technology related to the research for or production of such weapons and to take appropriate action to that end."[42] On April 28, 2004, the full Council unanimously "reaffirmed" that determination in a resolution passed under the Council's authority under Chapter VII of the Charter.[43] The resolution extends the reach of the nonproliferation regime to "non-state actors"—that is, to terrorists and criminal organizations.

---

[37]The bomb used to destroy the federal building in Oklahoma City on April 19, 1995, killing 168, was composed of ammonium nitrate, a fertilizer, and fuel oil (ANFO). In 1997 Timothy McVeigh was convicted of, among other charges, using, and of conspiring to use, a weapon of mass destruction in violation of 18 U.S.C.A. § 2332a. *See* Lois Romano & Tom Kenworthy, *McVeigh Guilty on All 11 Counts,* WASH. POST, June 3, 1997.

[38]European Union, *A Secure Europe in a Better World: The European Security Strategy, done* at Brussels, Dec. 12, 2003, pp. 3–4.

[39]*Ibid.*

[40]*See Nonproliferation of Weapons of Mass Destruction: A G-8 Declaration,* June 1, 2003.

[41]*See* G-8, *Statement on Non-proliferation,* July 16, 2006, *available at* http://www.g8.utoronto.ca/summit/2005gleneagles/nonprolif.pdf.

[42]United Nations Security Council, *Note by the President,* U.N. Doc. S/23500 (Jan. 31, 1992). It should be noted that declarations by the president of the Security Council do not in themselves authorize members to take action.

[43]Warren Hoge, *Ban on Weapons of Doom is Extended to Qaeda-Style Groups,* N.Y. TIMES, Apr. 29, 2004.

The United States has enacted criminal penalties for the use of WMD,[44] for producing and trafficking in WMD, and for a variety of terrorist activities.[45] The USA PATRIOT Improvement and Reauthorization Act of 2005 added a new offense of "transportation of explosive, biological, chemical, or radioactive or nuclear materials.[46] Moreover, shortly after the September 11 attacks, the attorney general of the United States was given authority to request assistance from the Department of Defense during an emergency situation "involving a weapon of mass destruction."[47]

Nuclear and Radiological Weapons

Well before President Eisenhower's epochal "Atoms for Peace" address to the United Nations in 1953,[48] the power of the atom had been harnessed for both peaceful and destructive ends.[49] The terrifying destructive potential of thermonuclear weapons is well known.[50] Peaceful uses for energy production, medicine, and

[44]18 U.S.C.A. § 2332a (West 2005). "Weapon of mass destruction" is defined in 18 U.S.C. §2332a(c)(2) to include any explosive devices defined in 18 U.S.C. § 921; any weapon designed or intended to cause death or serious bodily injury through the release or dissemination, or impact of toxic or poisonous chemicals or their precursors; any weapon involving a biological agent, toxin or vector, as defined in 18 U.S.C. § 178; or any weapon designed to release radiation or radioactivity at a level dangerous to human life. Conspiracy to use WMD or to kill a U.S. national in violation of 18 U.S.C. § 2332, or aiding and abetting such crimes, is also punishable. Conspiracy to kill or injure persons or damage property in a foreign country is prohibited by 18 U.S.C. § 956. WMD may also fall within the definition of a "destructive device" under 26 U.S.C. § 5845.

[45]*See, e.g.,* 18 U.S.C. § 2339 (harboring or concealing terrorists), § 2339A (providing material support to terrorists), § 2339B (providing material support to terrorist organizations), § 2339C (prohibitions against financing of terrorism) and § 2284 (transportation of terrorists). 18 U.S.C. § 2332b extends U.S. jurisdiction over certain transnational terrorism offenses —including threats, attempts and conspiracies—to acts within the U.S. territorial sea (defined by the statue as extending 12 miles seaward) and the "special maritime and territorial jurisdiction" of the United States, as defined in 18 U.S.C. § 7. The statute goes on to define "federal crimes of terrorism" to include, *inter alia,* 18 U.S.C. §§ 175, 175b (prohibitions on production, transfer or possession of biological weapons), 18 U.S.C. § 229 (prohibitions on production, transfer or possession of chemical weapons), 18 U.S.C. § 842(m), (n) (prohibitions on import, export or transport of unmarked plastic explosives), 18 U.S.C. § 1363 (injury to property in the special maritime and territorial jurisdiction), 18 U.S.C. § 2880 (violence against maritime navigation), 18 U.S.C. § 2881 (violence against maritime fixed platforms) and 18 U.S.C. § 2332a (use of weapons of mass destruction).

[46]USA PATRIOT Improvement and Reauthorization Act of 2005, Pub. L. No. 109–177 (Mar. 9, 2006), § 305 (codified at 18 U.S.C. § 2283).

[47]18 U.S.C.A. § 2332e (West 2005). *See also* U.S. Dep't of Defense, *Strategy for Homeland Defense and Civil Support,* June 2005, at 12, 18–19 (describing DoD CBRNE recovery mission and capabilities).

[48]President Dwight D. Eisenhower, *Atoms for Peace,* Address to the U.N. General Assembly, Dec. 8, 1953, *reprinted in* PUBLIC PAPERS OF THE PRESIDENT OF THE UNITED STATES 813 (1960).

[49]Reportedly, the United States and Russia each has over 100 nuclear power plants. The other 900 or so reactors in the world are located in other states.

[50]A simulation of a one-megaton explosion in Detroit projected 250,000 deaths, 500,000 more injured and devastation of all buildings within a 1.7-mile radius. Far more powerful weapons are plentiful in today's arsenals.

industrial processes remain controversial; however, such uses are not banned by international law. In fact, the nonproliferation regime discussed below expressly provides a means for states to acquire technology and materials to develop peaceful applications of nuclear technology and materials. As the demand for oil pushes prices to record levels and environmental concerns drive states to promote non-carbon energy sources, there is every reason to believe that states will increasingly turn to nuclear technologies to meet their energy needs in the coming years, thus accelerating the proliferation of nuclear technology and materials.

Although the possession and potential use of nuclear weapons is among the most contentious of the modern age, so far no rule of conventional or customary international law expressly prohibits their use in armed conflicts.[51] In a controversial and fractured 1996 advisory opinion, a majority of the jurists on the International Court of Justice agreed that the law of armed conflict (LOAC) governs the use of nuclear weapons.[52] The LOAC embodies a clear requirement for combatants to distinguish between military and civilian targets, and limits any use of force by the twin principles of necessity and proportionality. Nuclear weapons, like all WMD, present serious legal questions due to their potential for indiscriminate effects. Despite the near certainty that a nuclear weapon explosion and radiation release would cause collateral damage, the ICJ stopped short of concluding that their use could never be justified under existing international law. The tribunal's opinion, which is advisory and not binding, suggests, for instance, that the use of nuclear weapons might be justified where the very survival of the state is at risk.

The contemporary nuclear proliferation threat might come from an intentional transfer or security breach by a nuclear weapon state that results in a nonnuclear weapon state or non-state actor acquiring a working nuclear weapon. Alternatively, a nonnuclear weapon state or non-state actor might attempt to obtain the necessary technology, component parts and fissile material to construct its own nuclear weapon indigenously. Military delivery methods for strategic and tactical nuclear weapons include ballistic and cruise missile and aerial bombs. But a variety of other delivery methods are available to those lacking access to such delivery options, including smuggling a nuclear device in on one of the several million cargo containers that pass through U.S. seaports and airports and are trucked across the U.S. borders each year. An alternative strategy that must be considered is the "build-on-site" option, in which the user transports the weapon's component parts into the target state, where they are assembled, transported to the target site, and detonated.

---

[51]In any armed conflict, "the right of the Parties to the conflict to choose methods or means of warfare is not unlimited." Protocol Additional to the Geneva Conventions of Aug. 12, 1949, and Relating to the Protection of Victims of International Armed Conflict, art. 35, June 8, 1977, 1125 U.N.T.S. 3 [hereinafter "AP-I"]. The United States has rejected AP-I, primarily out of concern that it would give protected combatant status to terrorists. *See Denied: A Shield for Terrorists,* N.Y TIMES, Feb. 17, 1987, at A22 (recommending that the United States reject the protocol); *Hijacking the Geneva Conventions,* WASH. POST, Feb. 18, 1987, at A18 (same recommendation).

[52]*See* Advisory Opinion, Legality of the Threat or Use of Nuclear Weapons, 1996 I.C.J. REP. 226, para. 56 (July 8).

To produce and deploy a nuclear weapon requires acquisition of weapons-grade fissile materials[53] for the core, fabrication of the nuclear weapon (both the fissile core and the nonnuclear components), weapon testing, and delivery. Constructing a functional nuclear weapon generally requires a highly sophisticated technical capability, though low-yield devices may be constructed by persons with lesser skill levels, using plans that are now in the public domain.[54] Fissile materials, the fundamental ingredients of all nuclear weapons, are the most difficult to produce and most expensive component of a nuclear weapon.[55] The fissile materials typically weaponized are plutonium and highly enriched uranium (HEU).[56] The usual method for obtaining weapons-grade plutonium is through reprocessing spent fuel taken from nuclear reactors. A lump of plutonium no larger than a grapefruit and weighing just 10 pounds would be sufficient to construct a low-yield nuclear weapon, given sufficient technical knowledge and skill.[57] HEU, though more difficult to produce than plutonium,[58] is easier to weaponize into so-called improvised nuclear devices (IND), and arguably presents the greater danger if acquired by terrorist groups.[59] Enriched uranium and plutonium are occasionally transported by sea in multiton shipments over thousands of miles. Although security on the shipments is extremely tight, the materials are exposed to a risk of theft or diversion over a considerable period of time and distance.[60]

Reportedly, North Korea had, by 2004, processed some 8,000 spent fuel rods, which would produce enough plutonium for six atomic devices.[61] At the same time, it was secretly pursuing a uranium-enrichment operation. During a visit by a private group of Americans in early 2004, North Korea reportedly showed off a sample of

---

53"Fissile material" refers to an isotope that readily undergoes fission after absorbing neutrons.

54Government efforts to prevent public dissemination of such technology failed. *See* United States v. Progressive, Inc., 467 F. Supp. 990 (W.D. Wis.) (denying government's motion to enjoin publication of an article by a nuclear physicist explaining how to construct a thermonuclear weapon), *appeal dismissed,* 610 F.2d 819 (7th Cir. 1979).

55*See generally* U.S. Congress, Office of Technology Assessment, *Technologies Underlying Weapons of Mass Destruction,* Report No. OTA-BP-ISC-115 (1993).

56More specifically, plutonium (Pu-239) and concentrated (~90%) highly enriched uranium (U-235). Congressional Research Service, *North Korea's Nuclear Weapons: How Soon an Arsenal?,* CRS Rep. RS21391 (updated Feb. 2, 2004), at 2. The term "nuclear material" under U.S. federal law was extended to include all forms of plutonium. 18 U.S.C.A. § 831(f) (West 2005).

57The international standard is 8 kilograms of Pu per weapon, or 25 kilograms of HEU, but it might be technically possible to make a weapon with half that amount. CRS Rep. RS21391, at 4. Experts opine that nuclear weapons likely to be available to terrorist organizations or governments other than the great military powers would be in the 10- to 100-kiloton range. The bombs exploded over Hiroshima and Nagasaki in 1945 were in the 10- to 20-kiloton range.

58The most common uranium enrichment method uses a centrifuge process. A less common method employs laser technology.

59Graham Allison, *How to Stop Nuclear Terror,* 83 FOREIGN AFF. 64 (2004).

60David E. Sanger, *Japan's Plan to Import Plutonium Arouses Fear that Fuel Could be Hijacked,* N.Y. TIMES, Nov. 25, 1991, at D8 (reporting Japan's plan to import 30–40 tons of reactor-grade plutonium using 4–5 shipments by sea each year).

61*Proliferating Worries,* THE ECONOMIST, Mar. 1, 2004.

plutonium that was soon to be put into a nuclear weapon unless the United States met North Korean demands.[62] By the summer of 2005 it appeared likely that North Korea had 10 or more nuclear devices and the materials to manufacture more.[63] In 2006, North Korea developed and tested intermediate-range missiles and a low-yield (< 1 kiloton) nuclear device.[64] Neither test appeared to be particularly successful. The world has also learned that Iran, which is a party to the NPT,[65] has for years been working on a covert uranium-enriching capability, in violation of the International Atomic Energy Agency's (IAEA) safeguards.[66] In 2004, the IAEA discovered traces of weapons-grade fissile materials in Iran. At the conclusion of their 2004 summit, the G-8 expressed their serious concerns over North Korea's pursuit of nuclear weapons and urged it to "dismantle all of its nuclear weapons-related programs in a complete, verifiable, and irreversible manner."[67] The G-8 also indicated that they are "deeply concerned" about the situation in Iran and warned that they "deplore" Iran's delays, deficiencies in cooperation, and inadequate disclosures" to the IAEA.[68] A June 18, 2004, IAEA resolution reached the same conclusion.[69] Finally, in 2006, the U.N. Security Council took action, but so far Iran has ignored the Council. Nevertheless, in the fall of 2006, Iran admitted to having constructed a second uranium enrichment facility.

Radiological dispersal devices (RDD), one type of which is commonly referred to as a "dirty bomb," are sometimes included in the class of WMD. They are distinguished from nuclear explosive devices by the fact that an RDD relies on a conventional explosive device that is used to disperse radiological materials to cause destruction, damage, or injury.[70] They are capable of inflicting radiation-related

---

[62] *North Korea's Nuclear Taunts: Don't be Panicked,* THE ECONOMIST, Jan. 24, 2004, at 15.

[63] In fact, North Korean officials reportedly told the United States in early in 2003 that it "already had nuclear weapons and might test one, or sell one." *See North Korea: Playing With Plutonium,* THE ECONOMIST, Jan. 24, 2004, at 36.

[64] The North Korean missile inventory includes the medium range *No-Dong* class, capable of striking Japan, and the *Taep'o-Dong I* class, with an estimated range of 1,200 miles.

[65] Despite heavy pressure from Germany, France, and the United Kingdom, on August 10, 2005, Iran broke the IAEA seals at its Isfahan uranium-conversion plant. In November, 2004, Iran had agreed to at least temporarily shut down the process after the IAEA discovered trace amounts of weapons-grade fissile material in the facility. Although converting yellow cake into uranium-hexaflouride gas does not in itself violate the NPT, once the uranium has been converted it can then be enriched to weapons grade. Peter Grier, *Is a Bigger 'Nuke Club' Inevitable?,* CHRISTIAN SCI. MON., Aug. 11, 2005, available at http://www.csmonitor.com/2005/0811/p01s02-usfp.htm.

[66] *Proliferating Worries, supra.* Of course, the A.Q. Kahn network has demonstrated that an oil-rich state need not rely on indigenous sources for nuclear materials or technology.

[67] *G-8 Action Plan on Nonproliferation,* para. 4, June 9, 2004.

[68] *Ibid.*

[69] *See* Implementation of the NPT Safeguards Agreement in the Islamic Republic of Iran, Resolution Adopted by the IAEA Board of Governors on June 18, 2004, *available at* http://www.iaea.org/Publications/Documents/Board/2004/gov2004–49.pdf.

[70] Congressional Research Service, *Radiological Dispersal Devices: Select Issues in Consequence Management,* CRS Rep. RS21766, at 2; Congressional Research Service, *Terrorist "Dirty Bombs": A Brief Primer,* CRS Rep. RS21528.

illness and possibly death in the long term, while also causing widespread disruption and fear, possibly with long-term economic disruption in the affected area (causing some to label them a "weapon of mass disruption").[71] Unlike the more destructive nuclear weapons, which rely on a chain reaction, RDD do not require fissile material.[72] In fact, numerous medical and industrial processes employ radioactive materials that could be used in constructing a crude, low-level RDD. Some global security experts predict the next al Qaeda attack on a western city will involve an RDD.[73] The potential disruption by even the threat of an RDD incident was demonstrated through a Department of Homeland Security simulation in which two devices containing radioactive cesium wrapped around 30 pounds of C-4 explosive were "discovered" (as a part of the drill) in shipping containers; one in a California port and another in a Georgia port. Intelligence led homeland security officials participating in the exercise to suspect the two incidents were part of a larger coordinated attack involving other containers. In response, the department simulated the closure of all of the nation's seaports. The economic losses that would have been caused by such port closures lasting up to 45 days were estimated by the exercise participants at $66 billion.[74]

Chemical Weapons

Chemical weapons (CW) rely on the toxic characteristics of chemical compounds rather than their explosive properties to produce physical or psychological injury. CW agents include asphyxiating agents, such as chlorine; nerve agents, such as sarin (GB), soman (GD), tabun (GA), and VX; blister agents, such as mustard gas; and nonlethal agents designed to harass or incapacitate. CW agents are relatively easy to manufacture with basic equipment, trained personnel, and precursor materials (which often have dual uses). CW agents can be deployed by commercial handheld agricultural sprayers, crop dusters and spray tanks on ships or aircraft, and in munitions such as gravity bombs, artillery projectiles, and missile (cruise or ballistic) warheads. They can also be introduced directly into food and water supplies.

Chemical warfare agents can be extremely lethal and are capable of inflicting casualties in the tens of thousands. First used by the Axis powers in World War I, CW aerosols and vapors were eventually used by the Allies too. The use of CW agents was later banned by the 1925 Geneva Gas and Bacteriological Warfare Protocol, though many of the states that acceded to the protocol reserved a right to retaliate

---

[71] One scenario positing a device comprised of 220 kilograms of explosives and 50 kilograms of spent fuel rods projected a lethal dose of radiation for a one-kilometer range. *See* James L. Ford, *Radioactive Dispersal Devices,* 136 Strategic Forum 3 (1998).

[72] An RDD might use radioactive isotopes of cesium, iridium, cobalt, or strontium. Alternatively, it might incorporate spent reactor fuel rods or enriched uranium.

[73] *See Al Qaeda, Amorphous But Alive,* THE ECONOMIST, June 5, 2004.

[74] *See Port Shutdown for Terrorist Incidents Could Cost Billions, Drill Shows,* CQ HOMELAND SECURITY, Dec. 5, 2002.

against another state's first use of CW.[75] New prohibitions were added by the 1993 Chemical Weapons Convention. Notwithstanding the 1925 ban, between the two world wars, Italy used CW agents in Ethiopia, and Japan employed them in Manchuria and China. There are no reports of either side intentionally using CW agents in World War II, despite the fact that both sides had considerable stockpiles. The most notorious recent use of CW agents was by the Saddam Hussein regime, first against Iran in the 1982–1987 Iran-Iraq war, and later against its own Kurdish nationals. According to Iranian sources, Iraq's use of CW agents accounted for some 50,000 Iranian casualties, including roughly 5,000 deaths.[76] In 1988, Saddam Hussein ordered a gas attack on indigenous Kurds in Halabja, killing more than 5,000 with aerial and artillery bombardments of sarin, tabun, and VX. The use of asphyxiating, poisonous, or other gases is now a "war crime" under the Rome Statute establishing the International Criminal Court.[77]

Biological and Toxin Weapons

Throughout history, infectious diseases from natural causes or as a result of injuries have had a serious impact on military personnel. However, the prospect of an intentional exposure of military and civilian populations to "weaponized" infectious diseases is a relatively recent development.[78] The use of biological and toxin warfare (BTW) agents is banned under the law of armed conflict, and their development and stockpiling are controlled by a nonproliferation regime.[79]

Biological and toxin warfare agents include disease-causing microorganisms (pathogens) and toxins produced by living organisms. The common pathogen forms are disease-causing bacteria, viruses, rickettsiae, chlamydia, and fungi. "Biological toxin" agents are poisonous, nonliving chemical substances naturally produced by living organisms. BTW agents of concern include anthrax, plague, cholera, E. coli, Ebola, smallpox, ricin, tularemia, viral hemorrhagic fevers, and botulinum toxin. The range of BTW agents demonstrates that it will be difficult in many cases to distinguish a naturally occurring epidemic from a BTW attack. BTW agents are generally easier to produce than nuclear or chemical warfare materials and they can be prepared in smaller and less expensive facilities. They can be produced with rudimentary technical skills, easily acquired dual-use equipment, and a seed stock of pathogens, many of which are stored in culture banks. Modern laboratory and

---

[75]Protocol for the Prohibition of the Use in War of Asphyxiating, Poisonous, or Other Gases, and of Bacteriological Methods of Warfare, June 17, 1925, 26 U.S.T. 571, T.I.A.S. 8061, 94 L.N.T.S. 64 [hereinafter "1925 Geneva Gas and Bacteriological Warfare Protocol"].

[76]Mike Eisenstadt, *The Sword of the Arabs: Iraq's Strategic Weapons* 6 (Wash. Inst. Policy Papers No. 21).

[77]*See* Rome Statute of the International Criminal Court, July 17, 1998, art. 8(2)(b)(xviii), 2187 U.N.T.S. 3, *reprinted in* 37 I.L.M. 999 (1998).

[78]History does record incidents of small-scale use of "biological warfare" in antiquity; however, large-scale use did not occur until World War II, with the release of plague bacilli and so-called "yellow rain" (trichothecene mycotoxins).

[79]*See* Chapter 3.

biotechnology techniques have vastly changed the potential quantitative and qualitative threat from biological weapons. Some speculate that biotechnology and genetic modification innovations, much of which is in the public domain, now make it possible to produce "supergerms"—particularly virulent strains of pathogens that are robust, difficult or even impossible to detect, and immune to countermeasures. Some warn that application of nanotechnology to BW weapons development could significantly increase the effectiveness of such weapons and make them virtually impossible to detect with current inspection practices.[80]

BTW agents can be spread by a variety of pathways and means, including human vectors who might not display any symptoms of infection at the time of exposure or transmission. Releases can be targeted directly against humans and livestock or introduced into food and water supplies. BTW agents can be aerosolized and then spread through the air and inhaled. Some are absorbed through the skin. They are capable of inflicting widespread infection that can lead to illness, incapacity, and death when released in large quantities.

The use of biological weapons by terrorists (bioterrorism) is a relatively recent development, but one that raises grave concern.[81] A series of anthrax[82] releases, shortly after the September 11, 2001, attacks infected 25 people, five of them fatally. The attacks targeted media centers, Congress, and post offices, demonstrating the potential for a BTW attack to inflict illness, death, and massive economic disruption.[83] Although the death toll was minor compared to the September 11 airliner attacks, the releases resulted in evacuation of a number of Washington-area federal buildings, including the Capitol and Supreme Court, suspension of congressional sessions, disruption of mail services, and a widespread fear of that the mail system had become a vector for contamination, causing many to refuse to open incoming mail. In February 2004, the deadly biotoxin ricin was found in an envelope delivered to the mailroom of the U.S. Senate majority leader.[84] One year earlier, London police arrested six Algerians after being tipped off that they were producing ricin in a north London apartment.[85]

Bioterrorism exercises like *Dark Winter,* held just before the 2001 attacks, and *Atlantic Storm,* conducted on January 14, 2005, demonstrate why many homeland defense and security planners are so worried about the BTW potential. The exercises revealed that the threat from BTW releases includes both the immediate, acute effects, as well massive casualties well beyond the initial release site. Moreover, the panic over

---

[80]Juan Pablo Pardo-Guerra, *Nanotechnology and the International Regime on Chemical and Biological Weapons,* 2 NANOTECHNOLOGY, LAW & BUS. No. 1 (2005).

[81]Laurie Garrett, *The Nightmare of Bioterrorism,* 80 FOREIGN AFF. 76 (2001).

[82]One-millionth of a gram of anthrax is fatal within five to seven days after exposure.

[83]LEONARD A. COLE, THE ANTHRAX LETTERS: A MEDICAL DETECTIVE STORY (2003). The anthrax episode caused an estimated $60 billion in economic losses to the United States. Anthrax is caused by the bacterium bacillus anthracis. Eleven of the victims contracted the skin form of the disease. The other 11 contracted it in the respiratory system.

[84]*Early Tests Show Deadly Ricin in Senate Mailroom,* CNN.COM NEWS, Feb. 2, 2004.

[85]*See Terror Police Find Deadly Poison,* BBC NEWS.COM, Jan. 7, 2003.

infected carriers or other vectors would likely trigger a shutdown of international travel for a month or more.[86] Indeed, some predict that a large-scale BTW attack could shut down much of the world's economic activity, triggering a global recession.

WMD DELIVERY SYSTEMS

The threat posed by WMD is substantially increased when such weapons are mounted in a delivery vehicle capable of carrying its deadly payload over long distances, at high speed with relative accuracy. Nonproliferation concerns and countermeasures must therefore extend to missiles.[87] It should be noted, however, that it does not take an intercontinental ballistic missile to reach the United States, its forward deployed forces, or its allies. Any of the weapons described above could be transported to their target site by vehicle, vessel, conventional aircraft, or in one of the several million shipping containers passing through the United States each year. Shorter-range "cruise" missiles and unmanned aerial vehicles (UAV), some of which can be fitted with missiles (often referred to as unmanned combat aerial vehicles, or UCAVs), present a growing risk. Vulnerability assessments demonstrate that a cruise missile fired from a coastal freighter, or even a large fishing vessel, from a few hundred miles off the U.S. coast could reach any one of the nation's densely populated coastal cities.[88] Reports that Iran supplied Hezbollah, a designated terrorist organization, with UAVs and Noor C-802 cruise missiles that were later used against Israel demonstrate that access to this lethal technology is spinning out of control.[89]

Concerns over missile proliferation grew exponentially when North Korea test-fired a medium-range ballistic missile over Japan in 1998.[90] In response to international protests, North Korea defiantly asserted it has every right to develop a ballistic missile capability.[91] Indeed, as the discussion in Chapter 3 demonstrates, at the time no binding rule of international law stood in its way. The threat posed by North

---

[86]*See* Byron Spice, *Nations Vulnerable to Bioterror,* PITTSBURGH POST-GAZETTE, Jan. 16, 2005 (electronic edition).

[87]In the same spirit, the United States and other members of the G-8 and APEC are seeking to address the threat posed by terrorist use of Man Portable Air Defense Systems (MANPADS) through bilateral and multilateral initiatives to destroy excess stocks, enhance physical security and impose export controls. Both military and civilian aircraft are vulnerable to attacks by MANPADS, most of which rely on infrared targeting. *See* Tom Zeller, *Cheap and Lethal; It Fits in a Golf Bag,* N.Y. TIMES, Oct. 26, 2003, at A14. Concerns were raised following an attempted attack on an Israeli passenger jet taking off from Mombassa, Kenya with 271 passengers on board, using two shoulder-fired SA-7 missiles taken from the same batch used against U.S. military jets in Saudi Arabia. *See also* Intelligence Reform and Terrorism Prevention Act of 2004, Pub. L. No. 108–458, § 4026 (2004) (U.S. policy against proliferation of MANPADS).

[88]James M. Loy & Robert G. Ross, *Global Trade: America's Achilles' Heel,* 7 DEFENSE HORIZONS (Feb. 2002).

[89]*Hezbollah Drone Humiliates Israel,* IRAN DAILY, Nov. 8, 2004, http://www.iran-daily.com/1383/2135/html/index.htm; U.S. Dep't of State,*Country Reports on Terrorism, 2004,* April 2005 (Terrorist Group Profile on Hezbollah).

[90]Statement by Nobuyasu Abe, U.N. Under-Secretary-General for Disarmament Affairs, Dec. 3, 2003, *available at* http://disarmament.un.org:8080/speech/03dec2003.htm.

[91]*N. Korea Says Weapons Are Its Right,* CBS NEWS.COM, Mar. 3, 2003.

Korea's (and China's) missile program prompted the United States in the 1990s to re-examine the need for a missile defense system, to guard against attacks on the United States and its allies. In the aftermath of the Cold War, concerns about the ballistic missile threat of Russia and other former Soviet states had diminished if not disappeared. However, concern about the missile capabilities of states ruled by rogue regimes, such as North Korea and Iran, led U.S. Secretary of Defense William S. Cohen to announce on January 20, 1999, a six-year, $6.6 billion plan for the development of a land-based National Missile Defense (NMD) system.[92] In May 1999, Congress voted overwhelmingly in favor of going forward with an antimissile defense system.[93] The National Missile Defense Act of 1999, which was signed into law by President Clinton on July 22, 1999, provides:

> It is the policy of the United States to deploy as soon as is technologically possible an effective National Missile Defense system capable of defending the territory of the United States against limited ballistic missile attack (whether accidental, unauthorized, or deliberate) with funding subject to the annual authorization of appropriations and the annual appropriation of funds for National Missile Defense.

When President Bush came into office in 2001, he supported such a missile defense program. U.S. resolve hardened following the attacks of September 11, 2001, and the buildup in Chinese and North Korean missile programs.[94] By the time of the July 4, 2006, missile tests by North Korea, the United States had augmented its national ballistic missile defense system with a theater ballistic missile defense for the Western Pacific.

---

[92]Because deployment of such a system might be construed as a violation of the ABM Treaty, Secretary Cohen explained: "While our NMD program is being conducted consistent with the terms of the ABM Treaty to date, our deployment might require modifications to the treaty and the Administration is working to determine the nature and scope of these modifications... The ABM Treaty also provides, of course, for right of withdrawal with six months notice if a party concludes it's in its supreme national interests." R.W. Apple Jr., *Moscow and West Agree on Kosovo; Plan Given to U.N.,* N.Y. TIMES, June 9, 1999, at A1. On December 13, 2001, President Bush announced the United States had given formal notice to Russia, in accordance with the provisions of the ABM Treaty, that the United States was withdrawing from the treaty. On December 17, 2003, the Japanese Diet voted to move forward to develop a ballistic missile defense with the United States.

[93]National Missile Defense Act of 1999, Pub. L. No. 106–38, 113 Stat. 205.

[94]*See* Bill Gertz, *China Advances Missile Program,* WASH. TIMES, June 22, 2005 (electronic edition).

3

Grave Risks; Imperfect Protection: The WMD Nonproliferation Regime

Responses to the dangers posed by WMD, and more specifically the dangers they pose in the hands of rogue regimes and terrorist organizations, include the international arms control and nonproliferation regime, safeguards for materials while in storage or transit, domestic and multilateral export controls, a family of treaties on terrorism, U.N. Security Council resolutions, and a new, but not yet legally effective, protocol to the Convention for the Suppression of Unlawful Acts Against the Safety of Maritime Navigation.[1] The signature characteristic of the regime is its multilateral, but not always universal, approach.

The international arms control and nonproliferation security regime comprises four components. First, through arms control agreements it seeks to limit the kind and number of available WMD and to deter states from using them.[2] Second, it imposes limits on weapon testing.[3] Third, it prohibits the emplacement of nuclear

---

[1]Protocol of Amendment to the 1988 Convention for the Suppression of Unlawful Actsagainst the Safety of Maritime Navigation, Nov. 1, 2005, IMO Doc. LEG/CONF.15/21 [hereinafter "2005 SUA Protocol"]. The United States signed the 2005 Protocol on Feb. 17, 2006.

[2]Such treaties do not bind non-parties on their own force, or non-state actors. *See* Vienna Convention on the Law of Treaties, May 23, 1969, art. 34, U.N. Doc. A/CONF.39/39/27, 1155 U.N.T.S. 331; RESTATEMENT (THIRD) FOREIGN RELATIONS LAW OF THE UNITED STATES, Part III, Introductory Note (1987) [hereinafter "RESTATEMENT"].

[3]Even though the physical principles for constructing nuclear weapons are generally known, producing a reliable and effective nuclear weapon without testing poses significant challenges. Test ban treaties seek to eventually eliminate all nuclear weapons testing. The United States is party to the so-called Limited Test Ban Treaty of 1963. Treaty Banning Nuclear Weapon Tests in the Atmosphere, in Outer Space, and Under Water, Aug. 5, 1963, 14 U.S.T. 1313, T.I.A.S. 5433, 480 U.N.T.S. 43. In 1999, the U.S. Senate declined, 51:48, to give its advice and consent to ratification of the Comprehensive Test Ban Treaty. *See* Congressional Research Service, *Nuclear Weapons: Comprehensive Test Ban Treaty,* CRS Issue Brief IB92099, at 3. Ratification would have required an affirmative vote by two-thirds of those senators present.

weapons in the global commons, such as outer space and the seabed.[4] Finally, it seeks to halt and even reverse the proliferation of WMD and their delivery systems, with the long-term goal of a complete, irreversible, and verifiable disarmament of all weapons of mass destruction.

Within the United States, national and homeland security depend on both nonproliferation and counterproliferation measures. The distinction between nonproliferation and counterproliferation is far from clear, and often differs depending on the context, the identity and motivation of the person using the terms, and the times.[5] Proliferation looks at both the kind and quantity of weapons, and materials for producing weapons, as well as their distribution. Nonproliferation generally refers to the international and national regimes that seek to halt and eventually reverse the proliferation of WMD and their delivery systems.[6] The nonproliferation regime was recently expanded to include measures to identify and secure nuclear materials and other weapons of mass destruction, to prevent their use by terrorist organizations and criminal syndicates. Nonproliferation supplier and export control measures are pursued through arms control and other multilateral agreements,[7] threat reduction assistance programs, and domestic export controls.[8] Multilateral export control regimes by so-called "supplier states," while vital, only restrict exports of WMD materials from member states, and only to the extent those members choose to implement them. They do not restrict states that decline to join the export control regime. Nonproliferation and arms control regimes have long struggled with the problems posed by the dual-use of WMD technologies. The dual-use character of many

[4]*See* Treaty on the Prohibition of the Emplacement of Nuclear and Other Weapons of Mass Destruction on the Seabed and the Ocean Floor and in the Subsoil Thereof Feb. 11, 1971, 23 U.S.T. 701, T.I.A.S. 7337; U.N. Convention on the Law of the Sea, Dec. 10, 1982, art. 141 (reserving the international seabed for peaceful purposes); Treaty on Principles Governing the Activities of States in the Exploration and Use of Outer Space, Including the Moon and Other Celestial Bodies, Jan. 27, 1967, art. IV, 18 U.S.T. 2410, T.I.A.S. 6347.

[5]For one expert's distinction between nonproliferation and counterproliferation see Daniel H. Joyner, *The Proliferation Security Initiative: Nonproliferation, Counter-proliferation, and International Law,* 30 Yale J. Int'l L. 507, 519–20 (2005).

[6]*See* Nuclear Non-Proliferation Act of 1978, Pub. L. No. 95–242, 92 Stat. 120, *codified as amended at* 22 U.S.C.A. § 3201 (West 2005) (congressional declaration of non-proliferation policy). *See also* Exec. Order No. 12,058 (1978) (performance of duties relating to nuclear non-proliferation).

[7]Multilateral export control regimes by supplier states include the Nuclear Suppliers' Group, the Australia Group, and the Missile Technology Control Regime. As discussed more fully below, each is primarily a political commitment by responsible supplier states to restrict and regulate exports of specified WMD materials and delivery systems and does little to address the actual transport of such materials.

[8]Since 1991, the Nunn-Lugar Cooperative Threat Reduction (CTR) program has allocated over $400 million/year to deactivate nuclear weapons in the former Soviet Union. Those funds were used to deactivate 6,760 nuclear warheads and destroy 587 ballistic missiles, 483 ballistic missile silos, 150 bombers, 436 submarine missile launchers, and 28 strategic missile submarines. *See Nunn-Lugar Report 2005, available at* http://lugar.senate.gov/reports/Nunn-Lugar_Report_2005.pdf. *See also* [Senator] *Lugar Welcomes President's Support of Nunn-Lugar Expansion; Praises Nonproliferation Initiative,* Feb. 11, 2004, *available at* http://lugar.senate.gov/pressapp/record.cfm?id=217970 [hereinafter "Lugar Praises PSI"].

WMD and related equipment and precursors significantly complicates compliance verification and monitoring.[9] Moreover, they present complex "gray market" issues.[10] Finally, the national implementing measures for export control regimes often limit their application to sellers, exporters, and buyers, and typically exclude from their coverage transporters.[11] As a result, those aboard a vessel engaged in transporting illicit WMD or related materials might not be in violation of any laws, even though the actual export of those materials violated the source nation's export control regime.[12]

In contrast to nonproliferation, counterproliferation generally refers to proactive, focused measures to prevent the movement of WMD materials, technology, and expertise from states that fail to conform to nonproliferation norms to hostile states and terrorist organizations.[13] Counterproliferation measures include diplomacy, sanctions (granting/withholding of aid, financing, eligibility for government/military contracts, and trade)[14] and, in selected cases, interdiction. Interdiction actions that keep WMD out of the hands of rogue regimes and terrorist groups are now a key component in some counterproliferation strategies. Thus, counterproliferation strategies have expanded to include measures to be used in a preemptive sense to deny, disrupt, delay, or destroy proliferation capabilities. Such strategies may include law enforcement measures against those who traffic in or transport WMD and, more recently, who facilitate or finance the transactions.[15] As with nonproliferation measures, the dual-use character of many WMD and their related equipment and materials seriously complicates counterproliferation efforts.

---

[9]For example, a DNA synthesizer has any number of legitimate biotechnology applications, but might also be used to produce BTW agents.

[10]As used herein, "black market" goods are ones that are illegal to sell to any buyer. "Gray market" goods are ones that may be legally sold to some buyers, but are in fact—often through deceptive or fraudulent means—sold to an unqualified buyer. Dual-use materials are prime candidates for the gray market. When sold to a legitimate user who puts them to a legitimate, non-WMD use, they violate no laws. When sold to a user who intends to incorporate them into a WMD, however, the transaction may be illegal, depending on the relevant national laws. Gray market sellers are characterized by their willingness to ask no questions if the price is right.

[11]Some United States criminal statutes extend to persons who acquire, transfer, receive, possess, import, export, or use, or possess and threaten to use certain devices. *See, e.g.,* 18 U.S.C.A. § 2332g (West 2005). However, such laws are often limited in their application by the location or nationality of the actor.

[12]Although the 2005 SUA Protocol may extend criminal liability to certain transporters, that Protocol is not yet in force. In addition, it will require proof of knowledge or intent, which will make prosecution difficult. This is discussed in Chapter 7.

[13]*See generally* Omnibus Diplomatic Security and Antiterrorism Act of 1986, Pub. L. No. 99–399, 100 Stat. 853, *codified* at 22 U.S.C.A. § 3244 (West 2005) (actions to combat international nuclear terrorism).

[14]*See* Congressional Research Service, *Nuclear, Biological, Chemical and Missile Proliferation Sanctions: Selected Current Law,* CRS Rep. RL31502 (updated Oct. 21, 2005).

[15]On June 28, 2005, under authority of the International Emergency Economic Powers Act, 50 U.S.C. §§ 1701–1707, the president issued an executive order authorizing "blocking" (i.e., prohibiting the transfer, payment or withdrawal) of any assets in the United States owned by certain proliferators of WMD. *See* Exec. Order No. 13,382, 70 Fed. Reg. 38,567 (2005).

Early approaches to combating the threat of a strike by WMD focused on deterrence strategies and diplomatic efforts to negotiate and implement arms control treaties.[16] Arms control treaties—the diplomatic approach—seek to halt the proliferation of WMD and their delivery systems, with the long-term goal of disarmament.[17] Deterrence strategies—the principal military approach—rest on a threat of retaliation in kind, and are grounded in the belief that a rational state will be deterred from using WMD if it knows, or at least believes, that the enemy has the capability to survive a first strike and respond with similar weapons that will inflict an unacceptable level of damage. The Allies' threat of retaliation in kind against any first use of CW agents by Germany during World War II is believed to be the chief reason Germany never used any of its considerable stockpiles of such weapons. Similar threats are believed to have deterred Saddam Hussein from deploying WMD against coalition forces in the 1991 Gulf War to liberate Kuwait.

The growing threat of WMD use by terrorist groups and so-called rogue regimes, who may not be subject to internal and external political and legal controls or to the same deterrence rationale as responsible states, has added a new sense of urgency to proliferation security discussions. For some, it is becoming increasingly obvious that diplomatic measures and the nonproliferation regime will never be sufficient in themselves to curb the threats posed by WMD in the possession of these actors, and that deterrence strategies have little or no effect on rogue regimes and non-state actors. That realization has set in motion a shift in priority from nonproliferation and deterrence strategies to counterproliferation measures that are more proactive and may even include preemptive or preventive measures aimed at denying those groups access to WMD and their delivery systems.[18]

NONPROLIFERATION REGIME FOR NUCLEAR WEAPONS AND MATERIALS

The Nuclear Nonproliferation Treaty of 1968[19] (NPT) seeks to restrict the application of nuclear technology to peaceful purposes. Under the NPT, only five states—China, France, Russia, the United Kingdom, and the United States—may

---

[16]The law of armed conflict (LOAC) also limits the use of certain WMD. *See* Advisory Opinion, Legality of the Threat or Use of Nuclear Weapons, 1996 I.C.J. Rep. 226, paras. 55, 86 (July 8), 35 I.L.M. 80 (1996). Additionally, some uses of WMD could conceivably implicate the 1977 Convention on the Prohibition of Military or Other Hostile Use of Environmental Modification Techniques, 31 U.S.T. 233, T.I.A.S. 9614, 16 I.L.M. 90 (1977).

[17]Congressional Research Service, *Proliferation Control Regimes: Background and Status,* CRS Rep. RL31559 (updated Feb. 10, 2005); Barry Kellman, *Bridling the International Trade in Catastrophic Weapons,* 43 Am. U. L. Rev. 755 (1994).

[18]For an adversary who is immune to deterrence strategies, prevention may be a necessary strategic choice. *See generally* Lawrence Freedman, *Prevention, Not Preemption,* 26 Wash. Q. 105 (Spring 2003).

[19]Treaty on the Non-Proliferation of Nuclear Weapons, July 1, 1968, 21 U.S.T. 483, T.I.A.S. 6839, 729 U.N.T.S. 161 (1970) [hereinafter "NPT"]. The NPT was extended indefinitely in 1995.

lawfully manufacture and possess nuclear weapons.[20] These "nuclear weapon states" may not, however, transfer nuclear weapons or nuclear explosive devices to "any other recipient whatsoever," or in any way assist, encourage or induce any non-nuclear-weapon state to manufacture or otherwise acquire nuclear weapons or nuclear explosive devices.[21] The non-nuclear-weapon states agree not to acquire nuclear weapons in return for assistance in developing peaceful uses for nuclear power. At the same time, each of the "nuclear five" (who are also permanent members of the U.N. Security Council) is obligated under the NPT to undertake "general and complete disarmament under strict and effective international control."[22] Although considerable progress toward disarmament has been made over the last 20 years, the global inventory of strategic and tactical nuclear warheads still exceeds 10,000.[23] The failure of the nuclear weapon states to move more quickly on disarmament has been a recurring source of criticism by the non-nuclear-weapon states.[24]

Compliance with the nonproliferation and disarmament requirements of the NPT is monitored by the International Atomic Energy Agency (IAEA).[25] However, it has been frequently pointed out that promulgating safeguards and monitoring and verification measures do not by themselves ensure compliance. "The most air-tight verification regime is worthless if confirmed violations are ignored."[26]

---

[20]The five nuclear weapon states are those that had manufactured and tested a nuclear weapon prior to January 1, 1967.

[21]NPT, art. I

[22]*Ibid.* art. VI.

[23]In 2005, the United States nuclear stockpile stood at approximately 5,000 operational warheads (4,216 strategic and 780 nonstrategic). *U.S. Nuclear Forces, 2005,* 61 BULL. ATOMIC SCIENTISTS 73–75 (2005). The 2005 Russian nuclear stockpile stood at 3,814 operational warheads. *Russian Nuclear Forces, 2005,* 61 BULL. ATOMIC SCIENTISTS 70–72 (2005). The Soviet nuclear arsenal is thought to have reached as many as 35,000 warheads at the end of the Cold War in 1991. Estimated nuclear stockpiles for other states are: China, 410; France, 350; U.K., 185; India: 95; Israel, 75–200; and Pakistan, 52. *See* 14 CONG. Q. RESEARCHER 297, 300 (2004).

[24]*See, e.g.,* U.N. General Assembly, Res. 59/83, U.N. Doc. A/RES/59/83 (2004) (expressing the Assembly's deep concern with the lack of progress in the implementation of the 13 steps to implement article VI of the NPT).

[25]The IAEA's authority will be expanded as more states ratify and implement the Model Additional Protocol. The Protocol, which was adopted in 1997, strengthens the safeguards system by requiring states to provide the IAEA with broader information covering all aspects of their nuclear fuel-related activities and to permit broader access to inspect facilities and install verification technologies. To date, however, only 78 of the 180 NPT signatories have ratified the Additional Protocol. *See* IAEA, *Safeguards and Verification, available at* http://www.iaea.org/OurWork/SV/Safeguards/sg_protocol.html. President Bush transmitted the Additional Protocol to the U.S.-IAEA Safeguards Agreement to the Senate for advice and consent on May 9, 2002. *See* S. TREATY DOC. NO. 107–7 (2002). The Senate unanimously approved it on March 31, 2004. *See also* U.S. DEP'T OF STATE, DIGEST OF UNITED STATES PRACTICE IN INTERNATIONAL LAW 2002, at 1057–58 (2003).

[26]U.S. Dep't of State, Undersecretary of State for Arms Control and International Security John R. Bolton, *The NPT: A Crisis of Non-Compliance,* Statement to the Third Session of the Preparatory Committee for the 2005 Review Conference on the Treaty on the Non-Proliferation of Nuclear Weapons, Apr. 27, 2004 [hereinafter "*Statement to the 2005 Review Conference of the NPT*"].

Unfortunately, remedies for violations of the NPT are not as well developed as the verification regime. The IAEA may report violations to the U.N. Security Council,[27] which may then take appropriate action under Chapters VI or VII of the U.N. Charter,[28] but such measures are impossible without the support of at least all of the permanent members. Given the widely divergent interests expressed by those states over recent issues involving Iraq and longstanding support by some permanent members for North Korea and Iran, the prospects for Chapter VII measures to enforce the NPT were, until quite recently, not encouraging. The unanimous decision to impose mandatory import and export restrictions on North Korea, following its October 9, 2006, nuclear test, and to demand that Pyongyang return to the NPT and the IAEA safeguards, signals for some a new resolve, but others question whether China and Russia will ever agree to meaningful sanctions to back up the tough talk. U.N. observers will no doubt closely monitor the council in the coming months to see what actions it takes to "restore international peace and security" with respect to these proliferation threats.

All but four states (India, Israel, North Korea, and Pakistan) are party to the NPT.[29] India and Pakistan have both developed and tested nuclear weapons.[30] It is also likely that Israel possesses nuclear weapons,[31] though there is no proof that Israel has tested such weapons, nor has it formally declared it possesses (or denied that it possesses) nuclear weapons. Until quite recently, Israel has generally refused access to the IAEA. North Korea and Iran are at varying stages in the development of a nuclear weapons capability. As an NPT party, Iran is subject to IAEA compliance inspections.[32] Despite two years of negotiations with the European Union and Russia, Iran—whose president has called for the state of Israel to be wiped off the

---

[27]Statute of the International Atomic Energy Agency, Oct. 23, 1956, art. XII.A.7, 8 U.S.T. 1093, 276 U.N.T.S. 3 (amended Oct. 4, 1961, 14 U.S.T. 135, 471 U.N.T.S. 333).

[28]Charter of the United Nations, June 26, 1945, 59 Stat. 1031, T.S. No. 993, as amended in 1963 (16 U.S.T. 1134, T.I.A.S. No. 5857), 1965 (19 U.S.T. 5450, T.I.A.S. No. 6529) and 1971 (24 U.S.T. 2225, T.I.A.S. No. 7739).

[29]At last count, there were 189 states-parties. Despite widespread acceptance of the treaty, the parties are not in agreement over the treaty's future direction. *See Nuclear Nonproliferation Treaty Meeting Ends with Deep Divides,* U.N. WIRE, May 7, 2004, *available at* http://www.unwire.org/News/328_426_23598.asp.

[30]In early 2006, the United States and India entered into an agreement on civil nuclear cooperation. In return for a U.S. promise to permit India to engage in trade for civil nuclear technology, India agreed to take steps to bring its program into compliance with IAEA safeguards and Nuclear Suppliers' Group and Missile Technology Control Regime guidelines. *See* White House, *Fact Sheet: United States and India: Strategic Partnership,* Mar. 2006, *available at* http://www.whitehouse.gov/news/releases/2006/03/20060302–13.html.

[31]One estimate puts the Israeli nuclear arsenal at up to 200 warheads, deliverable by aircraft, missile and perhaps submarine. *Weapons of Mass Destruction: If You Push I'll Shove,* THE ECONOMIST, July 10, 2004, at 41.

[32]In June of 2004, after the IAEA inspectors discovered traces of highly-enriched uranium (HEU) on centrifuge parts from an Iranian facility Iran made an ambiguous assertion that it would demand that it be recognized as a "nuclear power." *See Iran Wants Recognition as Nuclear Nation,* CNN.COM NEWS, June 13, 2004.

map[33]—continues its enrichment program, ignoring a Security Council resolution calling for a "full and sustained" suspension of its enrichment and reprocessing activities by August 31, 2006.[34]

After the world discovered that North Korea had, for years, been systematically violating the 1994 "Agreed Framework" it reached with the United States,[35] and circumvented safeguards in the NPT system to hide its nuclear weapons programs, it withdrew from the NPT in early 2003 and denied further access to IAEA inspectors.[36] Pyongyang's renunciation of the NPT and expulsion of the IAEA inspectors were largely symbolic, since it had been violating the treaty for years despite IAEA oversight. In 2002, the Security Council members considered a resolution critical of North Korea's renunciation of the NPT; however, China blocked the action.[37] China relented, and voted for enforcement measures, after North Korea's 2006 nuclear device test.

Although the long-term goal of the NPT is to eliminate all nuclear weapons, it preserves and even promotes the "inalienable" right to peaceful use of nuclear technology, within a complex system of safeguards agreements entered into between 145 states and the IAEA and implemented through IAEA compliance inspections.[38] Rising oil prices and concern over carbon emissions seem certain to stimulate interest and investment in nuclear power projects that will significantly add to the challenge of NPT compliance monitoring.[39] The dual-use capability of the relevant nuclear technology presents thorny compliance verification problems, as the present situation in Iran demonstrates. The noncompliance by several states that exploit the benefits of NPT membership to develop nuclear weapons "under cover of supposed peaceful nuclear technology" has produced what a U.S. spokesman characterized

---

[33]Nazila Fathi, *Wipe Israel 'off the map' Iranian says,* N.Y. TIMES, Oct. 27, 2005.

[34]U.N. Security Council, Res. 1696, U.N. Doc. S/RES/1696 (2006). *See also* Int'l Atomic Energy Agency Board of Governors, *Implementation of the NPT Safeguards against the Islamic Republic of Iran,* IAEA Doc. GOV/2006/53, Sept. 16, 2006.

[35]The 1994 Geneva Accords, or "Agreed Framework," called for North Korea to freeze its plutonium nuclear program in Yongbyon in exchange for United States foreign aid, oil transfers and assistance in developing two civilian light water reactors. *See* Congressional Research Service, *North Korea's Nuclear Weapons Program,* CRS Issue Brief IB91141 (updated May 25, 2006).

[36]Some argue that North Korea's renunciation of the NPT was invalid when made, for substantive and procedural reasons. *See* Frederic L. Kirgis, *North Korea's Withdrawal from the Nuclear Proliferation Treaty,* ASIL INSIGHTS, Jan. 2003. In Resolution 1718, the Security Council "demanded" that the DPRK "immediately retract its announcement of withdrawal from the Treaty on the Non-Proliferation of Nuclear Weapons," and return to" the NPT and IAEA safeguards. U.N. Security Council Res. 1718, operative paras. 3, 4, U.N. Doc. S/RES/1718 (2006).

[37]Jean du Preez & William Potter, *North Korea's Withdrawal from the NPT: A Reality Check,* Center for Non-Proliferation Studies, Apr. 9, 2002, *available at* www.cns.miis.edu/pubs/week/030309/htm.

[38]NPT, arts. III & IV. The safeguards program will be enhanced by the Model Additional Protocol. *See*Int'l Atomic Energy Agency, IAEA*Safeguards: Stemming the Spread of Nuclear Weapons, available at* http://www.iaea.org/Publications/Factsheets/English/S1_Safeguards.pdf.

[39]The Energy Policy Act of 2005, Pub. L. No. 109–58, 119 Stat. 594 (2005), signed into law on August 8, 2005, included measures to "encourage investment in a new generation of safer, more reliable, and more proliferation-resistant nuclear power plants."

as a crisis.[40] As the president signaled in the *National Security Strategy of the United States,* the NPT parties must work together to close the "loophole in the Non-Proliferation Treaty that permits regimes to produce fissile material that can be used to make nuclear weapons under cover of a civilian nuclear power program."[41]

In 1974, shortly after the Indian nuclear test demonstrated how nuclear technology and materials transferred for peaceful purposes could be used to develop nuclear weapons, a number of supplier states (now up to 44) came together to form the "Nuclear Suppliers' Group" (NSG). The NSG is a voluntary multilateral export control regime for nuclear materials used in peaceful applications by other states.[42] The NSG scheme, which complements but is not formally part of the NPT, is a non-binding arrangement among like-minded nuclear materials supplier states designed to control exports of nuclear materials, equipment and technology, both dual-use and specially designed and prepared components. The primary control mechanism is a set of agreed upon guidelines. The NSG's guidelines are linked to the work of the 35-member Zangger Committee (also known as the Nuclear Exporters' Committee), which develops the "trigger list" of controlled items.[43] Any export of an item on the trigger list implicates not only the NSG's guidelines, but also the NPT safeguards established by the IAEA. The safeguards are implemented at the national level and enforced under domestic laws. At their 2004 summit, the G-8 member states—having declared that the "proliferation of weapons of mass destruction (WMD) and their means of delivery, together with international terrorism, remain the pre-eminent threat to international peace and security"—adopted an Action Plan for Nonproliferation that calls for significant changes to the NSG guidelines and a temporary suspension of transfers of enrichment and reprocessing equipment and technologies while the new guidelines are being developed.[44] The G-8 Action Plan would also require all states seeking supplies for peaceful applications of nuclear technology or materials to accede to the IAEA's Additional Protocol and comply with the more stringent safeguards currently under development.[45]

---

[40] *See* Bolton, *Statement to the 2005 Review Conference of the NPT.*

[41] White House, *The National Security Strategy of the United States* 20 (2006).

[42] Nuclear Suppliers' Group (also known as the London Group), *available at* http://www.nuclearsuppliersgroup.org/.

[43] *See* http://www.zanggercommittee.org. The European Union is a permanent observer. The criteria for listing materials that will fall within the IAEA safeguards are derived from Article III.2 of the NPT, which provides that:

> Each State Party to the Treaty undertakes not to provide: (a) source or special fissionable material, or (b) equipment or material especially designed or prepared for the processing, use or production of special fissionable material, to any non-nuclear-weapon State for peaceful purposes, unless the source or special fissionable material shall be subject to the safeguards required by this Article.

[44] G-8 *Action Plan on Nonproliferation,* para. 1, June 9, 2004 [hereinafter *"G-8 2004 Action Plan"*], *available at* http://www.whitehouse.gov/news/releases/2004/06/20040609–28.html. The G-8 reaffirmed their commitment at the 2006 summit in St. Petersburg, Russia. *See Statement on Non-proliferation,* July 16, 2006, *available at* http://www.g8.utoronto.ca/summit/2005gleneagles/nonprolif.pdf.

[45] *G-8 2004 Action Plan,* para. 1.

Advocates of a new Fissile Material Cut-Off Treaty[46] (FMCT) argue that a treaty banning production of fissile material for use in nuclear weapons is necessary to strengthen existing nonproliferation norms.[47] By one estimate, existing stockpiles of fissile materials total approximately 3,000 metric tons; enough to produce 200,000 weapons.[48] Negotiating a fissile materials cut-off treaty that advances the interests of the nation is an announced goal of the United States.[49] The draft FMCT presented by the United States at the May 2006 meeting of the U.N. Conference on Disarmament would not ban fissile materials used for nonexplosive purposes.[50] Nor does it include measures to reduce existing stockpiles. However, the treaty would do much to reduce availability of fissile material, and therefore the threat of such materials finding their way into a nuclear weapon.

Nuclear weapons and their components are vulnerable to diversion or theft while stored or in transport. A principal aim of the U.S. Department of Energy's Global Threat Reduction Initiative is to secure, remove, or dispose of nuclear and radiological materials around the world that are vulnerable to theft.[51] Recent efforts have focused on "repatriating" spent reactor fuel provided by the United States and Russia to other states and to convert research reactors that presently run on highly enriched uranium to nonfissile alternatives. The transport of nuclear materials and the standards for their protection were addressed in the Convention on the Physical Protection of Nuclear Materials (CPPNM), which requires states-parties to the convention to criminalize the theft or fraudulent obtaining of certain nuclear materials, or the use of such materials in attacks or threatened attacks.[52] The United States enacted criminal statutes to implement the CPPNM convention.[53] In 2003, the IAEA approved a revised Code of Conduct on the Safety and Security of Radioactive Sources.[54] The Safety of Life at Sea Convention

[46]The proposed treaty is sometimes referred to as FISSBAN.

[47]*See* U.N. General Assembly Res. A/48/75L (1993) (calling for negotiation of a nondiscriminatory, multilateral, and international, effectively verifiable treaty banning production of fissile material for nuclear weapons or other nuclear explosive devices).

[48]Bipartisan Security Group, *Status of the Non-Proliferation Treaty, Interim Report,* June 2003, at 5, *available at* http://www.middlepowers.org/gsi/pubs/06_03_npt_brief.pdf.

[49]White House, *National Strategy for Combating Weapons of Mass Destruction* 4 (2002) [hereinafter "NS-CWMD"]. India recently joined the U.S in supporting the conclusion of a Fissile Material Cut-off Treaty. *See White House Fact Sheet on India.*

[50]*See* John R. Cook, *Contemporary Practice of the United States Relating to International Law,* 100 Am. J. Int'l L. 690, 721–22 (2006).

[51]The Department of Energy program for nuclear and radiological materials complements and in some ways overlaps with the Nunn-Lugar Cooperative Threat Reduction Program.

[52]Convention on the Physical Protection of Nuclear Materials, Oct. 26, 1979, art. 7, T.I.A.S. 11080, 1456 U.N.T.S. 24631. Parties must also make such offenses extraditable. *Ibid.* art. 11. Materials of interest are plutonium, uranium 233, and uranium 235.

[53]*See* 18 U.S.C.A. § 831 (West 2005).

[54]*See also* United Nations, Oceans and the Law of the Sea, General Assembly Res. 58/240, U.N. Doc. A/RES/58/240 (2003) para. 26 (welcoming IAEA Res. GC(47)/RES/7 concerning measures for strengthening international cooperation in nuclear, radiation, and transport safety and waste management).

(SOLAS)[55] and the International Code for the Safe Carriage of Packaged Irradiated Nuclear Fuel, Plutonium and High Level Radioactive Wastes on Board Ships (INF Code)[56] prescribe requirements for the maritime transport of nuclear materials. Liability for maritime transporters is governed by the Convention Relating to Civil Liability in the Field of Maritime Carriage of Nuclear Material.[57]

In 2005, the U.N. General Assembly adopted the International Convention for the Suppression of Acts of Nuclear Terrorism.[58] When it enters into force, the new convention will extend the criminal regime applicable to proliferation-related offenses in several important respects. For example, the convention would require states-parties to criminalize the possession of radioactive material, or the making or possession of a nuclear or radioactive device, with the intent to use that material to cause death, serious bodily injury, or substantial damage to property or the environment.[59] The prohibitions would extend to attempts, and to those who participate as an accomplice, organize, or direct those who carry out acts of nuclear terrorism, or who in "any other way contributes to the commission" of a covered act, knowing of the intent to commit such acts or with the aim of furthering the general criminal activity or purpose of the group.[60] States-parties must also take all practicable measures to, *inter alia,* prohibit in their territories illegal activities by persons or groups that encourage, instigate, or organize acts of nuclear terrorism, or knowingly finance or provide technical assistance or information to persons or groups engaged in such acts.[61] The General Assembly's Convention plainly embraces a law enforcement approach to the threat posed by nuclear and radiological weapons in the hands of terrorists.[62] The convention would also eliminate, with significant exceptions, the political offense exemption to extradition.[63]

---

[55]International Convention for the Safety of Life at Sea, Nov. 1, 1974, 32 U.S.T. 47, T.I.A.S. 9700, 1184 U.N.T.S. 2; Protocol of 1978 Relating to the International Convention for the Safety of Life at Sea, 1974, Feb. 17, 1978, 32 U.S.T. 5577, T.I.A.S. 10009, 1226 U.N.T.S. 237 [hereinafter "SOLAS Convention"].

[56]Compliance with the INF Code is mandatory. *See ibid.* Reg. VII/16. *See also* International Maritime Organization, Res. A.853(20) (adopting updated INF Code).

[57]Convention Relating to Civil Liability in the Field of Maritime Carriage of Nuclear Material, Dec. 17, 1971, U.N.T.S. No. 14120. The Convention limits the transporter's liability for damage caused by a nuclear incident in cases where the operator of the related nuclear installation bears liability under the Paris or Vienna Conventions or national law. *Ibid.* arts. 1–2.

[58]International Convention for the Suppression of Acts of Nuclear Terrorism, annexed to U.N. General Assembly Res. 59/240, U.N. Doc. A/RES/59/240 (2005), 44 I.L.M. 815 (2005).

[59]*Ibid.* art. 2(1).

[60]*Ibid.* art. 2(2), (3), (4).

[61]*Ibid.* art. 7.

[62]The convention expressly mandates that all states-parties carry out the convention obligations in a manner "consistent with the principles of sovereign equality and territorial integrity of states and that of non-intervention in the domestic affairs of other States." *Ibid.* art. 21. The convention twice addresses the rights of individuals engaged in covered acts of nuclear terrorism (*ibid.* arts. 12 and 17) and requires the interdicting state to return any seized nuclear material or device to the state to which it belongs or of which the person owning it is a national. *Ibid.* art. 18(2).

[63]*Ibid.* arts. 6, 15. However, the grounds for refusing extradition in article 16 of the convention arguably provide a sympathetic state a nearly peremptory basis for denying extradition.

NONPROLIFERATION REGIME FOR CHEMICAL WEAPONS

Nearly 70 years after the 1925 Geneva Gas and Bacteriological Warfare Protocol banned the use of asphyxiating and poisonous gases in war,[64] the Chemical Weapons Convention of 1993 (CWC)[65] took the further step of forbidding parties to the CWC from developing, producing, stockpiling, or using chemical weapons. The Convention also requires member states not to permit any such activities to be conducted in any place under the state's control.[66] In contrast to the NPT, which has been ratified almost universally, a significant number of states, including many in the Middle East, are not yet a party to the CWC.

The CWC requires parties to destroy existing stockpiles by 2007. The United States recently stepped up its CW stockpile destruction program; however, it requested an extension on the 2007 destruction deadline.[67] The CWC includes provisions for verification and challenge inspections by the Organization for the Prohibition of Chemical Weapons (OPCW), located in The Hague. Although the OPCW has no enforcement powers, violations of the CWC can be reported to the CWC Conference of States-Parties, which can refer the matter to the U.N. Security Council. As with other WMD, however, the fact that many—perhaps most—CW agent precursors and technologies have legitimate dual-use applications complicates enforcement. For example, many chemical production plants exhibit an ability to engage in multiple uses, including production of pesticides, pharmaceuticals, and industrial chemicals.[68] In many cases, such plants may be converted to produce CW agents. Thus, in many cases, an intent to create CW cannot be inferred from the mere capability to produce them.

As with the NPT, the CWC requires states-parties to restrict exports of certain CWC materials and enforce those restrictions through their penal laws.[69] In the United States, the CWC is implemented through the Chemical Weapons Convention Implementation Act of 1998.[70] Federal prohibitions on possession and use of CW agents are prescribed in Chapter 11B of Title 18 of the U.S. Code.[71]

---

[64]Protocol for the Prohibition of the Use in War of Asphyxiating, Poisonous, or Other Gases, and of Bacteriological Methods of Warfare, 26 U.S.T. 571 (1925) [hereinafter "1925 Geneva Gas and Bacteriological Warfare Protocol"].

[65]Convention on the Prohibition of the Development, Production, Stockpiling and Uses of Chemical Weapons and on Their Destruction, Jan. 13, 1993, 1974 U.N.T.S. 45, 32 I.L.M. 800 (1993) [hereinafter "CWC"]. The United States ratified the CWC in 1997. *See* S. Exec. Rep. No. 104–33, Sept. 11, 1996.

[66]CWC, art. VII(1).

[67]See U.S. Dep't of State, *U.S. Requests to Extend Chemical Weapons Convention (CWC) Deadline for Complete Destruction of Chemical Weapons Stocks,* Apr. 20, 2006 (requesting an extension until 2012), available at http://www.state.gov/t/isn/rls/fs/64874.htm. Environmental concerns and community opposition have limited U.S. disposal options. *See* Rick Callahan, *Army to Begin Destroying Deadly Nerve Gas,* Assoc. Press, June 9, 2004 (reporting program to destroy 1,269 tons of VX nerve gas at the Newport, IN, facility).

[68]Chemical plants capable of manufacturing organic phosphorous pesticides or flame retardants could be converted to CW production in a matter of weeks.

[69]CWC, art. VII(1).

[70]22 U.S.C.A. § 6723 (West 2005).

[71]*See, e.g.,* 18 U.S.C.A. §§ 229, 229A-229F (West 2005).

The 1996 Antiterrorism and Effective Death Penalty Act enacted a number of changes to the prohibitions.[72] Nevertheless, the extraterritorial jurisdictional reach of the CW statute is limited, and would likely not extend to most foreign vessel situations likely to fall within the ambit of a maritime counterproliferation boarding.[73]

To better coordinate export controls, a group of 39 states concerned with the threats posed by CW (and BTW) agent proliferation have formed the "Australia Group," a voluntary multilateral export control regime.[74] Like the Nuclear Suppliers' Group, the Australia Group regime is a nonbinding arrangement among like-minded supplier states designed to control the risk of proliferation of WMD and their component materials. The primary purpose of the group is to ensure that industries of the participating states do not assist, either purposely or inadvertently, another state in acquiring CW or BTW capability. Participating states meet on a regular basis to consult on proliferation issues and harmonize their national export control regimes. The participants have agreed to restrict trade in CW and BTW materials through their national laws and regulations, by establishing a system to license the export of certain chemicals, biological agents, and dual-use equipment and facilities that might be used to produce CW or BTW. Finally, all of the states agree to exchange information with the other participants regarding proliferation trends and entities attempting to procure CW- or BTW-related materials.

The international regulatory regime for the transport of hazardous chemicals and explosives includes Chapter VII of the SOLAS Convention together with the International Maritime Dangerous Goods Code.[75] The IMDG Code prescribes standards for the packing, stowage, and labeling of dangerous goods transported by sea. Compliance with the IMDG Code is now mandatory.[76] Vessels carrying hazardous materials (including radioactive and biohazard materials) by sea are required to have available for inspection a "dangerous cargo manifest," which lists the weight, quantity, packaging, class, and stowage of all hazardous cargo on the vessel.[77] Enforcement, however, is generally limited to flag states and port states.

---

[72]Antiterrorism and Effective Death Penalty Act of 1996, Pub. L. No. 104–132, title V, subtitle C (1996), 110 Stat. 1214. *See also* Omnibus Diplomatic Security and Antiterrorism Act of 1986 (ODSAA), Pub. L. No. 99–399, 100 Stat. 853. Title IX of the ODSAA was the International Maritime and Port Security Act, 100 Stat. 889, *codified at* 46 U.S.C.A. §§ 1801–1809 (West 2005).

[73]*See* 18 U.S.C.A. § 229(c) (West 2005). Extraterritorial conduct to acquire WMD for use in the United States may, however, constitute a substantial step in furtherance of a conspiracy or an attempt. Providing CW agents or precursors to a terrorist organization might also implicate the "material support" prohibition in 18 U.S.C. § 2339B.

[74]Australia Group (for BTW and CW weapons), *available at* http://www.australiagroup.net/.

[75]*See* International Maritime Organization, *International Maritime Dangerous Goods Code*, IMO Pub. No. IE200E (2004) (new version to be released in 2007).

[76]*See* 49 C.F.R. pt. 176 (2006) (regulation for carriage of hazardous materials by water).

[77]*See* 49 C.F.R. § 176.30 (2006).

NONPROLIFERATION REGIME FOR BIOLOGICAL AND TOXIN WEAPONS

The use of bacteriological methods of warfare has been banned since 1925.[78] The Biological Weapons Convention of 1972 (BWC) takes the further step of banning the production, acquisition or stockpiling of biological agents or toxins (BTW agents).[79] Although the BWC includes a provision for reporting violations to the Security Council for possible action,[80] in contrast to the CWC, the BWC does not yet include provisions for verification and challenge inspections. The reasons for failing to close what many see as a potentially critical compliance gap are controversial. It is now known that the former Soviet Union systematically violated the BWC until at least 1992, by carrying on a massive program to produce BTW agents, which were then weaponized and stockpiled.[81] North Korea is believed to have the world's largest stockpiles of anthrax, cholera, and plague, along with programs for botulism, hemorrhagic fever, smallpox, typhoid, and yellow fever. Nevertheless, the United States has so far rejected a proposed protocol to the BWC that would add a verification scheme to increase compliance.[82] The grounds for rejection given by U.S. negotiators included concerns that outside inspections of government-sponsored research facilities would compromise the nation's BTW defensive efforts, which are deemed necessary to guard against known or suspected BTW programs by hostile states and non-state actors. Additionally, outside inspections of commercial facilities in the United States whose products would fall within the dual-use parameters of the protocol might endanger intellectual property rights held by the pharmaceutical and biotechnology companies.[83] Finally, given the nature and ubiquity of biological and pharmaceutical research facilities, and the difficulty of distinguishing prohibited BTW offensive activities from permitted defensive research,

---

[78]1925 Geneva Gas and Bacteriological Warfare Protocol, *supra* note 64.

[79]Convention on the Prohibition of the Development, Production, Stockpiling of Bacteriological (Biological) and Toxin Weapons and on Their Destruction, Apr. 10, 1972, 26 U.S.T. 583, T.I.A.S. 8062, 1015 U.N.T.S. 163 [hereinafter "BWC"]. President Nixon ordered an end to U.S. research in offensive use of biological weapons in 1969. *See* 5 Weekly Comp. Pres. Doc. 1659 61 (Nov. 26, 1969); U.S. Dep't of State Bull. 226–27 (1970). Research into defensive measures, primarily vaccine development, continues. *See* 18 Marjorie W. Whiteman, Digest of U.S. Practice in International Law 732–36 (1976).

[80]BWC, arts. VI & XIII.

[81]U.S. Arms Control and Disarmament Agency, Adherence to and Compliance with Arms Control Agreements and the President's Report to Congress on Soviet Noncompliance with Arms Control Agreements, Jan. 14, 1992, at 14.

[82]Rebecca Whitehair & Seth Brugger, *BWC Protocol Talks in Geneva Collapse Following U.S. Rejection,* Arms Control Today (Sept. 2001), *available at* http://www.armscontrol.org/act/2001_09/bwcsept01.asp.

[83]*See* Undersecretary of State for Arms Control and International Security John R. Bolton, *U.S. Efforts to Stop the Spread of Weapons of Mass Destruction,* Testimony before Committee on International Relations, U.S. House of Representatives, June 4, 2003, *in* U.S. Dep't of State, Digest of United States Practice in International Law 2002, at 1037–38 (2003).

some question the extent to which an outside inspection regime could ever be practical and sufficiently reliable.[84]

Some commentators are now propounding arguments for more onerous consequences when states fail to meet their international obligations to guard against BTW proliferation. For example, one writer argues that a state should bear international responsibility for failing to take adequate precautions against proliferation of BTW agents.[85] An argument might also be made that the criminal liability provisions of the Rome Statute of the International Criminal Court could extend to those who were complicit in putting BTW (or other WMD) or the means of delivery in the hands of those who later used them to commit crimes under the Statute.[86] On another front, an international convention proposed by the Harvard-Essex Program on CBW Disarmament would, if enacted, make it a crime under international law to develop, retain, acquire, transfer, or use biological or chemical weapons.[87] U.N. Security Council Resolution 1540 (discussed later in this chapter) calls for a similar approach at the national level. In the United States, federal prohibitions on possession and use of BTW agents are prescribed in Chapter 10 of Title 18 of the U.S. Code.[88] The 1996 Antiterrorism and Effective Death Penalty Act enacted a number of changes to the prohibitions.[89] Nevertheless, the extraterritorial jurisdictional reach of the BTW statute, like the CW statute, remains limited, and would likely not extend to most maritime counterproliferation boardings.[90]

MEASURES TO CURB AND CONTAIN MISSILE AND UAV PROLIFERATION

Despite the fact that the U.N. Security Council has concluded that the proliferation of missile delivery systems for WMD constitutes a threat to international peace

---

[84] *See* "The Debate over BWC Verification" in U.S. Congress, Office of Technology Assessment, *Technologies Underlying Weapons of Mass Destruction,* Report No. OTA-BP-ISC-115 (1993), at 74–75.

[85] Barry Kellman, *State Responsibility for Preventing Bioterrorism,* 36 INT'L LAWYER 29 (2002).

[86] *See* Rome Statute of the International Criminal Court, art. 25(3)(c), which extends individual criminal responsibility to one who "aids, abets or otherwise assists in [the commission of a crime under the Statute] or its attempted commission, including providing the means for its commission." Depending on the circumstances, use of a WMD could constitute the crime of genocide, a crime against humanity or a war crime.

[87] Harvard/Sussex program on CBW Disarmament and Arms Limitation, Draft Convention on the Prevention and Punishment of the Crime of Developing, Producing, Acquiring, Stockpiling, Retaining, Transferring or Using Biological or Chemical Weapons, Nov. 1, 2001, *available at* http://fas-www.harvard.edu/~hsp/crim01.pdf.

[88] *See, e.g.,* 18 U.S.C.A. §§ 175–178 (West 2005). The BTW prohibitions were expanded by the USA PATRIOT Act, Pub. L. No. 107–56, § 817, 115 Stat. 272, 385–86 (2001).

[89] Antiterrorism and Effective Death Penalty Act of 1996, Pub. L. No. 104–132, title V, subtitle B (1996), 110 Stat. 1214 (1996).

[90] *See* 18 U.S.C.A. § 175(a)(West 2005) ("There is extraterritorial Federal Jurisdiction over an offense under this section committed by or against a national of the United States"). Providing BW agents to a terrorist organization might, however, implicate the "material support" prohibition in 18 U.S.C. § 2339B.

and security,[91] international law does not presently prohibit the sale or transfer of missiles or missile technology. For that reason, the nonproliferation regime for missiles is the weakest of the four considered, as the 2002 M/V *So San* incident (discussed in Chapter 5) demonstrated.[92] A number of states concerned with the threats posed by missile proliferation have sought to at least partly fill this lacuna by establishing the Missile Technology Control Regime (MTCR).[93] Like the regimes established by the Nuclear Suppliers' Group and the Australia Group, the MTCR is a voluntary multilateral export control regime.[94] The MTCR consists of a set of guidelines and an equipment and technology annex. Participating states agree to regulate trade in missile technology through their national laws, which establish systems to license the exports of sensitive items. In general terms, the MTCR participants agree to refrain from selling missiles capable of specified ranges and payloads as follows:

> [The] greatest restraint is applied to what are known as *Category I* items. These items include complete rocket systems (including ballistic missiles, space launch vehicles and sounding rockets) and unmanned air vehicle systems (including cruise missiles systems, target and reconnaissance drones) with capabilities exceeding a 300km/500kg range/payload threshold; production facilities for such systems; and major sub-systems including rocket stages, re-entry vehicles, rocket engines, guidance systems and warhead mechanisms.
>
> The remainder of the annex is regarded as *Category II,* which includes complete rocket systems (including ballistic missiles systems, space launch vehicles and sounding rockets) and unmanned air vehicles (including cruise missile systems, target drones, and reconnaissance drones) not covered in item I, capable of a maximum range equal to or greater than, 300km. Also included are a wide range of equipment, material, and technologies, most of which have uses other than for missiles capable of delivering WMD. While still agreeing to exercise restraint, partners have greater flexibility in the treatment of Category II transfer applications.

---

[91] *See* U.N. Security Council Res. 1695, U.N. Doc. S/RES/1695 (2006) (reaffirming its finding in Resolution 1540 that missile proliferation constitutes such a threat and condemning the DPRK for test launching ballistic missiles capable of delivering WMD on July 5, 2006). The resolution goes on to require all member states to prevent the transfer of missile and missile related items to the DPRK's missile or WMD programs or the procurement of such items from the DPRK.

[92] The outcome of the M/V *So San* incident would not have been affected by U.N. Security Council Resolution 1540 because the resolution only directly addresses proliferation to non-state actors. The missiles on board the *So San* were destined for the government of Yemen. The transfer would almost certainly fall within the ambit of later resolutions, such as Resolution 1718, which was issued in 2006.

[93] The text of the MTCR is available at http://www.mtcr.info/english/. The MTCR has no secretariat or implementation organization. It is administered collectively by the participating states (thirty-four as of September, 2006). *See generally* U.S. General Accounting Office (since 2004, the "Government Accountability Office"), *Nonproliferation: Strategy Needed to Strengthen Multilateral Export Control Regimes,* GAO-03-43 (Oct. 25, 2002).

[94] Under the MTCR, export licensing requirements do not ban exports. The sole objective of export licensing is to prevent transfers contributing to delivery systems for WMD.

The efficacy of the MTCR depends on widespread adoption and adherence to the International Code of Conduct against Ballistic Missile Proliferation.[95] The Code, now referred to as the Hague Code of Conduct (HCOC), is, like the MTCR, a political commitment by the members, and is not legally binding. The HCOC calls on subscribing states to curb and prevent the proliferation of ballistic missiles capable of delivering WMD.[96] On November 25, 2002, the United States became an initial subscribing state to the Code.[97] Well over 100 states have similarly adopted the HCOC. The Code and the MTCR are key elements in the United States' multilateral strategy to impede and eventually roll back the missile proliferation threat.[98] Strengthening the MTCR is an announced goal of the United States.[99]

In addition to ballistic missiles, some 70,000 cruise missiles are in the world's inventory, and the inventory of unmanned aerial vehicles (UAVs) is rapidly growing. The utility of UAVs for reconnaissance, surveillance, targeting, and even weapon deployment has been convincingly demonstrated over the past decade.[100] In contrast to the technology for intermediate-range and long-range ballistic missiles, the technology for cruise missiles and UAVs is readily available and increasingly affordable.[101] Iran has reportedly supplied UAVs[102] and cruise missiles to Hezbollah,[103] which Hezbollah then used to attack an Israeli warship.

---

[95]*See* International Code of Conduct against Ballistic Missile Proliferation, Nov. 25, 2002 [hereinafter "HCOC"]. Congress adopted the Code in the International Arms Sales Code of Conduct Act of 1999, Pub. L. No. 106–113, § 1262. However, several missile-producing states, including China, India, Iran, and North Korea, as well as Taiwan, have so far declined to join the regime. *See generally* GAO, *Nonproliferation: Strategy Needed to Strengthen Multilateral Export Control Regimes,* at 9.

[96]*See* HCOC, para. 3(b).

[97]In announcing the support of the United States for the Code, former Undersecretary of State for Arms Control and International Security John Bolton notified the other participating states that this nation "regards the proliferation of ballistic missiles capable of delivering WMD as a *direct threat* to the U.S., our deployed forces, our friends and allies, and our interests in key regions of the world." *See* 2002 DIGEST OF U.S. PRACTICE IN INTERNATIONAL LAW, at 1063 (emphasis added).

[98]Congressional Research Service, *Missile Technology Control Regime (MTCR) and International Code of Conduct against Ballistic Missile Proliferation: Background and Issues for Congress,* CRS Rep. RL31848.

[99]NS-CWMD, at 4.

[100]On November 2, 2002, a Predator UAV fired a Hellfire missile at a carload of al Qaeda operatives in Yemen. The principal target of the strike was Qaed Salim Sinan al Harethi, who was identified as a key al Qaeda operative in the attack on the USS *Cole.* Jonathan Landay, *U.S. says CIA missile kills six from al-Qaeda,* PHILA. INQUIRER, Nov. 5, 2002.

[101]*Ibid.; see also* U.S. Government Accountability Office, *Nonproliferation: Improvements Needed for Controls on Exports of Cruise Missile and Unmanned Aerial Vehicle Technology,* GAO-04–493T (2004).

[102]*Hezbollah Drone Humiliates Israel,* IRAN DAILY, Nov. 8, 2004, http://www.iran-daily.com/1383/2135/html/index.htm; U.S. Dep't of State, *Country Reports on Terrorism, 2004,* April 2005 (Terrorist Group Profile on Hezbollah).

[103]The transfer likely violated two or more Security Council resolutions. See the discussion above concerning Security Council Resolutions 1373/1617 and 1540.

Cruise missile and UAV proliferation is addressed by both the MTCR and the Wassenaar Arrangement,[104] but neither is a binding international agreement, nor does either criminalize the sale, transfer, or transport of cruise missiles or UAVs.

Missile technology proliferation controls within the United States are implemented through various statutes, including the Arms Export Control Act,[105] the International Emergency Economic Powers Act,[106] and (at times) the Export Administration Act[107] and/or Trading with the Enemy Act.[108] The acts generally restrict exports of items on export control lists and shipments to enumerated states of missile proliferation concern.[109] The Missile Technology Control Act establishes a scheme of missile proliferation sanctions for "U.S. persons" who export, transfer, or otherwise engage in the trade of any item listed in the MTCR Annex in violation of the implementing U.S. licensing laws.[110] The Act also prescribes a more limited sanction scheme for "foreign persons" over whom the United States has jurisdiction.[111] In addition, the federal criminal code prohibits certain acts of importing, manufacturing, or dealing in nuclear or explosive materials,[112] as well as bringing, carrying, or possessing weapons or explosive devices aboard U.S. vessels.[113]

---

[104]The Arrangement has 33 subscribing states. Launched in 1996, it is the first multilateral institution covering both conventional weapons and sensitive dual-use goods and technologies. One of the Arrangement's current concerns is the proliferation of man-portable air defense systems (MANPADS), shoulder-fired weapons capable of destroying low-flying aircraft. *See* The Wassenaar Arrangement on Export Controls for Conventional Arms and Dual-use Goods and Technologies, *available at* http://www.wassenaar.org/.

[105]*See* 22 U.S.C.A. § 2797b (West 2005). Under authority of 22 U.S.C.A. § 2778, the Department of State has promulgated the International Traffic in Arms Regulations (ITAR). *See* 22 C.F.R. pt. 120 (2006); RESTATEMENT § 812.

[106]International Emergency Economic Powers Act, 50 U.S.C.A. §§ 1701–1707 (West 2005) [hereinafter "IEEPA"]. *See also* Exec. Order No. 13,206, 66 Fed. Reg. 18,397 (2001). IEEPA violations are punishable by civil and, in cases of willful violations, criminal penalties. 50 U.S.C.A. § 1705 (West 2005).

[107]Export Administration Act, 50 U.S.C. app. §§ 2401–2420 (expired) [hereinafter "EAA"]. Congress allowed the EAA to expire in 2001 (50 U.S.C. app. § 2419) and, at the time of this writing, had not yet renewed the act or replaced it with a suitable substitute. Accordingly, most export control measures are promulgated under a series of executive orders and Department of Commerce Bureau of Industry and Security regulations (15 C.F.R. pts. 730–774) issued under authority of the IEEPA, 50 U.S.C.A. §§ 1701, 1702, 1704 (West 2005).

[108]50 U.S.C.A. app. §§ 1–5 (West 2005).

[109]States "of missile proliferation concern" under the Export Administration Regulations are listed in 15 C.F.R. pt. 738. The export control program is administered by the Department of Commerce. *See* U.S. Dep't of Commerce, *Missile Technology Controls, available at* http://www.bis.doc.gov/PoliciesAndRegulations/04ForPolControls/Chap8_MTCR.htm.

[110]*See* Pub. L. No. 101–510, Div. A, Title XVII, § 1702(b), Nov. 5, 1990, 104 Stat. 1741; 50 App. U.S.C.A. § 2410b(a) (West 2005).

[111]50 App. U.S.C.A. § 2410b(b) (West 2005).

[112]*See* 18 U.S.C.A. §§ 831, 842 (West 2005).

[113]*See* 18 U.S.C.A. § 2277 (West 2005).

U.N. SECURITY COUNCIL RESPONSES TO PROLIFERATION AND TERRORISM

Multilateral efforts to combat terrorism have a long history.[114] Modernly, international obligations are established by 13 U.N.-sponsored counterterrorism conventions.[115] In early 2004, the growing threat posed by the proliferation of WMD and the potential for their use by terrorist organizations prompted the Security Council to invoke its authority under Chapter VII of the Charter. Resolution 1540—which is binding on all states—now forms an essential component of the international nonproliferation regime applicable to states.

Over the years, the Security Council has addressed the threats of global terrorism and weapons proliferation and trafficking in a number of resolutions. In Resolution 1368, issued the day after the September 11 attacks, the council implicitly found that an attack by non-state actors can trigger the inherent right of self-defense under Article 51 of the Charter.[116] The right was ultimately extended to actions against the states that harbored those non-state actors. Importantly, no state appears to have objected to extending the right of self-defense to non-state actors. Thus, the U.N. Charter is now understood by most to include a right of self-defense against attacks by non-state actors and, under some circumstances, those who harbor them.

On September 28, 2001, the council passed Resolution 1373, which requires all states to refrain from providing any kind of support to persons involved in terrorist acts and to eliminate the supply of weapons to terrorists.[117] Four years later, in Resolution 1617, the council reaffirmed the duty of all states to prevent the transfer of arms to listed terrorists.[118] Resolution 1373 notes the dangers posed by illegal movement of nuclear, chemical, biological, and other potentially deadly materials and emphasizes the need to enhance efforts on the international, regional, and national levels to strengthen the global response to the serious challenge and threat to international security posed by those weapons.

On September 23, 2003, President Bush—seeking further U.N. action—reported on the progress of the Proliferation Security Initiative to the U.N. General Assembly:

> Through our Proliferation Security Initiative, eleven nations are preparing to search planes and ships, trains and trucks carrying suspect cargo, and to seize weapons or missile shipments that raise proliferation concerns. The nations have agreed on a set of interdiction principles, consistent with current legal authorities. And we're working to expand the Proliferation Security Initiative to other countries. We're determined to keep the

---

[114]International measures to combat terrorism dates back at least to 1937, when the members of the League of Nations adopted the "Convention for Prevention and Punishment of Terrorism," League of Nations Doc. C.546 M.383 1937 (1937).

[115]For texts of the 12 conventions see "Conventions Against Terrorism," *available at* http://www.unodc.org/unodc/en/terrorism_conventions.html.

[116]U.N. Security Council, Res. 1368, U.N. Doc. S/RES/1368 (2001).

[117]U.N. Security Council Res. 1373, U.N. Doc. S/RES/1373 (2001).

[118]U.N. Security Council Res. 1617, para. 1(c), U.N. Doc. S/RES/1617 (2005).

> world's most destructive weapons away from all our shores, and out of the hands of our common enemies.[119]

The president announced to the General Assembly that he was asking the Security Council to adopt a new antiproliferation initiative that would call on all states to criminalize the proliferation of weapons of mass destruction, enact strict export controls consistent with international standards, and secure any and all sensitive materials within their borders, thus closing the loopholes in the existing antiproliferation regime.

In early 2004, the council specifically addressed the need for all states to prevent vessels or aircraft flying their flag from being used to transport arms and related materials of all types, including weapons and ammunition.[120] But many felt that specific measures calling for universal criminalization of WMD trafficking and transport were still needed. The council debated various proposed drafts of the resolution for several months,[121] before unanimously passing Resolution 1540 on April 28, 2004.[122] Resolution 1540 was cosponsored by France, the Philippines, Romania, Russia, Spain, and the United States. It includes the key finding under Article 39 of the U.N. Charter that the danger posed by proliferation of WMD threatens international peace and security. Arguably, the council's resolution therefore implicates Article 88 of the LOS Convention, which reserves the high seas for peaceful purposes.[123]

---

[119]White House, *Remarks by President George W. Bush to the United Nations General Assembly,* New York, NY, Sept. 23, 2003, at 3, *available at* http://www.whitehouse.gov/news/releases/2003/09/20030923–4.html.

[120]U.N. Security Council Res. 1526, para. 1(c), U.N. Doc. S/RES/1526 (2004). Paragraph 1 of the resolution provides that the Security Council:

> 1. *Decides* to improve. . .the implementation of the measures. . .with respect to Usama bin Laden, members of the Al-Qaida organization and the Taliban and other individuals, groups, undertakings and entities associated with them. . .to:
>
> (c) Prevent the direct or indirect supply, sale or transfer, to these individuals, groups, undertakings and entities from their territories or by their nationals outside their territories, or using their flag vessels or aircraft, of arms and related materiel of all types including weapons and ammunition, military vehicles and equipment, paramilitary equipment, and spare parts for the aforementioned and technical advice, assistance, or training related to military activities; and *recalls* that all States shall implement the measures with respect to listed individuals and entities. . .

[121]*See* U.N. Wire, *U.N. Draft Resolution Would Require States Deny Terrorists WMDs,* Mar. 25, 2004, *available at* http://www.unwire.org/UNWire/20040212/449_13079.asp.

[122]U.N. Security Council Res. 1540, U.N. Doc. S/RES/1540 (2004). *See also* U.N. General Assembly, Res. 59/80, U.N. Doc. A/RES/59/80 (2004) (urging all U.N. member states to strengthen national measures to prevent terrorists from acquiring weapons of mass destruction, their means of delivery, and materials and technologies related to their manufacture).

[123]Although "peaceful" is not defined in the LOS Convention, activities condemned by Security Council Resolution 1540 as a threat to international peace and security might well violate Article 88 of the LOS Convention. Nevertheless, Article 88 is not self-executing, and does not in itself confer a right to board vessels whose use of the high seas is not peaceful.

Resolution 1540 requires all states to "refrain from providing any form of support to non-State actors that attempt to develop, acquire, manufacture, possess, transport, transfer or use nuclear, chemical or biological weapons and their means of delivery," and to "adopt and enforce appropriate effective laws which prohibit any non-State actor to manufacture, acquire, possess, develop, transport, transfer or use nuclear, chemical or biological weapons and their means of delivery, in particular for terrorist purposes, as well as attempts to engage in any of the foregoing activities, participate in them as an accomplice, assist or finance them." Finally, all states must "take and enforce effective measures to establish domestic controls to prevent the proliferation of nuclear, chemical, or biological weapons and their means of delivery." To monitor compliance with the resolution, the council established a Nonproliferation Committee and required all states to submit reports on their compliance efforts to the committee. The United States submitted its first report on September 27, 2004.[124]

The message sent by the Security Council in Resolution 1540 seems clear: the burden of preventing proliferation is one shared by *all* states. Several Security Council members characterized the resolution as a measure to fill a gap in the existing system, particularly with respect to measures aimed at denying WMD access to terrorists and other non-state actors.[125] The president of the council emphasized that the disarmament, arms control, and nonproliferation regime played the key role for realizing the goals of the resolution, but he also pointed out that the resolution does not authorize unilateral enforcement measures if a given state fails to take effective and appropriate implementation action. Any such action would be the subject of further decisions of the council, which remains seized of the matter.[126] It is also important to note that the resolution directly addresses only proliferation to non-state actors, not to states. In 2006, the Security Council passed Resolution 1673, extending the program established by Resolution 1540 for two years.[127] It is too soon to predict, however, whether Resolution 1540 directed against non-state actors, Resolution 1696 against Iran, Resolution 1718 against North Korea, and the growing family of resolutions aimed at denying terrorists access to weapons will ever be effectively implemented and measurably strengthen the developing antiproliferation regime.

---

[124]*See* U.S. Dep't of State, *United States Report to the Nonproliferation Committee—Efforts Regarding United Nations Security Council Resolution 1540,* Sept. 27, 2004, available at http://www.state.gov/t/np/rls/37375.htm.

[125]U.N. Security Council Press Release SC/8076 (4956th meeting), Apr. 28, 2004, *available at* http://www.un.org/News/Press/docs/2004/sc8076.doc.htm. *See also* Report of the 4956th Meeting of the Security Council, Apr. 28, 2004, U.N. Doc. S/PV.4956 (2004).

[126]Reportedly China agreed to support the resolution only after a provision for interdiction at sea was removed, stating publicly that "That nasty word, interdiction, has been taken out." *See U.S. Wins China's Support for Ban on Proliferation,* BLOOMBERG.COM NEWS, Mar. 25, 2004; Warren Hodge, *Ban on Weapons of Doom is Extended to Qaeda-Style Groups,* N.Y. TIMES, Apr. 29, 2004 (reporting that China ended a threat to use its veto when language that called for interception at sea was dropped).

[127]U.N. Security Council, Res. 1673, U.N. Doc. S/RES/1673 (2006).

4

A Coalition of the Concerned and Committed: Post-9/11 Multilateral Counterproliferation Initiatives

A multilateral approach that includes both nonproliferation and counterproliferation measures will be essential to success in halting proliferation of weapons of mass destruction, particularly proliferation that might put WMD in the hands of a terrorist organization. The need for multilateralism was amply demonstrated by the Abdul Qadeer Kahn network, which operated out of Pakistan to sell nuclear weapons technology and equipment to North Korea, Libya, and Iran,[1] using components obtained or assembled in Europe, Dubai, and Malaysia.[2] The *National Security Strategy* and *National Strategy to Combat Weapons of Mass Destruction* recognize that the United States will promote and support nonproliferation and back up its commitment to nonproliferation with counterproliferation measures when appropriate. The national strategies recognize, however, that not all states can or will meet their nonproliferation responsibilities to the international community.[3] Most states are willing and able to do so. Some states are willing, but presently unable to meet the nonproliferation obligations. Finally, there is a third group of states that are either reluctant or unwilling to meet their obligations. Counterproliferation efforts like the Proliferation Security Initiative can be seen as an initiative by the nations within the first group, acting with the cooperation of the second group, to interpose an effective bulwark against the proliferation dangers created by the third group.

---

[1]Paul Reynolds, *Pakistan Leaks Prompt Western Resolve,* BBC NEWS.COM, Feb. 5, 2004.

[2]William J. Broad & David E. Sanger, *The Bomb Merchant: Chasing Dr. Kahn's Network,* N.Y. TIMES, Dec. 26, 2004, at A1.

[3]White House, *National Strategy for Combating Terrorism* 11–12 (2003, updated version Sept. 2006).

EVOLUTION OF THE PROLIFERATION SECURITY INITIATIVE

Roots of the Proliferation Security Initiative date back more than a decade. On December 7, 1993, Secretary of Defense Les Aspin announced the Clinton Administration's Defense Counterproliferation Initiative (DCI). According to Secretary Aspin, the spread of WMD represents one of the most direct and urgent threats facing U.S. national security. He contrasted the old nuclear danger of a massive Soviet first strike with that of "perhaps a handful of nuclear devices in the hands of rogue states or even terrorist groups. The engine of this new danger is proliferation."[4] He also asserted that "with this initiative, we are making the essential change demanded by this increased [proliferation] threat. We are adding the task of protection to the task of *prevention*. . . . At the heart of the Defense Counterproliferation Initiative, therefore, is a drive to develop *new military capabilities* to deal with this new threat."[5]

The September 11, 2001, attacks and the growing proliferation threats posed by North Korea, Iran, and Iraq highlighted the need to move beyond the initial counterproliferation efforts. President George W. Bush formally announced the multilateral Proliferation Security Initiative in a speech in Poland on May 31, 2003, just prior to the Group of Eight (G-8) Summit in Krakow.[6] In words reminiscent of Secretary Aspin's a decade earlier, the president first asserted that the "greatest threat to peace is the spread of nuclear, chemical and biological weapons," then announced:

> When weapons of mass destruction or their components are in transit, we must have the means and authority to seize them. So today I announce a new effort to fight proliferation called the Proliferation Security Initiative. The United States and a number of our close allies, including Poland, have begun working on new agreements to search planes and ships carrying suspect cargo and to seize illegal weapons or missile technologies. Over time, we will extend this partnership as broadly as possible to keep the world's most destructive weapons away from our shores and out of the hand our common enemies.[7]

The president's strategy built upon one of the core themes of his commencement address at the U.S. Military Academy one year earlier, and may well have gained momentum after the December 2002 incident involving the joint Spanish-U.S. boarding of the M/V *So San,* which was intercepted while carrying Scud missiles from North Korea to Yemen.[8]

---

[4]Secretary of Defense Les Aspin, *Speech to the National Academy of Sciences,* Washington, D.C., Dec. 7, 1993.

[5]*Ibid.* (emphasis added).

[6]White House, *Remarks by President George W. Bush to the People of Poland,* May 31, 2003, *available at* http://www.whitehouse.gov/news/releases/2003/05/20030531–3.html [hereinafter "President's PSI Remarks"].

[7]*Ibid.* at 2.

[8]*See* Carla Anne Robbins, *Why U.S. Gave U.N. No Role in Plan to Halt Arms Ships,* WALL ST. J., Oct. 21, 2003, at A1 (concluding that U.S. frustration over the 2002 M/V *So San* incident provided one incentive for launching a broader initiative to fight weapons proliferation).

Ten states initially joined the United States in the PSI, including Australia, France, Germany, Italy, Japan, the Netherlands, Poland, Portugal, Spain, and the United Kingdom.[9] The participating states met several times shortly after President Bush's May 2003 announcement.[10] In an address to the U.N. General Assembly on September 23, 2003, President Bush described the PSI, outlined the Statement of Interdiction Principles developed by all of the PSI participating states, and exhorted that "[b]ecause proliferators will use any route or channel that is open to them, we need the broadest possible cooperation to stop them."[11] By December 2003, the original 11 participating states were joined by Canada, Norway, and Singapore.[12] In 2004, Russia joined the initiative, bringing the number of participating states to 15, including all but one of the permanent members of the Security Council. Notably absent from the group of participating states are China, India, and South Korea.[13] Liberia, Panama, and the Marshall Islands became supporting players in the PSI in 2004 when they entered into bilateral shipboarding agreements with the United States to enforce nonproliferation measures. Belize, Croatia, and Cyprus entered into similar PSI boarding agreements in 2005. Sixty-two states indicated their support for the PSI at the first anniversary meeting in Krakow on May 31, 2004.[14] By the third anniversary in 2006 the number of states which had participated in the PSI had grown to 77.[15]

Although the framework established by the PSI is evolving, its members have made it clear that the initiative is intended to supplement, not displace, the existing nonproliferation regime. The initiative is a political commitment to implement effective measures, either individually or in concert with other

---

[9] *See* Proliferation Security Initiative, *Chairman's Statement, Brisbane Meeting,* July 9–10, 2003, *available at* http://www.dfat.gov.au/globalissues/psi/index.html.

[10] Plenary meetings were held in Madrid (June 2003), Brisbane (July 2003), Paris (Sept. 2003), London (Oct. 2003), Lisbon (Mar. 2004), and Krakow (May–June 2004). In addition, several "operational" meetings were conducted over the same period, including an experts' meeting in Washington, DC in December 2003 and another in Ottawa in April 2004. Information on subsequent meetings is published at U.S. Dep't of State, Bureau of Nonproliferation, *Calendar of Events, Proliferation Security Initiative Exercises, available at* http://www.state.gov/t/np/c12684.htm.

[11] White House, *President Addresses United Nations General Assembly,* Sept. 23, 2003, *available at* http://www.whitehouse.gov/news/releases/2003/09/20030923–4.html.

[12] *U.S., Allies Seek Right to Board Ships in WMD Search,* 34 Arms Control Today, Jan.–Feb. 2004, at 37.

[13] Although China has not supported the PSI, it did vote in favor of U.N. Security Council Resolution 1540 (after any mention of interdiction authority was removed) and agreed to join the Container Security Initiative. China has also joined the Zangger Committee, negotiations are underway for China to become a member of the NSG and the MTCR, and consultations between China and members of the Australia Group and the Wassenaar Arrangement have increased. Ye Ru'an & Zhao Qinghai, *The PSI: Chinese Thinking and Concern,* The Monitor 22 (Spring 2004), at 10.

[14] *Chairman's Statement at the First Anniversary Proliferation Security Initiative Meeting*, June 1, 2004, *available at* http://www.state.gov/t/rls/other/33208pf.htm.

[15] *See Proliferation Security Initiative: Chairman's Statement at High-Level Political Meeting,* June 23, 2006 ("the number of states that have expressed support for the PSI Principles and have committed to actively supporting interdiction efforts whenever necessary has increased to more than 75"), *available at* http://www.state.gov/t/isn/rls/other/69799.htm.

states, to interdict the transfer or transport of WMD, delivery systems, or related materials to or from countries of proliferation concern. The PSI is not simply an organization, but rather the framework for an active and evolving initiative of multiple players to accomplish a set of specific, shared, and vital goals through diplomatic, economic, legal, and military means. Elements of the PSI include strengthened export control, trade inspections, sharing information on suspected shipments, shippers, consignees, and carriers, and increased searches of vessels, planes, and vehicles. The initiative builds on the base established by existing non-proliferation norms, including applicable treaties and other regimes. It is also complemented by the World Customs Organization's 2005 "Framework of Standards to Secure and Facilitate Global Trade."[16] Ultimately, the PSI will focus on the transport phase of the exchange between illicit proliferators and their end-users. It will do so by taking full advantage of the legal authorities in the existing regime, obtaining cooperation and consent of other concerned states and offering resources to those states to assist them in meeting their international nonproliferation obligations, timely sharing information, and conducting frequent and realistic multinational exercises.

Each of the PSI members has committed not to transport or assist in the transport of WMD cargoes to or from states or non-state actors of proliferation concern, or to allow persons or entities subject to their jurisdiction to do so. The PSI thus implicates the jurisdiction and responsibilities of the participants in their roles as port states, coastal states, flag states, and transshipment states. The participating members also drafted a model boarding agreement and a Statement of Interdiction Principles (SIPs).[17] The SIPs (reproduced in Appendix B) includes both general practices and "specific actions" in support of interdiction efforts regarding cargoes of WMD, their delivery systems, or related materials."[18] The "specific actions" are to include vessel boardings at-sea and in port. All such boardings are to be conducted in compliance with applicable international and national laws.[19] At the same time, the participating states will seek to strengthen relevant international norms.[20] The SIPs encourage all concerned states to undertake "effective measures, either alone or in concert with other states, for interdicting the transfer or transport of WMD, their delivery systems, and related materials to and from states and non-state actors of proliferation

---

[16]*See* World Customs Organization, *Framework of Standards to Secure and Facilitate Global Trade, done* at Brussels, Belgium, June 23, 2005. This framework, by the 166-member WCO, is modeled on the CSI and C-TPAT. The goal is to detect weapons of concern in shipment before they arrive.

[17]*See Statement by the White House Press Secretary: Proliferation Security Initiative,* Sept. 4, 2003, *available at* http://www.state.gov/t/np/rls/prsrl/23809.htm. *See also* U.S. DEP'T OF STATE, DIGEST OF UNITED STATES PRACTICE IN INTERNATIONAL LAW 2003, at 1096–98 (2004).

[18]Interdiction Principles for the Proliferation Security Initiative, *done* at Paris, Sept. 4, 2003, para. 1, [hereinafter "Statement of Interdiction Principles"].

[19]*Ibid.* para. 4.

[20]Mohamed El Baradei, the IAEA Director-General, warned of a "very sophisticated and complex underground network of black market operators. . .not much different from organized crime cartels." Paul Reynolds, *Pakistan Leaks Prompt Western Resolve,* BBC NEWS.COM, Feb. 5, 2004.

concern."[21] Interdictions may be undertaken by states in their capacity as the competent flag, port, or coastal state, on their own initiative or, in some cases, "at the request and good cause shown by another state."[22]

The phrase "states or non-state actors of proliferation concern" refers to those countries or entities that the PSI participants involved determine should be subject to interdiction activities because they are engaged in proliferation through: (1) efforts to develop or acquire chemical, biological, or nuclear weapons and associated delivery systems; or (2) transfers (either selling, receiving, or facilitating) of WMD, their delivery systems, or related materials.[23] Although no particular states of interest are listed in the SIPs, North Korea and Iran were frequently referred to by the PSI states.[24] The fact that both states were later the subject of Security Council resolutions demonstrates that those early judgments were correct. The United States has also publicly indicated on several occasions that Syria is a state of proliferation concern.[25]

At its March 2004 meeting in Lisbon, the PSI members developed a set of "practical steps," which outline suggested ways that states can make concrete contributions to building the PSI's operational capacity. The practical steps invite states to issue a formal statement of support for the PSI and its Statement of Interdiction Principles, review and provide information on current national legal authorities, establish points of contact and good internal procedures, identify operational assets, engage in training efforts, and be willing to conclude relevant agreements or take other measures to facilitate cooperation.[26]

PSI MARITIME INTERCEPTION EXERCISES AND EVENTS

The PSI participating states initially agreed to hold 10 multilateral maritime, air, and ground training exercises. The operational exercises serve several purposes. First, they are designed and executed to improve the capabilities of the counterproliferation forces and coordination among the participants. Second, they demonstrate the depth of the political commitment of the PSI participants. Third, they provide an opportunity for states that support the PSI but are not yet participating states to attend and even take part in the exercises. Finally, the very willingness of so many states to commit significant resources to PSI exercises serves notice on current and would-be proliferators and their transporters that counterproliferation forces are now fully committed to an effective interdiction program.

---

[21] *Statement of Interdiction Principles, infra* Appendix B, para. 1.

[22] *Ibid.* para. 4.b. *See also ibid.* para. 4.e (interdiction of aircraft).

[23] *Ibid.* para. 1.

[24] Proliferation Security Initiative, *Chairman's Statement, Brisbane Meeting,* July 9–10, 2003, *available at* http://www.dfat.gov.au/globalissues/psi/index.html.

[25] George Jahn, *Bush Urges World to Stem WMD Trafficking,* Assoc. Press, June 1, 2004.

[26] *See* John R. Bolton, Undersecretary of State for Arms Control and International Security, *The Proliferation Security Initiative: A Vision Becomes Reality,* Remarks to the First Anniversary Meeting of the Proliferation Security Initiative, May 31, 2004, *available at* http://www.state.gov/t/us/rm/33046pf.htm.

More than 20 maritime PSI exercises involving participating and supporting states have been conducted since the initiative was launched.[27] Although several of the exercises focused on air and ground interdiction, most have involved maritime operations. From August 15–19, 2005, Singapore hosted Operation *Deep Sabre*, a 13-nation maritime exercise in the South China Sea. The exercise—the 18th since the PSI was launched and the first to be held in Southeast Asia—integrated an at-sea boarding (conducted by a combination of military and law enforcement forces) with a port search operation (conducted primarily by law enforcement).[28] *Deep Sabre* also marked New Zealand's first participation in a PSI maritime interdiction exercise.[29] Later maritime exercises were led by the Netherlands (Exercise *Top Port*), Turkey (Exercise *Anatolian Sun*), Australia (Exercise *Pacific Protector*), and Poland (Exercise *Amber Sunrise*). In addition, the eight states participating in U.S. Pacific Command's 2006 "Rim of the Pacific" (RIMPAC) exercise conducted a PSI exercise. In late October 2006, 25 states, including Japan, Pakistan, South Korea, Bahrain, Kuwait, Iraq, Qatar, and United Arab Emirates, participated in or served as observers in Operation *Leading Edge* in the Arabian Gulf, just 20 miles outside Iran's territorial sea.[30] The exercise was conducted on the same day that 13 states announced the new Global Initiative to Combat Nuclear Terrorism.[31]

Although the PSI participating states have been deliberately reticent about reporting on their actual interdiction activities, to guard against would-be proliferators or transporters using such reports to devise strategies to circumvent the measures, a U.S. government source reported that roughly a dozen interdictions had been carried out by the spring of 2004.[32] The following year, two dozen or so PSI operations were

---

[27]These include Operations *Pacific Protector I* (Coral Sea, September 2003), *Sanso* (Mediterranean Sea, October 2003), *Sea Saber* (Arabian Sea, January 2004), *Clever Sentinel* (Mediterranean Sea, April 2004), *Team Samurai* (Sagami Bay, Japan, October 2004), *Chokepoint '04* (Key West, FL, November 2004), *NINFA '05* (Portugal-led, April 2005), *Deep Sabre* (Singapore, October 2005), *Exploring Themis* (U.K.-led, November 2005), *Pacific Protector II* (Australia-led, April, 2006), and Exercise *Amber Sunrise* (Poland-led, September 2006). *See* U.S. Dep't of State, Bureau of Nonproliferation, *Calendar of Events, Proliferation Security Initiative Exercises, available at* http://www.state.gov/t/np/c12684.htm.

[28]*See* U.S. Dep't of State, *Singapore Hosts Proliferation Security Initiative (PSI) Interdiction Exercise (Deep Sabre), available at* http://www.state.gov/r/pa/prs/ps/2005/51032.htm.

[29]Janaki Kremmer, *For Security's Sake, Old Rift with New Zealand Overlooked by US,* CHRISTIAN SCI. MON., Aug. 19, 2005, *available at* http://www.csmonitor.com/2005/0819/p07s02-woap.html. A New Zealand security expert characterized the new situation "Since September 11, it's now all hands on the pump." *Ibid.*

[30]U.S. Dep't of State, *United States Hosts Proliferation Security Initiative Interdiction Exercise,* Oct. 27, 2006, *available at* http://www.state.gov/r/pa/prs/ps/2006/75274.htm.

[31]John Thorne, *U.S. 12 Others Join in Bid to Keep Nuclear Weapons from Terrorists,* PHILA. INQUIRER, Oct. 31, 2006. The initiative grew out of a joint agreement between President Bush and President Putin in July 2006. The member-states include Australia, Canada, China, France, Germany, Italy, Japan, Kazakhstan, Morocco, Russia, Turkey, the United Kingdom, and the United States.

[32]Judith Miller, *Panama Joins Accord to Stem Ships' Transport of Illicit Arms,* N.Y. TIMES, May 11, 2004.

carried out.[33] The first significant interdiction following announcement of the PSI involved the *BBC China,* a German ship that was transporting uranium enrichment equipment made in Malaysia to Libya, via Dubai.[34] The interdiction began when American and British intelligence services discovered in late September of 2003 that a freighter bound for Libya was transporting parts for a centrifuge which could be used to produce weapons-grade uranium. With the cooperation of the flag state (Germany) and the shipowner, the vessel was diverted to an Italian port shortly after entering the Mediterranean from the Suez Canal. Italian authorities boarded the vessel upon its arrival in Taranto and seized the centrifuge materials, which were not listed on the ship's cargo manifest. Libya's decision to abandon its WMD program may have been motivated in part by the *BBC China* interdiction and the evidence it provided on Libya's nuclear weapons ambition.[35]

IDENTIFYING AND RESOLVING PSI ISSUES

Issues raised by the PSI and the exercises and actual interdictions carried out to date have been examined in the various plenary sessions and at meetings of experts on operational, intelligence, and political questions. Experts' meetings are often attended by representatives from states that are not yet PSI participating states. At the first meeting of the participating states held in Madrid in June 2003, the United States urged the other participants to work together to (1) prevent the import or export of weapons of mass destruction and missile delivery systems, (2) interdict any vessels or aircraft believed to be transporting such materials through the participating states' territory or territorial sea or airspace, and (3) interdict vessels on the high seas where necessary. At the second meeting held in Brisbane, Australia, in July 2003, concerns over international law limits led the other states to oppose the initial proposal by the United States for high-seas boardings, at least in the absence of flag state consent. Accordingly, the list of "specific actions" in the Statement of Interdiction Principles issued at the September 2003 meeting in Paris omits any reference to nonconsensual boardings of foreign flag vessels on the high seas. At the London meeting in December 2003, the United States proposed to partially fill the high-seas enforcement gap by negotiating bilateral WMD boarding agreements with

---

[33]At the 2006 anniversary meeting, the U.S. representative reported that: "Between April 2005 and April 2006, the United States worked successfully with multiple PSI partners in Europe, Asia and the Middle East on roughly two dozen separate occasions to prevent transfers of equipment and materials to WMD and missile programs in countries of concern. For example, PSI cooperation has stopped the export to Iran's missile program of controlled equipment and dual-use goods. One PSI partner has also stopped the export of heavy water-related equipment to Iran's nuclear program." Robert G. Joseph, Under Secretary for Arms Control and International Security, *Broadening and Deepening Our Proliferation Security Initiative Cooperation,* June 23, 2006, *available at* http://www.state.gov/t/us/rm/68269.htm.

[34]Robin Wright, *Ship Incident May Have Swayed Libya,* WASH. POST, Jan. 1, 2004, at A18.

[35]*Ibid.* A Malaysian investigation traced the centrifuge parts to members of the A.Q. Kahn black market organization. *See* Ray Bonner, *Multinational Network Aided Pakistan's Nuclear Help to Libya,* INT'L HERALD TRIB. ONLINE (2002).

selected flag states. States participating in the 2004 meeting in Lisbon agreed to begin examining key steps necessary for expanding the PSI, including possible political actions, and to identify national law enforcement authorities and other assets that could be brought to bear to stop entities that facilitate or finance the proliferators.

Expert groups from PSI participating states have also met on several occasions to identify and resolve issues raised by the initiative. At the December 2003 operational meeting in Washington, DC, PSI experts were given briefings by a number of senior U.S. officials. A second experts' meeting in Ottawa in April 2004 challenged the participating states to identify all of the possible legal bases available to support PSI interdiction activities. A stated goal of the operational law review has been to identify any gaps in legal authorities needed to effectively carry out the initiative. Four more experts' meetings were conducted later in 2004, one of which focused on shipping container security. Three operational expert meetings were held in 2005 and again in 2006.[36]

FLAG STATE BOARDING AGREEMENTS

At the 2003 London meeting of the PSI participating states, the United States presented a proposal to the other participants to negotiate standing agreements with key flag states to put in place a framework for consensual boardings of vessels flying their flag. With the support of the other PSI members, the United States negotiated bilateral agreements with Liberia,[37] Panama,[38] the Marshall Islands,[39] Croatia,[40] Cyprus,[41] and Belize,[42] which together account for more than 60 percent of the world's commercial vessel tonnage. The agreements, which fall within the rubric of "specific actions" under paragraph 4.c of the Statement of Interdiction Principles, are broadly similar in their terms, though they take different forms. Most mirror the operative provisions of bilateral agreements already in place for counter-narcotics

[36] *See* U.S. Dep't of State, Bureau of Nonproliferation, *Calendar of Events, Proliferation Security Initiative Operational Experts Meetings, available at* http://www.state.gov/t/np/c12684.htm.

[37] *See* Agreement Between the Government of the United States of America and the Government of the Republic of Liberia, *available at* http://www.state.gov/t/np/trty/32403.htm.

[38] Amendment to the Supplementary Agreement Between the Government of the United States of America and the Government of the Republic of Panama to the Arrangement Between the Government of the United States of America and the Government of the Republic of Panama, *available at* http://www.state.gov/t/np/trty/32859.htm.

[39] Agreement Between the Government of the United States of America and the Government of the Republic of the Marshall Islands, *available at* http://www.state.gov/t/np/trty/35237.htm.

[40] Agreement between the Government of the United States of America and the Government of the Republic of Croatia, *available at* http://www.state.gov/t/np/trty/47086.htm.

[41] Agreement Between the Government of the United States of America and the Government of the Republic of Cyprus, *available at* http://www.state.gov/t/np/trty/50274.htm.

[42] Agreement Between the Government of the United States of America and the Government of Belize, *available at* http://www.state.gov/t/np/trty/50809.htm.

interdiction operations.[43] The agreement with Panama is an amendment to the existing arrangement between the two states, establishing a bilateral maritime law enforcement program.[44] Activities under the agreements are generally limited to waters seaward of any state's territorial sea. The agreements do not in themselves authorize boardings to interdict WMD shipments under all circumstances. They do, however, provide a mechanism for expedited review by the relevant flag state of a request by the United States to board one of its vessels and include a provision for presumed consent if the request is not denied within two hours of the request.[45] The agreements also address detention of vessels and their crews and cargoes pending instructions by the flag state's designated competent authority, as well as the allocation of jurisdiction in the event evidence of a violation is discovered.[46]

RESPONSES TO THE PSI

The Proliferation Security Initiative has been characterized by one global news source as the "best idea so far" in global efforts to curb proliferation.[47] One commentator favorably compared its development to that of the key multilateral export control regimes.[48] The 9/11 Commission's final report recommended that the PSI be expanded.[49] By 2004, more than 60 states had signaled their support for the PSI,[50] as did the 26 members of NATO in the

---

[43]In general, the bilateral counter-narcotics agreements operate within the framework established by Article 108 of the 1982 U.N. Convention on the Law of the Sea and Article 17 of the 1988 United Nations Convention Against Illicit Traffic in Narcotic Drugs and Psychotropic Substances.

[44]The preamble describes the underlying agreement as one that establishes "a program for conducting bilateral maritime law enforcement operations to stop illegal activities, such as the international trafficking of drugs, illegal fishing and transportation of contraband." U.S.-Panama WMD Shipboarding Agreements, *supra.*

[45]Although it would be more correct to refer to these as presumed consent agreements, for the sake of simplicity all such agreements will be referred to as shipboarding agreements.

[46]Under the terms of Security Council Resolution 1540, the flag state has an obligation to "adopt and enforce appropriate effective laws which prohibit any non-State actor to . . . transport, transfer or use nuclear, chemical or biological weapons and their means of delivery, in particular for terrorist purposes."

[47]*See Proliferating Worries,* The Economist, Mar. 1, 2004.

[48]Seema Gahlaut, *The PSI Will Parallel the Multilateral Export Control Regimes,* 10 The Monitor (Spring 2004), at 12–15.

[49]*Final Report of the National Commission on Terrorist Attacks Upon the United States* 381 (2004). The report also concluded "The PSI can be more effective if it uses intelligence and planning resources of the NATO alliance." *Ibid.* It goes on to recommend that membership should be open to non-NATO countries, including China and Russia. At the time the report was released, Russia was already a participating PSI state, as were non-NATO members Australia, Japan, and Singapore.

[50]Palacio Foz, *Proliferation Security Initiative: Chairman's Statement at the Fifth Meeting,* Lisbon Portugal, Mar. 5, 2004, *available at* http://www.state.gov/t/np/rls/other/30960.htm. By the time of the third anniversary meeting of PSI states in June 2006, participation had swelled to more than 70 states. *See* U.S. Department of State, Robert G. Joseph, Under Secretary for Arms Control and International Security, *Broadening and Deepening Our Proliferation Security Initiative Cooperation, available at* http://www.state.gov/t/us/rm/68269.htm.

2004 Istanbul Summit Communiqué.[51] Even the past president of the American Society of International Law has hailed the PSI as a step in the right direction.[52] The initiative is supported by the G-8, all of whom are now formal participants in the PSI.[53] At their June 2004 summit, the G-8 members adopted a new Action Plan on Nonproliferation that reiterated the members' "strong commitment to and support for" the PSI and the Statement of Interdiction Principles.[54] The members also pledged to work to broaden and strengthen the domestic and international laws supporting the PSI. At the 2005 summit in Gleneagles, Scotland, the G-8 members reaffirmed their commitment to countering the threat posed by proliferation.[55] In 2004, the U.S. Congress fully endorsed the PSI—including its provisions for physical interdictions—when it enacted the Intelligence Reform and Terrorism Prevention Act of 2004 and confirmed the establishment and missions of the National Counter Proliferation Center. The Act announced that:

> It is the sense of Congress that a central feature of counter proliferation activities, consistent with the President's Proliferation Security Initiative, should include physical interdiction, by air, sea, or land, of weapons of mass destruction, their delivery systems, and related materials and technologies, and enhanced law enforcement activities to identify and disrupt proliferation networks, activities, organizations, and persons.[56]

In all, the 109th Congress considered five different bills or resolutions that call for strengthening and expanding the PSI.[57]

---

[51]North Atlantic Treaty Organization, *Istanbul Summit Communiqué,* June 28, 2004, para. 15, *available at* http://www.nato.int/docu/pr/2004/p04–096e.htm. Preventing the proliferation of WMD is one of the potential anchor points of the 2006 NATO Response Force initiative. *See NATO 'Reinventing' Itself, General Says,* AM. FORCES PRESS SERV., Mar. 8, 2006, *available at* http://www.defenselink.mil/news/Mar2006/20060308_4431.html.

[52]Lee Feinstein & Anne-Marie Slaughter, *A Duty to Prevent,* 83 FOREIGN AFF. 136, 146 (2004).

[53]*See* The G-8 Global Partnership: *Principles to Prevent Terrorists, or Those that Harbor Them, From Gaining Access to Weapons or Materials of Mass Destruction,* para. 4 (Kananaskis, Alberta (Canada) June 26–27, 2002), *available at* http://www.G-8.gc.ca/2002Kananaskis/kananaskis/globpart-en.asp. The focus of the G-8 statement is on stabilizing nuclear materials of the former Soviet Union and preventing such materials from falling into the hands of terrorists. The G-8 agreed to contribute $20 billion to fight proliferation over the next ten years, half of which will come from the United States. Russia was the last of the G-8 members to join the PSI.

[54]*G-8 Action Plan on Nonproliferation,* June 9, 2004, *available at* http://www.whitehouse.gov/news/releases/2004/06/20040609–28.html.

[55]*G-8 Gleneagle's Summit, Chair's Summary,* July 8, 2005, *available at* http://www.g8.gov.uk/servlet/Front?pagename=OpenMarket/Xcelerate/ShowPage&c=Page&cid=1119518698846.

[56]Intelligence Reform and Terrorism Prevention Act of 2004, Pub. L. No. 108–458, Title I, Subtitle B, § 1022, 118 Stat. 3675 (2004).

[57]Congressional Research Service, *Proliferation Security Initiative,* CRS Rep. RS21881 (June 7, 2005), at 5.

The PSI is also consistent with a declaration by the European Union, which acknowledges that coherent and concerted efforts are needed to prevent the proliferation of WMD and their delivery systems.[58] Speaking to a 2003 conference on proliferation challenges, the U.N. Under-Secretary-General for Disarmament Affairs acknowledged the growing legitimacy of the PSI:

> This brings me to the "Proliferation Security Initiative"—the subject of a presentation at our second Plenary session. This initiative—announced by a group of states interested in interdicting illicit shipments of goods relating to missiles and WMD—may well become, as its membership grows and it gains greater international legitimacy, a foundation or framework for coordinated, multilateral action to enforce nonproliferation norms.
>
> Indeed, it would be most appropriate for such enforcement actions to be undertaken, in accordance with the UN Charter, as a result of decisions made in the Security Council. The fate of this Initiative—in particular its future relationship to the UN Security Council—offers a rich subject for discussion, for it is an issue with many profound implications for the future ability of the world community to enforce its most solemn disarmament and nonproliferation norms.[59]

The December 2, 2004, report of the U.N. Secretary-General's High-level Panel on Threats, Challenges and Changes similarly encouraged all states to join the PSI.[60] The report further suggests that the Security Council may need to consider mandatory action to implement the PSI if progress on amending the SUA Convention proves unsatisfactory.[61]

The PSI participating states have enlisted the cooperation of key coastal and flag states. As discussed above, Liberia, Panama, and the Marshall Islands, three of the world's largest shipping registries, have entered into standing agreements with the United States to conduct PSI boardings of vessels registered in those states, as have Croatia, Cyprus, and Belize. Additionally, the United States is reportedly negotiating agreements with numerous coastal states to gain authority for PSI-related boardings in the participating coastal states' waters.[62] In light of the sensitive nature of the

---

[58]Council of the European Union, *Basic Principles for an EU Strategy Against Weapons of Mass Destruction,* Doc. 10352/03, Brussels, June 10, 2003; *E.U.-U.S. Joint Statement on the Proliferation of Weapons of Mass Destruction,* June 25, 2003 (addressing states and non-state actors of proliferation concern, with particular reference to North Korea and Iran); *see also* European Union, *A Secure Europe in a Better World: The European Security Strategy, done* at Brussels, Dec. 12, 2003, *available at* http://ue.eu.int/uedocs/cmsUpload/78367.pdf.

[59]Statement by Nobuyasu Abe, U.N. Under-Secretary-General for Disarmament Affairs, Dec. 3, 2003, *available at* http://disarmament.un.org:8080/speech/03dec2003.htm.

[60]The United Nations' Secretary-General's High-Level Panel on Threats, Challenges and Change, Final Report: *A More Secure World: Our Shared Responsibility,* at 45, para. 132, U.N. Doc. A/59/565, Dec. 1, 2004.

[61]*Ibid.* para. 133.

[62]In 2002, the U.S. State Department reportedly began negotiating agreements with dozens of coastal states to permit U.S. Navy vessels to pursue and board suspect ships in the coastal states' waters. *See* Pauline, Jelinek, *U.S. Aims for More Power to Police Seas,* Assoc. Press, Aug. 10, 2002. As of 2005 there was no indication that any such agreements had been negotiated. However, it is unlikely that such agreements would be announced, alerting would-be proliferators.

operations involved and the potential for proliferators and their facilitators to use any information on the details on specific PSI operations and modalities to circumvent the initiative, it is unlikely that the identity of the cooperating coastal states and details regarding the location and methods of actual interdiction operations and seizures will be announced.[63] However, on August 15, 2005, Robert Joseph, the Undersecretary of State for Arms Control and International Security, reported that in the previous nine months alone the United States and 10 of its fellow PSI partners "have quietly cooperated on 11 successful efforts."[64] The maritime interception strategy embraced by the PSI states may have played a role in nudging Libya into renouncing its WMD ambitions.[65] Not long after a cargo of centrifuge parts en route to Libya were intercepted, Libya abandoned its long-standing WMD development programs.

Opinions on the PSI are not universally favorable, particularly among academics. The fact that the PSI is multilateral and its members have pledged to carry out their PSI activities in accordance with international law has not insulated the initiative from criticism. Some have decried the PSI as an encroachment on the LOS Convention principles of freedom of navigation and exclusive flag state jurisdiction, though the critics have yet to identify any PSI action that failed to comply with the Statement of Interdiction Principles or the relevant rules of international law.[66] Other critics have focused on an early statement by the United States indicating that the right of self-defense under Article 51 of the U.N. Charter might legitimate some WMD interdictions, ignoring the fact that the Statement of Interdiction Principles plainly states that PSI operations will be carried on consistently with international law.[67] Still others worried that the PSI would lead to a virtual blockade

---

[63]John Bolton, former Undersecretary of State for Arms Control and International Security, warned that PSI interdictions would likely not be publicized, to deny proliferators information they might use to circumvent PSI efforts. *See* Wade Boese & Miles Pomper, *The Proliferation Security Initiative: An Interview with John Bolton,* ARMS CONTROL TODAY, Dec. 11, 2003, at 37, *available at* http://www.armscontrol.org/act/2003_12/PSI.asp. If followed, this practice may slow the development of customary international law by withholding evidence of state practice. *See* The North Sea Continental Shelf Cases (F.R.G. v. Den./F.R.G. v. Neth.) 1969 ICJ REP. 3, 41, para. 71 (Feb. 20) (customary law evolves by general and consistent state practice followed out of sense of legal right or obligation).

[64]Robert Joseph, Undersecretary of State for Arms Control and International Security, *Transforming our Counterproliferation Efforts in the Asia Region,* remarks to the Institute of Defense and Strategic Studies, Aug. 15, 2005, *available at* http://www.state.gov/t/us/rm/51129.htm.

[65]*See* [Senator] *Lugar Welcome's President's Support of Nunn-Lugar Expansion; Praises Nonproliferation Initiative,* Feb. 11, 2004, *available at* http://lugar.senate.gov/pressapp/record.cfm?id=217970.

[66]In fact, any action that violated international law would, *ipso facto,* violate the Statement of Interdiction Principles agreed to by all of the PSI participating states.

[67]Charter of the United Nations, art. 51. Although when asked whether the United States would rely on Article 51 to justify the PSI, Secretary Bolton responded that nothing is "off the table," none of the other PSI participating states endorsed a self-defense rationale for the PSI and the Department of State guidance on the PSI does not include self-defense among its list of legal bases for the PSI. *See* U.S. Dep't of State, *Proliferation Security Initiative, Frequently Asked Questions,* May 26, 2005, *available at* http://www.state.gov/t/np/rls/fs/46839.htm.

of North Korea.[68] In fact, the North Korean government condemned one of the early PSI maritime exercises as "provocative," and labeled the PSI itself as evidence of the United States' "hostile" policy toward North Korea.[69] The decision by a unanimous Security Council to pass Resolution 1718, imposing a selective embargo on North Korea under Chapter VII of the U.N. Charter, moots those arguments.

Apart from the attacks on the PSI from the president's opponents within the United States, two Chinese officials listed China's five principal concerns with the PSI.[70] First, they argued that the PSI was not firmly grounded in international law. Second, they worried that some PSI interdictions might contravene existing legal instruments. Third, they complained that the PSI participating states had not sought Security Council support for their operations, and apparently planned to exclude the council from implementing and enforcing its resolution. Fourth, China was concerned that the states that take part in PSI interdictions must be prepared to provide compensation for unjustified boardings or seizures, a concern that likely stems from the 1993 incident involving the PRC-flag container ship *Yin He*.[71] Finally, they argued that the PSI does little to address the underlying causes of proliferation. One source of Chinese criticism was addressed in early 2004, when the U.N. Security Council invoked its Chapter VII authority, in Resolution 1540, to address the threat of WMD proliferation and terrorism.

SYNERGIES BETWEEN UNSC RESOLUTION 1540 AND THE PSI

U.N. Security Council Resolution 1540, which is reproduced in Appendix A, recognizes that WMD proliferation poses a threat to international peace and security, within the meaning of Article 39 of the U.N. Charter.[72] That finding was reiterated in Resolution 1718, directed against North Korea following its 2006 missile and nuclear device tests. The Article 39 finding serves as the predicate for further

---

[68]International Institute for Strategic Studies, *The Proliferation Security Initiative: An Interdiction Strategy,* 9 Strategic Comments, no. 10 (2003) ("others fear that [the PSI] will be a pervasive dragnet, tantamount to a naval blockade that in the case of North Korea risks inciting war"), *available at* http://www.iiss.org/stratcomfree.php?scID=282.

[69]John R. Bolton, former Undersecretary for Arms Control and International Security, *The Bush Administration's Nonproliferation Policy: Success and Future Challenges,* Testimony before the House International Relations Committee, Mar. 30, 2004, at 7.

[70]Ye Ru'an & Zhao Qinghai, *The PSI: Chinese Thinking and Concern,* at 22.

[71]In 1993, the United States alleged that the Chinese container ship *Yin He* was carrying chemical precursors used to produce mustard gas and sarin nerve gas from China to Iran. Secretary of State Warren Christopher publicly reiterated that the intelligence on the *Yin He* was reliable. A diversion and search of the vessel came up empty; yet the Clinton administration refused to issue an apology or compensate the vessel owner for the diversion and delay. Rone Tempest, *China Demands Apology: Search of Ship Fails to Find Warfare Chemicals,* Chi. Sun Times, Sept. 6, 1993, at 10. Beijing later blasted the U.S. for acting like a "self-styled world cop." Patrick E. Tyler, *No Chemicals aboard China Ship,* N.Y. Times, Sept. 6, 1993, at A4.

[72]On April 27, 2006, the Security Council reaffirmed its concern over WMD proliferation and extended the regime established by Resolution 1540 for an additional two years (until April 27, 2008). *See* U.N. Security Council Res. 1673, U.N. Doc. No. S/RES/1673 (2006).

measures by the Council under Articles 41 or 42. As drafted, Resolution 1540 is intended to supplement existing laws and regimes on disarmament and nonproliferation. In the words of the U.S. Department of State, the resolution and the PSI Statement of Interdiction Principles are mutually reinforcing and legally and politically compatible.[73] The resolution imposes new obligations on all states to take certain actions to prevent the proliferation of WMD, particularly to non-state actors.[74] It thus joins Resolutions 1373 and 1617, which require all states to take steps to prevent the transfer or sale of arms (conventional and WMD), or the use of ships or aircraft flying their flag in transporting such arms, to terrorist entities on the U.N. consolidated list.[75]

The resolution also "calls upon" states to cooperate, in accordance with their national legal authorities and legislation and consistent with international law, to take cooperative action to prevent illicit trafficking in nuclear, chemical, or biological weapons, their means of delivery, and related materials. Although it recognizes the risk posed by all proliferation, Resolution 1540 expressly refers only to non-state actors of proliferation concern. In contrast, the PSI refers to both states and non-state actors. Like the PSI, the resolution contemplates both unilateral and multilateral activities. It also imposes differential obligations on all nations in their capacities as port, coastal, flag, and transshipment states. Although the resolution does not include enforcement procedures, under Article 25 of the Charter, all members of the United Nations have an obligation to accept and carry out the decisions of the Council. Moreover, the committee established by Resolution 1540 to monitor efforts to combat WMD proliferation could potentially provide an important new forum for reporting, analysis, and discussion of global nonproliferation efforts.[76] Although Resolution 1540 should, if complied with, eventually lead to a strengthened and more universal global nonproliferation regime, by requiring all states to close some of the gaps in the existing scheme, the resolution does not confer any new authority or jurisdiction on states.

---

[73]*See PSI, Frequently Asked Questions, supra.*

[74]*See Special Report on Proliferation,* THE ECONOMIST, Feb. 28, 2004, at 27.

[75]U.N. Security Council Res. 1617, para. 1(c), U.N. Doc. S/RES/1617 (2005).

[76]The United States submitted its first report to the committee on September 27, 2004. The 41-page report details the steps taken by the United States with respect to each of the 10 operative paragraphs of Resolution 1540. *See* U.S. Dep't of State, *United States Report to the Nonproliferation Committee—Efforts Regarding United Nations Security Council Resolution 1540,* Sept. 27, 2004, *available at* http://www.state.gov/t/np/rls/37375.htm.

5

What's Your Evidence? The Role of Intelligence in Maritime Counterproliferation Operations

The long-term practical and political success of a counterproliferation initiative like the PSI will be determined in large measure by the availability of timely and accurate intelligence to the decision makers and their field operators. "Practical" success will turn on the extent to which, through inducement, deterrence, prevention, and interdiction, the production or transfer of weapons of mass destruction and their related materials and delivery systems from producer to the aspiring user is thwarted. Because the PSI is a "political" commitment and not a legally binding international obligation, actual and perceived legitimacy will be crucial to its long-term viability. Legitimacy will be enhanced if operations are grounded in accurate intelligence, interference with navigation rights is minimized, the use of force is strictly limited to that which is necessary and reasonable, and the interdicting states demonstrate their willingness to compensate those who suffer losses as a result of PSI interdictions that later prove unfounded. Intrusive interdictions based on intelligence that ultimately proves faulty will tend to erode public confidence in the program and may shake the resolve of other PSI participating states. Unjustified counterproliferation operations might also undermine the already fragile nonproliferation regime. It is readily apparent that the information demands of counterproliferation forces will present a daunting challenge for the intelligence community.

This chapter begins with an examination of the intelligence needs of those engaged in maritime counterproliferation efforts. It then turns to risk-management decision making under conditions of uncertainty, focusing on decisions at the operational level and exploring the question of whether decision strategies in the WMD context should seek to minimize false-negative or false-positive errors. It concludes that even vastly improved maritime intelligence will not obviate the need for national and operational commanders to make decisions under conditions of uncertainty and that such decisions should be made on the basis of established risk-assessment and management principles. At the same time, risk management analysis must be sensitive to the public's attitude toward risk. When possession of WMD is at stake, sound risk management that gives appropriate weight to the public's preferences might well call for action even where the relevant event probabilities are quite low. The chapter concludes with an examination of current issues regarding intelligence reform and information sharing.

INTELLIGENCE DEMANDS OF MARITIME COUNTERPROLIFERATION OPERATIONS

Maritime counterproliferation operations are but one component of the global and national WMD proliferation risk management strategy. Like all risk management strategies, the WMD strategy process begins with a risk assessment. Where possession or use of weapons of mass destruction is at stake, estimates must look beyond mere event probabilities; they must fairly weigh the extraordinary magnitude of the risks. It is often said that the detonation or release of a weapon of mass destruction, particularly a nuclear device, is a low-probability event—even an extremely low probability event—but one with destructive potential so enormous that it presents what most consider to be an unacceptable risk.[1] To this observation, risk management analysts often add the warning that in responding to WMD risks, managers must be successful in their risk management measures every time, while the malefactors who would unleash such weapons need be successful only once to annihilate millions and cast the world into a global recession or depression.[2]

The U.S. *National Strategy to Combat Weapons of Mass Destruction* establishes among its highest intelligence priorities "a more accurate and complete understanding of the full range of WMD threats."[3] It emphasizes that intelligence will be crucial in developing effective counterproliferation policies and capabilities and in deterring and defending against known proliferators and terrorist organizations.[4] The president's directive on maritime security policy similarly emphasizes the importance of a "robust and coordinated intelligence effort [that] serves as the foundation for effective security efforts in the maritime domain."[5] It was in response to this directive that a number of integrated maritime security planning documents, including the *National Strategy for Maritime Security* and the *National Plan for*

---

[1]*See* RICHARD A. POSNER, CATASTROPHE: RISK AND RESPONSE 120–22 (2004) (describing a "psychological asymmetry," which causes many to downplay low-probability/large-destructive-potential events, even when their expected costs are greater than some high-probability/lower-destructive-potential events).

[2]JOHN LEWIS GADDIS, SURPRISE, SECURITY, AND THE AMERICAN EXPERIENCE 75 (2004).

[3]White House, *National Strategy to Combat Weapons of Mass Destruction* 5 (2002) [hereinafter "NS-CWMD"].

[4]*Ibid.* at 5–6.

[5]White House, *National Security Presidential Directive 41/Homeland Security Presidential Security Directive 13,* NSPD-41/HSPD-13, at 5–6 (2004).

Achieving Maritime Domain Awareness, were produced. To more effectively meet the urgent demand for maritime domain intelligence integration and distribution, the president further tasked the involved agencies to prepare the document that became the *Plan for Global Maritime Intelligence Integration* (GMII Plan).[6] The closely related *Maritime Operational Threat Response Plan* (MOTR Plan) provides the framework for coordinated, unified, timely, and effective response planning and operational command and control of maritime security incidents.[7]

Decades of experience in narcotics interdiction and the testimony of thousands of boarding officers demonstrate the inestimable value of intelligence to maritime interception operations.[8] The forces available for maritime counterproliferation operations are finite, and not nearly adequate to cover the world's oceans or to board even a fraction of the vessels operating on those oceans. Moreover, the dangers and practical difficulties demand that at-sea boardings and searches be relied upon only when warranted by the circumstances. Finally, the president has made it clear that maritime interception and enforcement should be conducted in a manner that does not *unnecessarily* interfere with maritime commerce or the freedom of navigation. Better intelligence reduces the potential for unwarranted interference with those vital interests.

All agree on the essential importance of intelligence.[9] Indeed, intelligence has been called the nation's "first line of defense."[10] As used here, intelligence includes data collection, processing, predictions, assessments and analysis, and the use of those intelligence products by those with the authority to act.[11] The modern intelligence collection approach has been characterized as "all source," drawing as it does on human intelligence (HUMINT), signals intelligence (SIGINT), measurement and signature intelligence (MASINT), and imagery intelligence (IMINT) from satellites, aircraft, and unmanned aerial vehicles. Intelligence may also be obtained from "open" sources (OSINT), commercial and proprietary sources, and information held by law enforcement, customs, commerce, energy, and maritime safety agencies. Information collection efforts draw on and provide support to the integrated "C4ISR" system: command, control, communications, computing, intelligence,

---

[6]White House, *Global Maritime Intelligence Integration Plan for the National Strategy for Maritime Security* (2005). The GMII Plan was one of the eight plans promulgated in support of the National Strategy for Maritime Security.

[7]White House, *Maritime Operational Threat Response Plan for the National Strategy for Maritime Security* (2005); MOTR Protocols, Apr. 4, 2006.

[8]Many interdictions of vessels engaged in human and narcotics trafficking are based almost entirely on what some would call "organic," self-generated intelligence—or, simply being at the right place at the right time. Such techniques are inefficient and will rarely be relevant to WMD interception operations.

[9]*See* Jason D. Ellis & Geoffrey D. Kiefer, Combating Proliferation: Strategic Intelligence and Security Policy (2004).

[10]*See* White House, *President's Statement on the Intelligence Reform and Terrorism Prevention Act of 2004,* Dec. 8, 2004, *available at* http://www.whitehouse.gov/news/releases/2004/12/20041208–11.html.

[11]The "intelligence cycle" is typically said to comprise planning and direction, collection, processing, analysis and production, dissemination and operations planning, decision making, and action. *See* Mark A. Lowenthal, Intelligence: From Secrets to Policy 135 (2d ed. 2003).

surveillance, and reconnaissance. The system is designed to process the collected data into "information," which is then analyzed and integrated into a real-time common operating picture or reported through usable intelligence products.

The intelligence community, including any organic components of the operating forces involved, provides (in the framework of what is commonly known as the "OODA loop") the "observe" and "orient" foundation by which those charged with control over operations are to "decide" and "act."[12] The intelligence demands of counterproliferation decision makers and operators will likely differ in several respects from those of their nonproliferation counterparts. Not least among the differences will be the timeliness demands of a forward-leaning counterproliferation strategy that contemplates the interdiction of WMD shipments during transit. The nonproliferation program relies chiefly on relatively long-term, strategic intelligence. By contrast, counterproliferation operations demand timely indications and warnings intelligence for each component in a layered defense scheme. The inverse relationship between certainty and speed is readily apparent: any additional time allocated to the observe and orient phases comes at the expense of the time remaining to decide and act. Not everyone agrees with how the time available should be allocated. Those charged with tactical thinking tend to emphasize speed of decision making ("faster is better"), while those entrusted with strategy are more inclined to prefer accuracy ("smarter is better").

Multilateral activities introduce an additional consideration. Multilateral decision processes virtually always take longer to develop, and they generally raise the intelligence bar, because the level of certainty for multilateral actions must meet the standard set by the most demanding participant. Interagency consultation processes like the scheme established by the MOTR Plan may have the same effect. Additionally, if the intercepting forces must first obtain the consent of the vessel's flag state or a coastal state, that government's information requirements must be met. The flag state will likely demand more information and greater certainty where the vessel must be diverted to accomplish the boarding or when force might be necessary to compel compliance.

Intelligence in support of counterproliferation must be adequate to answer the most pressing questions that maritime interception forces will pose regarding shipments of WMD and related materials.[13] The intelligence challenge will often begin with the "What?" question. It is improbable (but nonetheless possible) that proliferators will attempt to transport an assembled and operational WMD device via commercial seagoing vessels. It is more probable that maritime shipments will consist of components, precursors, or small quantities of fissile or radiological materials. In some cases those materials will be dual-use in nature, presenting additional

---

[12]The construct of the observe-orient-decide-act (OODA) cycle was developed by U.S. Air Force Colonel John Boyd.

[13]Not considered here are the equally important applications of intelligence to WMD defense, reducing infrastructure vulnerability, and response and mitigation planning, each of which is a recognized element in the "counterproliferation" pillars of the NS-CWMD, at 3.

challenges for analysts and operators, who might not be familiar with the characteristics and applications of the materials or equipment.

The second challenge will be to provide answers to the "Who?" question: Who are the parties to the suspected WMD transfer and transport transaction? It is necessary to know the identities of the consignor, consignee, and the owner and flag of the vessel, in order to assess the risk and determine which states might have jurisdiction over the vessel and whose consent or cooperation would therefore facilitate interdiction. Closely related to "Who?" is the question of the actors' intent: Why are they seeking the materials or equipment? Intent—which unlike "Who?" and What?" always requires analysis—is critical where dual-use materials or equipment are involved. Whether a given shipment is illicit and a candidate for interdiction may turn on the identity of the end user and the nature of the intended end use. Moreover, analysts and commanders evaluating possible courses of action and the urgency of the need for action understand that the risk posed by the availability of WMD is in part determined by the present willingness of the entity in possession to deploy the weapon.

The next questions the commander is likely to ask in forming an estimate of the situation and choosing a course of action concern time and space factors: Where and when will the illicit WMD likely be transported, and, perhaps, how will it be carried out? Interdictions at sea can present significant legal and practical problems. The intelligence community must be prepared to provide, if possible, accurate information on both the location of the transporting ship and of the illicit materials on board. The "When?" question should produce an assessment of the last practicable opportunity to prevent the delivery of WMD materials to the state or non-state actor of proliferation concern. For a variety of reasons, dockside inspections are preferable to at-sea boardings. For example, maritime interception forces in receipt of information that a ship under charter to a well-known commercial carrier is believed to have 10 drums of chemical warfare component materials in one or more of 5,000 containers will likely explore alternatives to boarding at sea, perhaps raising the always contentious question of whether the intelligence is sufficiently reliable to justify diverting the vessel to a port.

Decision makers and operators will also want to know who else might be involved in the transaction. Interdicting a shipment is only one element of the larger counterproliferation strategy. The emergence of proliferation networks, such as the lucrative multinational enterprise operated out of Pakistan by A.Q. Kahn, amply demonstrates that non-state actors now participate as both suppliers and consumers of WMD technology. Those global networks must be identified and interdicted as well. Finally, decision makers will want to know the degree of confidence in the intelligence assessment. In many cases, it will be based on analysts' subjective judgment of probability. In contrast to objective probabilities, derived from accurate and reliable sources, subjective probabilities involve events the likelihood of which can only be estimated, based in part on the judgment and experience of the analyst. (For example, President John F. Kennedy is said to have estimated the probability of war with the Soviet Union during the Cuban missile crisis as one in three.) Because such judgments are influenced by a variety of factors and are subject to cognitive errors, they are likely to differ from one person to another.[14] Candid evaluations that are clear about the bases of the probability assessment, any ambiguities in the evidence relied on, the degree of uncertainty, and whether competing theories or dissenting views exist are indispensable to decision makers, who must evaluate the assessment (and the assessors), weigh the respective event probabilities, and project the potential consequences of an erroneous decision.

RISK ASSESSMENT WHEN POSSESSION OF WMD IS AT STAKE

The geostrategic environment of the twenty-first century is frequently described as one fraught with uncertainty and subject to rapid and sometimes dramatic change. If one defines certainty as precluding any possibility of subsequent challenge in light of additional or more accurate observations or more comprehensive reasoning, uncertainty seems inevitable in the maritime counterproliferation operating environment.

Although we must accept that national security decisions will on occasion be made on the basis of incomplete or uncertain information, we may nevertheless expect them to be tempered with practical wisdom and mature judgment. Even so, we must admit that the time for making decisions is not unlimited. The commander must be prepared to complete the observation-to-action decision loop before the adversary can deliver or acquire that weapon of mass destruction. The greater certainty accruing from multiple corroborating sources may increase confidence but also impose delays the commander might not be able to afford.

It is important to bear in mind also that even "correct" decisions do not ineluctably produce desired outcomes. Whether a decision was correct must be judged by the quality and quantity of information reasonably available at the time it was made, not by that which was only revealed later.[15] The goal, of course, is timely reaching of the correct conclusion despite any information deficit; however, the possibility of error can rarely be eliminated altogether.[16]

Under international law and the PSI Statement of Interdiction Principles, boardings must generally be predicated upon some level of suspicion of illicit activity described by such vague formulae as a "reasonable ground" to suspect or "good cause" to believe that the vessel is engaged in the illicit activity.[17] Under U.S. law,

---

[14]*See* JOHN S. HAMMOND ET AL., SMART CHOICES 209 (1999). Cognitive errors may result from a variety of causes, including experience bias, selective perception, wishful thinking, and overconfidence.

[15]*See* PETER F. DRUCKER, THE ESSENTIAL DRUCKER 251 (2001). ("A decision is a judgment. It is a choice between alternatives. It is rarely a choice between right and wrong. It is at best a choice between 'almost right' and 'probably wrong.'")

[16]It would be naïve to suggest that this standard controls in the political arena, where judgments (and elections) are based on perceptions regarding the outcome. A carefully considered and broadly supported decision based on the best available information will not shield elected officials if it fails to produce a popular outcome.

[17]1982 U.N. Convention on the Law of the Sea, art. 110 ("reasonable ground for suspecting" basis for right of visit); 2005 Protocol to the Convention for the Suppression of Unlawful Acts against the Safety of Maritime Navigation, art. 8 *bis* ("reasonable ground for believing"); *Proliferation Security Initiative: Statement of Interdiction Principles,* paras. 4(b) ("good cause shown") and 4(d) ("reasonably suspected of").

the standard for arrest or seizure is typically "probable cause" to believe a crime has occurred. It is noteworthy that none of these measures require for field action anything approaching certainty "beyond a reasonable doubt." The practical reasons are apparent. A requirement for prior certainty that a vessel is engaged in piracy sets the bar impossibly high; permitting a vessel to operate without fear of interdiction so long as it conceals the evidence reasonably well. Moreover, the degree of intrusion represented by a boarding is far less than that of seizure or arrest. The information that warrants visit or boarding might also be necessary to persuade the vessel's flag state or a coastal state through whose waters it will pass to authorize yet another state, which is willing and able to board, search, and perhaps seize the vessel, to do so. That second state is, of course, free to set its own standard for information reliability, either by treaty or ad hoc agreement.

THE VALUE OF "GOOD" INTELLIGENCE

The intelligence community's predilection for modest silence is well known. With few exceptions, intelligence agencies are not given to self-promoting publicity following intelligence "successes." The transparency that is otherwise the hallmark of constitutional democracies is antithetical to the long-term success of the intelligence community. It should come as no surprise that states participating in the PSI, knowing that illicit proliferators would take advantage of such announcements to probe for weaknesses, have given notice that they may never reveal many of their interdiction activities.[18] Unfortunately, denying proliferators and transporters such an opportunity means that the public and nonparticipating states often will often have no direct means of learning of the program's accomplishments.[19]

There is no shortage of books, articles, and congressional or commission reports documenting actual or perceived intelligence "failures."[20] Almost none salute the intelligence community's many successes. Modern critics might offer a brief tip of the hat to the courage and resourcefulness of the Office of Strategic Services operatives and code breakers in World War II, and perhaps to the U-2 pilots who risked (and, in one case, lost) their lives obtaining the photo images of the Soviet missile sites in Cuba that Ambassador Adlai Stevenson displayed so effectively to the Security Council, but then they tend to focus their attention quickly on the

---

[18]Wade Boese and Miles Pomper, *The Proliferation Security Initiative: An Interview with John Bolton,* ARMS CONTROL TODAY, Dec. 11, 2003, at 37.

[19]The U.S. Department of State provided a thumbnail sketch of 11 "successful efforts" by the PSI partners between August 2004 and May 2005, mostly involving ballistic missile and nuclear technology shipments bound for Iran. The report does not indicate whether any of the interdictions took place at sea. *See* Robert Joseph, Undersecretary of State for Arms Control and International Security, *Transforming our Counterproliferation Efforts in the Asia Region* (remarks to the Institute of Defense and Strategic Studies, Aug. 15, 2005, Singapore), *available at* http://www.state.gov/t/us/rm/51129.htm.

[20]Commonly cited intelligence "failures" in nonproliferation monitoring efforts include the surprise 1998 nuclear tests in South Asia and, for some, the nuclear weapons program in North Korea.

failures. Accordingly, it is fitting to acknowledge briefly two recent intelligence success stories involving maritime counterproliferation operations. The first involved the interdiction of the cargo vessel *So San.*

In late 2002, American intelligence agencies had good reason to believe that a vessel later identified as the *So San* was transporting missiles from North Korea. They were uncertain, however, of the cargo's destination. The U.S. Navy eventually requested that a Spanish warship intercept the vessel and board it on the high seas off the coast of Yemen. A team of Spanish Marines from the frigate *Navarra,* later joined by U.S. Navy personnel, conducted a noncompliant boarding of the *So San* and during the subsequent search discovered North Korean–made Scud missiles and components hidden beneath the cargo of bagged cement. Not surprisingly, the missiles were not listed in the vessel's manifest. Although the ship and cargo were eventually released at the request of the government of Yemen, to which it was learned that the missiles were being shipped, the interdiction demonstrated the capability of the intelligence community to detect and track maritime WMD shipments over considerable distances. Much of the information on the *So San* interdiction remains classified; however, publicly available accounts suggest that intelligence assets detected the missiles being loaded in North Korea and tracked the vessel from there to the interception point.[21] Apparently, however, the intelligence community was unable to determine the buyer's identity before the boarding.[22]

The second incident involved the multilateral interdiction of the German-flag *BBC China* in October 2003, which was described briefly in Chapter 4. American and British intelligence agencies concluded that the *BBC China* was transporting component parts for uranium enrichment centrifuges from Dubai to Libya. Demonstrating the kind of cooperation the PSI was designed to foster, Germany agreed to order the vessel to divert to a port in Italy for inspection. The vessel's owner and master readily complied with the flag state's order. Italy then agreed to allow the vessel to enter one of its ports and to conduct the search. The intelligence proved accurate, leading to the discovery of thousands of parts for gas centrifuges of a kind that can be used to enrich uranium. Some suggest that the *BBC China* interdiction contributed to Libya's decision in late 2003 to abandon its WMD program.

INTELLIGENCE, INFERENTIAL ERRORS, AND RISK MANAGEMENT DECISIONS

The fulcrum of the debate over intelligence and WMD counterproliferation in the coming years will likely be the relationship between the tolerance for risk and error,

---

[21]*See* Nuclear Threat Initiative, *North Korea: U.S., Spanish Forces Seize Scud Shipment,* Dec. 11, 2002, *available at* http://www.nti.org/d_newswire/issues//2002/12/11/7p.html.

[22]Thus, the intelligence community's assessment can be said to be accurate but incomplete. Nevertheless, decision makers decided to go forward with the interdiction, exercising the internationally recognized "right of visit." *See* 1982 U.N. Convention on the Law of the Sea, art. 110.

on the one hand, and our willingness to bear the financial, societal, and political costs of enhanced security measures, on the other.[23] As President Bush remarked in response to the report of the 9/11 Commission, "There is no such thing as perfect security in our vast, free Nation."[24]

Nor do security decision makers often have the luxury of waiting for complete and perfect information, or for intelligence that provides the kind of assurance Israelis have described (in the *Karine A* war materiel interdiction) as "unequivocal, clear, and undeniable."[25] The goal therefore cannot be perfect security but rather optimal security, and optimal security decisions will inevitably be based not on perfect knowledge but the most accurate intelligence assessment available within the time window for effective action.[26]

On occasion, the assessments made by the intelligence community will later prove to be wrong. Error might result from information that is incomplete, conflicting, or susceptible to more than one plausible interpretation or inference. To simplify the analysis in this counterproliferation setting, it will be helpful to posit that the "wrong" inference or conclusion might take one of two hypothetical forms. In the first, a ship that intelligence analysts have concluded is transporting WMD components is intercepted and boarded at sea; an exhaustive, daylong search reveals that the intelligence assessment was wrong and the vessel's cargo is entirely legitimate.[27] In the second, a ship that is in fact transporting a WMD to a densely populated port city is not boarded because the decision maker concludes that there is insufficient evidence. Surveillance of the vessel is later lost when it enters a crowded traffic lane, and the weapon is delivered and later detonated in the city. Those charged with responsibility for the decision must be prepared to determine which of the two erroneous outcomes poses the more serious risk.

---

[23]Kenneth Rogoff, *The Cost of Living Dangerously: Can the Global Economy Absorb the Expenses of Fighting Terrorism?*, FOREIGN POL'Y, Nov.–Dec. 2004, at 70.

[24]White House, *Bush Administration Actions Consistent with 9/11 Recommendations*, July 30, 2004, *available at* http://www.whitehouse.gov/news/releases/2004/07/20040730-18.html.

[25]*Israelis Say They Seized Palestinian Arms Ship*, CNN.COM, Jan. 4, 2002. The freighter *Karine A* was intercepted by the Israel Defense Forces in the Red Sea on January 3, 2002, carrying Katyusha rockets, mortars, sniper rifles, bullets, antitank mines, antitank missiles, and explosives. Although the ship was carrying conventional weapons, not WMD, when the IDF interdicted it en route to its Palestinian buyers, the operation stands out prominently in the annals of successful applications of intelligence to maritime interdiction operations.

[26]*See* Congressional Research Service, *Port and Maritime Security: Background Issues for Congress*, CRS Report RL31733, at 17 (updated May 27, 2005) ("Perfect maritime security can only be achieved by shutting down the transportation system.").

[27]It is rare indeed to hear an intelligence assessment characterized as a "slam dunk." It will no doubt be rarer still in the coming years. It is far more common for such assessments to be cast in terms of probabilities. Where an estimate concludes that it is "probable" that a given ship is carrying a cargo of WMD concern, a boarding that turns up nothing does not render the assessment "wrong." It had, after all, been couched in terms of a probability of less than 100 percent.

The False Positive Error

Statistical decision theory recognizes two types of inferential error. The false positive, or *Type I,* error refers to a conclusion that a condition exists or a proposition is true when in fact the condition does not exist or the proposition is not true. Prewar intelligence estimates of Iraq's WMD, characterized on one occasion as a "slam dunk," present a recent and notorious example of such a "false positive" error, as was the less well publicized four-day boarding of the container ship *Palermo Senator* in 2003.[28]

A 1993 incident involving the Chinese containership *Yin He* and the 1998 cruise missile strike on a Sudanese chemical plant in Al Shifa are cited as examples of the kind of international embarrassment the United States can expect to suffer by taking action based on a false positive intelligence assessment.[29] The United States alleged that the *Yin He* was carrying chemical precursors that could be used to produce mustard and sarin nerve gases from China to Iran.[30] Secretary of State Warren Christopher publicly asserted that the intelligence on the *Yin He* was reliable. In fact, an American intelligence official went so far as to declare, "We know these chemicals are bound for Iran's chemical weapons plants, and it is a lot of tonnage, tens of tons."[31] China disputed the U.S. allegation, but it eventually agreed to a boarding of the vessel in a Saudi Arabian port. The inspection by Saudi officials, accompanied by American technical advisers, uncovered no trace of the precursors American intelligence officials had alleged were aboard. Beijing blasted the United States for acting like a "self-styled world cop."[32] Nevertheless, the United States refused to offer either an apology or compensation for the vessel's delay;[33] Washington asserted that it had "had sufficient credible evidence that those items were in the cargo."[34] In the latter incident, the United States struck the Al Shifa plant in the belief, based on intelligence, that the plant was engaged in producing chemical warfare agents. Post-strike investigations revealed that the assessment was almost certainly wrong.

Decision makers who rely on a false positive assessment may be accused of being rash or alarmist and may be required to issue apologies or compensate the owner of

---

[28]The German-flag containership *Palermo Senator* was delayed for four days while the Coast Guard and other federal agencies conducted a boarding to determine the source of radiation emissions from the vessel's cargo. Ultimately, it was determined that the radiation was being emitted from a cargo of clay tiles. The Coast Guard was later criticized for relying on obsolete radiation detection equipment. Ronald Smothers, *Ship's Radiation Is Traced to Harmless Tiles,* N.Y. TIMES, Sept. 14, 2003, at A7.

[29]ELLIS & KIEFER, COMBATING PROLIFERATION, at 149–53, 156–66.

[30]An officer from U.S. Central Command asserted that the vessel was transporting thiodiglycol and thionyl chloride to Iran. *Ibid.* Both chemicals are dual-use products.

[31]*Ibid.*

[32]*Ibid.,* citing Patrick E. Tyler, *No Chemicals aboard China Ship,* N.Y. TIMES, Sept. 6, 1993, at A4.

[33]Rone Tempest, *China Demands Apology: Search of Ship Fails to Find Warfare Chemicals,* CHI. SUN TIMES, Sept. 6, 1993, at 10.

[34]ELLIS & KIEFER, COMBATING PROLIFERATION, at 152. One possible explanation for why no chemicals were found during the boarding in Saudi Arabia was that they had been dumped over the side before the ship arrived.

a vessel or cargo. Frequent or egregious actions taken on the basis of erroneous intelligence will eventually undermine public and partner states' confidence in the program. False positive errors can also demoralize members of the intelligence community and may cause them (and operational commanders) to be more cautious, more guarded, and less willing to pass on preliminary or tentative findings in the future.[35] Such wariness might also lead to errors of the opposite kind, demonstrating the interdependence of errors caused by too much and too little caution. Finally, false positives, like false negatives, can educate would-be proliferators and transporters on the tactics and methods employed by counterproliferation forces, providing them with information useful in circumventing the regime's strengths and exploiting its weaknesses.

The False Negative Error

The false negative, or *Type II,* error is committed by concluding that a condition does not exist or that a proposition is not true when in fact the condition does exist or the proposition is true. For example, a provocative quarantine might be imposed around Cuba on the assumption, later proven to be seriously in error, that even if the situation escalates, Soviet troops on the island number only 3,000 and no nuclear weapons or missile delivery systems are available to them.[36] Or, a hypothesis that a handful of religious extremists have enrolled in flying lessons in preparation for turning airliners into instruments of mass devastation might be erroneously dismissed as too far-fetched. At best, erroneous false negative decisions simply delay responsive action.[37] At worst, they may convince those with blind spots or a high tolerance for risk that it is safe to open the city's gates and wheel that massive wooden horse inside.

ACTING ON UNCERTAIN RISK ASSESSMENTS WHEN POSSESSION OF WMD IS AT STAKE

Risk assessments help us categorize and quantify a risk, but they do not tell us what, if anything, to do about it. That second question falls in the domain of risk

---

[35]In a rare public speech explaining some of the intelligence failures regarding Iraq's WMD programs, former CIA director William Tenet warned that "we cannot afford an environment to develop where analysts are afraid to make a call, where judgments are held back because analysts fear they will be wrong." Remarks as prepared for delivery by Director of Central Intelligence George J. Tenet at Georgetown University on Feb. 5, 2004, *available at* http://www.cia.gov/cia/public_affairs/speeches/2004/tenet_georgetownspeech_02052004.html.

[36]Decades after the Cuban missile crisis ended, the United States learned that the Soviet forces had actually totaled approximately 40,000 men (20 times the estimate) and that tactical nuclear devices—nine *Luna* missiles and six launchers—were already on the island.

[37]*See* Richard K. Betts, *Analysis, War, and Decision: Why Intelligence Failures Are Inevitable,* in THE ART AND PRACTICE OF MILITARY STRATEGY 378–79 (1984) (noting that "making warning systems more sensitive reduces the risk of surprise, but increases the risk of false alarms, which in turn reduces sensitivity").

management, which nearly always entails a policy judgment. Decisional "purists" will ground their decision on objective risk-management principles. The purist's approach evaluates the various alternative courses of action, applying decisional criteria that include an alternative's predicted effectiveness in producing the desired result and the cost of achieving that result in that fashion. Those who define their decisional criteria more broadly will also consider the public's likely reaction to the decision. Where the decision is a binary one—between interdicting a vessel and taking no action, where a subjective probability assessment indicates a risk that it is transporting WMD—the latter group will factor in the public's attitude toward risk. Put another way, these analysts will ask how cautious the public expects its national and homeland-security leadership to be in the face of uncertainty.

The nation's reaction to the September 11, 2001 attacks and to the 9/11 Commission hearings and report suggest that as a nation the United States is risk averse, preferring the embarrassment of an occasional false positive to the potential horrors of a false negative. To the extent they were willing to accept errors of any kind, the majority of Americans appeared to demand that the risk of "false negatives" be minimized, if not eliminated—at least when the threat is to the homeland itself. Some would characterize their preference as one akin to the "precautionary approach" advocated by many environmentalists, which takes the position that lack of certainty regarding a risk does not excuse failure to take avoiding action in cases where the harm may be irreversible. Two critical considerations are less clear, however. The first concerns the cost the public is willing to bear for a true precautionary approach to homeland security. That cost includes not only the financial costs of an enhanced security system but also possible criticism from abroad and encroachments on civil liberties. The second concerns the chronic tendency toward short-term thinking, what some derisively refer to as "strategic attention deficit disorder," perhaps coupled with what cognitive psychologists call the "availability heuristic"—the tendency to make judgments about the future based not upon a broad body of historical evidence but on recent, vivid events that skew perceptions. The cautionary preferences manifested in late 2001 or when the 9/11 Commission first denounced a collective "failure of imagination" may not reflect preferences five or 10 years after the traumatic event.

In assessing the public's attitude toward risk and the consequences of error, we must also be mindful of the political and media reaction to the most significant false positive error in recent history—the prewar intelligence assessments of Iraq's WMD program. Like the pre-9/11 risk assessment of the homeland's vulnerability to large-scale terrorist attacks, they may be reduced for analytic purposes to an intelligence judgment that presented decision makers with two possible "truths": either Iraq was engaged in a clandestine program to produce and stockpile WMD, or it had abandoned its earlier design and production activities and disposed of its stockpiles. In this light, a rational decision maker following accepted risk management principles would have to consider, among other things, the respective consequences of a false positive and a false negative error.[38] As Philip Bobbitt, former strategic planning director of the National Security Council, has argued, judgments regarding the consequences of an erroneous decision might actually cause a decision maker to pursue a course of action that is *not* based on the state of affairs analysts have concluded is the most probable.[39] Under accepted risk management principles, if a scenario with a lesser, but still significant, probability presents an overall risk that the decision maker deems unacceptable (as measured by the magnitude of the expected harm, discounted by the event's probability), the "correct" course may be to abate or at least reduce that risk. Bobbitt further warns that in judging a decision we must avoid "Parmenides' fallacy," which occurs when one assesses the correctness of a decision based solely on the state of affairs it produced, without comparing that state of affairs to the outcomes that would have been produced if one of the alternative courses of action had been chosen.[40] One need not delve deeply into notions of efficient or proximate cause to understand that any given end state is the product of a multitude of causes and factors, many of which are not under the control of the decision maker.

INTELLIGENCE COLLECTION AND SHARING IN MARITIME COUNTERPROLIFERATION OPERATIONS

Access to classified information and other protected but unclassified information may be protected from disclosure for a variety of reasons, including the need to protect intelligence sources, methods and analytical processes or out of concerns for individual privacy.[41] The protections take a variety of forms, including requirements that only persons with an appropriate security clearance and need-to-know and who enter into a nondisclosure agreement will be granted access. The need to restrict access to classified and sensitive information is often in tension with the goal of ensuring that intelligence is timely disseminated to one with authority to take action on that intelligence.

A recurring privacy issue under U.S. law flows from the fact that the collection of foreign intelligence information[42] is subject to a lower constitutional standard than is

---

[38]In a response to the leading investigations into the British and American prewar WMD assessments, Professor Philip Bobbitt reminds the reader that the U.N. inspectors had been "fooled" by Saddam's claim in 1995 that he had abandoned his program. Philip Bobbitt, *How Proof Became a Burden: Saddam's Intentions Had to Be Part of the Spook's Judgment Call,* Guardian, Oct. 28, 2004. They realized their mistake only after Saddam's son-in-law, Hussein Kamal, defected and revealed the details of a new clandestine WMD program.

[39]Philip Bobbitt, *Seeing the Futures,* N.Y. Times, Dec. 8, 2003.

[40]Philip Bobbitt, *Today's War against Tomorrow's Iraq,* N.Y. Times, Mar. 10, 2003. The relevant question would therefore not be whether we are better off or safer today than we were before an action was taken, but whether we are better off or safer than we would have been had we pursued an alternative course, including no action.

[41]*See, e.g.,* Exec. Order No. 13,292 (2003); Exec. Order No. 13,356 (2004).

[42]"Foreign intelligence information" is defined in 50 U.S.C.A. § 1801(e) (West 2005).

evidence gathered for law enforcement purposes.[43] In 1978, Congress stepped into the breach by enacting the Foreign Intelligence Surveillance Act (FISA).[44] In the ensuing three decades, the U.S. Attorney General,[45] the Foreign Intelligence Surveillance Court established by FISA,[46] and Congress[47] have at various times—and particularly after the September 11 attacks—sought to strike an appropriate balance between security and privacy interests that are implicated when foreign intelligence information is "shared" with law enforcement officers and prosecutors.[48] The fact that counterproliferation intelligence collection and analysis will now be integrated by a single National Counter Proliferation Center,[49] at the same time that Congress calls for "enhanced" counterproliferation law enforcement efforts, may increase the likelihood of conflict.

Even before the September 11, 2001, attacks on the United States, the need to set a more cooperative tone in information collection and sharing among the maritime sector participants was documented. The August 2000 report by the Interagency Commission on Crime and Security in U.S. Seaports concluded that "[o]ne of the key concerns in information sharing is that intelligence on terrorist threats to port facilities and, maritime transportation systems, and other critical port infrastructure must reach appropriate personnel."[50]

The Interagency Commission concluded with four recommendations for improving information and intelligence collection, integration, and dissemination.[51] In the aftermath of the September 11 attacks on the United States, virtually all of the committees, commissions, and oversight agencies that engaged in the search for causes and remedies identified the need to promote greater sharing of relevant information

---

[43] *See, e.g.*, United States v. United States District Court (Keith), 407 U.S. 297, 321 (1972).

[44] 50 U.S.C.A. §§ 1801–1811 (West 2005); 18 U.S.C.A. §§ 2511, 2518, 2519 (West 2005).

[45] National security investigations and foreign intelligence collection activities are governed by the Attorney General's Guidelines for FBI National Security Investigations and Foreign Intelligence Collection, Oct. 31, 2003, *available at* http://www.usdoj.gov/olp/nsiguidelines.pdf.

[46] FISA established the Foreign Intelligence Surveillance Court and the Foreign Intelligence Surveillance Court of Review.

[47] The so-called "wall" that formerly barred sharing between the national security and law enforcement communities was brought down but not eliminated by the 2001 USA PATRIOT Act, which replaced "the purpose" test in the pre-9/11 version of the FSIA with "a significant purpose." *See* Pub. L. No. 107–56, §§ 218, 233(b), 115 Stat. 272 (2001), *codified in* 50 U.S.C.A. § 1804(a)(7)(B) (West 2005). The Foreign Intelligence Surveillance Court of Review unanimously upheld the constitutionality of that section of the PATRIOT Act. In re Sealed Case No. 02–001, 310 F.3d 717 (FISCR 2002).

[48] The 9/11 Commission was particularly critical of the failure of the various offices of the FBI and the CIA to share intelligence and other information, which collectively might have revealed the emerging "mosaic." *See Final Report of the National Commission on Terrorist Attacks Upon the United States*, ch. 13 (2004) [hereinafter "9/11 Commission Report"].

[49] *See* 50 U.S.C.A. § 404o-1 (West 2005).

[50] *Report of the Interagency Commission on Crime and Security in U.S. Seaports,* ch. 7 (Intelligence and Information Management), at 150 (Aug. 2000).

[51] *Ibid.* at 155.

and intelligence.[52] In response, both Congress and the president have taken steps to promote greater cooperation in intelligence collection, analysis, and sharing. The 2001 USA PATRIOT Act relaxed some of the restrictions on sharing foreign intelligence with domestic law enforcement personnel.[53] The 2002 Homeland Security Act[54] requires the department's Information Analysis and Infrastructure Protection Directorate to share information with other members of the intelligence community and with state and local police.[55] The 2004 Intelligence Reform and Terrorism Prevention Act reaffirms Congress's commitment to increased intelligence sharing.[56] Anticipating the 2004 Intelligence Reform Act by several months, the president directed, by executive order, federal agencies to strengthen the sharing of terrorism-related information.[57] Threat-specific cooperation and information sharing among involved agencies in the intelligence, military, law enforcement, and diplomatic agencies is further enhanced by the National Counterterrorism Center and National Counter Proliferation Center, established by executive order and legislation.[58]

The conclusions reached by the 9/11 Commission regarding the risk of not sharing information among the U.S. intelligence and law enforcement communities are also relevant on the international level. The "mosaic" of a WMD attack comes into view only when sufficient pieces are in place. If those pieces are held by different states and those states are reluctant to share them and permit them to be fused with intelligence held by other states, the picture might not emerge until it is too late for any state to take effective action. A strict need-to-know limit on information sharing fails to acknowledge that the "need" might not be apparent until one piece is linked to another.[59] It is therefore not surprising that the G-8 states, all of which are PSI-participating states, recognized the importance of intelligence sharing in their efforts

[52]*See, e.g., 9/11 Commission Report,* at 416–17; General Accounting Office, *Transportation Security, Post–September 11th Initiatives and Long-Term Challenges,* Apr. 1, 2003, GAO-03-616T; Congressional Research Service, *Port and Maritime Security: Background Issues for Congress,* updated May 27, 2005, at 20–21, CRS Rep. RL31733.

[53]Pub. L. No. 107–56, §§ 218 & 233(b), 115 Stat. 272–403, (October 26, 2001) (amending relevant provisions of the Foreign Intelligence Surveillance Act, 50 U.S.C. §§ 1801, *et seq*). *See also* Congressional Research Service, *Intelligence and Law Enforcement: Countering Transnational Threats to the U.S.,* CRS Rep. No. RL 30252 (updated Dec. 3, 2001).

[54]Homeland Security Act of 2002, § 892, Pub. L. No. 107–296, 116 Stat. 2135 (2002), *codified at* 6 U.S.C. § 482.

[55]6 U.S.C.A. § 141 (West 2005). *See also* Exec. Order No. 13,311 (2003) ("Homeland Security Information Sharing").

[56]Intelligence Reform and Terrorism Prevention Act of 2004, § 1016, Pub. L. No. 108–458, 118 Stat. 3638 (2004), *codified at* 6 U.S.C. § 485.

[57]Exec. Order No. 13,356 (2004).

[58]The centers, established earlier by executive order, were given a legislative basis in Sections 1021 and 1022 of the Intelligence Reform and Terrorism Prevention Act of 2004.

[59]*Cf. 9/11 Commission Report,* at 417 (arguing that the present "need-to-know" approach should be replaced with a "need-to-share" approach).

to combat transnational terrorism.[60] The need for information sharing was also recognized in the 2005 Protocol to the SUA Convention.[61] The question that must be asked in each case is whether the benefits of information sharing are outweighed by the risk of intentional or inadvertent disclosure. The question could prove as vexing in counterproliferation efforts as it has been in the counterterrorism context.

The *National Strategy to Combat Weapons of Mass Destruction* recognizes that "it is vital that we work closely with like-minded countries on *all elements* of our comprehensive proliferation strategy."[62] That comprehensive national strategy vows that a more accurate and complete understanding of the full range of WMD threats is among the "highest" intelligence priorities of the United States.[63] It follows that working closely with the intelligence agencies of like-minded states on WMD proliferation issues is a key part of the U.S. strategy. Information sharing among the PSI participants will be critical for several reasons. Intelligence sharing promotes information integrity, by permitting others to verify and corroborate data collected by a partner state or agency. Intelligence sharing also helps guard against "groupthink" in the analysis stage, by giving others the opportunity to draw their own conclusions from the data. Sharing can and often does lead to synergistic outcomes. Pieces of information may be distributed among several agencies, states, or international organizations (such as the International Atomic Energy Agency), and the true picture may spring into view only after those pieces are shared and assembled.[64] The commonly employed "link analysis" method for discerning patterns or relationships in data often requires access to databases maintained only by partners.[65] Sharing puts the intelligence in the hands of those who are able and willing to act on it. For example, the agency or state in possession of the information or intelligence concerning a WMD shipment might lack the legal or practical capability to act on it. As the Director of National Intelligence remarked on the occasion of the second anniversary of the PSI:

> There is no need to spell out in any detail the role intelligence plays in supporting PSI. That is obvious to us all. On the occasion of the second anniversary of PSI, it makes

[60]*See G-8 Ministers Want Intelligence Sharing,* NEWSMAX.COM, May 12, 2004, *available at* http://www.newsmax.com/archives/articles/2004/5/11/225427.shtml. The agreement calls for the states to pass legislation if necessary to ensure that terrorism information can be shared internally with police and prosecutors and externally with other countries. The G-8 group also recommended that each state ensure it can legally use a variety of "special investigative techniques" such as wiretaps, audio and visual surveillance, and interception of electronic communications.

[61]*2005 SUA Protocol,* art. 12, para. 1(b).

[62]NS-CWMD, at 6.

[63]*Ibid.* at 5.

[64]Intelligence sharing protocols must recognize that nations will participate in PSI interdictions through a variety of public security and safety entities, including intelligence, diplomatic, military, coast guard, customs/border patrol and treasury agencies, as well as port authorities.

[65]*See Report on the Commission on the Intelligence Capabilities of the United States Regarding Weapons of Mass Destruction* (Mar. 31, 2005), at 523 (highlighting importance of databases maintained by the Department of Homeland Security in mapping and link analysis), *available at* http://www.wmd.gov/wmd_report.pdf. Linking databases to leverage access provides one solution. *See 9/11 Commission Report,* at 418.

> more sense to note that PSI makes intelligence "actionable." That is a signal accomplishment, and it should be a great stimulus to all nations concerned about the menace of WMD. Through PSI, intelligence can be coupled to governmental actions in whatever way is judged to be maximally effective by the responsible authorities.[66]

Providing the necessary information to a flag state or a coastal state through whose waters the vessel will transit might be the key to successful interdiction. Finally, intelligence and information sharing is an invaluable method for building trust with and educating PSI partners. When intelligence is hoarded, the unavoidable message is that trust is lacking. Intelligence sharing fosters trust while also educating sister agencies in partner states on the nature and extent of the risk and the basis for decision making.[67]

The 2003 Paris Statement of Interdiction Principles called upon the PSI states to:

> adopt streamlined procedures for rapid exchange of relevant information concerning suspected proliferation activity, protecting the confidential character of classified information provided by other states as part of this initiative, dedicate appropriate resources and efforts to interdiction operations and capabilities, and maximize coordination among participants in interdiction efforts.[68]

The participating states agreed to the following guidelines for exchanging information:[69]

- Countries commit to seek to release information to other PSI participants to facilitate timely sharing of information to identify, monitor, disrupt or interdict proliferation activities of concern;
- Countries will release information to other PSI participants—and receiving countries agree to accept information—in accordance with existing national rules of release of operationally sensitive information or intelligence to third parties;
- Countries agree not to release any information received from a PSI country for PSI purposes to a third party—including other PSI countries—without the specific consent of originating country;

[66]John D. Negroponte [Director, National Intelligence], *Remarks from the Second Anniversary of the Proliferation Security Initiative,* May 31, 2005, *available at* http://www.dni.gov/proliferation.html.

[67]At present, the U.S. approach does not reach this far. In explaining the U.S. position, the Department of State announced that sensitive information on specific interdiction cases will ordinarily be shared only with those states involved in the actual interdiction effort. There is no intent to make such intelligence available to other PSI states, nor does the Department envision "multilateral" sharing of intelligence to facilitate the PSI. *See* U.S. Dep't of State, *Proliferation Security Initiative, Frequently Asked Questions,* May 26, 2005, *available at* http://www.state.gov/t/np/rls/fs/46839.htm.

[68]*Statement of Interdiction Principles,* para. 2.

[69]*See* U.S. Dep't of State, John R. Bolton, Undersecretary of State for Arms Control and International Security Affairs,*Remarks at Proliferation Security Initiative Meeting,* Paris, France, Sept. 4, 2003, *available at* http://www.state.gov/t/us/rm/23801.htm.

- Countries agree to afford protection to any information received from a PSI country for PSI purposes at substantially the same level it would receive in the originating country; and
- Countries agree to provide feedback on PSI operations conducted as a result of information supplied by another PSI country to the originating country.

Each state that seeks to participate in the PSI is asked to identify an appropriate point of contact for sharing information, in the event a specific interdiction effort requires their active efforts or support. Similar information-sharing provisions were included in the bilateral PSI shipboarding agreements.[70] The PSI Paris Guidelines are complemented by the G-8 Intelligence Sharing Agreement. Although it is too soon to tell if the Paris Guidelines or the G-8 Intelligence Sharing Agreement will live up to their promise, there is every reason to believe that the savagery of recent terrorist attacks and growing concern over the threat of radical groups gaining access to WMD will enhance the reform measures' chances of success.

Although the PSI establishes a framework for cooperation, there is little doubt that some WMD interdiction decisions will be unilateral. Assuming each nation's leadership will adopt some form of rational choice methodology in approaching proliferation policy decisions regarding what action, if any, to take in response to a threat, it seems clear that national leaders will often come to differing conclusions. The balance of interests is likely to vary from one state to another and even from one nation's leader to the next, according to their assessment of the quantity and quality of intelligence, the risks presented to international peace and security and to their nation in particular, and the various consequences of alternative courses of action.

Multilateral decisions take longer and generally raise the bar on certainty because the level of certainty for such actions must meet the test set by the most demanding decision maker, particularly if the operation may require the use of force to compel compliance. Recent U.N. Security Council debates highlight the fact that international consensus will break down if the most demanding state's evidentiary requirements are not met. Risk-averse states will tend to favor decisions that minimize the risk of false negatives, while risk tolerant states, and those not within the cross hairs of those wielding WMD, might be more concerned about avoiding false positives. Moreover, as the United States learned after its retaliatory attack on the Al Shifa plant in Sudan that was believed to be engaged in making CW agents, world opinion may compel a state to disclose the intelligence upon which its actions were based, to avoid opprobrium or censure.

The U.S. Department of State[71] points out that any judgment regarding the reliability of information used for interdictions is a national decision that must be made by each PSI participant government. For its part, the United States will only

[70] *See* Bilateral WMD Shipboarding Agreement, U.S.-Liberia, art. 6. "Operational information" is not defined in the agreement; however, the context in which it is used (detection and location of suspect vessels) suggests that the parties envisioned tactical information, not necessarily intelligence.

[71] *See* U.S. Dep't of State, *PSI Frequently Asked Questions.*

pursue interdiction efforts where it believes there is a "solid case" for doing so.[72] It bears repeating, however, that whether a particular case is "solid" enough to warrant action must be determined by risk assessment and management methods grounded in the best available—but likely imperfect—intelligence, and guided by judgments regarding the probability and consequences of an erroneous decision.

[72] *Ibid.*

6

Making WMD Transport Prohibitions Effective: A Primer on the Conduct of Maritime Security Operations

Contemporary national and homeland security strategies call for a layered defense capable of identifying, interdicting, and neutralizing threats to national or homeland security before they reach the nation's borders whenever possible. Counterproliferation and enhanced nonproliferation efforts form two of the central pillars of the U.S. *National Strategy to Combat Weapons of Mass Destruction* (NS-CWMD),[1] supplementing traditional nonproliferation regimes. Counterproliferation operations in the maritime domain seek to deter, disrupt, and deny use of maritime pathways by potential or actual proliferators and transporters. Although the NS-CWMD document does not refer to the Proliferation Security Initiative (PSI), which was launched the year after the NS-CWMD was promulgated, it is now clear that multilateral or consistent unilateral operations taken within the framework for activities established by the PSI will be the principal counterproliferation activity applied in the maritime domain, to intercept and neutralize the threat posed by WMD in the hands of states or non-state actors of proliferation concern.[2]

Maritime counterproliferation operations will be carried out within a complex scheme of international and national laws, U.N. Security Council resolutions, multilateral export control arrangements, and political agreements. When conducted at sea, such operations are often referred to by the generic labels "maritime interception," "visit, board, search, and seizure," and "maritime law enforcement" operations, but

---

[1]White House, *National Strategy to Combat Weapons of Mass Destruction* (2002) [hereinafter "NS-CWMD"].

[2]U.S. Dep't of State, *United States Initiatives to Prevent Proliferation,* DOS Pub. No. 11,254 (2005), *available at* http://www.state.gov/t/np/rls/other/46896.htm.

applying those labels indiscriminately may obscure important distinctions in the legal basis for the operation. Whether any given component of the complex legal scheme referred to above will apply in a given case will often turn on the actual nature of the operation. For example, in the United States the *posse comitatus* statutes and regulations limit the participation of Department of Defense (DoD) personnel in maritime law enforcement boardings, but not in maritime interception operation boardings conducted outside the United States.[3] Similarly, rules on the use of force apply in peacetime operations, while the rules of engagement apply in combat operations.

To provide the reader with the necessary background on the principal features of maritime interception and enforcement operations and the specialized terminology they employ, this chapter begins with a brief description of the mechanics of the vessel approach and boarding. It then examines the nature of the various conceptual frameworks under which at-sea boardings are conducted, to provide a context for the materials on international law in Chapter 7 and a more detailed examination of the legal issues raised by maritime counterproliferation boardings in Chapter 8. Three of the frameworks covered—self-defense, the belligerent right of visit and search, and blockade—are generally limited to situations involving an armed conflict. Two others, the peacetime right of visit and maritime law enforcement operations, apply primarily in peacetime or among neutrals during an armed conflict involving other states. The sixth framework, maritime interception operations (sometimes a subset of maritime security operations), is an increasingly generic term applied most often in the context of peace maintenance or restoration measures imposed by the U.N. Security Council.

THE AT-SEA APPROACH, BOARDING AND SEARCH

Maritime interception and enforcement actions are an indispensable element in maintaining public order in the oceans. No one has yet suggested a feasible substitute for an adequate and effective at-sea monitoring and enforcement presence. The law of the sea has long recognized that warships engage in a variety of activities that can be grouped under the rubric "military activities other than war." Those activities include several that seek to promote and enforce public order by suppressing piracy, the slave trade, narcotics trafficking, and other threats to international peace, security, and public safety. A number of states rely on naval vessels to enforce fisheries, customs, and immigration laws,[4] while others might rely on a coast guard or other law enforcement agency for such constabulary tasks.[5] The law of the sea recognizes that "warships"

---

[3] *See* 18 U.S.C.A. § 1385 (West 2005). H.R. Rep. No. 97–71, pt. 2, *reprinted in* 1981 U.S.C.C.A.N. 1785.

[4] In the United States, customs and immigration enforcement operations are conducted by elements of the Department of Homeland Security. Department of Defense units play a limited role in detecting and responding to incidents of maritime smuggling of undocumented aliens and naval vessels, like all vessels, have an obligation to render assistance to vessels or persons in distress at sea.

[5] *See* Ivan A. Shearer, *The Development of International Law with Respect to the Law Enforcement Role of Navies and Coast Guards in Peacetime,* 71 U.S. Nav. War Coll., Int'l L. Studies 429 (1998).

and certain other designated public vessels may approach vessels in ocean waters and, under some circumstances, take enforcement action against the vessel and those on board. Although at first blush it would appear to make little difference to the boarded vessel or its flag state whether a boarding is carried out by a traditional warship or a law enforcement vessel, boardings conducted by warships are more likely to raise questions regarding the purpose of the boarding and whether any coercive or forceful measures employed to carry out the boarding constitute a use of armed force rather than an arguably less provocative exercise of the state's police power.

Vessel interceptions and boardings by naval vessels are generally carried out by visit, board, search, and seizure (VBSS) teams drawn from the U.S. Maritime Forces[6] or the analogous forces of another government. Boarding teams from U.S. Navy platforms may include Navy, Marine Corps, and Coast Guard personnel. Coast Guard interception and boarding teams may also operate from Coast Guard cutters or from allied naval vessels. In most cases, Coast Guard law enforcement detachments (LEDETs) on naval vessels serve under the operational or tactical control of the cognizant Coast Guard command authority when conducting boardings.[7] In cases not calling for law enforcement measures, however, the LEDET may operate under DoD control, drawing on the Coast Guard's statutory authority to provide assistance to other agencies.[8]

It should be noted at the outset that not all approaches lead to boardings and not all boardings extend to a search of the vessel, particularly when a more thorough search can be conducted in the vessel's next port of call. The degree of intrusion that will be necessary and appropriate in each case turns on a variety of legal, informational, and operational considerations. Typically, the interception of a vessel suspected of transporting WMD or delivery systems will be based on an intelligence finding that is progressively developed through surveillance and reconnaissance by organic intelligence assets, before moving to the "stop-and-search" phase of MIO. For example, a vessel observed loading suspicious cargo in a port might later be tracked by satellite, aircraft, unmanned vehicles, radar, surface ship, submarine, or seabed sensors.[9] When the vessel is encountered by an intercepting vessel or aircraft exercising the right of approach, it will be visually inspected for evidence of

---

[6]The term "U.S. Maritime Forces" includes the U.S. Navy, Marine Corps, and Coast Guard. *See* U.S. Navy, *Naval Doctrine for Military Operations Other-Than-War,* 1–1, NWP 3–07 (1998) [hereinafter "U.S. Navy, *MOOTW Doctrine*"].

[7]*See* 10 U.S.C.A. § 379 (West 2005).

[8]14 U.S.C.A. § 141 (West 2005). The fact that a given boarding is conducted under the MIO/VBSS framework does not indicate the nature or scope of the boarding or the legal authority on which it relies. Similarly, the fact that a Coast Guard LEDET accompanies a Navy VBSS team does not necessarily indicate that the boarding falls within the maritime law enforcement rubric. *See* U.S. Navy, *Maritime Interception Operations*, para. 2.2.4, NTTP 3–07.11/CGP 3–07.11 (2003) [hereinafter "U.S. Navy, *MIO Doctrine*"].

[9]The Department of Defense's role in maritime detection, monitoring, reconnaissance, communications, and interceptions in counter-narcotics operations is defined by statute. *See* 10 U.S.C.A. §§ 371–378, 124 and note (West 2005).

identity and flag. Visual surveillance might be followed by a radio inquiry, to determine or confirm the vessel's name, registry, homeport, last port, next port, cargo, and number of crew and passengers.[10] The information obtained can then be checked against available information and intelligence databases. The vessel's registry might also be confirmed with the flag state (if cooperative), and its claimed next port of call might be contacted to determine whether the vessel has filed an advance notice of arrival and a copy of its cargo manifest. If suspicions remain, consent to board may be requested from the flag state or the master, or a nonconsensual boarding may be conducted, perhaps under the right of visit.

Depending on the vessel's location, flag, and type, the threat level presented, whether a state of belligerency exists, and the goals of the mission, maritime security, detection, interception, and enforcement operations involving vessels suspected of transporting WMD could potentially be carried out under one or more of the following frameworks: the peacetime right of visit, maritime interception or interdiction operations, maritime law enforcement operations, self-help countermeasures, individual or collective self-defense, the belligerent's visit and search for contraband, or blockade enforcement.

THE PEACETIME RIGHT OF APPROACH AND VISIT

The importance of timely and actionable intelligence in any counterproliferation operation is discussed in Chapter 5. Frequently, however, patrol vessels or aircraft encounter a vessel about which there is little or no prior intelligence, but whose appearance or actions raise suspicion. The peacetime right of visit can, in some instances, provide the patrol vessel with a legal ground for taking action, including boarding, to allay those suspicions. The peacetime right of visit under the LOS Convention should not be confused with a belligerent's right of visit and search for contraband under the law of neutrality (discussed below).[11]

As the materials in Chapters 7 and 8 describe more fully, Article 110 of the 1982 LOS Convention confers on a warship the limited right to approach, board (i.e., "visit"), and possibly search a foreign vessel located on the high seas under circumstances set out in the convention. In its exercise of the customary international law "right of approach," a warship may intercept a vessel, inspect it from a safe distance to determine its name, flag, and home port, receive and review any data the vessel might be emitting from its automatic identification system

---

[10]Enforcement vessels will no doubt recognize the security risks posed by requiring vessels to transmit sensitive information by radio transmissions that are easily intercepted by other vessels or shore stations.

[11]*See* The *Marianna Flora,* 4 U.S. (11 Wheat.) 1 (1826)(distinguishing between a belligerent's right of visitation and search in time of war and the peacetime right of approach). Contemporary U.S. Navy doctrine acknowledges there are "crucial differences between MIOs and belligerent acts of interdiction such as blockade and visit and search during international armed conflict." *See* U.S. Navy, *MOOTW Doctrine,* para. 3.2.2.1.

(AIS)[12] or long-range identification and tracking (LRIT)[13] equipment, perhaps scan other electromagnetic emissions if so equipped,[14] and finally hail it on the radio.[15] Information obtained during the approach may reveal that the vessel is subject to the jurisdiction of the approaching vessel (i.e., of the same flag), is registered in a state with which the flag state of the approaching vessel has a bilateral boarding agreement or which generally agrees to consensual boardings on a case-by-case basis when requested.[16] In such cases, there is no need to formally rely on the "right of visit" to justify a boarding, should one be called for. A refusal to answer the hail or any questions posed does not in itself constitute a violation or give the approaching vessel a right to board.[17] The failure to hoist a flag or to provide requested information may, however, give rise to suspicions that justify boarding.[18]

Right-of-visit boardings are most commonly triggered by suspicions regarding the vessel's nationality. An approach and boarding undertaken to resolve such questions may ripen into one of the other maritime operations described below if, for example, evidence of criminal activity or violation of a U.N. Security Council embargo is discovered in the course of a visit to investigate questions regarding the vessel's flag. Application of the international law right of visit in a maritime counterproliferation scenario is illustrated by the 2002 encounter with the M/V *So San,* which was visited to resolve nationality questions and then found to be carrying Scud missiles from North Korea to Yemen. The incident, and application of the right of visit in counterproliferation operations, is analyzed in Chapter 8.

---

[12]AIS equipment, designed primarily for collision avoidance, automatically transmits a data stream of information such as the vessel's identity, location, course, and speed. The transmissions can be received and displayed on other AIS-equipped vessels in the immediate vicinity. Most commercial vessels over 300 registered tons are now required to carry and use AIS equipment.

[13]LRIT equipment will, when installed, serve much the same function as AIS equipment, but is capable of being received as much greater distances. Like AIS, LRIT is one of the tools that facilitates and enhances maritime domain awareness.

[14]Some naval vessels are equipped to obtain measurement and signature (MASINT) intelligence from other vessels.

[15]The information obtained during such approaches is normally reported and added to databases kept by law enforcement and intelligence agencies.

[16]Under the ILC Draft Articles on State Responsibility, valid consent by a state to a given act by another state precludes the wrongfulness of the act in relation to the consent-granting state, to the extent that the act remains within the limits of consent. *See* Draft Articles on Responsibility of States for Internationally Wrongful Acts, art. 20, adopted by the International Law Commission at its Fifty-third session (2001), U.N. GAOR, 53d Sess., Supp. No. 10, U.N. Doc. A/56/10 (2001) [hereinafter "ILC Draft Articles on State Responsibility"].

[17]The *Marianna Flora,* 4 U.S. (11 Wheat.) 1, 44 (1826).

[18]*See, e.g.*, United States v. Alvarez-Mena, 765 F.2d 1259 (5th Cir. 1985); Robert C.F. Reuland, Note, *Interference with Non-National Ships on the High Seas: Peacetime Exceptions to the Exclusivity of Flag-State Jurisdiction*, 22 VAND. J. TRANSNAT'L L. 1161, 1229 (1989). For the requirement that a ship sail under a flag see LOS Convention, art. 92(2)("a ship shall sail under the flag of one State only...") (emphasis added).

MARITIME INTERCEPTION/INTERDICTION OPERATIONS

The phrase "maritime interception operations" (MIO) was originally used by the United States in a narrow sense to refer only to naval operations taken to enforce U.N. Security Council resolutions. Under the U.N. Charter, the Security Council may take measures under Chapter VI to promote peaceful settlement of disputes.[19] Such measures include peacekeeping or humanitarian operations and are carried out with the consent of the target state and generally do not include the use of armed force by the peacekeepers except in self-defense. When an incident threatens international peace or security or constitutes a breach of the peace or an act of aggression, the Council may exercise its authority under Chapter VII to impose "prevention" or "enforcement" measures.[20] Chapter VII measures are divided into those not involving the use of force, such as complete or partial interruption of economic relations, transportation or communication and severance of diplomatic relations,[21] and measures that include the use of force as necessary to maintain or restore international peace and security.[22] The measures imposed may be punitive or preventative. Punitive economic sanctions are designed to coerce the sanctioned state into complying with specific requirements established by the sanctioning authority. By contrast, preventative measures are those designed to deny the sanctioned state the military and/or economic means necessary to threaten or breach the peace.

The Charter imposes an obligation on all states to refrain from giving assistance to any state against which the United Nations is taking preventative or enforcement action,[23] and to accept and carry out decisions of the Security Council.[24] However, the level of participation varies according to the respective national interests, capabilities, location, and political will. As a result, maritime patrols to enforce Security Council embargoes have traditionally been carried out by a single nation, an established alliance like NATO, or relatively small coalitions of willing states.

Over the years, the MIO concept has expanded in response to the growing array of peacekeeping and peace enforcement measures. International law does not define "interception" or "interdiction." The U.S. Navy defines "maritime interception operations" as the "legitimate action of denying suspect vessels access to specific ports for import or export of prohibited goods to or from a specified

---

[19]Charter of the United Nations, art. 36.

[20]The terms "preventative" and "enforcement" are not used in article 41 or 42, but rather in articles 2(5), 5, and 50.

[21]*Ibid.* art. 41.

[22]*Ibid.* art. 42.

[23]*Ibid.* art. 2(5).

[24]*Ibid.* art. 25. Article 25 is part of Chapter V of the Charter and therefore applies to "security measures" under Chapters VI and VII.

nation or nations, for purposes of peacekeeping or to enforce imposed sanctions."[25] The United States has also developed the concept of "expanded" maritime interception operations, which may be authorized even when no collective security measures have been imposed.[26] In addition, the U.S. Navy increasingly participates in what has come to be known as maritime security operations.[27] One of the better known maritime security operations is Combined Task Force 150. CTF 150 is comprised of the navies of up to 17 nations, which patrol the offshore waters in and around the Arabian Gulf, North Arabian Sea, Gulf of Oman, Gulf of Aden, and parts of the Indian Ocean and Red Sea, in support of Operation Enduring Freedom.

Other NATO states sometimes prefer the phrase maritime "interdiction" operations to maritime "interception" operations.[28] States participating in the Proliferation Security Initiative have similarly adopted the term "interdiction" in their Statement of Interdiction Principles.[29] For some states, however, the term interdiction signifies more intrusive measures than does the term interception. For example, China reportedly insisted that the term interdiction be deleted from an early draft of U.N. Security Council Resolution 1540. MIO and counterproliferation measures fall within the class of activities known as "military operations other than war" (MOOTW).[30] The classification takes MIO out of the armed conflict legal structure.[31] MOOTW tasking may constitute a substantial part of the operational requirements for some naval vessels. It is not unusual in some theaters for a naval ship to conduct up to 100 MIO boardings during a six-month deployment. However, few of those operations are expressly related to WMD counterproliferation missions.

---

[25]*See* U.S. Navy, *MIO Doctrine,* para. 1.5.12.

[26]*See ibid.* para. 1.5.6. "Expanded MIO," when authorized by the Secretary of Defense, are designed to intercept targeted personnel or material that pose an imminent threat to the U.S. Expanded MIO may involve multinational forces. The most complete working definition of "maritime security operations" is set out in the Naval Operations Concept. It states that the goals of such operations are to "ensure freedom of navigation, the flow of commerce and the protection of ocean resources" and to "secure the maritime domain from nation-state threats, terrorism, drug trafficking and other forms of transnational crime, piracy, environmental destruction and illegal seaborne immigration." Chief of Naval Operations-Commandant of the Marine Corps, *Naval Operations Concept 2006,* Sept. 1, 2006, at 14, *available at* http://www.mcwl.usmc.mil/concepts/ServiceConcepts/NOC%20FINAL%2014%20Sep.pdf.

[27]See *Naval Operations Concept,* at 14.

[28]In U.S. military parlance "interdiction" is defined as activities designed to "divert, disrupt, delay or destroy" the adversary's potential to inflict harm before it can be used effectively against friendly forces. *See* Joint Chiefs of Staff, *Joint Interdiction Operations,* Jt. Publ'n 3–03 (1997). Within the *National Strategy for Maritime Security* framework interdiction relates to actions taken to divert, delay, intercept, board, detain, or destroy, as appropriate, suspect vessels, people or cargo.

[29]*See Statement of Interdiction Principles* (reproduced in Appendix A).

[30]The Navy MIO doctrine does not apply to naval blockades in time of war. U.S. Navy, *MIO Doctrine,* para. 1.3. Note, however, that the Security Council may impose a blockade under its Chapter VII authority even in peacetime. *See* Charter of the United Nations, art. 42.

[31]The statutory scheme for U.S. participation in Chapter VII enforcement actions is found in the United Nations Participation Act of 1945, 22 U.S.C.A. §§ 287d, 287d-1 (West 2005).

WMD maritime interception operations by the United States can be traced back at least as far as the 1962 quarantine proclaimed by President Kennedy and enforced by the U.S. Navy to halt the shipment of Soviet offensive missiles to Cuba.[32] Navy doctrine notes that the term "quarantine" was later dropped from the planning terminology in favor of maritime interception operations.[33] Contemporary maritime interception operations by the Navy are characterized by: (1) the source of their legal authority (usually a U.N. Security Council resolution); (2) the principle of proportionality between means and ends; (3) the principle of impartiality;[34] and (4) a commitment to effectiveness.[35]

Between 1977 and 2000 the U.N. Security Council invoked its power under Article 41 of the Charter to impose economic sanctions on states more than a dozen times.[36] Six of those sanction resolutions entailed maritime enforcement of an embargo, principally in the Arabian Gulf, Gulf of Oman, Arabian Sea, and Red Sea (Resolutions 661, 665), Adriatic (Resolution 787),[37] and waters surrounding Haiti (Resolution 875).[38] In most cases, the implementing maritime interception operations were carried out by multinational forces.[39] In the course of patrols to enforce applicable Security Council resolutions, multinational interception forces may, of course, conduct boardings under circumstances falling within their jurisdiction as the flag or coastal state, or with the consent of the flag or coastal state.

---

[32]Proclamation No. 3504, 27 Fed. Reg. 10,401 (Oct. 23, 1962). The proclamation authorized the use of force only in cases of failure or refusal to comply, after reasonable efforts had been made to communicate directly with the vessel, or in cases of self-defense, and then only to the extent necessary.

[33]*See* U.S. Navy, *MOOTW Doctrine,* at 3–2 n.4.

[34]The principle of impartiality is also manifested in the 1982 Law of the Sea Convention's articles banning discrimination. *See, e.g.,* U.N. Convention on the Law of the Sea, arts. 24(1)(b), 25, 26, 42(2), 52(2) & 227.

[35]U.S. Navy, *MIO Doctrine,* at 3–3. The principle of impartiality does not require that all vessels be stopped. Effectiveness is measured by the extent to which MIO furthers compliance with the sanctions.

[36]It is not always clear whether the Security Council resolution is based on Article 41, which authorizes imposition of economic sanctions and embargoes, or Article 42, which includes the use of armed force. *See* Alfred H.A. Soons, *Enforcing the Economic Embargo at Sea,* in UNITED NATIONS SANCTIONS AND INTERNATIONAL LAW 307–24 (W. Gowlland-Debbas, ed., 2001). Professor Soons raises the question whether U.N. Security Council Chapter VII resolutions in themselves provide authority for a state other than the flag state of a vessel to conduct nonconsensual boardings of vessels to enforce the resolution. *Ibid.* at 316–17.

[37]*Operation Sharp Guard* operations were carried out in the Adriatic Sea by NATO (*Operation Maritime Guard*) and Western European Union (*Operation Sharp Fence*) elements in response to the conflicts in the former Yugoslavia.

[38]The six include Southern Rhodesia, Iraq, the territory of the former Yugoslavia, Haiti, and Sierra Leone. Soons, at 307–08. The United Kingdom's Beira patrol, in support of the Southern Rhodesia sanctions, lasted more than a decade. *See* Richard Mobley, *The Beira Patrol,* 55 NAVAL WAR COLL. REV. 63 (2002).

[39]The Iraq operations have been carried out since 1990 by the 15 nations that have contributed to the Multinational Interception Force. *See generally* Horace B. Robertson, *Interdiction of Iraqi Maritime Commerce in the 1990–1991 Persian Gulf Conflict,* 22 OCEAN DEV. & INT'L L. 289 (1992). Over the years, MIO patrols have extended at various times from the Persian Gulf south to the northern Arabian Sea and west to the Red Sea.

MIO patrols are also being carried in other regions, outside the U.N. Security Council umbrella. For example, NATO launched its *Operation Active Endeavor* (OAE) in the eastern Mediterranean shortly after the attacks of September 11, 2001.[40] The stated purpose of OAE is to "deter, defend, disrupt and protect against terrorism through maritime operations in the Area of Operations."[41] In the first three years of OAE, NATO vessels hailed more than 41,000 vessels.[42] NATO announced in early 2004 that it was extending its antiterrorism naval patrols to the entire Mediterranean and perhaps the Black Sea as well. At the same time, NATO members announced they were seeking permission from a number of Mediterranean states to stop and search merchant vessels that appear suspicious.[43]

Increasingly, vessels engaged in maritime security operations are intercepting vessels smuggling drugs, triggering maritime law enforcement actions (discussed below). If evidence of a crime is discovered in the course of a visit, boarding or search personnel with law enforcement authority (the Coast Guard LEDET or foreign law enforcement agents) may be called on to arrest the offenders and seize the vessel and cargo.

MARITIME LAW ENFORCEMENT OPERATIONS

Many of the counterproliferation actions envisioned under the PSI Statement of Interdiction Principles and U.N. Security Council Resolution 1540, which requires all states to prohibit certain proliferation activities, will be carried out under a law enforcement framework. As this chapter's introductory materials highlight, classifying a given counterproliferation interception as a law enforcement operation can affect the respective roles of U.S. Departments of Defense and Homeland Security. The law enforcement classification also implicates a number of issues regarding the controlling legal authorities for the use and disclosure of classified material[44] and gathering evidence.[45] In transitioning between an interception operation based on classified intelligence and a law enforcement operation that may require

---

[40] *Operation Active Endeavor* is one of the NATO counterterrorism measures carried out under Article 5 of the Washington Treaty, invoked immediately following the September 11 attacks. *See NATO to Expand Operation Active Endeavor to the Whole Mediterranean,* NATO Press Release (2004) 039, Mar. 16, 2004.

[41] *Ibid.*

[42] *Ibid.* OAE boardings beyond coastal state waters are carried out with the consent of the flag state.

[43] *NATO Allies Expanding Antiterror Naval Patrols,* INT'L HERALD TRIB., Mar. 17, 2004.

[44] The use of classified information at trial is controlled by the Classified Information Procedures Act (CIPA), 18 U.S.C.A. app. §§ 1–12 (West 2005). As discussed in Chapter 5, case managers must also be alert to the legal limits regarding the sharing of information gathered using foreign intelligence methods with law enforcement officers and prosecutors.

[45] Evidence gathered during a boarding using unconstitutional methods might be excluded at trial. However, the constitutional standards for search and seizure at sea and on internal navigable waters vary from those applicable to terrestrial searches. *See, e.g.,* United States v. Villamonte-Marques, 462 U.S. 579 (1983) (warrantless and suspicionless boarding and search of a U.S. vessel in the internal waters of the U.S. under authority of 19 U.S.C. § 1581 customs statute upheld against a Fourth Amendment challenge).

presentation of evidence at trial, those involved must be alert to the issues created by that transition.

The phrase maritime law enforcement (MLE) operations refers to activities by officials with the legal authority to detect crimes, apprehend violators, and gather the evidence necessary to support prosecution.[46] Legitimate MLE activities must be grounded on lawful authority and an applicable basis for jurisdiction. However, boardings often are conducted pursuant to consent by the vessel's flag state, the coastal state or vessel master, flag state, or costal state.

Laws that might be relevant in a WMD interdiction incident include those dealing with the transfer or transport of such weapons and related materials, including the export control laws now mandated by U.N. Security Council Resolution 1540, as well as laws regarding licensing and that prohibit false or fraudulent documentation. In addition, some transfer or transport activities could constitute a violation of laws prohibiting the provision of material support to terrorists, aiding and abetting violent crimes, and conspiracies. In the future, some WMD transfer or transport schemes might also trigger national prohibitions enacted in response to the draft 2005 SUA Protocol (discussed in Chapter 7). In carrying out MLE actions in support of counterproliferation programs, it is important to recognize that the relevant laws are often very focused in their application, and liability may be imposed on the exporter, buyer, transporter, or other parties who financed or otherwise provided support for the illicit transaction, or who made false statements in the course of the transaction. Thus an ocean carrier or vessel crew should not be presumed to be responsible for all violations found on board the vessel. Finally, it should be noted that under the "protective principle" a state has jurisdiction to prescribe and enforce laws against acts that threaten vital state interests.[47] Such laws against conduct by non-state entities might also implicate issues regarding countermeasures or self-defense measures against states.[48]

FORCIBLE AND NONFORCIBLE COUNTERMEASURES

The term "countermeasures" refers to unilateral self-help measures directed at another state to coerce the state into complying with international law. Such countermeasures against states should not be confused with law enforcement measures taken against individuals or other non-state actors. Historically, a distinction was drawn

---

[46]The U.S. Coast Guard defines "law enforcement" as "all Coast Guard functions or actions carried out pursuant to the legal authorities described in" the Maritime Law Enforcement Manual. *See* U.S. Coast Guard, Maritime Law Enforcement Manual, para. 4.A.2, COMDTINST M16247.1C (2003) [hereinafter "Coast Guard MLEM"].

[47]*See* Restatement § 402(3) & comment *f.* The general rules regarding jurisdiction under customary international law must, however, be applied in light of more specific treaty provisions, such as those in the LOS Convention regarding the allocation of jurisdiction among flag states, coastal states and other states.

[48]In times of armed conflict, individuals whose acts might otherwise constitute crimes proscribed on the basis of protective jurisdiction might be deemed combatants under the relevant law of armed conflict.

between forcible and non-forcible countermeasures. The line of demarcation between countermeasures and the use of armed force is one that has historically turned more often on rhetoric than discernable legal principles. Moreover, there remains considerable disagreement over the range of legitimate countermeasures and the violations that justify their application. Finally, the availability of countermeasures in cases involving matters of which the U.N. Security Council is seized is unsettled.

The predicate for lawful countermeasures is a prior breach of an international obligation by the state against which the countermeasures will be directed. Chapter 7 discusses a number of provisions in the LOS Convention authorizing a state (usually a coastal state) to take countermeasures to protect its interests. Several commentators have analyzed the interplay between the customary law of self-help countermeasures and U.N. Security Council resolutions. One reasoned that the legal authority for the maritime interception operations carried by the United States and United Kingdom shortly after Iraq invaded Kuwait and the Security Council issued its first resolution (which did not authorize force) could be found in the customary law of collective, forcible self-help.[49] Another commentator argued that in the event a state fails to meet its obligations under an applicable Security Council resolution or otherwise violates international law, a state harmed by that breach might be justified in exercising its right to take self-help measures, to the extent such a countermeasure was both necessary and proportionate.[50] Still another raises the question whether a flag state that refuses to grant consent to a boarding to enforce a Security Council resolution might thereby be committing a breach of its obligation under the U.N. Charter, providing the justification for countermeasures by another state.[51] It is not entirely clear, however, what state or states are harmed by the flag state's breach under those circumstances, and would therefore be entitled to obtain relief by countermeasures,[52] or whether such a state would first be required to consult with the Security Council.[53]

---

[49]Richard Zeigler, *Ubi Sumus? Quo Vadimus? Charting the Course of Maritime Interception Operations*, 43 NAVAL L. REV. 1, 4, n.12 (1996).

[50]*See* Wolff Heintschel von Heinegg, *The Proliferation Security Initiative: Security vs. Freedom of Navigation*, 35 ISRAEL Y.B. HUMAN RIGHTS 181 (2005). Professor Heintschel von Heinegg argues that a target state would be entitled to take defensive countermeasures short of Article 51 against a state that is actively or passively furthering WMD proliferation. *Ibid.* at 198. Countermeasure reprisals involving visit and search could be taken against vessels for the mere reason that they are flying the violating state's flag. *See also* Gilbert Guillaume, *Terrorism and International Law*, 53 INT'L & COMP. L. Q. 537, 544 (2004) (discussing extrajudicial countermeasures not involving the use of armed force in response to acts of terrorism).

[51]*See* Soons, at 317 & n.33.

[52]*See* ILC Draft Articles on State Responsibility, arts. 33(1) & 42–43 (addressing issues regarding breach of an international obligation owed to the international community as a whole). *But see* RESTATEMENT § 905, comment *a*(distinguishing between such *erga omnes* obligations and obligations arising under Security Council measures).

[53]*See* Soons, at 318.

INDIVIDUAL OR COLLECTIVE SELF-DEFENSE

It will come as no surprise that navies and coast guards take action to defend the nation and its allies. Self-defense is a form of armed or forcible self-help in response to an actual or imminent act of armed aggression.[54] It appears clear that the inherent right of individual and collective self-defense can now be invoked against non-state entities. In the post-9/11 world, the U.N. Security Council has invoked its powers under Chapter VII of the Charter and collective self-defense agreements, such as Article 5 of the Washington Treaty of the NATO states,[55] Article IV of the ANZUS Treaty,[56] and the Inter-American Treaty of Reciprocal Assistance among OAS members,[57] have also been triggered by attacks by the al Qaeda organization operating out of bases in Taliban-controlled Afghanistan. The response has included, among other things, extended naval patrols throughout the Arabian Gulf, Gulf of Oman, Arabian Sea, Red Sea, and the Mediterranean. The legal basis on which actions by the U.N. Security Council and NATO states are engaged clearly suggests that the threat posed by international terrorism and proliferation of WMD, related materials, and delivery systems might in some cases cross the threshold from peacetime counterproliferation operations to the domain of individual or collective self-defense. The test for determining which fall within the self-defense domain is a matter of disagreement.

Most maritime counterproliferation operations will likely be conducted by a flag state or coastal state with jurisdiction over the suspect vessel, or with the consent of such a state or of the master of the suspect vessel. Alternatively, in some regions the initial boarding may be conducted pursuant to an applicable U.N. Security Council Resolution. In early statements describing the PSI, the United States indicated that the inherent right of self-defense recognized under Article 51 of the U.N. Charter might also serve as a legal basis for WMD interdictions in some cases. However, no mention of the right of self-defense was

---

[54] *See* 5 MARJORIE M. WHITEMAN, DIGEST OF INTERNATIONAL LAW §§ 24–26 (1965); 12 MARJORIE M. WHITEMAN, DIGEST OF INTERNATIONAL LAW § 2–3 (1968). *See also* YORAM DINSTEIN, WAR, AGGRESSION AND SELF-DEFENCE 159 (3d ed., 2001), which explains:

> The essence of self-defence is self-help: under certain conditions set by international law, a State acting unilaterally—perhaps in association with other countries—may respond with lawful force to unlawful force (or, minimally, to the imminent threat of unlawful force). The reliance on self-help, as a remedy available to States when their rights are violated, is and always has been one of the hallmarks of international law. Self-help is a characteristic feature of all primitive legal systems, but in international law it has been honed to art form.

[55] U.S. DEP'T OF STATE, DIGEST OF UNITED STATES PRACTICE IN INTERNATIONAL LAW 2001, at 861 (2002).

[56] *Ibid.* at 862.

[57] *Ibid.*

included in the Statement of Interdiction Principles prepared later.[58] That does not rule out the possibility that a case might arise where a WMD shipment to a given state or non-state actor poses such a serious risk to the national security of the United States or one of its allies that the nations' leaders will invoke the right of individual or collective self-defense. Any interdiction carried out in accordance with the right of self-defense, as recognized by Article 51 of the U.N. Charter, would be in accordance with international law, as the Statement of Interdiction Principles require.

The contours of the right of self-defense are beyond the scope of this chapter. It is noteworthy, however, that it is sometimes said that national security is the "high politics" of international relations: a subject where legal rules have less force, and a subject trumping all lesser interests. Indeed, as situational urgency grows from everyday national interests, to vital national interests, and finally to the state's very survival, the state is less likely to sacrifice effectiveness for perceived legitimacy. In the aftermath of the 1962 Cuban missile crisis, former Secretary of State Dean Acheson commented on the role of law in a crisis that may threaten the very survival of the state:

> I must conclude that the propriety of the Cuban quarantine is not a legal issue. The power, position and prestige of the United States had been challenged by another state; and law simply does not deal with such questions of ultimate power—power that comes close to the sources of sovereignty... No law can destroy the state creating the law. The survival of state is not a matter of law.[59]

Echoes of Secretary Acheson's pronouncement can be heard in the *National Security Strategy of the United States.* But those who argue for a right of self-help and self-defense without any apparent legal limit must be prepared to distinguish the legitimacy of those actions from what many consider similar "necessity" rationales forcefully espoused by terrorists and rogue regimes or similar arguments by a "rational" state that concludes only a preventative strike on the nascent nuclear capability of an intractable regional or global rival can insure the state's security. Chapter 7 examines the international law of self-defense framework. Chapter 8 then applies that framework to the maritime counterproliferation setting.

---

[58]John Bolton, former Undersecretary of State for Arms Control and International Security, included the right of self-defense among the possible justification for PSI interdictions in an early statement; however, none of the other PSI-participating states endorsed his comment and the U.S. Department of State guidance on the PSI does not include self-defense on its list of legal bases for the PSI. *See* Chapter 5.

[59]Remarks of Hon. Dean Acheson, American Society of International Law, PROC. OF AM. SOC. INT'L L. at its 57th Annual Mtg., 1963, at 14.

BELLIGERENTS' VISIT AND SEARCH FOR CONTRABAND

Should an armed conflict arise,[60] the law of neutrality[61] recognizes the right of a warship of any of the belligerents to visit and search neutral shipping, other than neutral vessels enjoying sovereign immunity, outside of neutral waters, in order to intercept contraband destined for the enemy.[62] The belligerent's right of visit and search during an armed conflict must be distinguished from the related tactic of blockading the enemy's ports to prevent vessels from entering or leaving (discussed below). "Visit" refers to the act of ordering a vessel to heave to and submit to an inspection of its papers. "Search" refers to the questioning of the vessel's captain and crew and examining the vessel's spaces and cargo. If a search at sea is impossible or unsafe, the vessel may be diverted to an appropriate port.[63] "Contraband" is defined as goods that are ultimately destined for territory under the control of the enemy and which may be susceptible for use in armed conflict.[64] A vessel found to be carrying contraband may be captured (seized) and delivered to a prize court, where the vessel and its contraband cargo may be confiscated and condemned (forfeited) as a prize.[65] This "prize" scheme bears some similarity to the asset forfeiture aspects in criminal laws. The civilian crew members of the vessel taken as a prize are repatriated, not treated as prisoners of war.

---

[60]France relied on its claimed legal right to exercise visit and search powers on the high seas during the Algerian independence conflict of 1956–1962 to conduct nearly 5,000 boardings in one year. Robin R. Churchill & A. Vaughan Lowe, The Law of the Sea 217 (2d ed. 1999); Reuland, *Interference with Non-National Ships,* at 1218. In contrast, during the Falklands Islands armed conflict, the United Kingdom did not invoke the right of self-defense to interdict a shipment of arms from France to Argentina. It seems clear that the United Kingdom could have exercised a belligerent's right of visit and search under the circumstances.

[61]The law of neutrality, which addresses the relationship between belligerents and neutrals, concerns questions of contraband, blockade and visit and search. The law of neutrality must be distinguished from the law of armed conflict, which governs actions between and among belligerents. *See generally* 10 Marjorie M. Whiteman, Digest of International Law 644 (1968); 11 Marjorie M. Whiteman, Digest of International Law ch. XXXIII (1968).

[62]San Remo Manual on International Law Applicable to Armed Conflicts at Sea 31–32, paras. 118–121 (Louise Doswald-Beck, ed. 1995). *See also* 11 Digest of International Law §§ 1–6; Annotated Supplement to the Commander's Handbook of the Law of Naval Operations, para. 7.6 (1997); Wolff Heintschel von Heinegg, *Visit, Search, Diversion, and Capture in Naval Warfare, Pts. I & II,* 29 Can. Y.B. Int'l L. 283 (1991) & 30 Can. Y.B. Int'l L. 89 (1992).

[63]San Remo Manual, para. 121.

[64]*Ibid.* at 215. Historically, contraband was in turn divided into "absolute" contraband and "conditional" contraband; however, that distinction is no longer in favor. *Ibid.* at 215–16. *See also* 10 Digest of International Law § 4.

[65]During the 1990–1991 Gulf War, the United States set up two prize courts: one in the federal district court for the southern district of New York and one in the northern district of California.

BLOCKADE

Brief mention should be made of the extant, but seldom invoked,[66] blockade doctrines. Blockade under the law of armed conflict (LOAC) is a method of naval warfare and is defined as "a belligerent operation to prevent vessels and/or aircraft of all nations, enemy as well as neutral, from entering or exiting specified ports, airfields, or coastal areas belong to, occupied by, or under the control of an enemy nation.[67] Under the LOAC, one belligerent might choose to blockade another belligerent to deny the enemy the arms and other resources needed to sustain the conflict.[68] Because a blockade involves the use of or threat to use military force by one state against another state, the action meets the definition of an international armed conflict within the meaning of common Article 2 of the 1949 Geneva Conventions. Accordingly, such actions will be governed by the relevant maritime law of armed conflict,[69] and the twin requirements of necessity and proportionality. Under Article 42 of the U.N. Charter, "blockade" is among the enforcement measures the Security Council may impose to maintain or restore international peace or security when Article 41 measures (including embargoes discussed above) would be or have proved to be inadequate.

The distinct doctrine of "pacific blockade" is grounded in the law of peacetime countermeasures; specifically, the claimed right to take reprisals in response to another state's breach of its international law obligations.[70] Accordingly, the legality of such a blockade would be controlled in the first instance by the customary law of countermeasures, to the extent they survive the 1982 LOS Convention. The pacific blockade is distinguished from the wartime blockade in that the former is not intended as a belligerent act. It operates in a similar fashion, however, in preventing ships from entering or leaving specified areas of the blockaded state. However, unlike wartime blockades, pacific blockades did not extend to ships of third party states.[71] The 1962 "quarantine" on Cuba to prevent emplacement of offensive missiles in that state is sometimes mistakenly referred to as a pacific blockade because the involved states were not at war. However, because the Cuban quarantine extended to all ships,[72] public and private, without regard to the flag they flew,

---

[66]One recent application was Israel's "blockade" of Lebanon during the 2006 armed conflict with Hezbollah.

[67]ANNOTATED COMMANDER'S HANDBOOK, para. 7.7.1. *See also* 10 DIGEST OF INTERNATIONAL LAW, at 861–78.

[68]Wolff Heintschel von Heinegg, *Naval Blockade,* 75 U.S. Nav. War Coll., INT'L L. STUDIES 203–230 (2000); Zeigler, *Ubi Sumus?* at 10.

[69]The U.N. General Assembly included blockades of the ports or coasts of a state by the armed forces of another states among the acts that constitute "aggression" within the meaning of Article 2(4) of the Charter. *See* U.N. General Assembly, *Definition of Aggression,* Resolution 3314 (XXIX) of Dec. 14, 1974, G.A.O.R. 29th Sess., Supp. No. 31 (A/9631), at para. 3(c).

[70]2 OPPENHEIM'S INTERNATIONAL LAW §§ 33–35, 46–47 (Robert Jennings & Arthur Watts, eds., 9th ed. 1992).

[71]C. JOHN COLOMBOS, THE INTERNATIONAL LAW OF THE SEA 465–69 (6th rev. ed. 1967).

[72]4 MARJORIE M. WHITEMAN, DIGEST OF INTERNATIONAL LAW 676–77 (1965).

the action could not be grounded in the pacific blockade doctrine. Moreover, because there was no state of belligerency (and everyone concerned hoped to avoid that very thing), the United States rejected the "blockade" terminology and its martial overtones, and relied instead on a controversial application of collective action under Chapter VIII of the Charter to quarantine the island.

7

A Finely Wrought Balance: International Laws Applicable to Maritime Counterproliferation Operations

The PSI Statement of Interdiction Principles[1] makes it clear that actions carried out by the participating states are to be consistent with "relevant international law and frameworks, including the Security Council." At the same time it calls upon participating states to "strengthen" the relevant international law and frameworks in appropriate ways, in order to support the PSI commitments. This chapter examines the principal sources of international law relevant to maritime counterproliferation operations,[2] including the U.N. Charter, the 1982 Convention on the Law of the Sea, customary international law and, to a lesser extent, selected conventions developed at the International Maritime Organization. The intent is to provide readers, both lay and law-trained, with the legal background to assess the more detailed analysis of PSI boardings in Chapter 8.

Any examination of the international law sources that will govern PSI activities must begin with the U.N. Charter. By its terms, the Charter is paramount international law. As a matter of international law, in the event of a conflict between the obligations of members of the United Nations under the Charter and their obligations under any other international agreement, their obligations under the Charter prevail.[3] *A fortiori,* if a nation's obligation under customary international law conflicts with its obligations under the Charter, the Charter obligations take precedence.

---

[1] *Interdiction Principles for the Proliferation Security Initiative, done* at Paris, Sept. 4, 2003 [hereinafter "*Statement of Interdiction Principles*"] (reproduced in Appendix A).

[2] A distinction is made between the "sources" of international law (treaties, customary law and general principles of law) and "evidence" of international law (judicial decisions and the writings of the most highly qualified legal commentators). RESTATEMENT (THIRD) FOREIGN RELATIONS LAW OF THE UNITED STATES §§ 102–103 (1987) [hereinafter "RESTATEMENT"].

[3] Charter of the United Nations, art. 103.

The 1982 Convention on the Law of the Sea provides the legal framework for peacetime uses of the oceans, where the PSI activities of concern will take place.[4] The United States has formally acknowledged that the Convention's articles on navigation and other ocean's uses "generally confirm existing maritime law and practice and fairly balance the interests of all states."[5] The extensive family of treaties developed under the auspices of the International Maritime Organization, including the International Convention on the Safety of Life at Sea (SOLAS),[6] the codes that complement SOLAS,[7] and the Convention on Suppression of Unlawful Acts Against the Safety of Maritime Navigation (SUA Convention),[8] also play a significant role in the maritime security field.[9] Navigation and access rights and responsibilities may also be prescribed by global trade treaties, such as the General Agreement on Tariffs and Trade,[10] applicable treaties of friendship, commerce, and navigation, regional port state control agreements, and customs agreements.[11] Such agreements must be consistent with the LOS Convention.[12] Finally, despite the prevalence of applicable treaties, customary international law continues to play an important role in public maritime law.[13]

The international legal regime seeks to accommodate the respective interests of states and to strike an appropriate balance when those interests come into conflict.

---

[4]U.N. Convention on the Law of the Sea, Dec. 10, 1982. All of the PSI participating states except the United States are party to the LOS Convention.

[5]Statement Accompanying Proclamation of Exclusive Economic Zone (Proclamation 5030, Mar. 10, 1983), 19 WEEKLY COMP. OF PRES. DOCS. 383 (1983), 22 I.L.M. 461 (1983) [hereinafter "Ocean Policy Statement"].

[6]International Convention for the Safety of Life at Sea, Nov. 1, 1974.

[7]They include, for example, the International Ship and Port Facility Security Code (ISPS Code) of 2002, IMO Pub.I116E, the International Code for the Safe Carriage of Packaged Irradiated Nuclear Fuel, Plutonium and High Level Radioactive Wastes on Board Ships (INF Code), and the International Maritime Dangerous Goods Code (IMDG Code).

[8]Convention for the Suppression of Unlawful Acts Against the Safety of Maritime Navigation, Mar. 10, 1988, 1678 U.N.T.S. 201, S. TREATY DOC. No. 101–1 (1988), 27 I.L.M. 668 (1988) [hereinafter "SUA Convention"]; Protocol for the Suppression of Unlawful Acts Against the Safety of Fixed Platforms Located on the Continental Shelf, Mar. 10, 1988, 1678 U.N.T.S. 304, 27 I.L.M 685 (1988). Two new SUA protocols were adopted at an IMO-sponsored diplomatic conference held in October 2005.

[9]*See* Rosalie Balkin, *The International Maritime Organization and Maritime Security*, 30 TUL. MAR. L. J. 1 (2006).

[10]*See* General Agreement on Tariffs and Trade, Oct. 30, 1947, 61 Stat. A-3, 55 U.N.T.S. 187 [hereinafter "GATT"].

[11]*See, e.g.*, the bilateral agreements entered into as part of the U.S. Container Security Initiative. http://www.customs.gov/xp/cgov/border_security/international_activities/csi/.

[12]*See* LOS Convention, art. 293(1). If, however, the LOS Convention conflicts with the Charter of the United Nations, the Charter takes precedence. Charter of the United Nations, art. 103.

[13]*See ibid.*, Preamble, para. 8 ("Affirming that matters not regulated by this Convention continue to be governed by the rules and principles of general international law"); U.S. Ocean Policy Statement, *supra;* M/V "Saiga" (No. 2) (Saint Vincent and the Grenadines v. Guinea), para. 155, 38 I.L.M. 1323 (ITLOS 1999) (referring to customary international law in the absence of an applicable treaty). Use of force issues are largely governed by customary law.

The states' sovereign interest in territorial integrity and political independence are expressly protected by the U.N. Charter.[14] The principle of freedom of navigation, which facilitates naval mobility and maritime commerce, is emphasized throughout the LOS Convention and "jealously safeguarded" by states.[15] Indeed, the *mare liberum* (freedom of the seas) doctrine espoused by the Dutch jurist Hugo Grotius in 1608 was principally motivated by his nation's maritime trading interests.[16] In an era in which global trade has become so vital to the state's economic well-being and supply chains are linked by just-in-time deliveries, cargo mobility plays an increasingly important role. Any interference with freedom of navigation by vessels or cargo mobility impinges on the economic interests of the involved states.[17] All states also share an interest in healthy and productive marine ecosystems. Finally, all states share an interest in a level of public order in the oceans sufficient to provide the safety and security on which their territorial integrity, freedom of navigation, and the marine ecosystems depend. Threats to the public order come from an array of states and non-state actors, including those engaged in or supporting piracy, armed attacks on vessels, organized crime, and transnational terrorism. Trafficking in weapons,[18] particularly weapons of mass destruction, significantly adds to the lethal potential of those groups.[19]

RIGHTS AND OBLIGATIONS OF STATES UNDER INTERNATIONAL LAW

States are the principal subjects of international law. Under the U.N. Charter, all states have the legal status of sovereign equality and are entitled to have their territorial integrity and political independence respected.[20] The LOS Convention

---

[14]Charter of the United Nations, art. 2.

[15]*See* RESTATEMENT § 521, note 1.

[16]HUGO GROTIUS, THE FREEDOM OF THE SEAS OR THE RIGHT WHICH BELONGS TO THE DUTCH TO TAKE PART N THE EAST INDIAN TRADE, at 7 (James Brown Scott ed., 1916) (1608) (finding an "unimpeachable axiom" of the law of nations that "[e]very nation is free to travel to every other nation, and to trade with it").

[17]*See generally* Daniel Moran, *The International Law of the Sea in a Globalized World*, in GLOBALIZATION AND MARITIME POWER (Sam J. Tangredi, ed., 2002).

[18]*See* Protocol against the Illicit Manufacturing of and Trafficking in Firearms, Their Parts and Components and Ammunition, supplementing the United Nations Convention against Transnational Organized Crime, adopted by the U.N. General Assembly June 8, 2001, U.N. Doc. A/RES/55/255. Because the Protocol focuses on conventional firearms (portable barreled weapons), it is unlikely to find direct application in this context; however, the WMD materials targeted by the maritime counterproliferation forces might well be part of a larger shipment that includes firearms within the prohibitions of the Protocol. The U.S. Senate gave its advice and consent to the Convention against Transnational Organized Crime in October 2005 while also attaching understandings and declarations limiting its application to states within the United States.

[19]Activities that seek to deny access to weapons are sometimes defended on the basis of their tendency to preserve or restore the peace or at least reduce the level of violence.

[20]Charter of the United Nations, Preamble & art 2.

reserves the high seas for peaceful purposes.[21] Indeed, all states must, in exercising their rights and performing their obligations under the Convention, refrain from any threat or use of force against the territorial integrity or political independence of any State, or in any manner inconsistent with the principles of international law embodied in the U.N. Charter.[22] By logical extension, any use of the sea for an activity the Security Council has found poses a threat to international peace and security may be deemed to be inconsistent with the reservation of those seas for peaceful purposes. All states must fulfill their Convention obligations in good faith and exercise their rights, jurisdiction, and freedoms recognized in the Convention in a manner that would not constitute an abuse of rights.[23]

In analyzing law of the sea issues, it is important to distinguish the legally protected rights from legally imposed obligations. It is equally important to distinguish the rights held by a state from direct or derivative rights which might be held by individuals and non-state entities.[24] In the analysis that follows, the reader must also distinguish rights under the LOS Convention from jurisdiction conferred or recognized by the Convention. For example, the LOS Convention confers on a state's warship and other duly authorized public vessels the "right" of approach and visit vessels on the high seas under certain circumstances, even though the state might not have jurisdiction to prescribe and enforce laws against the vessel visited. A final point that will help frame the analysis of rights and obligations under international law derives from the earlier-mentioned sovereign equality of all states. In what has become the classic positivistic characterization of international law, the Permanent Court of International Justice in the *S.S. Lotus* case held that the court would not presume international law limits a sovereign state's freedom of action, and that the burden therefore falls on the one challenging a state's exercise of jurisdiction to prove

---

[21]LOS Convention, art. 88; *see also* RESTATEMENT § 521, comment *b*. Article 88 of the LOS Convention is not more restrictive than the U.N. Charter. *See U.N. Disarmament Study Series—The Naval Arms Race, Report of the Secretary-General,* para. 188, U.N. GAOR, 40th Sess., Annexes, Agenda Item 68(b), U.N. Doc. No. A/40/535 (1985) (concluding that nothing in the LOS Convention prohibits military activities which are consistent with the principles of international law embodied in the Charter of the U.N., in particular with Articles 2(4) and 51). The report goes on to conclude that:

> In the exercise of the right of collective self-defense it is clear that parties to [collective] security arrangements may use force upon the high seas, with the limits prescribed by international law, to protect their armed forces, public vessels or aircraft.

Ibid. para. 178. The report is silent regarding attacks on non-public vessels. When the U.S. Senate Foreign Relations Committee reported out the LOS Convention for advice and consent it recommended the following understanding: "The United States understands that nothing in the Convention, including any provisions referring to "peaceful uses"...impairs the inherent right of individual or collective self-defense or rights during armed conflict." Senate Foreign Relations Committee, Report on the United Nations Convention on the Law of the Sea, S. EXEC. REP. NO. 108–10 (Mar. 11, 2004), understanding 1.

[22]LOS Convention, art. 301.

[23]*Ibid.* art. 300.

[24]ROBIN R. CHURCHILL & A. VAUGHAN LOWE, THE LAW OF THE SEA 257 (2d ed. 1999) [hereinafter "CHURCHILL & LOWE"].

the existence of a positive rule of law, consented to by the acting state, that legally bars the assertion of jurisdiction.[25]

In addition to the shared interests and obligations common to all states, port states and coastal states have differential interests in their ports, internal waters, and the seas adjacent to their coasts. In most cases, the interests are not exclusive; that is, the port state or coastal state interest can be fully realized without necessarily excluding use of those ports or waters by other states. However, those interests can and sometimes do conflict with the interests of flag states and cargo states in freedom of navigation, port access and cargo mobility.

Port State Rights and Obligations

A state's territorial sovereignty extends to its internal waters and the ports within those waters.[26] In the *Corfu Channel* case, the International Court of Justice defined sovereignty as the whole body of rights and attributes that a state possesses in its territory, to the exclusion of all other states.[27] Sovereignty extends to all persons within the state's territory, but is subject to an international obligation to protect from harm nonnationals within the state's territory.[28] Vessels and cargoes passing through a state's internal waters and ports could pose actual or perceived risks to the safety or security of other vessels in the port, port facilities, surrounding infrastructure, and populations, as well as the waterways themselves. Accordingly, port states may and do prescribe and enforce laws designed to manage those risks, subject to the established rules of immunity for public vessels and diplomats. Such measures may include access restrictions, entry conditions, and port state control screening and inspection requirements.

The LOS Convention does not confer a right of access to foreign ports,[29] though the customary law of the sea has recognized a limited right of access for vessels in cases of *force majeure* or distress. However, at least two other legal sources address access to foreign ports and internal waters. Article V of the General Agreement on Tariffs and Trade provides:

> There shall be freedom of transit through the territory of each contracting party, via the routes most convenient for international transit, for traffic in transit to or from the territory of other contracting parties. No distinction shall be made which is based on the flag of vessels, the place of origin, departure, entry, exit or destination, or on any

[25]Case of the S.S. *Lotus* (Fr. v. Turk.), 1927 P.C.I.J. (ser. A) No. 10, at p. 18 (Sept. 7). The legal bar to exercising jurisdiction must be distinguished from decisions to abstain from exercising that jurisdiction as a matter of comity or courtesy. *See* Hilton v. Guyot, 159 U.S. 113, 163–64 (1894).

[26]LOS Convention, art. 2(1). *See also ibid.* arts. 11–12.

[27]The Corfu Channel case (U.K. v. Alb.) 1949 I.C.J. REP. 1 (Apr. 9). *See also* The Schooner *Exchange* v. McFadden, 11 U.S. (7 Cranch) 116, 136 (1812) ("The jurisdiction of a nation within its own territory is necessarily exclusive and absolute.").

[28]RESTATEMENT § 511, comment *e,* § 512, comment *c* & note 3, & § 711.

[29]Nor is there a general customary right of access to ports or internal waters (except in cases of distress). *See* Patterson v. The Bark *Eudora,* 190 U.S. 169, 178 (1903).

> circumstances relating to the ownership of goods, of vessels or of other means of transport.[30]

In addition, many states have entered into bilateral treaties of friendship, commerce, and navigation (FCN treaties) that may address port access and extend "national treatment" and/or "most favored nation treatment" to the contracting parties on a reciprocal basis.[31] The right of access does not preclude application of entry conditions, port state regulations, or port state enforcement (often called "port state control") of international safety and security regimes, such as those imposed by SOLAS and the ISPS Code to promote port and vessel security.[32]

Although ports states have broad power to promulgate *bona fide* safety and security regulations, the LOS Convention bans discriminatory treatment of foreign vessels (as does GATT Article V).[33] Despite that general ban, virtually all port state control regimes more closely scrutinize vessels registered in states that have been found to be lax in exercising jurisdiction and control over their vessels. Nothing in the LOS Convention bans consideration of a vessel's flag state and the degree of diligence historically exercised by that flag state in controlling its vessels. Limited resources, practical necessities, and concern for vessel and cargo mobility in fact compel port state control authorities to employ risk management measures that focus enforcement actions on the known or most probable violators.[34] Port state control measures that "blacklist" certain flag states and classification societies have long recognized this.

Coastal State Rights and Obligations

Under the 1982 LOS Convention, the seas are divided into four juridical "zones" (not including the internal waters or archipelagic waters), the boundaries of which are reckoned from the territorial sea "baseline."[35] Beginning at the baseline and moving seaward, those zones are the territorial sea, the contiguous zone, the exclusive economic zone and the high seas. The rights and obligations of the coastal state and the various flag states vary from one zone to another. Coastal states are "sovereign" in the adjacent territorial sea,[36] which may extend up to 12

---

[30]GATT, art. V(2).

[31]A 1923 multilateral convention would have provided a right of port access, but attracted relatively few significant ratifications. *See* Convention and Statute on the International Regime of Maritime Ports, July 26, 1926, 58 L.N.T.S. 287.

[32]*See* George C. Kasoulides, Port State Control and Jurisdiction: Evolution of the Port State Regime (1993).

[33]*See, e.g.*, LOS Convention, arts. 24(1)(b), 25, 26, 42(2), 52(2) & 227.

[34]*See generally* Congressional Research Service, *Port and Maritime Security: Background Issues for Congress*, at 4, updated May 27, 2005, CRS Rep. RL31733 (emphasizing vital importance of freight mobility and "intolerable" cost of slowing down that flow for increased inspections).

[35]*See* LOS Convention, arts. 5–7.

[36]LOS Convention, art. 2; Restatement § 512.

nautical miles seaward from the baseline.[37] The sovereignty of coastal states over their territorial seas is, however, subject to two servitudes in favor of foreign vessels: a right of innocent passage[38] and a right of transit passage through any portion that constitutes an international strait. These servitudes, which attempt to balance the common interest in freedom of navigation with the coastal state's heightened interest in the immediately adjacent sea, are discussed below.[39] The contiguous zone (if claimed) extends from the outer edge of the territorial sea up to 24 nautical miles seaward of the baseline. A coastal state's exclusive economic zone (EEZ) extends from the outer edge of the territorial sea to a distance of up to 200 nautical miles from the baseline (and may therefore overlap with the contiguous zone, if claimed). Within its EEZ, the coastal state has sovereign rights in the natural resources and jurisdiction over a limited range of activities. For other purposes, all waters seaward of the territorial sea are treated much the same as the high seas.[40] Beyond the above-mentioned maritime zones lie the high seas, which are not subject to the sovereignty of any state.[41]

The coastal state may prescribe and enforce laws and regulations applicable to foreign vessels in innocent or transit passage through its territorial sea (covered in the jurisdiction section below); however, it may not "hamper" the innocent passage of a foreign vessel, except "in accordance with" the LOS Convention.[42] That means it cannot impose requirements on foreign vessels which have the practical effect of denying or impairing the right of innocent passage, nor can it discriminate in form or fact against the vessels of any state or vessels carrying cargo to, from, or on behalf of any state.[43] The coastal state may suspend innocent passage temporarily, but only in specified areas where such suspension is "essential" to the protection of the coastal state's security.[44] The coastal state may also take "necessary steps" in its territorial sea to prevent passage that is not innocent.[45] At the very least, those steps would include the full range of measures available to a state exercising a right of approach and visit

---

[37]LOS Convention, art. 3.

[38]*Ibid.* art. 17; RESTATEMENT § 513. The innocent passage regime also applies in most archipelagic waters. LOS Convention, art. 52.

[39]Article 17 actually provides that "ships of all States. . . enjoy the right of innocent passage." By contrast, the "right of navigation" on the high seas in Article 90 is cast in terms of the right of states, not vessels. *Ibid.* art. 90. Similarly, Article 87(2) conveys the principle that the high seas freedoms "shall be exercised by States," implying that such rights are held by states, not vessels of states. The distinction is important in determining who has standing to challenge a state's interference with navigation rights.

[40]The LOS Convention makes it clear that the high seas articles in Articles 88 to 115 of the Convention apply within the EEZ insofar as they are not inconsistent with the EEZ regime.

[41]LOS Convention, art. 89.

[42]*Ibid.* art. 24.

[43]*Ibid.*

[44]*Ibid.* art. 25.

[45]*Ibid.* art. 25(1). *See also* 2 UNITED NATIONS CONVENTION ON THE LAW OF THE SEA 1982: A COMMENTARY 229 (Satya N. Nandan & Shabtai Rosenne eds. 1993).

on the high seas.[46] Chapter 8 analyzes the interplay between the transit rights of foreign vessels in the territorial sea and the announced goal of the PSI states to board vessels within those waters.

The LOS Convention is even more solicitous of vessels (and aircraft) passing through a "strait used for international navigation" that lies within a state's territorial sea, conferring on such vessels a more liberal right of "transit passage."[47] The right of transit passage differs from innocent passage in several important respects. Transit passage rights extend to aircraft as well as vessels. Aircraft have no right of innocent passage under the LOS Convention. In contrast to innocent passage, the right of transit passage may not be suspended.[48] Vessels have a right to transit in their "normal mode,"[49] meaning that submarines need not surface and display their national flag, as they must while in innocent passage.[50] As with the right of innocent passage, vessels in transit passage must comply with the principles of international law embodied in the U.N. Charter and must refrain from the use of force or threats to use force against the sovereignty, territorial integrity or political independence of the states bordering the strait.[51] Finally, the coastal state is more limited in the range of laws and regulations it may apply to foreign vessels in transit passage than to those in innocent passage.[52] In comparing the two transit regimes, it is noteworthy that the transit passage regime does not include a provision similar to Article 23 in the innocent passage regime applicable to foreign nuclear-powered ships and ships carrying nuclear or other inherently dangerous or obnoxious materials.[53]

Coastal states enjoy limited enforcement jurisdiction over vessels in their contiguous zone.[54] Within its contiguous zone a coastal state may exercise the control necessary to prevent infringement of its customs, fiscal, immigration, or sanitary laws and regulations within its territorial seas or punish such infringements when the violation is committed within its territory or territorial sea.[55] It is important to note that the

---

[46]*See* Ivan A. Shearer, *The Development of International Law with Respect to the Law Enforcement Role of Navies and Coast Guards in Peacetime,* 71 U.S. Nav. War Coll., Int'l L. Studies 429, 433 (1998) (the necessary steps likely encompass the "standard procedures of approach, stopping, boarding, investigation and possibly arrest").

[47]LOS Convention, art. 38. The definition for the phrase "strait used for international navigation" is derived from Articles 37 and 38(1). "Transit passage" is defined in Article 39(2).

[48]*Ibid.* art. 45(2).

[49]*Ibid.* art. 39(1)(c).

[50]*Ibid.* art. 20.

[51]*Ibid.* art. 39(1)(b).

[52]*Compare* Article 21 (laws and regulations applicable to foreign vessels in innocent passage) *with* Article 41 (laws and regulations applicable to foreign vessels in transit passage).

[53]Such vessels are required to carry documents and observe special precautionary measures established by international agreement while in innocent passage. *Ibid.* art. 23. Vessels in transit passage may nevertheless be required to comply with relevant provisions of the IMO and IAEA conventions and codes, was well as any applicable conditions of entry imposed by the port state.

[54]*Ibid.* art. 33.

[55]*Ibid. See also M/V Saiga,* paras. 150–52.

contiguous zone regime under the peacetime law of the sea does not extend to security interests,[56] though the competency to enforce "customs" laws certainly extends to cargo import and export controls motivated by security concerns.[57] Finally, the coastal state has sovereign rights in the natural resources, together with a limited jurisdiction and control over vessels in an exclusive economic zone.[58] As in the contiguous zone regime, the coastal state's jurisdiction over the waters of the EEZ does not extend to security interests.

Flag State Rights and Obligations

All states, whether coastal or landlocked, have the right to sail ships flying their flag on the high seas.[59] Additionally, all states enjoy certain freedoms on the high seas, including the freedom of navigation and fishing.[60] The high seas freedoms must, like most internationally recognized rights and freedoms, be exercised with due regard for the interests of other states.[61] Those "other state" interests include the shared interest in safety and security. The flag state must exercise its rights in a manner that would not constitute an abuse of rights.[62]

Ships may sail under the flag of one state only. A ship that is not validly registered in any state is deemed "stateless."[63] A ship that sails under two or more flags may not claim either of the nationalities, and may be "assimilated" to a ship without a nationality.[64] No state has standing to assert diplomatic protection on behalf of stateless vessels.[65] In fact, the crews of such vessels have on occasion been labeled

---

[56] 2 U.S. Dep't of State, Cumulative Digest of United States Practice in International Law 1981–88, at 1860–61 (1994). Nevertheless, some states have asserted the right to establish military security zones in waters seaward of the territorial sea. *See* Annotated Commander's Handbook, Annotated Supplement to the Commander's Handbook of the Law of Naval Operations, para. 1.5.4 & n.54 (1997).

[57] Restatement § 511, comment *k*.

[58] *See* David J. Attard, The Exclusive Economic Zone in International Law (1987).

[59] LOS Convention, art. 90. This principle is a corollary to the sovereign equality of states.

[60] LOS Convention, art. 87; Restatement § 521. The United States repeatedly demonstrated its commitment to preserving freedom of navigation and overflight on the seas by, among other things, its "freedom of navigation" program. 2 Cumulative Digest Int'l Law 1981–88, at 1832–33. The U.S. need for those freedoms is no less urgent today, particularly as overseas basing increasingly gives way to sea-based forces.

[61] *See* Fisheries Jurisdiction cases (U.K. v. Iceland) 1974 I.C.J. Rep. 22, 29 (July 25). The freedoms are also subject to express limitations imposed by the LOS Convention. *See, e.g.*, LOS Convention, art. 116 (limitations on high seas fishing).

[62] LOS Convention, art. 300.

[63] In holding that a stateless vessel has no rights under the law of the sea, the court in United States v. Cortes, 588 F.2d 106 (5th Cir. 1979), explained that: "To secure the protection afforded merchant vessels on the high seas, a vessel must accept the duties imposed by registration. This the [defendant's vessel] failed to do; her crew cannot complain of the results." *Ibid.* at 110.

[64] LOS Convention, art. 92.

[65] *See* Churchill & Lowe, at 214 (citing, but questioning, *Molvan v. Attorney General for Palestine*). The vessel's stateless status should not preclude a state from asserting diplomatic or consular protection on behalf of its national on board the vessel. *Ibid.*

by the courts as "international pariahs."[66] It is for each state to fix the conditions for the grant of nationality to ships, for the registration of ships, and for the right to fly its flag.[67] Although the LOS Convention requires that there must exist a "genuine link" between the flag state and ships that are entitled to fly its flag,[68] the Convention provides no criteria for evaluating whether a genuine link exists,[69] nor is there any mechanism for enforcing the genuine link requirement other than to report the matter to the flag state for action.[70] For that reason, much of the international focus has shifted from the genuine link requirement to the requirement that each flag state exercise jurisdiction and control over its vessels.

Under the LOS Convention flag states have an international duty to exercise effective jurisdiction and control over vessels registered in the state.[71] The LOS Convention provides little guidance on the scope of the concepts of "jurisdiction" and "control." Indeed, the two concepts are often conflated. "Jurisdiction," which is discussed more fully below, is the capacity to exercise legal authority.[72] The requirement to effectively "control" vessels registered in the state entails much more than an exercise of jurisdiction.[73] In fact, the flag state duties extend beyond the ship itself, to include at a minimum the master, officers, and crew.[74] When the International Tribunal on the Law of the Sea held that the flag state had standing to assert claims on behalf of the vessel's crew, even though they were not nationals of the flag state, it explained that "the ship, everything on it, and every person

---

[66]United States v. Caicedo, 47 F.3d 370, 371 (9th Cir. 1995).

[67]LOS Convention, art. 91; *M/V Saiga,* paras. 64–65. The ship's flag is *prima facie* evidence of its nationality. C. John Colombos, The International Law of the Sea 291–93 (6th rev. ed. 1967). In the United States, a certificate of documentation is conclusive evidence of nationality for international law purposes, but not in a proceeding conducted under U.S. laws. *See* 46 U.S.C.A. § 12104 (West 2005). Ultimately, the nationality of a ship under international law is a question of fact if contested. *See M/V Saiga,* para. 66.

[68]LOS Convention, art. 91.

[69]*See M/V Saiga,* paras. 80–88. *See also* 9 Marjorie M. Whiteman, Digest of International Law 7–11, 13–16 (1968).

[70]*M/V Saiga,* paras. 80–86.

[71]LOS Convention, art. 94; Restatement § 520. A flag state's interest in its nonpublic vessels is one of jurisdiction and control, not sovereignty. Accordingly, the U.N. Charter provisions regarding noninterference with the sovereignty of another state should not be applicable where such interferences are directed at a foreign nonpublic vessel. *But see* The Owners of the Jessie, Thomas F. Bayward and Pescawha (G.B. v. U.S.), U.N. Rep., vol. 6, at 57 (stating that under "international maritime law" an illegal enforcement boarding "constitutes a violation of the sovereignty of the country whose flag the vessel flies"). It is suggested that the arbitrator's view is outdated.

[72]In contrast to sovereignty and sovereign rights, which are generally understood to apply to territory and natural resources, "jurisdiction" generally extends to non-state entities, such as individuals, corporations, offshore facilities, and nonpublic vessels and aircraft. Jurisdiction over states implicates the doctrine of sovereign immunity. *See* Restatement § 522, comment *a.*

[73]The term "control" is also used in Article 33 on the contiguous zone.

[74]LOS Convention, art. 94(2)(b). *See* Restatement § 502, comment *g* (concluding that a failure to exercise effective jurisdiction and control "may be a factor in determining a lack of a 'genuine link' between the flag state and the vessel").

involved or interested in its operations are treated as an entity linked to the Flag State. The nationalities of the persons are not relevant."[75]

The LOS Convention requires flag states to ensure vessels flying their flag conform to generally accepted international regulations, standards, procedures, and practices for safety and protection of the marine environment.[76] The flag state must exercise its jurisdiction and control in a manner that would not constitute an abuse of rights.[77] Sadly, however, even the U.N. General Assembly has formally acknowledged the failure of some flag states to effectively fulfill their obligations to exercise effective jurisdiction and control over vessels flying their flag and urged:

> flag states without an effective maritime administration and appropriate legal frameworks to establish or enhance the necessary infrastructure, legislative and enforcement capabilities to ensure effective compliance with, and implementation and enforcement of, their responsibilities under international law and, until such action is undertaken, to consider declining the granting of the right to fly their flag to new vessels, suspending their registry or not opening a registry.[78]

Although not suggested by the General Assembly, flag states that are unable to discharge their obligations may also enlist the assistance of other states, and some do so through bilateral boarding agreements. Port state control arrangements may actually compel such enforcement "assistance" for any vessels entering a port within the control regime.

The Ubiquitous Duty of All States to "Cooperate"

The 1982 LOS Convention calls upon all states, including flag states, to cooperate in suppressing a variety of activities deemed inimical to the public order. For example, since the nineteenth century all states have had an obligation to cooperate in the suppression of piracy[79] and slave trading.[80] In its 1970 *Declaration on Principles of International Law Concerning Friendly Relations and Cooperation among States,* the U.N. General Assembly listed the duties to cooperate in accordance with the

---

[75]*M/V Saiga,* para. 106. Doubtless, the ITLOS did not intend to suggest that the actual state of nationality of any persons on board the vessel lacked even *concurrent* capacity to exercise diplomatic protection on behalf of their nationals, subject to the flag state's primacy. *See* CHURCHILL & LOWE, at 209 ("A state retains jurisdiction over its nationals wherever they might be, whether on a foreign ship or anywhere else").

[76]LOS Convention, art. 94(3)-(5). *See* U.N. Division of Ocean Affairs and the Law of the Sea, *The Law of the Sea: Obligations of States Parties under the United Nations Law of the Sea and Complementary Instruments* 49–50 (2004).

[77]LOS Convention, art. 300.

[78]U.N. General Assembly Resolution 58/240, para. 27, U.N. Doc. A/RES/58/240 (2004).

[79]LOS Convention, art. 100 (requiring all states to cooperate "to the fullest possible extent in the repression of piracy on the high seas or in any other place outside the jurisdiction of any state"). *See also Harvard Research Draft Convention on Piracy,* reprinted in 26 AM. J. INT'L L. 739 (Supp. 1932); 6 MARJORIE M. WHITEMAN, DIGEST OF INTERNATIONAL LAW § 5 (1968).

[80]LOS Convention, art. 99 (requiring states to take "effective measure to prevent and punish the transport of slaves in ships authorized to fly its flag and to prevent the unlawful use of its flag for that purpose").

U.N. Charter and to fulfill in good faith the obligations assumed in the Charter as two of its seven "principles."[81] In the twentieth century, a requirement for all states to cooperate in suppressing illicit traffic in narcotic drugs and psychotropic substances was added.[82] Similarly, states now have a duty to suppress unauthorized broadcasting from the high seas.[83] The 2005 Protocol to the SUA Convention will bind its parties to cooperate in the suppression and prevention of unlawful acts covered by the Convention.[84] Finally, the LOS Convention requires states to cooperate to conserve and manage living marine resources on the high seas[85] and to protect and preserve the marine environment.[86] Additional duties have been imposed on flag states by other treaties, particularly those developed under the auspices of the IMO and IAEA and the family of multilateral terrorism conventions that require states to prosecute or extradite persons suspected of committing an offense under the convention.

All states have an obligation under the U.N. Charter to comply with resolutions of the Security Council.[87] Three recent Chapter VII resolutions by the Security Council impose both individual state obligations and duties to cooperate in suppressing global terrorism and WMD proliferation.[88] Each resolution triggers the Charter's Article 1 obligation for all states to take effective collective measures to prevent and remove threats to the peace and the Article 2 obligation to refrain from giving assistance to any state and, by necessary implication, any non-state entity against which the United Nations takes preventative or enforcement action.[89] Resolution 1373 calls upon states to cooperate "particularly through bilateral and multilateral arrangements and agreements, to prevent and suppress terrorist attacks and take actions against perpetrators of such acts."[90] Resolution 1526, which directly responded to the September 11, 2001, attacks on the United States, among other things calls upon flag states to prevent the direct or indirect supply or transfer of arms or related materials and the use of their vessels or aircraft in the transport of arms and related materials to the individuals or organizations on a "consolidated list" that

---

[81] U.N. General Assembly, Declaration on Principles of International Law Concerning Friendly Relations and Cooperation Among States in Accordance with the Charter of the United Nations, UNGA Res. 2625 (XXV) (Oct. 24, 1970).

[82] LOS Convention, art. 108.

[83] *Ibid.* art. 109.

[84] 2005 SUA Protocol, *infra* Appendix E, art. 8 (adding Article 8*bis* to the SUA Convention).

[85] LOS Convention, arts. 117–119.

[86] *See ibid.* art. 197.

[87] Charter of the United Nations, art. 49 ("[t]he Members of the United Nations shall join in affording mutual assistance in carrying out the measures decided upon by the Security Council").

[88] The principal resolutions of interest include 687 (Iraq), 1172 (affirming that the proliferation of WMD constitutes a threat to international peace and security), 1373, 1540, and 1617. *See also* Jochen Frowein & Nico Kirsch, *Introduction to Chapter VII, in* THE CHARTER OF THE UNITED NATIONS: A COMMENT 701–716 (Bruno Simma, et al. eds. 2d ed. 2002).

[89] Charter of the United Nations, arts. 1(1) & 2(5).

[90] U.N. Security Council Resolution 1373, *infra*, Appendix C, para. 3(c). The "calls upon" language suggests the action called for is recommended, not mandatory.

includes the Taliban, al Qaeda, and other individuals, groups, undertakings, and entities associated with them.[91] Although not explicit in the resolution, the obligation to "prevent" the "direct or indirect supply" of arms and related materials is cast in language sufficiently broad to impose affirmative obligations on port states from which such arms might be shipped. The obligation of flag states to prevent the use of their vessels or aircraft to transport arms and related material to those on the consolidated list is clearly mandatory under Resolution 1617.[92] Moreover, individuals or entities that supply, sell, or transfer arms and related material to those on the consolidated list will be deemed to be "associated with" al Qaeda, Bin Laden, or the Taliban.[93] Resolution 1540, discussed below, calls upon all states to "take cooperative action to prevent illicit trafficking in nuclear, chemical or biological weapons, their means of delivery, and related materials."[94] Several additional resolutions address proliferation by individual states, including North Korea and Iran.

The nature of the duty to cooperate has not been adequately defined, rendering any discussion of how a breach of such a duty should be assessed and what remedies are available for such breaches problematic.[95] Chapter 9 examines the question whether a state that fails to carry out the universal obligation imposed by a Security Council resolution should bear international responsibility for any harm suffered by the breach. A state might fail to fulfill its obligation to exercise effective jurisdiction and control or to carry out obligations under another treaty or a binding resolution issued by the Security Council for reasons of inability or unwillingness. In assessing the magnitude of any violation, the distinction is a critical one. A flag state may be unwilling to fully discharge its obligations due to a lack of resources or the location of the vessel. Under such circumstances, the flag state can meet its obligation by requesting assistance from an "able" state. The "unwilling" state presents a thornier question of state responsibility and may invite intervention by other states. The circumstances under which such an intervention might be legally justified are discussed below.

JURISDICTION UNDER INTERNATIONAL LAW

Jurisdiction refers to the authority of a state to affect the legal interests of individuals and entities. The subject is often broken down into prescriptive jurisdiction (the state's power to make laws applicable to certain actors, events, things, and places),

---

[91]U.N. Security Council Resolution 1526, para. 1(c), U.N. Doc. No. S/RES/1526 (2004).
[92]U.N. Security Council Resolution 1617, para. 1(c), U.N. Doc. No. S/RES/1617 (2005).
[93]*Ibid.* para. 2.
[94]U.N. Security Council Resolution 1540, *infra*, Appendix B, para. 8.
[95]Those who advocate for an expansive interpretation of the duty to cooperate might point to the International Tribunal for the Law of the Sea's decision in Southern Bluefin Tuna cases (N.Z. v. Japan; Austl. v. Japan), 38 I.L.M. 1624, 1627–28 (ITLOS 1999). The implicit premise of the tribunal's decision seems to suggest that the duty to "cooperate" in good faith might include an obligation to actually reach an agreement with the other involved states. In essence, a failure to agree might constitute a breach of the duty to cooperate.

enforcement jurisdiction (the state's power to compel compliance with its laws and punish violations), and adjudicative jurisdiction (the power to subject certain persons or things to the state's judicial process). Under international law, jurisdiction may derive from or be limited by customary international law or a treaty, such as the LOS Convention.[96]

Like the rights and duties discussed above, maritime jurisdiction is divided among port states, coastal states, and flag states, together with what might be characterized as the "patrol states," the vessels of which are engaged in extraterritorial interception and enforcement activities. Jurisdiction may be exclusive or concurrent. Jurisdiction over vessels is distinct from, but closely related to, navigation rights and the competence of a state other than a flag state to "interfere" with a vessel in navigation. As the right of visit demonstrates, the warship of a state might have an adequate legal basis for interfering with a foreign vessel's navigation—extending to a right to board and search the vessel—even though the warship's flag state has no jurisdiction over the vessel.

Under the LOS Convention, jurisdiction over vessels depends on the vessel's flag, location, and activity.[97] Three overarching principles govern vessel boarding and related actions. The first is the well-established principle that a vessel's flag state has jurisdiction over its vessels wherever the vessel is located.[98] Flag state jurisdiction over nonpublic vessels is concurrent when the vessel is located in another state's ports or coastal waters.[99] The second principle is that in times of peace, a vessel on the high seas is subject to the exclusive jurisdiction of the flag state except in "exceptional cases expressly provided for in international treaties or in [the LOS] Convention."[100] The final principle is that warships and other public vessels not engaged in commercial activities enjoy sovereign immunity.[101]

In analyzing jurisdiction in any given case one must distinguish jurisdiction over the vessel from jurisdiction over persons on board the vessel. A state might have jurisdiction over an individual on board a vessel under the nationality principle,

---

[96] *See* 4 Marjorie M. Whiteman, Digest of International Law § 2 (1965); U.S. Coast Guard, Maritime Law Enforcement Manual, ch. 2, sec. B, COMDTINST M16247.1C (2003) [hereinafter "Coast Guard MLEM"].

[97] Jurisdiction is sometimes organized into three classes: jurisdiction *ratione personae* (limited by the nationality of the person), *ratione loci* (limited by location), and *ratione materiae* (limited by the subject matter or activity).

[98] *See* Restatement § 502, comment *a;* 1982 LOS Convention, art. 94. The rule does not preclude self-help and self-defense actions.

[99] *See* Boleslaw A. Boczek, Flags of Convenience: An International Legal Study ch. 6 (1960); United States v. Flores, 289 U.S. 137 (1933) (U.S. has jurisdiction over murder committed on board a U.S. flag vessel located on Congo River, 250 miles inland). The Court held that for purposes of criminal jurisdiction over persons on board, vessels are deemed to be part of the territory of its flag state.

[100] LOS Convention, art. 92(1); Case of the S.S. *Lotus* (Fr. v. Turk.), 1927 P.C.I.J. (ser. A) No. 10, at p. 25 (Sept. 7); Restatement § 521, note 1.

[101] LOS Convention, arts. 32, 95, 96, & 110; *see also* Restatement § 522. Like warships, vessels owned or operated by the government and used only for government noncommercial service enjoy "complete immunity" wherever located. *See* LOS Convention, arts. 32 & 96; The Schooner *Exchange* v. McFaddden, 11 U.S. (7 Cranch) 116 (1812); Coast Guard MLEM, para. 2.B.2. When in the territorial sea, such vessels may, however, be directed to leave and must comply. *Cf.* LOS Convention, art. 30.

but will generally be unable to exercise that jurisdiction while the individual is on board the vessel and outside the state's territory.[102] The LOS Convention also imposes prudential and mandatory limits on a coastal state's jurisdiction to enforce criminal laws or civil claims on a foreign vessel in transit through its territorial sea, thus highlighting the importance of distinguishing prescriptive and enforcement jurisdiction.[103]

Customary international law recognizes several bases for a state to apply its municipal laws.[104] The first and universally accepted basis is the territoriality principle, which recognizes that a state is competent under international law to apply its municipal law to persons and acts within its territory. A variant of territorial jurisdiction extends to extraterritorial acts that have an effect within the state's territory (sometimes called objective territoriality). A state may also apply its laws to nationals of the state, even when they are located outside the state. Under the passive personality principle, a state has jurisdiction to apply its laws to conduct injuring one of its nationals.[105] The protective principle recognizes that a state may apply its laws to protect vital state interests, such as the state's national security or governmental functions.[106] U.S. courts have invoked the protective principle for drug trafficking on the high seas.[107] Although the matter is not free from doubt, the protective principle may extend to attempts to smuggle WMD or delivery equipment. So far, however, the statutes enacted by the U.S. Congress to address global terrorism and WMD proliferation rely principally on territoriality, nationality, and passive personality.[108] Moreover, few of those statutes apply in the special maritime and territorial jurisdiction of the United States.[109]

---

[102]Recall, however, that the ITLOS emphasized in the *M/V Saiga* case that the flag state has standing to assert claims on behalf of all those on board the vessel.

[103]In the multinational setting in which maritime counterproliferation operations are conducted, it is helpful to distinguish prescriptive jurisdiction and enforcement jurisdiction. *See* RESTATEMENT §§ 402 & 431. For example, the United States has jurisdiction to *prescribe* certain criminal laws applicable to U.S. flag vessels wherever they are located, yet it would not have jurisdiction to *enforce* those laws while the vessel is located in another state's territorial sea or internal waters unless the coastal state consented.

[104]*See* RESTATEMENT § 402. *See also Harvard Research in International Law, Jurisdiction With Respect to Crime,* 29 AM J. INT'L L. (Supp. 1935).

[105]RESTATEMENT § 402, note 3 (highlighting application of the passive personality principle to cases involving terrorist acts directed against the state's nationals).

[106]United States v. Gonzalez, 776 F.2d 931, 938 (11th Cir. 1985).

[107]United States v. Romero-Galue, 757 F.2d 1147, 1154 (11th Cir. 1985).

[108]*See, e.g.,* 18 U.S.C.A. § 229(c)(3) (West 2005).

[109]One prominent exception is 18 U.S.C.A. § 831, which implements the Convention on Physical Protection of Nuclear Material. The statute prohibits certain transactions involving nuclear materials, and extends to acts in the special maritime and territorial jurisdiction of the United States. *See also* 18 U.S.C.A. § 2283 (West 2006) (prohibiting the transportation of explosive, biological, chemical, or radioactive or nuclear materials "aboard any vessel within the United States and on waters subject to the jurisdiction of the United States or any vessel outside the United States and on the high seas or having United States nationality").

The last recognized basis for extraterritorial jurisdiction is the universality principle.[110] A crime of universal jurisdiction is enforceable by any state, regardless of the location of the prohibited activity or the nationality of those involved. In fact, no nexus between the crime and the enforcing state is required. The rationale is that some crimes are recognized by the community of nations as of universal concern.[111] As might be expected, such crimes are few in number.[112] Universal jurisdiction presents additional problems when extended beyond the principals who actually committed the crimes, to accessories and to those who, while not accessories, provide material support to those who commit crimes of universal jurisdiction, and to conspiracies and attempts.

Some offenses may be universally condemned and even made the subject of a prosecute or extradite obligation, yet still not be a crime of universal jurisdiction.[113] Crimes prohibiting "terrorist" acts have been cited by the courts as examples.[114] Similarly, the U.N. Convention against Illicit Traffic in Narcotic Drugs and Psychotropic Substances[115] requires states-parties to criminalize certain drug-related activities, provide for severe penalties, and cooperate with other states in enforcement and extradition. Moreover, Article 108 of the LOS Convention requires all states to cooperate in the suppression of illicit drug trafficking. It further provides that any state that has reasonable grounds for believing a ship flying its flag is engaged in such trafficking may request the cooperation of other states to suppress it. The LOS Convention stops short, however, of making maritime drug trafficking a crime of universal jurisdiction, or a basis in itself for exercising a right of visit.

Port State Jurisdiction

As the previous section highlighted, states possess full sovereignty over their internal waters and ports within those waters.[116] They also enjoy broad jurisdiction over

---

[110]*See* RESTATEMENT § 404. The *Restatement,* which some have observed too often takes on a prescriptive role that undermines its utility as a true restatement of the law, adopts the position in Section 404 that the universality principle "perhaps" includes certain acts of terrorism.

[111]RESTATEMENT § 404.

[112]In *United States v. Yousef,* the court of appeals reversed the trial court's holding that universal jurisdiction extended to a conspiracy by terrorists to bomb 12 U.S. commercial aircraft while in southeast Asia, reasoning that the trial court improperly relied on the opinions of commentators and the *Restatement of Foreign Relations Law* instead of the actual practice of states. United States v. Yousef, 327 F.3d 56 (2d Cir.), *cert. denied,* 540 U.S. 933 (2003).

[113]*Yousef,* 327 F.3d at 96, n.29.

[114]*Ibid.* at 97 (holding that "customary international law currently does not provide for the prosecution of 'terrorist' acts under the universality principle, in part due to the failure of States to achieve anything like a consensus on the definition of terrorism").

[115]U.N. Convention against Illicit Traffic in Narcotic Drugs and Psychotropic Substances, Dec. 20, 1988, art. 17,1696 U.N.T.S. 449, S. TREATY DOC. NO. 101–4 (1989), *reprinted in* 28 I.L.M. 493 (1989). *See also* U.S. DEP'T OF STATE, DIGEST OF UNITED STATES PRACTICE IN INTERNATIONAL LAW 1989–1990, at 128–33 (2003).

[116]LOS Convention, arts. 2(1), 8, 11. The LOS Convention does not define "sovereignty."

nonpublic foreign vessels voluntarily in their ports, subject to any limits imposed by relevant treaties.[117] In addition, the port state may impose entry and exit conditions applicable to the vessel while transiting the territorial sea and enforce relevant port, vessel, and cargo security measures.[118] In itself, the LOS Convention imposes few limits on the authority of port states to inspect foreign vessels voluntarily in port. The port state's jurisdiction may, however, be limited by other treaties, such as the GATT, an applicable bilateral FCN or consular relations treaty, or one of the many IMO-sponsored conventions. In addition, port states may abstain from exercising their jurisdiction over internal matters on the ship, pursuant to treaty or as a matter of comity, unless the consequences extend to the port state.[119]

In 2004 a new, comprehensive security regime for international shipping was adopted by a 2002 diplomatic conference convened by the IMO. The conference approved a number of amendments to the SOLAS Convention, the most far-reaching of which makes mandatory the new International Ship and Port Facility Security Code (ISPS Code).[120] The ISPS Code contains detailed security-related requirements for states, port facilities, and shipping companies. The purpose of the Code is to provide a standardized, consistent framework for evaluating risk. The Code requires all covered ships to have a ship security plan, ship security officer, company security officer and certain onboard equipment. Covered vessels are required to carry an International Ship Security Certificate attesting to the vessel's compliance with the requirements of SOLAS chapter XI-2 and part A of the ISPS Code. When a ship is at a port or is proceeding to a port of Contracting Government, the Contracting Government has the right to exercise various control and compliance measures with respect to that ship.[121] The ship may also be subject to additional control measures if the port state exercising the control and compliance measures has reason to believe that the security of the ship has, or the port facilities it has served have, been compromised.

Port states necessarily play an indispensable role in stemming the proliferation of WMD, related materials, and delivery devices. In fact, the day-to-day role of port

---

[117]The "voluntariness" qualifier acknowledges the exceptions for vessels entering due to *force majeure* or distress. Port states may be constrained by applicable treaties of friendship, commerce and navigation, bilateral treaties on consular affairs and by Article V of the GATT (providing for nondiscriminatory freedom of transit). *See* GATT, art. V. *See also Jurisdiction over Vessels*, in 2 CUMULATIVE DIGEST INT'L LAW 1981–88, at 1374–82.

[118]LOS Convention, art. 25. Examples of entry conditions include advance transmission of cargo manifests and compliance with notice of arrival requirements, applicable IMO vessel and port safety regimes, the U.S. Container Security Initiative, the ISPS Code, the IMDG Code, and applicable export controls.

[119]*See* Mali v. Keeper of the Common Jail ("Wildenhus's case"), 120 U.S. 1 (1887) (acknowledging jurisdiction over foreign nonpublic vessels voluntarily in port, but abstaining from interference with internal discipline on such vessels unless conduct disturbs peace of the port); Cunard S.S. Co. v. Mellon, 262 U.S. 100, 124 (1923).

[120]The ISPS Code was implemented in the United States by the Maritime Transportation Security Act of 2002, Pub. L. No. 107–295, 101, 116 Stat. 2064 (2002), *codified at* 46 U.S.C.A. ch. 701 (West 2005). *See also* 33 C.F.R. pt. 103 (2005) (implementing regulations).

[121]SOLAS, regulation XI-2/9.

states arguably dwarfs that of flag states, which generally lack the means to control the cargo loaded and carried on their nonpublic vessels.[122] Port states, by contrast, have both the legal authority and means of control over the facilities relied upon for the export, transshipment, or import of cargo and the all-important opportunity to screen and inspect cargo before it is packed and loaded. It therefore falls to port states to administer the nonproliferation export control regimes and other vessel and cargo security measures. Both the IMO and the World Customs Office (WCO) recognize the importance of the port state in maritime and cargo security. Member states of the IMO, for example, recognized that port facilities must be included in any maritime security scheme and therefore extended the security measures in the ISPS to port facilities.[123] The Code includes a requirement for port facility security assessments.[124] Those assessments must be reported to the IMO[125] and could be used by other states in determining the extent to which ships calling on or receiving cargo from ports for which security measures are deemed to be inadequate should be denied entry or subjected to additional security measures before being allowed to berth or offload cargo.[126] In 2005, the WCO adopted the "Framework of Standards to Secure and Facilitate Global Trade."[127] The framework serves the layered defense approach by incorporating measures to detect weapons of concern in shipments before they arrive. The framework calls for systems that will electronically capture shipping data before the cargo embarks from a port, use risk management techniques to sort out which containers to inspect, and employ outbound cargo inspections using large-scale, X-ray type imaging and radiation detection equipment.

Coastal State Jurisdiction

Coastal states are sovereign in their territorial sea and archipelagic waters. The sovereignty of coastal states over their territorial seas is subject to the two earlier mentioned "servitudes" for the benefit of foreign vessels: a right of innocent passage and of transit passage. States that legally claim "archipelagic waters" must also permit vessels to transit certain lanes within those waters in conformance with the right of archipelagic sea lanes passage.[128] The right of hot pursuit and constructive

---

[122] *Cf.* Alfred H.A. Soons, *Enforcing the Economic Embargo at Sea,* in UNITED NATIONS SANCTIONS AND INTERNATIONAL LAW 307, 308 (W. Gowlland-Debbas, ed., 2001) (observing that with respect to supervision of shipments of articles prohibited by Security Council–imposed embargoes, enforcement is primarily carried out in port; however, at-sea enforcement is essential to address inadequate port state supervision, fraud and corruption).

[123] *See generally* the ISPS Code. *See also* SOLAS, ch. XI-2 and IMO Res. A924(22).

[124] ISPS Code, para. A-15.

[125] *Ibid.* para. A-15.7.

[126] *See generally* International Maritime Organization, Maritime Safety Committee, *Guidance Relating to the Implementation of SOLAS Chapter XI-2 and the ISPS Code,* MSC Cir. 1111, June 7, 2004.

[127] *See* World Customs Organization, *Framework of Standards to Secure and Facilitate Global Trade, done* at Brussels, Belgium, June 23, 2005, *available at* http://www.wcoomd.org/ie/En/en.html. This framework, by the 166-member WCO, is modeled on the CSI and C-TPAT.

[128] LOS Convention, art. 53.

presence doctrines may extend the coastal state's jurisdiction under some circumstances.[129] In addition to the duty to accommodate the transit rights of foreign ships, a coastal state is also subject to limits on its exercise of jurisdiction over criminal matters[130] and civil matters of vessels transiting its territorial sea.[131]

In the near term, PSI boardings are likely to be conducted in the ports, internal waters, or territorial sea of participating or cooperating states.[132] As several commentators have observed,[133] PSI boardings of foreign vessels in the territorial sea must be mindful of the rights of innocent passage and transit passage.[134] Ships enjoy a right of innocent passage through waters of the territorial sea and transit passage through any such waters that constitute a strait used for international navigation.[135] The right of innocent passage in Article 17 is set out in Subsection 3.A of Part II of the Convention, and is therefore applicable to "all ships," a class that includes warships and other public vessels, as well as nuclear-powered vessels or vessels transporting nuclear or other inherently dangerous or noxious substances. Whether a vessel is in innocent passage requires a two-step analysis. First, Article 18 of the LOS Convention defines the acts that qualify as "passage." It provides:

Article 18
Meaning of passage

1. Passage means navigation through the territorial sea for the purpose of:
   (a) traversing that sea without entering internal waters or calling at a roadstead or port facility outside internal waters; or
   (b) proceeding to or from internal waters or a call at such roadstead or port facility.
2. Passage shall be continuous and expeditious. However, passage includes stopping and anchoring, but only in so far as the same are incidental to ordinary navigation or are

[129]On hot pursuit, see LOS Convention, art. 111; NICOLAS M. POULANTZAS, THE RIGHT OF HOT PURSUIT IN INTERNATIONAL LAW (2d ed. 2002). On "constructive presence" see CHURCHILL & LOWE, at 215. The LOS Convention implicitly incorporates the constructive presence doctrine in Article 111(1).

[130]LOS Convention, art. 27. The "limit" on criminal jurisdiction is partly precatory (based on well-established principles of comity) and partly mandatory. For states party to the Brussels Convention on Penal Jurisdiction in Matters of Collision, May 10, 1952, 439 U.N.T.S. 233, a coastal state's criminal jurisdiction is further limited in collision matters.

[131]*Ibid.* art. 28. *See also* International Convention on the Arrest of Ships, Mar. 12, 1999 (arrest of ship vice person aboard ship); RESTATEMENT § 513, comment *e.*

[132]*See* Statement of Principles, *infra,* Appendix A, para. 4(d); *The Proliferation Security Initiative: An Interview with John Bolton,* 33 ARMS CONTROL TODAY 37 (Dec. 2003).

[133]*See, e.g.,* Samuel E. Logan, *The Proliferation Security Initiative: Navigating the Legal Challenges,* 14 J. TRANS. L. & POL'Y 253 (2005).

[134]For some, in fact, PSI actions that erode the right of innocent or transit passage are more troubling than those that infringe on high seas navigation freedoms and flag state primacy. Chapter 8 includes an examination of the limits on such boardings.

[135]LOS Convention, art. 38.

rendered necessary by *force majeure* or distress or for the purpose of rendering assistance to persons, ships or aircraft in danger or distress.[136]

Article 19 then provides a definition of "innocence" that focuses on the vessel's activity while it is in the territorial sea and the effect of that activity:

Article 19
Meaning of innocent passage

1. Passage is innocent so long as it is not prejudicial to the peace, good order or security of the coastal State. Such passage shall take place in conformity with this Convention and with other rules of international law.
2. 2. Passage of a foreign ship shall be considered to be prejudicial to the peace, good order or security of the coastal State if *in the territorial sea it engages* in any of the following activities:

(a) any threat or use of force against the sovereignty, territorial integrity or political independence of the coastal State, or in any other manner in violation of the principles of international law embodied in the Charter of the United Nations;

(b) any exercise or practice with weapons of any kind;

(c) any act aimed at collecting information to the prejudice of the defense or security of the coastal State;

(d) any act of propaganda aimed at affecting the defense or security of the coastal State;

(e) the launching, landing or taking on board of any aircraft;

(f) the launching, landing or taking on board of any military device;

(g) the loading or unloading of any commodity, currency or person contrary to the customs, fiscal, immigration or sanitary laws and regulations of the coastal State;

(h) any act of wilful and serious pollution contrary to this Convention;

(i) any fishing activities;

(j) the carrying out of research or survey activities;

(k) any act aimed at interfering with any systems of communication or any other facilities or installations of the coastal State;

(l) any other activity not having a direct bearing on passage.[137]

It can be seen that the question of "innocence" does not turn on a violation of the laws of the coastal state. Such a violation is neither necessary nor sufficient to render a vessel's passage non-innocent. It is not clear whether Article 19 is to be strictly or

---

[136] *Ibid.* art. 18.

[137] *Ibid.* art. 19 (emphasis added to highlight the present tense "engages in" and that the activity must take place while the vessel is in the territorial sea). *See generally* 4 MARJORIE M. WHITEMAN, DIGEST OF INTERNATIONAL LAW 343–417 (1968).

liberally construed,[138] and whether the list of activities in Paragraph 2, which lacks the tell-tale *"inter alia"* qualifier (included, for example, in the list of high seas freedoms in Article 87), is exhaustive or suggestive. The United States and the former Soviet Union formally took the position that the list of activities in Article 19 that render passage non-innocent was exhaustive.[139] In the final analysis, the debate might be largely academic since the last listed activity, "any other activity not having a direct bearing on passage," is potentially broad enough to be considered a "catch-all" clause by a coastal state inclined to a narrow view of innocence.

When the U.S. Senate Foreign Relations Committee reported out the LOS Convention for advice and consent in 2004, it recommended that the president attach the following understanding: "any determination of non-innocence of passage by a ship must be made on the basis of acts it commits while in the territorial sea, and not on the basis of. . .cargo, armament, means of propulsion, flag, origin, destination, or purpose."[140] The U.S. position is consistent with the World Court's decision in the *Corfu Channel* case, in which the Court held that the inquiry into whether a vessel's passage was "innocent" turns on the manner of passage, not the vessel's motive.[141] Article 19 emphasizes that passage must take place in conformity with the LOS Convention and "with other rules of international law."

Even vessels (other than warships and other public vessels) entitled to transit the territorial sea in innocent passage under the two-step test set out above may be subject to a limited class of laws and regulations and safety measures prescribed by the coastal state.[142] Article 21 imposes limits on the coastal state's prescriptive

[138] *See* CHURCHILL & LOWE, at 87 (concluding that a coastal state's right to suspect passage "has been interpreted liberally, as is often the case where rights protect security interests"). Those concerned with the shared interest in freedom of navigation would favor a broad construction of the right of innocent passage, while those who focus on the coastal state's sovereignty over the waters would favor a narrow reading of any passage rights in derogation of state sovereignty. On the burden and quantum of proof question see Thomas D. Lehrman, *Note: Enhancing the Proliferation Security Initiative: The Case for a Decentralized Nonproliferation Architecture*, 45 VA. J. INT'L L. 223, 231–32 (2004).

[139] *See* Uniform Interpretation of Norms of International Law Governing Innocent Passage (U.S.-U.S.S.R), *reprinted in* 14 LAW OF THE SEA BULL. 12–13 (1989) *&* 28 I.L.M. 1444 (1989). Paragraph 3 of the so-called Jackson Hole agreement provides: "Article 19 of the Convention of 1982 sets out in paragraph 2 an exhaustive list of activities that would render passage not innocent. A ship passing through the territorial sea that does not engage in any of those activities is in innocent passage." 28 I.L.M. 1444 (1989). Some commentators highlight the fact that the U.S.-U.S.S.R. interpretation is not binding on other states. At the same time, the joint Uniform Interpretation has been labeled "very influential," in light of the position of the two parties. CHURCHILL & LOWE, at 86.

[140] Senate Foreign Relations Committee, Report on the United Nations Convention on the Law of the Sea, S. EXEC. REP. NO. 108–10 (Mar. 11, 2004), understanding 2(c). The United States has long taken the position that, because the listed activities must take place in the territorial sea (Article 19(2)), the vessel's cargo, destination or the purpose of its voyage can not be used as a criterion for determining whether its passage is innocent. *See* Admiral Horace B. Robertson, Testimony before the House Merchant Marine and Fisheries Comm., 97th Cong., Hearings on the Status of the Law of the Sea Treaty Negotiations, July 27, 1982, Ser. 97–29, at 413–14; *see also* Bernard Oxman, *The Regime of Warships Under the United Nations Convention on the Law of the Sea,* 24 VA. J. INT'L L. 813, 853 (1984).

[141] *See* 4 WHITEMAN, DIGEST OF INTERNATIONAL LAW, § 19.

[142] LOS Convention, arts. 21–25.

jurisdiction with respect to foreign public and nonpublic ships in innocent passage. The limits apply only to foreign vessels in innocent passage. All such coastal state laws must be in conformity with other rules of international law including other relevant provisions of the LOS Convention. The article includes a list of eight subjects over which the coastal state is competent to legislate. Those eight subjects are extended for foreign nuclear-powered ships and ships carrying nuclear or other inherently dangerous or noxious substances by Articles 22 and 23. It is noteworthy that Article 23 recognizes that nuclear-powered ships and ships carrying nuclear or other dangerous or noxious cargoes are eligible to exercise the right of innocent passage; however, that provision does not in itself mean that navigation by such vessels constitutes "passage" under Article 18 or is "innocent" under Article 19. It must also be noted that Article 24 forbids discrimination in form or in fact against vessels of any particular state or ships carrying cargoes to, from, or on behalf of any state.

Coastal state control over vessels engaged in transit passage through waters of the territorial sea that constitute a strait used for international navigation is even more restricted than over vessels merely in innocent passage.[143] Under the right of transit passage, vessels of all nations have the right to unimpeded transit, in their ordinary mode of travel, through international straits.[144] At least during peacetime, the coastal state may not suspend or hamper the right of transit.[145] Transit passage must be conducted without delay, and ships in transit passage must refrain from using or threatening to use force, and may not engage in any activities other than those incident to their normal and expeditious travel.[146] As with innocent passage, the right of transit passage is subject to other applicable rules of international law,[147] presumably including binding resolutions of the Security Council. The coastal state may establish traffic lanes through such straits and require transiting vessels to follow them.[148] The coastal state may also adopt a limited class of laws and regulations relating to vessels in transit passage.

In the contiguous zone, a coastal state has jurisdiction to prevent or punish violations of its customs, fiscal, immigration, or sanitary laws in the territorial sea.[149] The fact that the state's competency is limited to preventing and punishing violations *within the territorial sea or territory* of the coastal state makes it clear that the

---

[143]LOS Convention, art. 37 (transit passage regime "applies to straits used for international navigation between one part of the high seas or an exclusive economic zone and another part of the high seas or an exclusive economic zone"). *See also ibid.* art. 36 (excluding certain straits where an alternative route of similar convenience exists).

[144]*Ibid.* art. 38. *See also* William L. Schachte, Jr. & J. Peter A. Bernhardt, *International Straits and Navigational Freedoms,* 33 VA. J. INT'L L. 527 (1993).

[145]LOS Convention, art. 44. *See also* The Corfu Channel case (U.K. v. Alb.) 1949 I.C.J. REP. 1 (Apr. 9).

[146]LOS Convention, art. 39(1).

[147]*Ibid.* art. 39(1)(b).

[148]*Ibid.* art. 41.

[149]*See* LOS Convention, art. 33; 4 WHITEMAN, DIGEST OF INTERNATIONAL LAW § 2; RESTATEMENT § 513, comment *f;* A Vaughan Lowe, *The Development and Concept of the Contiguous Zone*, 1981 BRIT. Y.B. INT'L L. 109 (1982). The term "sanitary" comes from the French "sanitaire," which is limited to health and quarantines measures.

contiguous zone regime is not an independent basis for the coastal state to exercise prescriptive jurisdiction.[150] Moreover, it does not include defense and security interests, as does the Article 19 definition of "innocence" for passage through the territorial sea.[151]

Flag State Jurisdiction and Control

The flag state's positive obligation to exercise effective jurisdiction and control over its vessels was emphasized above. A flag state's prescriptive jurisdiction over its vessels exists regardless of the vessel's location.[152] However, when such vessels enter the exclusive economic zone, contiguous zone, territorial sea, archipelagic waters, or internal waters of another state, they are subject to the coastal state's sovereignty, sovereign rights, or jurisdiction, depending on the vessel's location and status. Prescriptive jurisdiction in such cases may be shared concurrently between the coastal state and the flag state.

Despite the global reach of a flag state's prescriptive jurisdiction as a matter of international law, national courts do not always favor extraterritorial application of municipal laws. For example, U.S. courts have adopted a presumption that Congress does not intend that U.S. statutes apply extraterritorially.[153] Accordingly, the courts will look for clear evidence that Congress did intend extraterritorial application before applying it to conduct occurring outside U.S. territory. When Congress makes plain its intent that a statute is to apply extraterritorially, courts must enforce the statute as written, unless it would violate the U.S. Constitution. Crimes that apply in the "special maritime and territorial jurisdiction of the United States"[154] plainly fall in that category. Similarly, Congress made clear its intent that the Maritime Drug Law Enforcement Act applies extraterritorially, even in cases involving foreign vessels and nonnationals.[155] In the absence of explicit provision in a statute for extraterritorial application, courts apply one or more canons of construction to determine the

---

[150]Shigeru Oda, *The Concept of the Contiguous Zone*, 11 INT'L & COMP. L.Q. (1962). Because the contiguous zone generally lies entirely within the coastal state's EEZ (if one is claimed), the coastal state may exercise its prescriptive jurisdiction under Article 56 of the Convention over those waters. In addition, for vessels bound for the coastal state's ports or internal waters, the coastal state may enforce conditions on entry in the contiguous zone.

[151]*See* 2 UNITED NATIONS CONVENTION ON THE LAW OF THE SEA 1982: A COMMENTARY 266–75 (Satya N. Nandan & Shabtai Rosenne, ed. 1995).

[152]RESTATEMENT § 502, comments *a* & *d*. The flag state's jurisdiction may be concurrent, particularly when the vessel is within waters over which another state has jurisdiction. *See* United States v. Rodgers, 150 U.S. 249, 266 (1893), United States v. Flores, 289 U.S. 137, 153 (1933).

[153]EEOC v. Arabian Am. Oil Co., 499 U.S. 244, 248 (1991); National Transp. Safety Bd. v. Carnival Cruise Lines, Inc., 723 F. Supp. 1488 (S.D. Fl. 1989) (holding that statute establishing NTSB authority to investigate marine casualties was presumed not to extend to foreign vessel casualties outside U.S. waters, even though jurisdiction might be appropriate under the customary law "effects doctrine").

[154]18 U.S.C.A § 7 (West 2005).

[155]*See* 46 U.S.C.A. app. § 1903 (West 2005). The statutory definition of "vessel subject to the jurisdiction of the U.S." is also incorporated into High Seas Fishing Compliance Act. *See* 16 U.S.C.A. § 5502(10) (West 2005).

statute's reach. First, the courts will presume that Congress did not intend to violate principles of international law.[156] Thus, courts may refer to the above-listed bases under international law for a state to extend application of its laws beyond its territory. Second, in construing the terms of an ambiguous statute, the court will not construe it "to violate the law of nations if any other possible construction remains."[157] The *Charming Betsy* canon is wholly independent of the first canon.[158] Finally, in the absence of express congressional intent that the statute applies extraterritorially, some courts, drawing on the 1987 U.S. *Restatement (Third) of Foreign Relations Law,*[159] further require that application of U.S. law be "reasonable" under the circumstances;[160] at least for theories other than the universality principle.

Congress has the power to define and punish piracy and crimes "against the law of nations."[161] In addition, Congress has the authority to regulate interstate and foreign commerce.[162] Finally, Congress has the power to enact legislation necessary and appropriate to implement a treaty to which the United States is a party.[163] Notwithstanding the broad constitutional grant of legislative power, the Court of Appeals for the Ninth Circuit has held that extraterritorial application of a criminal statute to those aboard a foreign flag vessel violates the Due Process Clause of the Constitution if the offense charged lacks an adequate nexus to the United States.[164] Most other circuits that have considered the question have rejected the Ninth Circuit's approach,[165] while commentators have pointed out the irony of invoking

---

[156]*EEOC,* 499 U.S. at 248 (holding that, unless a contrary intent appears, legislation of Congress is meant to apply only within the territorial jurisdiction of the U.S.); McCulloch v. Sociedad Nacional de Marineros de Honduras, 372 U.S. 10, 21–22 (1963).

[157]Murray v. The Schooner *Charming Betsy,* 6 U.S. (2 Cranch) 64, 81 (1804).

[158]*EEOC,* 499 U.S. at 264 (Marshall, J. dissenting).

[159]Restatement §§ 403(2), 421, 431.

[160]United States v. Vasquez-Velasco, 15 F.3d 833, 840 (9th Cir. 1994). The U.S. Supreme Court's position is uncertain. *Compare* Hartford Fire Ins. Co. v. California, 509 U.S. 764 (1993) (majority rejecting reasonableness test) *with* Hoffman-La Roche Ltd. v. Empagran S.A., 124 S. Ct. 2359 (2004) (majority applying reasonableness test).

[161]U.S. Const. art. I, § 8; *see also* United States v. Smith, 18 U.S. (5 Wheat.) 153 (1820); United States v. Flores, 289 U.S. 137 (1933) (the power to define and punish piracy does not preclude additional jurisdiction over admiralty and maritime matters).

[162]U.S. Const. art. I, § 8.

[163]Missouri v. Holland, 252 U.S. 416 (1920).

[164]*See* United States v. Klimavicius-Viloria, 144 F.3d 1249, 1257 (9th Cir. 1998). *See also* A. Mark Weisburd, *Due Process Limits on Federal Extraterritorial Legislation?,* 35 Colum. J. Transnat'l L. 379 (1997); Lea Brilmayer & Charles Norchi, *Federal Extraterritoriality and Fifth Amendment Due Process,* 105 Harv. L. Rev. 1217 (1992). The government need not demonstrate a nexus to prosecute U.S. nationals (citizens or resident aliens) on board a stateless vessel. United States v. Caicedo, 47 F.3d 370, 371 (9th Cir. 1995); United States v. Juda, 46 F.3d 961 (9th Cir. 1995).

[165]*See, e.g.,* United States v. Suerte, 291 F.3d 366 (5th Cir. 2002). *But see* United States v. Yousef, 327 F.3d 56, 100 (2d Cir. 2003) (following Ninth Circuit, in arguable *dicta*) *cert. denied,* 540 U.S. 933 (2003). In some cases, the nexus requirement was deemed to be unnecessary where the flag state consented to assertion of U.S. jurisdiction. United States. v. Cardales, 168 F.3d 548 (1st Cir. 1999); United States v. Martinez-Hidalgo, 993 F.2d 1052, 1056 (3d Cir. 1993). The Ninth Circuit disagrees, and requires a nexus even under those circumstances. *Klimavicius-Viloria,* 144 F.3d at 1257.

extraterritorial application of the Constitution to defeat extraterritorial application of a criminal statute.[166] Alternatively, some argue that extending a criminal statute to a person under circumstances where the person had no way of foreseeing that his conduct was subject to U.S. law violates the prohibition on *ex post facto* laws.[167] Such arguments are unpersuasive where the conduct is a universal crime or one made criminal under the laws of all of the states with an interest in the matter.

Properly registered vessels sailing on the high seas are said to be subject to the exclusive jurisdiction of their flag state, save under exceptions provided by international treaty or the LOS Convention.[168] As the Permanent Court of International Justice explained in the *S.S. Lotus* dispute between France and Turkey: "It is certainly true that—apart from certain special cases which are defined by international law—vessels on the high seas are subject to no authority except that of the State whose flag they fly."[169] Some commentators have taken the view that in any case where an exception to the general rule is asserted, the burden of proof falls upon the party relying on the exception.[170] The customary law principle was later codified into the 1958 Convention on the High Seas[171] and the 1982 LOS Convention, though those articles of the conventions speak in terms of "jurisdiction" rather than "authority."[172]

Article 92(1) of the LOS Convention provides: "Ships shall sail under the flag of one State and, save only in exceptional cases expressly provided for in international treaties or in this Convention, shall be subject to its exclusive jurisdiction on the high seas. A ship may not change its flag during a voyage or while in a port of call, save in the case of a real transfer of ownership or change in registry."[173] Flag state jurisdiction

---

[166]Curtis A. Bradley, *Universal Jurisdiction and U.S. Law,* 2001 U. Chi. Legal Forum 323, 338.

[167]*See* United States v. Aikins, 946 F.2d 608 (9th Cir. 1990) (rejecting argument); United States v. Gonzalez, 776 F.2d 931 (11th Cir. 1985) (same).

[168]U.S. law raises the possibility of concurrent jurisdiction over some crimes where the vessel is owned in whole or in part by a U.S. citizen or corporation, even if the vessel is registered in another state. *See* 18 U.S.C.A. § 7(1) (West 2005). *But see* Restatement § 502, note 2 (concluding that the ownership provision of 18 U.S.C. § 7(1) apply to only to vessels either registered in the United States or not registered in any state).

[169]Case of the S.S. *Lotus* (Fr. v. Turk.), 1927 P.C.I.J. (ser. A) No. 10, at p. 25 (Sept. 7).

[170]Colombos, at 311 (6th rev. ed. 1967); Henry W. Halleck, International Law 239 (S. Baker, ed., 3d ed. 1967). *See also* Churchill & Lowe, at 12, who treat the principle of exclusive flag-state jurisdiction as a "residual presumption for the resolution of doubtful claims." They explain that: "[h]ere any doubt over the existence of the non-flag state's rights is settled in favor of exclusiveness of the flag state's jurisdiction, by reference to the general principle." *Ibid.*

[171]Convention on the High Seas, Apr. 29, art. 6, 1958, 13 U.S.T. 2313, 450 U.N.T.S. 82.

[172]LOS Convention, art. 91. The principle of exclusive flag state jurisdiction over vessels on the high seas was sorely tested in Canada's enforcement actions against the Spanish F/V *Estai* in 1995, causing some to question whether the Grotian freedom to fish would endure. *See* Wolfgang Munchan, *EU Brands Seizure of Spanish Trawler an Act of Piracy,* Times (London), Mar. 11, 1995, at 15.

[173]*See* LOS Convention, art. 92; Restatement § 522; Robert C. F. Reuland, *Note, Interference with Non-National Ships on the High Seas: Peacetime Exceptions to the Exclusivity of Flag-State Jurisdiction,* 22 Vand. J. Transnat'l L. 1161 (1989). The predecessor article in the 1958 Convention on the High Seas was held not to be self-executing. Accordingly, an individual could not assert a violation of the article as a defense to prosecution. United States v. Postal, 589 F.2d 862, 873 (5th Cir.), *cert. denied,* 444 U.S. 832 (1979).

extends to the vessel, her crew and passengers, and the cargo.[174] In recognizing exclusive flag state jurisdiction over its vessels located on the high seas, neither the 1958 Convention on the High Seas nor the 1982 UNCLOS specifies the customary international law basis of jurisdiction.[175] However, since exclusive jurisdiction is lost when the vessel enters another state's waters,[176] the basis cannot be strictly said to be territorial. Because it includes jurisdiction over the persons on board, flag state jurisdiction might be most accurately characterized as "quasi-territorial."[177]

The LOS Convention seeks to preserve freedom of navigation on the high seas by limiting states from "interfering" with foreign flag vessels. Article 110 of the LOS Convention provides that "[e]xcept where acts of interference derive from powers conferred by treaty," states other than the flag state may not interfere with a vessel on the high seas unless the interfering vessel has grounds for believing the situation falls within one of the four grounds enumerated in Article 110.[178] In addition, the flag state may authorize interference or even waive primary jurisdiction over its vessels by agreement. Such agreements may take the form of standing treaties or *ad hoc* agreement by an exchange of notes.[179] Those agreements are examined in Chapter 8.

Extraterritorial Jurisdiction by "Patrol States"

For centuries, some states have dispatched their vessels to patrol distant waters. Such patrols were indispensable in regions where piracy and slave-trading flourished. Jurisdiction to enforce laws in the maritime domain is governed by both international law and by the enforcing state's constitution and statutory laws. This section examines

---

[174]For excerpts of the Department of State memorandum on maritime interdiction and law enforcement, including the exceptions to exclusive flag state jurisdiction on the high seas, see DIGEST OF U.S. PRACTICE IN INTERNATIONAL LAW 1989–1990, at 448–52.

[175]In the *S.S. Lotus* case, the Permanent Court reasoned that a ship on the high seas is "assimilated" to the territory of the state the flag of which flies. Case of the S.S. *Lotus* (Fr. v. Turk.), 1927 P.C.I.J. (ser. A) No. 10, at p. 18 (Sept. 7) ("It follows that what occurs on board a vessel upon the high seas must be regarded as if it occurred on the territory of the State whose flag the ship flies").

[176]*See* RESTATEMENT § 502, comment *d.*

[177]*See* 1 JOHN BASSETT MOORE, A DIGEST OF INTERNATIONAL LAW § 174 (1906) (adopting the "quasi-territorial" label). If ships truly were "floating territory," nonpublic vessels could serve as platforms for asylum while in another state's internal waters, but this is not the case. *Cf.* Lam Mow v. Nagle, 24 F.2d 316 (9th Cir. 1928) (holding that a person born on a U.S. flag ship was not born in U.S. territory and was therefore not entitled to U.S. citizenship). *See generally* 9 MARJORIE M. WHITEMAN, DIGEST OF INTERNATIONAL LAW 22–23, 37, 39 (1968).

[178]Professor Colombos takes the position that non–flag state interferences with vessels on the high seas are presumed to be illegitimate and that the burden is on the state asserting an exception. COLOMBOS, at 311.

[179]In the nineteenth century Great Britain relied on flag state consent for its boarding of vessels transporting slaves. *See* Louis Sohn, *Peacetime Use of Force on the High Seas,* 64 U.S. Nav. War Coll., INT'L L. STUDIES 38 (1991). Modernly, Article 99 of the LOS Convention requires all states to criminalize the transport of slaves on vessels flying their flag, though it stops short of conferring universal jurisdiction over the offense.

the conventional and customary international laws applicable to maritime interception and enforcement operations. Customary law and the LOS Convention recognize two classes of vessels that do not, or potentially do not, enjoy the protection of exclusive flag state jurisdiction: vessels that are without a nationality[180] and vessels that have been "assimilated" to a vessel without a nationality.[181] Some argue that a stateless vessel is not, by virtue of its stateless condition alone, subject to the jurisdiction of every state.[182] They argue for an examination of the recognized bases for jurisdiction under international law, including the territoriality, nationality, protective, and passive personality principles. They further argue that any state exercising jurisdiction over the vessel must have enacted laws applicable to that vessel.

Even for lawfully registered vessels, the often-heard assertion that the flag state's jurisdiction or authority over its vessels while on the high seas is always "exclusive," is not quite true. The Convention includes several exceptions that permit non-flag states to "interfere" with vessels on the high seas or to exercise jurisdiction over such vessels.[183] The *chapeau* to Article 110, which prohibits states other than the flag state from interfering with a vessel's navigation, recognizes that acts of interference may be authorized "from power conferred by treaty." Although some sources limit the term "treaty" to written agreements between states,[184] there is no reason to conclude that Article 110 was meant to exclude oral, *ad hoc* agreements between states or Security Council resolutions.[185] Oral international agreements, while rare, can be valid and binding "treaties."[186] The United States has long recognized the validity of *ad hoc* oral ship boarding agreements with flag states.[187] Moreover, the state's consent would estop it from later asserting that the boarding encroached on the right waived.

---

[180]*See* LOS Convention, art. 92(2); *see also* 46 U.S.C.A. § 1903(c)(2) (defining "vessel without a nationality"); 9 WHITEMAN, DIGEST OF INTERNATIONAL LAW, at 6, 7, 21, 25–26, 34–35.

[181]9 WHITEMAN, DIGEST OF INTERNATIONAL LAW, at 7, 16, 22, 25–27, 34–35. The "assimilation" mechanism is also incorporated into Article 102, which addresses the status of warships engaged in piracy. The question whether inconsistent registry claims by those on board a vessel relieves the flag state of its obligation to exercise effective jurisdiction and control is beyond the scope of this project.

[182]*See* CHURCHILL & LOWE, at 214. The United States takes the position that stateless vessels engaged in drug trafficking or the use of high seas driftnets are subject to U.S. jurisdiction. 46 U.S.C.A. app. § 1903(c) (West 2005); 16 U.S.C.A. § 1802(44) (West 2005); RESTATEMENT § 522, note 7.

[183]Few will argue that any "interference" with a merchant vessel on the high seas is tantamount to a use of armed force against the territorial integrity or political independence of a state, in violation of Article 2(4) of the U.N. Charter. Indeed, the civil remedies provisions for unjustified or unlawful detentions built into the LOS Convention evidences an intent to bring such actions within the umbrella of state responsibility for acts in violation of international law.

[184]Vienna Convention on the Law of Treaties, art. 2(1)(a).

[185]*See* 14 MARJORIE M. WHITEMAN, DIGEST OF INTERNATIONAL LAW 5 (1968).

[186]Legal Status of Eastern Greenland (Den. v. Nor.) 1933 P.C.I.J. Ser. A/B No. 53 (holding that an oral promise by the Norwegian foreign minister to renounce Norwegian claims to Greenland was enforceable).

[187]*See* 9 WHITEMAN, DIGEST OF INTERNATIONAL LAW, at 65–66; 46 U.S.C.A. § 1903(c)(1) (West 2005).

In addition to authorizing another state to interfere with one of its vessels, a flag state may waive its primary jurisdiction.[188] Article 92 of the LOS Convention acknowledges that exceptions to the exclusivity rule may arise within the LOS Convention itself or some other international agreement.[189] U.N. Security Council resolutions imposing economic embargoes trigger maritime enforcement actions by so-called coalitions of the willing.[190] Other conventions such as the U.N. Convention on Narcotic Drugs, Straddling Fish Stocks Agreement, and the Human Trafficking and Illegal Migrant Smuggling Protocols, extend that principle. Finally, state practice, as evidenced by Canada's enforcement action against the F/V *Estai* and actions by European Union states in the post-*Prestige* oil spill response demonstrate that not all states categorically accept the exclusivity of flag state jurisdiction and control in waters beyond the coastal state's control.[191] It is the case that, in most circumstances, the flag state's jurisdiction and control over the vessel will be exclusive of other states and that in those situations in which another state shares concurrent prescriptive jurisdiction, the flag state will be given primacy in any exercise of enforcement jurisdiction. For one reason or another, however, the flag state may be unable or unwilling to exercise the necessary jurisdiction and control.

Universal Jurisdiction over Vessels

The concept of universal jurisdiction was introduced in the previous section. The universality principle is a unique basis for a state to exercise jurisdiction in that it permits, perhaps even requires, a state to prescribe penal laws respecting conduct even if that conduct has no nexus with the enforcing state.[192] For example, the fact that a pirate ship flies a foreign flag, sails with a foreign crew, and harms no nationals of the enforcing state is no bar to a state prescribing laws against such conduct and enforcing them, even though all of the activities took place outside

---

[188]United States v. Robinson, 843 F.2d 1, 3, 4 (1st Cir.) (holding that "[i]t is clear, under international law's 'territorial principle,' that a 'state has jurisdiction to prescribe and enforce a rule of law in the territory of another state to the extent provided by international agreement with the other state"), *cert. denied*, 488 U.S. 834 (1988); *see also* RESTATEMENT § 522, comment *e* (under the U.S. view, "interference with a ship that would otherwise be unlawful under international law is permissible if the flag state has consented"). There is also authority for the notion that jurisdiction may be "ceded" or "transferred" from one state to another. *See, e.g.,* Model Treaty on the Transfer of Criminal Proceedings in Criminal Matters, U.N.G.A. Res. 45/118, U.N. GAOR, 45th Sess., Supp. No. 49A, at 219 (1991). *In Rasul v. Bush*, 542 U.S. 466 (2004), the U.S. Supreme Court examined the validity of "transferring" jurisdiction by agreement in the context of the 1903 lease between the United States and Cuba. The lease confers on the United States "complete jurisdiction and control" over the leased area, while Cuba retained "ultimate sovereignty."

[189]Article 92 sets a demanding standard for waivers of the flag state's primacy: "save in exceptional cases expressly provided for in international treaties or in this Convention").

[190]The validity of interdictions under authority of the U.N. Security Council resolutions turns on the text of the resolution.

[191]The rapid expansion of port state control regimes throughout the 1990s further eroded the primacy of flag state jurisdiction and control.

[192]*Bradley*, at 323.

the enforcing state's waters.[193] The commonly cited rationale for this expansive jurisdictional reach is that the conduct involved renders the violator *hostis humani generis*—the enemy of all mankind. Universal jurisdiction is said to extend to "offenses recognized by the community of nations as of universal concern."[194] Modernly, the principal point of disagreement is not so much whether there is a class of crimes for which jurisdiction is "universal," but rather what crimes are included in that class.[195]

Any application of universal jurisdiction principles must acknowledge that people (and in rare case, juridical entities like corporations) commit crimes, not vessels. While it is true that a vessel may be used to commit or facilitate a crime, and may therefore be subject to arrest, seizure, and even forfeiture, the criminal statute is enforced against the individuals who engaged in the conduct. A passenger ship might be carrying a notorious war criminal, whose conduct might give rise to universal jurisdiction; but a state other than the flag state could not invoke universal jurisdiction to board the vessel on the high seas to arrest the suspect without the flag state's consent. It should also be noted that the competence to prescribe laws prohibiting conduct can be "universal," but the competence to enforce that law is still limited. For example, a vessel engaged in piracy could not be boarded and seized by a warship while the vessel was in the territorial sea of another state. Nevertheless, any discussion of the allocation of jurisdiction among port states, coastal states, and flag states must recognize that the offenses falling within universal jurisdiction to some extent cut across that allocation.

Peacetime Right of Approach and Visit

Article 110 of the 1982 LOS Convention confers on warships[196] and other duly authorized ships or aircraft the right to approach, board, and possibly search a foreign vessel located on the high seas under circumstances set out in the convention.[197] The scope of such boardings is limited by the LOS Convention.[198]

---

[193]This principle shares some features with the concept of *erga omnes* norms, the violation of which permits any state to seek a remedy without regard to the ordinary requirement for standing.

[194]RESTATEMENT § 404.

[195]*Bradley*, at 324 & 329.

[196]*See* LOS Convention, art. 29 (defining "warship"). Coast Guard vessels under the command of a commissioned officer qualify as warships. *See* United States v. Cadena, 585 F.2d 1252, 1260 n.16 (5th Cir. 1978).

[197]4 WHITEMAN, DIGEST OF INTERNATIONAL LAW, § 7.

[198]LOS Convention, art. 110(2). The warship may send over a boat with a boarding team to check the suspect vessel's documents. If suspicion remains after inspecting the documents, the team may further examine the vessel. *See generally* 4 WHITEMAN DIGEST INT'L LAW, at 515–22; Z. Wanenberg, *Interference with Ships on the High Seas,* 10 INT'L & COMP. L. Q. 785 (1961).

Some commentators,[199] and even many of the early court decisions, distinguish between an "approach" on a vessel and a "visit" or boarding of the vessel.[200] The "right of approach" (sometimes call "reconnaissance"), which predates what is now referred to as the right of visit, is said to include the right to intercept the vessel, inspect it from a safe distance to determine its name, flag, and home port, and (modernly) to hail it on the radio and request information. The "right of visit" is expressly set out in Article 110 of the LOS Convention, which provides that:

Article 110
Right of visit

1. Except where acts of interference derive from powers conferred by treaty, a warship which encounters on the high seas a foreign ship, other than a ship entitled to complete immunity in accordance with articles 95 and 96, is not justified in boarding it unless there is reasonable ground for suspecting that:
   (a) the ship is engaged in piracy;
   (b) the ship is engaged in the slave trade;
   (c) the ship is engaged in unauthorized broadcasting and the flag State of the warship has jurisdiction under article 109;
   (d) the ship is without nationality; or
   (e) though flying a foreign flag or refusing to show its flag, the ship is, in reality, of the same nationality as the warship.
2. In the cases provided for in paragraph 1, the warship may proceed to verify the ship's right to fly its flag. To this end, it may send a boat under the command of an officer to the suspected ship. If suspicion remains after the documents have been checked, it may proceed to a further examination on board the ship, which must be carried out with all possible consideration.
3. If the suspicions prove to be unfounded, and provided that the ship boarded has not committed any act justifying them, it shall be compensated for any loss or damage that may have been sustained.
4. These provisions apply *mutatis mutandis* to military aircraft.
5. These provisions also apply to any other duly authorized ships or aircraft clearly marked and identifiable as being on government service.[201]

---

[199] *See, e.g.*, IAN BROWNLIE, PRINCIPLES OF PUBLIC INTERNATIONAL LAW 232 (5th ed. 2003) (a right of approach is recognized "in all circumstances" under customary international law); 4 WHITEMAN, DIGEST OF INTERNATIONAL LAW, at 670.

[200] *Reuland*, at 1169–70. Professor Brownlie concludes that as a "matter of customary law visit, search, and capture are a legal unity." BROWNLIE, at 232, n.59. *See also* Coast Guard MLEM, § 2.C.1 & § 3.B.1 ("right of approach questions").

[201] *See* 1982 LOS Convention, art. 110. By its terms, Article 110 applies only to vessels on the high seas; however, Articles 88 to 115 also apply within a coastal state's exclusive economic zone insofar as such an application would not be incompatible with the EEZ regime. LOS Convention, art. 58(2). *See also* 33 C.F.R. § 2.05–1 (2005); 16 U.S.C.A. § 5502(4)(A) (West 2005).

Strictly speaking, the right of visit is an exception to the noninterference rule, not a basis for exercising jurisdiction.[202] However, an approach and boarding initiated under the right of visit might reveal a basis for the boarding state to exercise jurisdiction. On the other hand, if the suspicions that prompted the visit prove to be unfounded, and the boarded vessel did not commit any act that would have justified the boarding, the vessel's owner must be compensated for any loss or damage sustained.

The right of visit is not necessarily triggered by suspicions relating to all of the activities that states have an obligation to suppress and/or prohibit. For example, all states have an obligation to suppress illicit traffic in drugs; however, there is no right of visit against vessels suspected of engaging in such trafficking. The *Restatement* goes so far as to "suggest" that the right to inspect foreign ships on the high seas can be extended to "ships carrying stolen nuclear materials or escaping terrorists."[203] It admits, however, that "the present international law on the subject is unclear,"[204] and is less than clear about whether its suggestion is based on jurisdictional competence to take law enforcement action or the customary law of countermeasures.

CONSENSUAL BOARDINGS

A warship or other authorized vessel which encounters a foreign vessel that would otherwise be immune from interference with its navigation might nevertheless intercept, board, and even search the vessel pursuant to consent. The consent must be given by a party competent to do so, such as the flag state, the coastal state in whose waters the vessel is located, or the master of the vessel. In fact, the best way to honor the principle of flag state primacy and the sovereignty and paramount interest of coastal states in their adjacent waters—while at the same time conforming to relevant duties to "cooperate" in maintaining the public order—is for patrolling states to request consent to enforcement actions that infringe on the rights and interests of other states and for the requested state to agree.[205]

Flag State Consent

Although Article 92 of the LOS Convention characterizes the jurisdiction of the flag state of vessels on the high seas as "exclusive," Article 110 recognizes that a warship which encounters a foreign ship on the high seas may be justified in "interfering" with that vessel when the "acts of interference derive from *powers conferred by*

[202] RESTATEMENT § 522. If, however, the vessel meets the liberalized definition of a "pirate ship" under Article 103 (which includes vessels not presently engaged in piracy), the vessel is subject to universal jurisdiction.

[203] RESTATEMENT § 522, n.6.

[204] *Ibid.* The reporters cited no legal authority for the "suggestion."

[205] *See generally* COAST GUARD MLEM, § 2.C.2; 2 CUMULATIVE DIGEST INT'L LAW 1981–88, at 1386–99.

treaty."[206] Treaties authorizing foreign vessel boardings in waters beyond national jurisdiction have become increasingly common. The United States has in fact concluded some two dozen ship boarding agreements under the frameworks of the 1988 U.N. Convention against Illicit Traffic in Narcotic Drugs and Psychotropic Substances[207] and the Protocol against the Smuggling of Migrants by Land, Sea and Air.[208] The family of counter-narcotics enforcement agreements between coastal states and patrolling states take a variety of forms, some of which are prior standing agreements while others are concluded on an *ad hoc* case-by-case basis.[209] Ship boarding arrangements are also permitted under the 1995 Straddling Fish Stocks Implementation Agreement.[210] If it enters into force, the SUA Convention Protocol may provide similar boarding authority to interdict shipments of weapons of mass destruction and their delivery systems.

In the counter-narcotics context, U.S. courts have held that an enforcement vessel may lawfully detain a foreign vessel on the high seas while awaiting consent from the flag state to board.[211] Any law enforcement actions based on consent must be conducted within the scope of the consent given, and with the understanding that consent may generally be withdrawn at any time. If, however, during a consensual boarding the boarding team develops an independent basis for exercising jurisdiction

---

[206]LOS Convention, art. 110.

[207]U.N. Convention on Narcotic Drugs, art. 17; BROWNLIE, at 232; DIGEST OF U.S. PRACTICE IN INTERNATIONAL LAW 1989–1990, at 128–33. A U.S. Senate Committee report emphasizes that Article 17 of the U.N. Convention "is based on the traditional rule of flag State duty to exercise its jurisdiction and control over ships flying its flag." Staff of Sen. Comm. on Foreign Relations, 101st Cong., 1st Sess., Report on United Nations Convention Against Illicit Traffic in Narcotic Drugs art. 17 (Comm. Print 1989). *See also* Council of Europe Agreement on Illicit Traffic by Sea implementing Article 17 of the U.N. Convention against Illicit Traffic in Narcotic Drugs and Psychotropic Substances, European T.S. No. 156.

[208]Protocol against the Smuggling of Migrants by Land, Sea and Air, Supplementing the U.N. Convention against Transnational Organized Crime, Dec. 14, 2000, arts. 7–9, U.N. Doc. A/55/383, 40 I.L.M. 335 (2001). The Protocol is Annex III to the parent convention. *See* 40 I.L.M. 335, 384–94. Article 17 ("Agreements and arrangements") provides:

> States Parties shall consider the conclusion of bilateral or regional agreements or operational arrangements or understandings aimed at:
>
> (a) Establishing the most appropriate and effective measures to prevent and combat the conduct set forth in article 6 of this Protocol; or
>
> (b) Enhancing the provisions of this Protocol among themselves.

Executive Order 12,807 expressly requires the Coast Guard to obtain flag state consent to interdict foreign vessels on the high seas believed to be smuggling aliens. 3 C.F.R. pt. 303 (1992).

[209]*See* DIGEST OF U.S. PRACTICE IN INTERNATIONAL LAW 1989–1990, at 450; Joseph E. Kramek, *Bilateral Maritime Counter-Drug and Immigration Interdiction Agreements: Is this the World of the Future?,* 31 U. MIAMI INTER-AM. L. REV. 121, 133–34 (2000).

[210]Agreement for the Implementation of the United Nations Convention on the Law of the Sea of 10 December 1982 relating to the Convention and Management of Straddling Fish Stocks and Highly Migratory Fish Stocks, arts. 20, 21, 60, U.N. Doc. No. A/CONF. 164/37 (1995).

[211]United States v. Kahn, 35 F.3d, 426, 430 (9th Cir. 1994) (holding that the Coast Guard may legally detain a vessel while awaiting consent of the flag state to exercise jurisdiction over the vessel).

and control, law enforcement actions may continue even if consent is withdrawn or is otherwise terminated.

Flag state consent may extend to boardings on the high seas or to vessels flying the consenting state's flag while in innocent passage through another state's territorial sea (essentially waiving the innocent passage protection). The bilateral PSI ship boarding agreements entered into by the United States and some of the major flag states implicitly recognize that a coastal state may, consistent with international law, authorize a third state to board a foreign flag vessel in its waters.[212] It is important to distinguish enforcement actions in which the boarding state is assisting the flag or coastal state in *that* state's exercise of its jurisdiction (essentially acting as a surrogate enforcer) from the cases in which the flag or coastal state waives its jurisdiction and authorizes the boarding state to exercise jurisdiction over the vessel.

As a matter of U.S. law, a flag state's consent renders the vessel "subject to the jurisdiction of the United States" and its crew subject to prosecution in U.S. courts. In the Maritime Drug Law Enforcement Act (MDLEA), Congress defines the phrase "vessel subject to the jurisdiction of the United States" to include "a vessel registered in a foreign nation where the flag nation has consented or waived objection to the enforcement of United law by the United States."[213] Under the MDLEA, consent may be provided by treaty or *ad hoc* "special agreements."[214] The Act expressly provides that flag state consent may be obtained by radio, telephone, or similar or electronic means.[215] U.S. courts have upheld enforcement actions against foreign vessels and crews based on boardings conducted with the consent of the flag state.[216]

The United States has already concluded treaties with six flag states that grant reciprocal rights to board vessels of the other party to implement the PSI.[217] The agreements are modeled upon existing agreements used for counter-narcotics boardings.[218] Interestingly, the PSI agreements are couched in terms of the flag state having the "primary right to exercise jurisdiction," but the right can be waived.[219]

---

[212] *See, e.g.,* Bilateral WMD Shipboarding Agreement, U.S.-Liberia, *infra,* Appendix D, art. 4(6). The provision certainly does not foreclose the argument that a ship in innocent or transit passage would be exempt from such boardings.

[213] 46 U.S.C.A. app. § 1903(c)(1)(C) (West 2005). The same definition is applied to fishing violations. 16 U.S.C.A. § 1802(44) (West 2005).

[214] *See, e.g.,* 46 U.S.C. app. § 1903(c)(1), defining "vessel subject to the jurisdiction of the United States" to include vessels registered in a foreign nation where the flag nation has consented or waived objection to U.S. enforcement actions. Consent may be obtained by radio, telephone or similar oral or electronic means. The agreement may be formal or informal. United States v. Robinson, 843 F.2d 1, 10–11 (1st Cir. 1988) (Breyer, J.).

[215] 46 U.S.C.A. app. § 1903(c)(1) (West 2005).

[216] United States v. Suerte, 291 F.3d 366 (5th Cir. 2002) (rejecting defendant's due process violation argument); *see also* RESTATEMENT § 522, comment *e*.

[217] The six states are Belize, Croatia, Cyprus, Liberia, Marshall Islands, and Panama.

[218] Andrew C. Winner, *The Proliferation Security Initiative: The New Face of Interdiction*, 28 WASH. Q. 129, 135 (Spring 2005).

[219] *See, e.g.,* Bilateral WMD Shipboarding Agreement, U.S.-Liberia, *infra,* Appendix D, art. 5.

Reportedly, the government of the United Kingdom has similarly initiated efforts to reach PSI boarding agreements.[220]

Coastal State Consent

Enforcement actions based on consent by a coastal state are less common than those based on flag state consent. Nevertheless, such agreements already serve an important function in contemporary efforts to combat illegal smuggling[221] and to facilitate enforcement of U.N. Security Council embargoes.[222] Although U.S. courts have long condemned nonconsensual enforcement actions taken in the territory of another state, they upheld enforcement actions based on coastal state consent.[223] Coastal state cooperation and consent could prove to be just as vital to the success of PSI operations. For example, a vessel suspected of transporting WMD or delivery systems to state or non-state actors of proliferation concern that was originally intercepted on the high seas might try to flee into the territorial waters of a third state to escape pursuit. Under existing law, the pursuing vessel could not continue its pursuit in the territorial sea of the coastal state in the absence of consent by that state.

In evaluating the role and effect of coastal state consent to a boarding by a third state, one must be mindful of the principle that, as a matter of international law, the boarding state (unless it is also the flag state or it has the joint consent of the flag state) has no greater rights or jurisdiction than the coastal state would have under the circumstances. The derivative nature of its authority means that the enforcing state's vessel is limited in its jurisdiction over the pursued vessel not only by the scope of the coastal state's consent, but also by the innocent and transit passage doctrines, if applicable.

In 2002, the U.S. State Department reportedly began negotiating agreements with dozens of coastal states to permit U.S. Navy vessels to pursue and board suspect ships in the coastal states' waters.[224] NATO has launched a similar initiative with a

---

[220] *See UK Wants to Search Ships for WMD*, Maritime Executive, Mar. 2, 2004, *available at* http://www.newsletterscience.com/marex/readmore.cgi?issue_id=28&article_id=220&cid-2 625.

[221] Enforcement actions are further facilitated by a family of Mutual Legal Assistance in Criminal Matters Treaties (MLATs). For information on MLATs entered into by the United States *see* U.S. Dep't of State, Mutual Legal Assistance and Other Agreements (MLAT), *available at* http://www.travel.state.gov/law/info/judicial/judicial_690.html.

[222] For example, Albania expressly consented to enforcement of the Yugoslavian embargo in its territorial sea and a number of Gulf States entered into similar agreements with respect to the embargo on Iraq. *See* Soons, at 323.

[223] *See* United States v. Conroy, 589 F.2d 1258 (5th Cir.) (Coast Guard enforcement actions against a U.S. flag vessel in Haitian territorial sea), *cert. denied,* 444 U.S. 831 (1979).

[224] Pauline Jelinek, *U.S. Aims for More Power to Police Seas*, Assoc. Press, Aug. 10, 2002. It is unlikely that the United States or any of its PSI partners will announce which coastal states have granted consent to enforcement actions in their waters. To do so would surely invite traffickers to move to states that do not cooperate. *See also U.S., Allies Seek Right to Board Ships in WMD Search,* 34 Arms Control Today 37 (Jan.–Feb, 2004).

number of Mediterranean states. The U.S. consensual arrangements reportedly extend to vessels suspected of being involved with al Qaeda or other terrorist organizations of global reach or which are thought to be carrying weapons or other contraband in support of terrorist organizations. They are apparently modeled after similar agreements for counter-narcotics boardings.

Consent by Vessel Master

Consent by a vessel's master, a private individual, must be distinguished from consent or authorization from a state having jurisdiction over the vessel. Consent by the master might justify the boarding state in "interfering" with the vessel's freedom of navigation or other high seas freedoms, but the master's consent does not bind the flag state or strip the flag state of its primary jurisdiction over the vessel.[225] It should be noted that some states object to boardings of their vessels on the high seas based only on consent of the master. The rationale typically offered for that position—a position at odds with overwhelming state practice carried out with little or no objection—is that the right of noninterference with navigation attaches to the flag state, not the vessel owner or master, and that only the flag state may legally consent to boardings. The sounder view is that any boarding carried out with the master's consent does not constitute "interference" with the vessel's navigation or fishing rights and, because it does not constitute an exercise of jurisdiction by the boarding state, does not encroach on the flag state's primary jurisdiction over its vessels. As with all consensual boardings, those conducted only on the basis of the master's consent are limited in their reach to the scope of that consent. At any point at which the master withdraws consent, the boarding must be terminated unless another legal basis for the boarding is present. Finally, it should also be noted that consent by the vessel's master does not in itself confer jurisdiction over the vessel as a matter of U.S. law.[226]

MARITIME ENFORCEMENT OF U.N. SECURITY COUNCIL RESOLUTIONS

Under the Charter of the United Nations, the 15-member Security Council is assigned primary responsibility for the maintenance of international peace and security.[227] The Council generally acts under the authority conferred by Chapter VI (pacific settlement of disputes) or Chapter VII (actions in response to threats to

---

[225] Digest of U.S. Practice in International Law 1989–1990, at 449 ("No enforcement jurisdiction, such as arrest or seizure, may be exercised during a consensual boarding of a foreign flag vessel without the permission of the flag state (whether or not the master consents), even if evidence of illegal activities is discovered").
[226] *See, e.g.,* 46 U.S.C.A. app. § 1903(c) (West 2005); 18 U.S.C.A. § 7 (West 2005).
[227] Charter of the United Nations, art. 24(1).

the peace, breaches of the peace, and acts of aggression).[228] If it finds, pursuant to Article 39, that a situation threatens the peace or constitutes a breach of the peace or an act of aggression, the Council has the authority to, *inter alia,* impose an economic embargo (and interrupt rail, sea, and air communications) under its Article 41 authority.[229] If it finds that Article 41 measures will be or have been inadequate, the Council may impose more severe measures under Article 42, including a blockade or the use of armed force.

All members of the United Nations are required to accept and carry out the decisions of the Security Council.[230] Because the United Nations does not have its own armed force (or law enforcement agency), enforcement measures are carried out by member states. The Security Council further determines whether the enforcement of its decision will be undertaken by all member states, or only by those designated by the Council.[231] The applicable resolution will generally define the means that may be employed by the participating states to carry out the enforcement measures imposed by the resolution. Absent express authorization in the resolution, maritime enforcement measures normally may not be carried out in the territorial sea of any state without the consent of the coastal state.[232] Most commentators reject the notion that the laws of neutrality are relevant in the context of an embargo or blockade imposed by the Security Council under Chapter VII.[233] But that leaves open questions as to which states are bound by the measures, which may enforce them,

---

[228]The General Assembly is delegated limited dispute settlement (peacekeeping) authority under Chapter VI. *See ibid.* arts. 34, 35 & arts. 11–12 & 14. The General Assembly defined "aggression" to include, *inter alia,* the sending, by or on behalf of a state, armed bands, groups, irregulars or mercenaries, which carry out acts of armed force against another state of such gravity as to amount to acts of aggression committed directly by the state or its substantial involvement therein. U.N. General Assembly Resolution 3314, Dec. 14, 1974, 29 U.N. GAOR, 6th Comm., 29th Sess., Supp. No. 31, art. 3(g), at 143, U.N. Doc. A/9631 (1975).

[229]On one occasion, the Council expressly authorized the "use of force" to prevent ships from violating an embargo it imposed under Article 41. *See* Wolff Heintschel von Heinegg, *Naval Blockade,* in 72 U.S. Nav. War Coll., INT'L L. STUDIES 203, 229–30, n.127 (1998) (citing the 1966–1979 embargo on Rhodesia imposed by Resolutions 217, 221, and 232). Paragraph 5 of Resolution 221 authorized the United Kingdom to "prevent, *by the use of force if necessary*" the arrival of tankers in Beira. By its terms, Article 41 of the Charter is limited to measures "not involving the use of armed force." Accordingly, any resolution authorizing "armed force" must be issued under Article 42, not Article 41. However, it is important to distinguish the "use of force" from "armed force." *See Soons,* at 311–12, 321. Law enforcement agencies often use force to compel compliance, in circumstances not amounting to "armed force."

[230]Charter of the United Nations, art. 25.

[231]*Ibid.* art. 48.

[232]There are unconfirmed reports that U.S. Fifth Fleet or Multinational Interception Forces may have taken the position that the U.N. embargo on Iraq could be enforced even in the territorial sea of neighboring Iran. The author is not aware of any official acknowledgment of that conclusion and the records remain classified. *See* Lois E. Fielding, *Maritime Interception" Centerpiece of Economic Sanctions in the New World Order,* 53 LA. L. REV. 1191, 1223–24 & n.182 (1993).

[233]In 1945 the French government was the first to take the position that with respect to actions by a state in violation of the Charter no nation could be neutral. *See* 6 DOCUMENTS OF THE UNITED NATIONS CONFERENCE ON INTERNATIONAL ORGANIZATIONS 312, 400–01 (1945).

what waters they may be enforced in, and what means may be employed in their enforcement. Answers to those questions must of course begin with the terms of the particular resolution. In construing and applying Security Council resolutions, it may be helpful to draw upon the methods employed in construing international agreements set out in the Vienna Convention on the Law of Treaties.[234]

The history of U.N. Security Council resolutions imposing selective or full embargoes against states embroiled in conflicts now spans almost four decades.[235] One of those resolutions authorized seizure and forfeiture of vessels and cargoes found to be in violation of the resolution.[236] Recent Chapter VII measures, including those imposed in response to conflicts in the former Yugoslavia and in Iraq,[237] required prolonged maritime enforcement measures. Whether the measures imposed on North Korea and Iran will follow that path is unclear. It must be borne in mind that not all Chapter VII resolutions expressly authorize participating states to take extraterritorial enforcement measures against nonnationals. Whether express authorization is required for third-party enforcement of a mandatory Chapter VII measure, without flag state consent, remains a subject of dispute.[238] One view holds that a warship would not be acting unlawfully if it boarded and diverted a foreign ship to enforce a Security Council resolution, even if the resolution did not expressly provide for third party enforcement.[239]

THE 2005 PROTOCOL TO THE SUA CONVENTION

The PSI members and a number of supporting states have committed themselves to strengthening relevant international norms while also conforming their present activities to existing international law. One of the most recent legal initiatives in the PSI effort was launched in the International Maritime Organization, where the 1988 Convention for the Suppression of Unlawful Acts Against the Safety of

---

[234]Vienna Convention on the Law of Treaties, arts. 31–32; Restatement § 325.

[235]*See Soons,* at 307–08 (identifying 14 such resolutions, six of which entailed maritime enforcement measures).

[236]*See, e.g.,* U.N. Security Council Res. 820, U.N. Doc. S/RES/820 (1993), para. 25 (directing that vessels in violation "shall be impounded and, where appropriate, they and their cargoes may be forfeited to the detaining state"). Such authority is rare. More commonly, vessels in violation of the embargo are diverted and prevented from delivering cargo to the target state.

[237]*See, e.g.,* U.N. Security Council Res. 665, U.N. Doc. S/RES/665 (1990), which calls upon member-states that have deployed maritime forces to the Iraq-Kuwait theater to use such measures as a necessary to halt all inward and outward maritime shipping in order to inspect and verify their cargoes and destinations, to ensure compliance with the embargo imposed by Resolution 661.

[238]*See Soons,* at 316–17 (identifying two views on the question).

[239]*Ibid.* at 317. Professor Soons relies on the duty of all states to comply with resolutions of the Security Council. If the flag state fails to comply, third party action may be justified as a lawful countermeasure or, alternatively, under the principle of necessity. He further implies that any dispute over whether the action was lawful would be decided by the Security Council.

Maritime Navigation ("SUA Convention")[240] was put under review in 2001.[241] The importance of the IMO's task was recognized by the U.N. Secretary-General's High Level Panel on Threats, Challenges and Change, which urged prompt completion of the SUA Protocol to reinforce international legal provisions against illicit tracking in WMD, and cautioned that if progress is not satisfactory, the Security Council may need to be prepared to consider mandatory action.[242]

The security review efforts came to fruition on October 14, 2005, when an IMO diplomatic conference approved the text of a new protocol to the SUA Convention.[243] The 2005 SUA Protocol will, if and when effectively implemented, criminalize the transport of WMD, their delivery systems, and related materials on vessels at sea.[244] The protocol, selected articles of which are included in Appendix E, calls attention to the "international will" to combat terrorism in all its forms and manifestations, as expressed in U.N. Security Council Resolutions 1368 and 1373. It also cites Resolution 1540 as evidence of the "urgent need" for all states to take additional effective measures to prevent the proliferation of WMD and their means of delivery.

The 2005 SUA Protocol would add a new Article 3*bis,* which provides that a person commits an offense within the meaning of the SUA Convention if, *inter alia,* that person unlawfully and intentionally transports[245] on board a ship:[246]

- any explosive or radioactive material, knowing that it is intended to be used to cause, or in a threat to cause, death or serious injury or damage for the purpose of intimidating a population, or compelling a government or an international organization to do or to abstain from doing any act;
- any biological, chemical or nuclear (BCN) weapon,[247] knowing it to be a BCN weapon;

---

240 SUA Convention. *See also* 18 U.S.C. §§ 2280–2281; Violent Crime Control and Law Enforcement Act of 1994, Pub. L. No. 103–322, Title VI, § 60019(a), 108 Stat. 1975–1977 (1994).

241 IMO Res. A.920(22) of Nov. 29, 2001 (calling for a review of the SUA Convention). The reader should bear in mind that this section concerns an instrument that has not yet entered into legal force. Nor can it be considered as reflective of existing customary law. The information provided on the Protocol is designed to alert the reader to a possible direction the international regime might take.

242 United Nations, *A More Secure World: Our Shared Responsibility,* High-Level Panel on Threats, Challenges and Change, Final Report, U.N. Doc. A/59/565, Dec. 1, 2004.

243 H.E. José Luis Jesus, *Protection of Foreign Ships against Piracy and Terrorism at Sea: Legal Aspects,* 18 INT'L J. MARINE & COASTAL L. 363, 388–95 (2003); DIGEST OF U.S. PRACTICE IN INT'L LAW 2002, at 104–110.

244 *See* Protocol of 2005 to the Convention for the Suppression of Unlawful Acts against the Safety of Maritime Navigation, *adopted* Oct. 17, 2005, IMO Doc. LEG/CONF.15/DC/1 [hereinafter "2005 Protocol to the SUA Convention"], partially reproduced in Appendix E.

245 "Transport" is defined in Article 1 of the 2005 Protocol to the SUA Convention. *See infra* Appendix E.

246 The Protocol broadly defines "ship" as "a vessel of any type whatsoever not permanently attached to the sea-bed, including dynamically supported craft, submersibles, or any other floating craft." *Ibid.* art. 1.

247 "BCN weapon," "biological weapons," and "chemical weapons" are defined in Article 1 of the Protocol.

- any source material, special fissionable material, or equipment or material especially designed or prepared for the processing, use or production of special fissionable material, knowing that it is intended to be used in a nuclear explosive activity or in any other nuclear activity not under safeguards pursuant to an IAEA comprehensive safeguards agreement; and
- any equipment, materials or software or related technology that significantly contributes to the design, manufacture or delivery of a BCN weapon, with the intention that it will be used for such purpose.[248]

The protocol's prohibition on the transport of component materials is rather narrowly drawn. Paragraph 1(b)(iii) of the new Article 3*bis* extends to any source material, special fissionable material (the definitions of "source material" and "special fissionable material" are taken from the Statute of the IAEA[249]), or equipment or material "especially designed or prepared for the processing, use or production of special fissionable material." The offense is limited, however, to transportation of such material "knowing that it is intended to be used in a nuclear explosive activity or in any other nuclear activity not under safeguards pursuant to an IAEA comprehensive safeguards agreement." The requirement to prove that the transporter knew the end-user's intent means there will likely be very few prosecutions under this article. Paragraph 1(b)(iv) of the new Article 3 appears to be broader in its coverage of materials, extending to "any equipment, materials or software or related technology that significantly contributes to the design, manufacture or delivery of a BCN weapon." However, the *mens rea* component of the article is confusing. When read in conjunction with the *chapeau* for Article 3*bis,* the prohibition only extends to the act of intentionally transporting such material "with the intention that it will be used for" a BCN weapon purpose. Although the "intent" component might be read by some to refer to the intent of the shipper or end-user of the materials, it is drafted in a way that would require proof that the transporter held or shared such intent. Accordingly, this section of the article is likely to apply only in cases where the transporter is also the end-user, or working closely with the end-user.

The transportation of nuclear material is not considered an offense if such item or material is transported to or from the territory of, or is otherwise transported under the control of, a state party to the Treaty on the Non Proliferation of Nuclear Weapons (subject to certain conditions listed in the Protocol). The protocol would also amend Article 8 of the SUA Convention facilitate boardings by states other than the vessel's flag state. The Protocol's boarding provisions are discussed in Chapter 8.

Under the 2005 Protocol, a person also commits an offense within the meaning of the SUA Convention if he unlawfully and intentionally transports another person on board a ship knowing that the person has committed an act that constitutes an

---

[248] *Ibid.* art. 4, para. 5 (adding Article 3*bis* to the SUA Convention).

[249] 2005 Protocol to the SUA Convention, *infra* Appendix E, art. 1, para. 1(b).

offense under the SUA Convention or an offense set forth in any treaty listed in the Annex.[250] The Annex lists nine such treaties.[251] The 2005 Protocol also makes it an offense to unlawfully and intentionally injure or kill any person in connection with the commission of any of the offenses in the SUA Convention; to attempt to commit an offense; to participate as an accomplice; to organize or direct others to commit an offense; or to contribute to the commissioning of an offense.[252] Finally, the 2005 Protocol will require states-parties to take necessary measures to enable a legal entity (this could be a company or organization, for example) to be made liable and to face sanctions when a person responsible for management of control of that legal entity has, in that capacity, committed an offense under the SUA Convention.[253]

A state party in which a person is suspected of committing an offense under the amended SUA Convention will have a duty to prosecute the individual or extradite him to another state with jurisdiction to do so.[254] The 2005 Protocol further instructs that none of the offenses should be considered a "political offense" for the purposes of extradition.[255] The protocol will also require states-parties to afford one another assistance in connection with criminal proceedings brought in respect of offenses under the amended SUA Convention.[256] The obligation to extradite or afford mutual legal assistance is not mandatory if the request is believed to have been made for the purpose of prosecuting or punishing a person on account of that person's race, religion, nationality, ethnic origin, political opinion, or gender, or that compliance with the request would cause prejudice to that person's position for any of these reasons. It is easy to foresee that the "political opinion" exception has the potential to negate the attempt to exclude covered crimes for the "political offense" exception to extradition.

The 2005 Protocol will enter into force 90 days after 12 states have formally indicated their consent to be bound.[257] Implementation and enforcement will raise a number of questions, such as the potential effect of the new regime on states that are not party to the SUA Convention or that reject the 2005 Protocol, as well as the resolution of any conflicts between the LOS Convention and the SUA Convention, as *lex specialis* and *lex posteri*. Chapter 8 examines the principal legal issues surrounding potential applications of the 2005 Protocol in counterproliferation boardings.

---

[250] 2005 Protocol to the SUA Convention, art. 4, para. 6 (adding Article 3*ter* to the SUA Convention).

[251] *Ibid.* art. 7.

[252] *Ibid.* art. 4, para. 7 (adding Article 3*quater* to the SUA Convention).

[253] *Ibid.* art. 5, para. 2 (adding Article 5*bis* to the SUA Convention).

[254] *Ibid.* art. 6, para. 3 (providing a substitute Article 6, para. 4 to the SUA Convention).

[255] *Ibid.* art. 10 (adding Article 11*bis* to the SUA Convention). Offenses under the Protocol are also deemed to be included as extraditable offenses in any extradition treaty existing between the states-parties.

[256] *Ibid.* art. 11 (providing a substitute Article 12, para. 1 to the SUA Convention).

[257] *Ibid.* art. 18.

CUSTOMARY LAW OF UNILATERAL SELF-HELP COUNTERMEASURES

The term "countermeasures" refers to unilateral self-help measures taken by one state and directed at another state to coerce the latter to comply with an international law obligation owed to the former. Countermeasures overlap somewhat with the "necessity" exemption from state responsibility.[258] The customary law of countermeasures applies only to breaches of international law by states, not legal violations by non-state actors,[259] though this limitation may change as non-state actors increasingly become subjects of international law.

The *Restatement (Third) of Foreign Relations Law of the United States* summarizes the customary law of self-help countermeasures:

(1) Subject to Subsection (2), a state victim of a violation of an international obligation by another state may resort to countermeasures that might otherwise be unlawful, if such measures,

> (a) are necessary to terminate the violation or prevent further violation, or to remedy the violation; and
>
> (b) are not out of proportion to the violation and the injury suffered.

(2) The threat or use of force in response to a violation of international law is subject to prohibitions on the threat or use of force in the United Nations Charter, as well as Subsection (1).[260]

Historically, a state injured by the breach of an international law obligation owed to it by another state had the option of responding with self-help or by seeking redress through a recognized dispute settlement procedure. Many believe that in a horizontally structured world of sovereign states, self-help countermeasures are necessitated by the absence of a global executive.[261] Extrajudicial self-help measures have a long pedigree in municipal law of many states, including well-recognized

---

[258] *See* ILC Draft Articles on State Responsibility, art. 25.

[259] Actions by non-state actors may, however, be attributed to a state, or may have been made possible by a state's breach of its duty to exercise effective control over the entity, and might therefore give rise to a right of self-help against that state. *See* ILC Draft Articles on State Responsibility, arts. 4–11.

[260] RESTATEMENT § 905. The Draft Articles on State Responsibility provisions on countermeasures are controversial. Although the Articles acknowledge that some countermeasures are lawful, the drafters take a very narrow view of the range of permissible countermeasures. DIGEST OF U.S. PRACTICE IN INT'L LAW 2002, at 364–71 (2002) (objecting to ILC draft provisions on countermeasures on grounds the draft articles are not consistent with customary law); *see also* David J. Bederman, *Counterintuiting Countermeasures,* 96 AM. J. INT'L L. 817 (2002) (commenting on the countermeasures articles in the ILC Draft Articles on State Responsibility).

[261] *See* Myres S. McDougal, *Authority to Use Force on the High Seas,* 61 U.S. Nav. War Coll., INT'L L. STUDIES 551, 555 (1979) ("International law has depended largely upon the unorganized, unilateral making and enforcement of law by nation-states"); Report of the International Law Commission to the General Assembly, 2 [2000] Y.B. INT'L L. COMM'N, pt. 2, at 53, para. 308.

common law self-help remedies like ejection and recovery of chattels, which may be invoked against private actors. Like provisional measures, countermeasures can be employed in combination with other, more formal, dispute settlement measures to preserve the status quo or prevent irreversible harm.[262]

The customary right to invoke unilateral or self-help remedies—what one commentator refers to as the "muscular version of what is practically required to enforce international norms"[263]—included the forcible countermeasures of rescue,[264] reprisal,[265] intervention,[266] and self-defense,[267] as well as nonforcible measures of rebuke, retorsion,[268] and nonforcible reprisals.[269] Although the use of forcible countermeasures is now constrained by the U.N. Charter,[270] which requires all states to settle their disputes by peaceful means,[271] and bans the threat or use of force against the territorial integrity or political independence of a state,[272] the right to engage in countermeasures, not including the use of armed force, has not been extinguished.[273]

---

[262] *See* ILC Draft Articles on State Responsibility, art. 52(2) (injured state may take such urgent countermeasures as may be necessary to preserve its rights). *But see* United States Diplomatic and Consular Staff in Tehran case (U.S.-Iran), 1980 I.C.J. REP. 3, 43 (May 24), in which the ICJ criticized the United States for resorting to self-help measures to free the hostages while the case was before the court.

[263] *Bederman,* at 818.

[264] "Rescue" is distinguished from "intervention" in that the former is directed at the protection of the rescuing state's own nationals while the latter is directed at the safety of the nationals of other states, most often the nationals of the intervened-in state. The *Restatement* cites the Israel Defense Force Entebbe hostage rescue intervention as a lawful, forcible self-help measure. *See* RESTATEMENT § 905, comment *g.* Articles 49–50 of the Draft Articles on State Responsibility take a narrower position.

[265] "Reprisals are acts which are in themselves illegal and have been adopted by one state in retaliation for the commission of an earlier illegal act by another state." *See also* MALCOLM M. SHAW, INTERNATIONAL LAW 1023 (5th ed. 2003).

[266] *See* The Corfu Channel case (U.K. v. Alb.) 1949 I.C.J. REP. 1, 4, 35 (Apr. 9). (rejecting the U.K. argument that it had a right to intervene and clear mines in the Albanian territorial sea to facilitate innocent passage of U.K. warships). *See* SHAW, at 1021–22.

[267] *See* RESTATEMENT § 905. Professor Colombos examined these in a chapter titled "forcible measures short of war used in time of peace." *See* COLOMBOS, ch. X. The U.S. government took the position that sending U.S. Marines into Cambodia to recover the American merchant vessel S.S. *Mayaguez* and its crew after it was illegally seized by Cambodian gunboats constituted a legitimate act of forcible self-help. *See* U.S. DEP'T OF STATE, DIGEST OF UNITED STATES PRACTICE IN INTERNATIONAL LAW 1975, at 423–26 (1976).

[268] "Retorsion is the adoption by one state of an unfriendly and harmful act, which is nevertheless lawful, as a method of retaliation against the injurious legal activities of another state." *See* SHAW, at 1022. *See also* RESTATEMENT § 905, comment *f* ("Retorsion is to be distinguished from 'reprisal'; traditionally, reprisal was punitive in character and commonly involved the use of force").

[269] SHAW, at 1023 (concluding that nonforcible reprisals "may still be undertaken legitimately").

[270] *See* RESTATEMENT § 904(2); ILC Draft Articles on State Responsibility, art. 50(1)(a).

[271] Charter of the United Nations, arts. 2(3) & 33; LOS Convention, arts. 280–81.

[272] Charter of the United Nations, art. 2(4); *see also* LOS Convention, art. 301; 3 UNITED NATIONS CONVENTION ON THE LAW OF THE SEA 1982: A COMMENTARY 90, ¶ 88.7(a) (Satya N. Nandan & Shabtai Rosenne, ed. 1995) (concluding that LOS Convention Article 301 is broader than Article 2(4) of the Charter).

[273] *See* Gabčíkovo-Nagymaros Project (Hung. v. Slovk.), 1997 I.C.J. REP. 7, 55, para. 83 (Sept. 25). The Draft Articles do not apply where and to the extent the matter is governed by a *lex specialis,* such as the LOS Convention. *Ibid.* art. 55.

Any countermeasures chosen, however, must be necessary to terminate or remedy the violation or to prevent a further violation, and must be proportionate to the violation and the injury suffered.[274]

In distinguishing between forcible and nonforcible countermeasures, it must be emphasized that forcible countermeasures do not include those in which "police force" is used against a private entity or vessel to carry out legitimate law enforcement measures. Professor Myres McDougal, for example, clearly distinguishes the use of force in law enforcement measures taken against private actors from forcible self-help and self-defense measures taken against states for violations of international law.[275]

The 1982 LOS Convention recognizes the right of states to take several self-help measures.[276] For example, Article 25 provides that a coastal state may take the "necessary steps" within its territorial sea to "prevent" passage that is not innocent. Such steps may include the use of force when necessary.[277] Although warships enjoy sovereign immunity, Article 30 recognizes that a coastal state may "require" a warship to leave the coastal state's territorial sea if the warship fails to comply with regulations applicable in those waters.[278] Finally, Article 221 recognizes the existing right of a coastal state to "take and enforce" measures beyond their territorial sea to protect their coastline or related interests" from pollution or the threat of pollution.[279] Such measures must be proportionate to the actual or threatened damage posed. By their

---

[274]*See* RESTATEMENT § 905; ILC Draft Articles on State Responsibility, art. 51. *See also* Guy B. Roberts, *The Counterproliferation Self-Help Paradigm: A Legal Regime for Enforcing the Norm Prohibiting the Proliferation of Weapons of Mass Destruction,* 27 DEN. J. INT'L L. & POL'Y 483, 507 (1999).

[275]*See* Myres S. McDougal, *Authority to Use Force on the High Seas,* 61 U.S. Nav. War Coll., INT'L L. STUDIES 551, 557–58 (1979) (concluding that the use of force in law enforcement activities does not constitute forcible countermeasures); *Soons,* at 311–12 & 321, n.45 (distinguished the use of "police force" in maritime interception operations from the use of "armed force" and concluding that potential measures taken under Article 41 of the Charter can include police force). Many states would consider the use of armed force against a vessel flying its flag as an attack upon the state, justifying the use of armed force in self-defense. The use of "police force" in the course of a legitimate law enforcement action is not included. Distinguishing between the two cases is not always easy.

[276]Forcible measures against pirate attacks are authorized by U.S. law outside of the traditional Title 10 national defense structure. *See, e.g.,* 33 U.S.C.A. § 381 (West 2005) (authorizing the president to employ warships to protect U.S. vessels from "piratical aggressions and depredations").

[277]Article 25 is in subsection A of section 3, and therefore applies to all ships, including warships. Accordingly, the "necessary steps" could be taken against a state's warship, making it a true self-help measure, not one directed against a nonpublic vessel. *See also* ANNOTATED COMMANDER'S HANDBOOK, at para. 2.3.2.1.

[278]*See* CHURCHILL & LOWE, at 99 (concluding that the coastal state may use force to expel a warship for violations of "customs, navigation and pollution" laws).

[279]An often-cited example of such a countermeasure was the destruction of the tanker *Torrey Canyon* by British warplanes to abate the pollution threat posed by the stricken tanker. London justified the action on the basis of "self-defense." Professor Brownlie concluded that the "action may be justified on the ground of necessity (but not of self-defence)." BROWNLIE, at 239. Because the action was taken against a nonpublic vessel (and therefore not against a state), most would question whether the customary right of self-help is applicable.

terms, all three articles contemplate the possibility that the coastal state may resort to extrajudicial countermeasures.[280]

INDIVIDUAL OR COLLECTIVE SELF-DEFENSE

International law governing the use of force in self-defense consists of both customary and conventional sources. Article 2 and Article 51 of the U.N. Charter provide the starting point for any self-defense analysis.[281] The U.N. Charter was founded upon the belief in the promise of "collective security" measures administered primarily by the Security Council and carried out by member states or forces made available to the Council under Article 43 agreements. For a variety of reasons, the promise was never fulfilled. Judge Philip Jessup was one of the first to acknowledge the conditional relationship between the "surrender" of some elements of the customary right of self-help and the promise that collective security would step in to fill the void.[282] To the extent that the Security Council and its Military Staff Committee were unable to respond timely to a threat to a state,[283] forcible self-help might be permissible.[284] Later writers openly challenged the failure of the Charter-based collective security regime to effectively remove threats to international peace and security and call for a reexamination of the limits on the noncollective use of force by member states.[285] Nevertheless, in the words of one commentator, Article 2(4) is shrinking, while Article 51 is expanding.[286]

The "inherent right" of individual or collective self-defense under the *jus ad bellum* is recognized in Article 51 of the U.N. Charter.[287] The International Court of

---

[280]It is noteworthy that Article 219 of the LOS Convention, which provides authority for measures relating to seaworthiness of vessels, limits the available measures to "administrative measures." LOS Convention, art. 219.

[281]*See* ILC Draft Articles on State Responsibility, art. 21.

[282]Philip C. Jessup, A Modern Law of Nations 162 (1952).

[283]The General Assembly formally recognized the Security Council's failure in the 1950 "Uniting for Peace" resolution. U.N. General Assembly, Res. 337A (V 1950). The Assembly was moved to action by the "failure of the Security Council to discharge its responsibilities on behalf of Member States."

[284]Richard B. Lillich, *Forcible Self-Help Under International Law,* 62 U.S. Nav. War Coll., Int'l L. Studies 129, 135 (1980).

[285]Robert F. Turner, *Operation Iraqi Freedom: Legal and Policy Considerations,* 27 Harv. J. L. & Public Pol'y 765, 767 (2004) (concluding that "*unenforced* international law will not maintain the peace") (emphasis in original).

[286]Philip Bobbitt, The Shield of Achilles: War, Peace, and the Course of History 474 (2002).

[287]*See* Dieter Fleck, *Rules of Engagement for Maritime Forces and the Limitation of the Use of Force Under the UN Charter,* 31 German Y.B. Int'l L. 165 (1988). For an analysis of the self-defense arguments see Michael Byers, *Comment, Policing the High Seas: The Proliferation Security Initiative,* 98 Am. J. Int'l L. 526–45 (2004). It is an established principle that "the first and foremost restriction imposed by international law upon a State is that—failing the existence of a permissive rule to the contrary—it may not exercise its power in any form in the territory of another State." Case of the S.S. *Lotus* (Fr. v. Turk.), 1927 P.C.I.J. (ser. A) No. 10, at p. 18 (Sept. 7).

Justice holds that the U.N. Charter confirms the established customary law rule on self-defense; it does not purport to supervene the existing rule.[288] U.S. courts have long recognized the right of a state to "secure itself from injury" through actions on the high seas, beyond the state's own waters.[289] Customary law also recognizes the state's right of anticipatory self-defense. However, the status of the customary right of anticipatory self-defense vis-à-vis Article 2(4) of the Charter and the contours of such a right in situations short of an armed attack are a matter of dispute.[290] For some, being forced to absorb a first blow is an unattractive prospect, particularly if the blow might be delivered by a nuclear weapon or an untreatable strain of anthrax. On the other hand, a strict test is felt by many to be necessary to guard not only against the aggressive use or force, in violation of the U.N. Charter, but also a pre-emptive use of force that turns out to be premature, unnecessary, or a mere pretext for aggression.

Historically, claims of a right of anticipatory self-defense have been tested by the standards articulated by U.S. Secretary of State Daniel Webster in the *Caroline* incident. British forces entered the United States and destroyed the *Caroline* in 1837 after concluding that the vessel was going to be used to assist Canadians in their rebellion against the British. The United States and Great Britain were not at war at the time. In an exchange of notes on the question of British responsibility for the vessel's destruction, Webster articulated the most commonly cited standard for anticipatory self-defense. In the U.S. view, as articulated by Webster, the use of armed force before, but in anticipation of, an armed attack was legally justified only if "the necessity of that self-defense is instant, overwhelming, and leaving no choice of means, and no moment for deliberation."[291] The standard thus looks at both the imminence of the attack and the necessity of the use of force to preempt that attack.

The chief deficiency in the standard, and one easily explained by the circumstances of the *Caroline* incident itself, is that it focuses almost entirely on the imminence of the blow without factoring in the magnitude of the harm likely to flow from it.[292]

---

[288]*See* Case Concerning Military and Paramilitary Activities in and Against Nicaragua (Nicar. v. U.S.) 1986 I.C.J. Rep. 14, 94 (June 27) (it cannot "be held that article 51 is a provision which 'subsumes and supervenes' customary international law").

[289]*See* Church v. Hubbard, 6 U.S. (2 Cranch) 187, 234–35 (1804) (Marshall, C.J.) (upholding legality of Portugal's seizure of a U.S. vessel off the coast of Brazil, explaining that a state's "power to secure itself from injury may certainly be exercised beyond the limits of its territory. . . Any attempt to violate the laws made to protect this right, is an injury to itself which it may prevent, and it has a right to use the means necessary for its prevention"). *See also Reuland,* at 1206–22 (concluding on the basis of state practice and works of publicist that a state may meet a threat to its political security or territorial integrity where such threat may be found, including on the high seas).

[290]Michael J. Glennon, *Why the Security Council Failed,* 82 Foreign Aff. 16 (2003); Jack M. Beard, *America's New War on Terror: The Case for Self-Defense under International Law,* 25 Harv. J. L. & Pub. Pol'y 559 (2002).

[291]Letter from Daniel Webster to Lord Ashburton (Aug. 6, 1842), quoted in 2 John Bassett Moore, A Digest of International Law 412 (1906).

[292]*See* Annotated Commander's Handbook, para. 4.3.2.1.

The potential magnitude of the harm is of course the distinguishing characteristic of weapons of mass destruction, particularly nuclear weapons. The U.S. *National Security Strategy* recognizes this deficiency, concluding that "[t]he greater the threat, the greater is the risk of inaction—and the more compelling the case for taking anticipatory action to defense ourselves, even if uncertainty remains as to the time and place of the enemy's attack."[293] The conclusion is bolstered by U.N. Security Council Resolution 1373, which declares that terrorism presents the most serious threats to international peace and security in the twenty-first century; and Resolution 1540, issued under the council's Chapter VII authority, which declares that WMD in the hands of non-state actors threatens international peace and security.

Characterizing an action involving the use of force as an application of armed force (rather than police force) carries with it several important legal consequences. If the situation is one of armed conflict, the use of force is governed by the law of armed conflict (LOAC). Under the LOAC, any use of armed force is constrained by the principles of necessity and proportionality.[294] Serious breaches of the LOAC may be prosecuted as war crimes[295] and may fall within the jurisdiction of the International Criminal Court. The justification for the use of force under such circumstances is lost when hostilities cease. Like other forms of self-help, self-defense has traditionally been confined to acts by states, not individuals or even organized criminal syndicates. However, the threat posed by international terrorism has challenged the orthodox view. Terrorist attacks on the Marine barracks in Lebanon, an Air Force dormitory in Saudi Arabia, the USS *Cole* in Yemen, and, more recently, al Qaeda's unsuccessful rocket attack on U.S. Navy warships in Aqaba, Lebanon, all demonstrate the willingness of terrorists to attack even military targets.[296]

OBLIGATIONS OF STATES TAKING ENFORCEMENT ACTION

The peacetime law of the sea—both conventional and customary—incorporates several established limits on states taking enforcement actions against vessels and their crews. The municipal laws of enforcing states commonly impose even greater restrictions. Vessels other than warships when engaged in maritime interception and enforcement operations must be clearly marked and identifiable as such.[297] As mentioned above, states may not discriminate in their enforcement actions. Under what some loosely refer to as a "rule of reasonableness" embodied in Article 300 of

---

[293] *See generally Byers,* at 532–33 & 541. *See also* Michael N. Schmitt, *Preemptive Strategies in International Law,* 24 MICH. J. INT'L L. 513 (2003).

[294] Advisory Opinion, Legality of the Threat or Use of Nuclear Weapons, 1996 I.C.J. REP. 226, 245 (July 8), *reprinted in* 35 I.L.M. 80 (1996). *See also* RESTATEMENT § 905.

[295] *See* 18 U.S.C.A. § 2441 (West 2005).

[296] *Al Qaeda Claim for Red Sea Attacks,* CNN NEWS.COM, Aug. 19, 2005, *available at* http://www.cnn.com/2005/WORLD/meast/08/19/jordan.blasts/index.html. (the warships, the amphibious assault ships USS *Ashland* and USS *Kearsarge,* were in port with members of the 26th Marine Expeditionary Unit to conduct joint training with Lebanon).

[297] *See, e.g.,* LOS Convention, art. 110(5).

the LOS Convention,[298] enforcing states are held to be limited in their enforcement actions to measures that are reasonably necessary.[299] The reasonableness limit is nowhere more evident or more important than in the rules regarding the use of force.[300] State responsibility and liability for harm caused by an unwarranted enforcement measure or other breach of international law is briefly reviewed in Chapter 9.

The LOS Convention requires that the enforcing state notify the flag state when one of its vessels has been arrested or detained.[301] The notification requirements are even more specific in cases where the coastal state is contemplating the exercise of criminal jurisdiction over a person on board a vessel in innocent passage.[302] The LOS Convention also requires that if the enforcing state detains a foreign vessel for a possible violation of the enforcing state's laws, it shall promptly release the vessel and its crew upon the posting of reasonable security for any penalty that may be imposed for the violation.[303] To the extent feasible, innocent cargo should be released for transshipment to its consignee or owner. Enforcement actions taken under the authority of a bilateral shipboarding treaty may be subject to additional safeguards set out in the agreements.[304] Additionally, should the 2005 Protocol to the SUA Convention enter into force, it will incorporate a number of safeguards on boardings by non-flag states.[305] Those safeguards impose an obligation not to endanger the safety of life at sea; to ensure that all persons on board are treated in a manner that preserves human dignity and is in keeping with human rights law, taking due account of safety and security of the ship and its cargo; and to ensure that

---

[298]Article 300 provides that "States Parties shall fulfil in good faith the obligations assumed under this Convention and shall exercise the rights, jurisdiction and freedoms recognized in this Convention in a manner which would not constitute an abuse of right." All states have a similar obligation with respect to obligations assumed under the U.N. Charter. *See* U.N. General Assembly Declaration on International Law Principles Concerning Friendly Relations among States, *supra.*

[299]Chief Justice John Marshall explained the rationale for a rule of reasonableness more than two centuries ago. *See* Church v. Hubbard, 6 U.S. (2 Cranch) 187, 235 (1804) (reasoning that other states will oppose measures that are unreasonable, but if a state's enforcement measures are "reasonable and necessary to secure their laws from violation, they will be submitted to").

[300]*See* Craig H. Allen, *Limits on the Use of Force in Maritime Operations in Support of WMD Counter-Proliferation Initiatives,* 81 U.S. Nav. War Coll., Int'l L. Studies 77 (2006).

[301]*See, e.g.,* LOS Convention, art. 73(4), 231. Similar requirements to notify the vessel's flag state are included in some of the IMO-sponsored conventions.

[302]*Ibid.* art. 27(3). If the master of the vessel so requests, the coastal state is required to notify a diplomatic agent or consular officer of the flag state before taking action. Concurrent notification is acceptable in cases of emergency.

[303]*Ibid.* arts. 73, 220, 292. Prompt release cases have so far dominated the docket of the International Tribunal for the Law of the Sea. As a non-party to the LOS Convention, the U.S. is not subject to Article 292 proceedings in the ITLOS; however, arguably, the duty to promptly release a detained vessel and crew upon payment of reasonable security is a duty binding as a matter of customary law.

[304]*See, e.g.,* Bilateral WMD Shipboarding Agreement, U.S.-Liberia, *infra* Appendix D, art. 8 & 12–14.

[305]2005 Protocol to the SUA Convention, *infra* Appendix E, art. 8, para. 2 (adding Article 8*bis* to the SUA Convention).

measures taken are environmentally sound and reasonable efforts are taken to avoid a ship being unduly detained or delayed.

Other international law instruments—including, for example, the International Covenant on Civil and Political Rights (ICCPR),[306] the International Labor Organization's 2006 Maritime Labor Convention, and the Vienna Convention on Consular Relations (VCCR)[307]—may be relevant if crew members or others on board the vessel are detained or prosecuted. Importantly, the human rights and consular notification obligations under those conventions have the potential to involve states other than the flag state of the vessel.[308] Finally, in any case where one or more individuals are suspected of having committed an offense that is subject to an obligation to prosecute or extradite the individual, still another class of states may become involved in the follow-on enforcement measures.

[306]International Covenant on Civil and Political Rights, Dec. 16, 1966, arts. 9, 10, 14, 15, 999 U.N.T.S. 171.

[307]Vienna Convention on Consular Relations (1969), Apr. 24, 1963, art. 36, 21 U.S.T. 77, T.I.A.S. 6820, 596 U.N.T.S. 261.

[308]Article 292 of the LOS Convention limits standing for actions seeking prompt release of a vessel *or* its "crew" to the flag state. Interestingly, the article does not actually require participation by the flag state, but rather permits a private party (often an attorney retained by the shipowner) to appear "on behalf of" the flag state. LOS Convention, art. 292(2).

8

Preserving the Rule of Law: Legal Issues in PSI Interceptions and Boardings

Chapter 7 examined the principal legal authorities and frameworks relevant to maritime counterproliferation activities. It also identified some of the state interests that the international regime is designed to serve, while highlighting the fact that those interests may at times be in conflict. It is clear, for example, that maritime interception operations to enhance proliferation security carry the potential to erode freedom of navigation and impede freight mobility.[1] At the same time, only a layered defense, which includes at-sea interdictions when necessary and appropriate, offers an adequate level of assurance that the nonproliferation regime will be effectively enforced.[2] That realization may explain why flag states representing more than 60 percent of the world's vessel tonnage have entered into treaties with the United States to facilitate PSI boardings of their vessels.

A threshold question in any maritime interception or enforcement activity is the legal authority for the action. Over the past three years, participating states and legal analysts have suggested several possible bases for PSI boardings by states other than the flag state of the target vessel. Early suggestions included boardings based on consent of a state with jurisdiction over the vessel (the flag or coastal state, as appropriate), the stateless vessel doctrine, the right of visit, and, more controversially, the universal jurisdiction principle, justification by necessity, and the customary law of countermeasures, including the inherent right of forcible countermeasures taken in self-defense.[3] To this initial list, at least two more grounds can now be added: the right and obligation of all states to comply with and cooperate in implementation of

---

[1] *See* Thomas D. Lehrman, Note, *Enhancing the Proliferation Security Initiative: The Case for a Decentralized Nonproliferation Architecture,* 45 Va. J. Int'l L. 223, 229 (2004).

[2] On the "layered" approach see Andrew C. Winner, *The Proliferation Security Initiative: The New Face of Interdiction,* 28 Wash. Q. 129, 136 (2005).

[3] Congressional Research Service, *Weapons of Mass Destruction Counterproliferation: Legal Issues for Ships and Aircraft,* Oct. 1, 2003, CRS Rep. RL32097, at 21–22.

enforcement measures promulgated by the U.N. Security Council and the possible new legal authority conferred by the 2005 Protocol to the 1988 SUA Convention. This chapter explores those bases, drawing on the background materials provided in earlier chapters, particularly Chapter 7. It focuses solely on operations involving vessels, even though interdiction operations involving aircraft raise similar questions.

A LEGITIMATE SECURITY COUNCIL RESOLUTION ENFORCEMENT MEASURE?

In early 2004, shortly after news of Doctor Abdul Qadeer Khan's Pakistan-based WMD black market network broke, the U.N. Security Council legitimated the core principles of the year-old PSI by unanimously passing Resolution 1540.[4] In passing Resolution 1540 (and Resolution 1373 three years earlier[5]), the Council invoked the triggering clause of Article 39 of the Charter, declaring that acts of international terrorism and proliferation of WMD to such actors constitute a threat to international peace and security. It follows that the Security Council now has the primary obligation under the Charter to take steps to remove the threats described in the resolution,[6] and that all states have an obligation to carry out the Council's implementing measures.[7] The initial inquiry, then, turns to what Resolution 1540 requires (and, by extension, Resolution 1718 against North Korea).

The meaning and effect of any Security Council resolution must begin with its text. In this case, the text of the resolution calls upon all states to take certain actions to prohibit and prevent the proliferation of WMD, particularly to non-state actors.[8] The resolution's mandate has three compulsory components. It requires all states, in accordance with their national legal authorities and legislation and consistent with international law, to: (1) refrain from any supporting role in WMD proliferation to non-state actors,[9] (2) enact nonproliferation legislation (i.e., exercise prescriptive jurisdiction),[10] and (3) prevent and punish any violations of the nonproliferation

---

[4]U.N. Security Council Res. 1540, U.N. Doc. No. S/RES/1540 (2004) (reproduced in Appendix C).

[5]In Resolution 1373, the Council had earlier directed all states to, *inter alia,* act to eliminate the supply of weapons to terrorists. U.N. Security Council Res. 1373, para. 2(a), U.N. Doc. No. S/RES/1373 (2001) (reproduced in Appendix B).

[6]*See* Charter of the United Nations, arts. 1(1) & 24. Article 1(1) affirmatively calls for the "removal" of threats to international peace and security.

[7]Although the resolution does not include enforcement procedures, under Article 25 of the Charter, all members of the United Nations have an obligation to accept and carry out the decisions of the Council.

[8]The resolution defines a "non-state actor" as an "individual or entity, not acting under the lawful authority of any State in conducting activities which come within the scope of this resolution." U.N. Security Council Res. 1540, *infra* Appendix C.

[9]The actual text of the Resolution provides that all states shall "refrain from providing any form of support to non-state actors that attempt to develop, acquire, manufacture, possess, transfer or transport nuclear, biological or chemical weapons and their means of delivery..." *Ibid.,* operative para. 1.

[10]The text provides that all states shall "adopt and enforce appropriate effective laws which prohibit any non-State actor to manufacture, acquire, possess, develop, transport, transfer or use nuclear, chemical or biological weapons and their means of delivery, or to attempt, assist or finance such an act, or otherwise act as an accomplice to such acts..." *Ibid.,* operative para. 2.

legislation (exercise enforcement jurisdiction).[11] Resolution 1540 focuses on preventing the transfer of WMD to non-state actors[12] without directly addressing the related problem of transfers to "states of proliferation concern."[13] By contrast, the PSI Statement of Interdiction Principles and the ship boarding agreements between the United States and the governments of several flag states also address proliferation to states of proliferation concern. For example, the agreement between the United States and Liberia, which addresses proliferation to both states and non-state actors, adopts the following definition, taken largely from the PSI Statement of Interdiction Principles:[14] "States or non-state actors of proliferation concern" means those countries or entities that should be subject to interdiction activities because they are or are believed to be engaged in: (1) efforts to develop or acquire WMD or their delivery systems; or (2) trafficking (either selling, receiving, or facilitating) of WMD, their delivery systems, or related materials.[15]

Resolution 1540 provides important guidance on the thorny problem posed by the dual-use character of many materials of WMD concern.[16] It defines WMD and delivery system "related materials" as "materials, equipment and technology covered by relevant multilateral treaties and arrangements, or included on national control lists, which could be used for the design, development, production or use of nuclear, chemical and biological weapons and their means of delivery," thus limiting the class to previously listed materials. It bears repeating, however, that nothing in the governing nonproliferation treaties (NPT, CWC, and BWC) or in the missile technology control regimes categorically prohibits the possession, transfer or transport of dual-use materials. In informal guidance, the United States makes it clear that the PSI is not aimed at legitimate commerce, dual-use or otherwise, and declares that legitimate dual-use commerce "will very rarely be affected by" the PSI.[17] However, the guidance also states that if the United States has adequate information that

---

[11]The text provides that all states shall "take and enforce effective measures to establish domestic controls to prevent the proliferation of nuclear, chemical, or biological weapons and their means of delivery, including by establishing appropriate controls over related material. When necessary states are to develop and maintain appropriate law enforcement efforts to "detect, deter, prevent, and combat" the illicit trafficking and brokering in WMD and their means of delivery, in accordance with their national legal authorities and legislation and consistent with international law." *Ibid.,* operative para. 3.

[12]The non-state actors of greatest concern are the entities listed on the U.N. "consolidated list" produced in response to Security Council Resolutions 1267, 1373 and 1617. U.N. Security Council Res. 1540, *infra* Appendix C, 8th preambular paragraph.

[13]Other regimes, such as the NPT, provide a mechanism for bringing proliferation concerns involving states before the Security Council. *See, e.g.,* U.N. Security Council Resolutions 1696 (Iran) and 1718 (North Korea).

[14]Statement of Interdiction Principles, *infra* Appendix A, operative paragraph 1.

[15]U.S.-Liberia WMD Shipboarding Agreement, *infra* Appendix D, para. 5. Note the qualifying phrase "or are believed to be." This qualifier is not included in the Statement of Interdiction Principles.

[16]U.N. Security Council Res. 1540, *infra* Appendix C.

[17]*See* U.S. Dep't of State, Proliferation Security Initiative, *Frequently Asked Questions,* May 26, 2005, *available at* http://www.state.gov/t/np/rls/fs/46839.htm.

a shipment is destined for an end-use or end-user of proliferation concern, the United States will work to stop that shipment. Thus, dual-use materials will likely be of interest only when accompanied by information indicating a WMD use or user of proliferation concern.[18]

It is clear from the operative paragraphs that Resolution 1540 is intended to supplement and more fully implement existing laws and regimes on disarmament and nonproliferation—as well as the related Security Council resolutions on international terrorism—while also requiring all states that have not already done so to enact "effective" laws to fill gaps in the proliferation regime and to enforce those laws. Those laws must prohibit the manufacture, acquisition, possession, or transfer of WMD, as well as assisting in or financing such acts. The resolution imposes differential obligations on nations in their capacities as port, coastal, flag, and transshipment states. Like the PSI, the resolution contemplates both unilateral and multilateral activities. In calling for all states to develop effective laws as well as border, national export, transshipment, end-user, and physical protection controls to prevent proliferation, Resolution 1540 is fully consistent with and, in fact, complements the PSI in its call for nations to "review and work to strengthen" their relevant national legal authorities where necessary and international law and frameworks in appropriate ways to support these commitments.

In assessing its effect on PSI operations, it is important to note, however, that Resolution 1540 stopped short of conferring on non-flag states any new interdiction authority over vessels engaged in transporting WMD and delivery systems on the high seas.[19] As the Pakistani representative on the Council emphasized, Resolution 1540 is not a piece of international legislation.[20] As drafted, the resolution cannot be enforced by any state extraterritorially against foreign vessels. It does not confer a new right of visit or otherwise interfere with foreign flag vessels, nor does it confer jurisdiction to enforce laws against them.[21] Rather, it calls on states to establish effective export controls and enact national laws providing for the prosecution of actors who supply designs and key elements required to make nuclear, biological, or chemical weapons. Like the national strategies of the United States, the resolution recognizes that some states lack the means necessary to carry out the resolution's call

---

[18]The definition of "related materials" in the U.S.-Liberia WMD Shipboarding Agreement is limited to material "related to *and destined for use in* the development, production, utilization or delivery of WMD," suggesting that any interdiction of dual-use materials must be based on reasonable suspicion of a WMD *use.* The nature of the related materials alone will not be sufficient. *See* U.S.-Liberia WMD Shipboarding Agreement, *infra* Appendix D, art. 1, para. 3.

[19]Given China's insistence that any mention of interdictions be removed from Resolution 1540, there is no reason to believe that the Council will order or authorize more aggressive maritime operations in the near future. *See* Chapter 3.

[20]Cassady Craft, *Challenges of UNSCR 1540: Questions About International Export Controls,* CENTER FOR INTERNATIONAL TRADE AND SECURITY BRIEF, at 5, n.9 (2004).

[21]*See* ROBIN R. CHURCHILL & A. VAUGHAN LOWE, THE LAW OF THE SEA 19 (2d ed. 1999) (observing that "[r]ights pass into customary international law more readily than obligations").

for strengthening control. Under the resolution's terms, such states will be eligible for assistance.

Resolution 1540 has been criticized by some as a vague compromise that fails to provide for enforcement measures commensurate to the risks to international peace and security identified in the resolution. While there is some truth to that assessment, there is little reason to think the Security Council is likely to do more under present circumstances. It does not take much imagination to foresee the fate of future initiatives in the Security Council if the Council's resolutions are seen to be increasingly used legislatively, to address diffuse, ongoing problems, or if those resolutions are providing certain proactive and operationally capable states with the authority to act as what China once denounced as a maritime "world cop."[22]

At the same time, there is a danger in allowing 1540 or similar resolutions directed against individual states to be ignored at a time when the integrity and efficacy of the U.N. system and the NPT regime is being called into question. The Charter calls for *effective* collective measures to *remove* threats to international peace.[23] Having found that the proliferation of WMD presents such a threat, the Council's obligation under the Charter is clear. The fact that the Council remains seized of the issue by the express terms of Resolution 1540 certainly implies it has assumed ongoing responsibility for monitoring implementation and making necessary adjustments to ensure the action is effective. It is an open question, however, whether the Council can muster the consensus necessary to discharge its obligation. The fate of the collective security system may well hinge on how it responds to the combined threats of global terror and WMD proliferation.[24]

A CRIME OF UNIVERSAL JURISDICTION?

Before turning to an examination of law of the sea issues raised by potential maritime counterproliferation operations, it might be helpful to first deal with the suggestion that trafficking in WMD or transporting such weapons or related materials is a crime of universal jurisdiction. The argument can be quickly dismissed. In fact, as the *So San* Scud missile incident described below painfully demonstrates, trafficking in or transporting WMD, related materials, or missile delivery systems might not be a crime at all under any law applicable to the incident.[25] Moreover, the lessons from the *So San* incident could be extended to demonstrate that even if the *transfer* of

[22]Such was China's public reaction to the U.S. concern of the M/V *Yin He* discussed in Chapter 5.

[23]Charter of the United Nations, art. 1(1) (emphasis added).

[24]As U.N. Secretary-General Kofi Annan stated in 2003: "it is not enough to denounce unilateralism, unless we also face up squarely to the concerns that make some states feel uniquely vulnerable. . . We must show that these concerns can, and will, be addressed effectively through collective action. We have come to a fork in the road. This may be a moment no less decisive than 1945 itself, when the United Nations was founded." Kofi Annan, U.N. Secretary-General, *Address to the 58th Session of the U.N. General Assembly*, Sept. 23, 2003, *available at* http://www.un.org/webcast/ga/58/statements/sg2eng030923.htm.

[25]North Korea and Yemen are not parties to the Missile Technology Control Regime, and North Korea is not a party to the 1982 LOS Convention or the 1988 SUA Convention.

WMD or delivery systems to a state or non-state actor of proliferation concern had been a crime, even a crime of universal jurisdiction, it does not follow that the vessel *transporting* the cargo is subject to an enforcement action at sea by any state other than the flag state. In the absence of consent by the flag state (or perhaps a coastal state), any enforcement action would therefore likely have to await the vessel's arrival in a port.

It is safe to say that international law favors jurisdiction founded on either the territorial or nationality principles. Universal jurisdiction, while certainly not an infant theory, is not free from controversy. Moreover, as the discussion in Chapter 7 reveals, some offenses may be universally condemned, and even made the subject of a "prosecute or extradite" obligation, and yet not be enforceable as a crime of universal jurisdiction. Most crimes falling within the terrorism prohibition family, as well as those prohibiting narcotics trafficking, are commonly cited examples. What about activities that are "prohibited" by a Security Council Chapter VII resolution? Renowned Dutch law of the sea scholar Alfred Soons was one of the first to examine the question whether a Chapter VII resolution of the U.N. Security Council confers universal jurisdiction over the matters found by the Council to pose a threat to international peace and security.[26] There can be no categorical answer to the question, for it is clear that the effect of any given resolution must turn on its terms. Presumably, the Council could authorize any and all states to interdict and neutralize a threat to international peace and security. But Security Council Resolution 1540 plainly does not reach that far. It requires all states to prevent and prohibit certain WMD proliferation activities. In some ways, it therefore parallels the international regimes applicable to the transport of slaves or trafficking in narcotic drugs, neither of which is yet a crime of universal jurisdiction.[27]

It is worth observing that even if a colorable argument could be made in favor of a universal jurisdiction to enforce a Security Council ban on transporting WMD to states and non-state actors of proliferation concern, there is no inherent or customary law right of visit to determine if a vessel is in violation.[28] Although many will find it remarkable that the right of visit extends to vessels engaged in unauthorized broadcasting but not to vessels suspected of activities prohibited by the Security Council,

---

[26]*See* Alfred H.A. Soons, *Enforcing the Economic Embargo at Sea,* in UNITED NATIONS SANCTIONS AND INTERNATIONAL LAW 307, 318 (W. Gowlland-Debbas, ed., 2001).

[27]Article 99 of the LOS Convention requires all states to take effective measures to prevent and punish the transport of slaves in ships authorized to fly their flag. Although the Convention does not confer universal jurisdiction over such vessels (as it does for vessels and aircraft engaged in piracy), it does provide for a right of visit in situations where a foreign warship has reasonable grounds for believing a vessel is engaged in the slave trade. LOS Convention, art. 110. Article 108 requires all states to cooperate in the suppression of illicit drug trafficking. Anomalously, however, Article 110 provides no right of visit against a vessel suspected of engaging in such trafficking. The present WMD regime more closely approximates the approach to drug trafficking than the approaches to slave trading or piracy.

[28]The distinction between prescriptive and enforcement jurisdiction is an important one. States other than the flag state might have a valid basis for prescribing laws applicable to an activity condemned by Resolution 1540, while lacking jurisdiction to enforce those laws while the vessel is on the high seas or the coastal waters of another state.

Article 110 is clear in its reach.[29] Accordingly, unless the Security Council resolution itself can be read to permit boardings based on a standard of reasonable suspicion or some other basis, it may well be the case that a vessel operating in contravention of a resolution could escape even a "visit" by any state other than its flag state.

UNILATERAL COUNTERPROLIFERATION OPERATIONS AND THE LAW OF THE SEA

The PSI is a commitment by the participating states to take unilateral actions within their international and national legal authorities as well as a framework for co-operative action. It will be recalled from Chapter 4 that the Statement of Interdiction Principles (SIPs) do not expressly address high seas boardings. The omission certainly does not mean that no WMD interdictions will take place on the high seas. It merely means that any such interdictions will fall within some other framework. For example, a PSI-participating or supporting flag state would have no need to invoke or rely on the PSI framework to board one of its own vessels on the high seas. Indeed, it has an international obligation under the LOS Convention to exercise effective jurisdiction and control over vessels flying its flag and an independent duty to carry out applicable resolutions of the Security Council. In addition, states other than the flag state may carry out unilateral counterproliferation operations on the high seas under the authority of several well-established bases under the international law of the sea. This section addresses two of those bases for conducting high seas boardings: the peacetime right of visit and the stateless vessel doctrine. A third basis, boardings conducted with the consent of the flag state, is discussed below. It is noteworthy that the bilateral PSI ship boarding agreements entered into by the United States were drafted to preserve nonconsensual legal bases for taking action against vessels of the other party,[30] and expressly preserve the internationally recognized right of visit.[31] Accordingly, right-of-visit boardings and actions against stateless vessels continue to operate alongside treaty-based boarding schemes.

THE RIGHT OF APPROACH AND VISIT

As the materials in Chapters 6 and 7 explained, the customary right of approach allows a warship to intercept a vessel on the high seas and determine its nationality.[32] The "approach" generally consists of a visual inspection of the vessel for evidence of its name and nationality, and may also include questions put to the intercepted vessel by loudhailer or radio. Article 110 of the LOS Convention implicitly incorporates

[29]It is also remarkable that many human rights norms set out in the International Covenant of Civil and Political Rights are derogable in times of national emergency under Article 4 of the Covenant, but vessel high seas navigation rights are not similarly derogable.

[30]U.S.-Liberia Ship Boarding Agreement, *infra* Appendix D, art. 4, para. 6.

[31]*Ibid.* art. 4, para. 4.

[32]3 United Nations Convention on the Law of the Sea 1982: A Commentary 237–46 (Satya N. Nandan & Shabtai Rosenne, ed. 1995) [hereinafter "3 UNCLOS 1982 Commentary"].

the customary right of approach, and then turns to the "visit" phases of an interception, for vessels suspected of being within one of the categories enumerated in Article 110. The Article 110 categories are strictly limited, however. Unless the initial approach provides the intercepting vessel with reasonable grounds for suspecting that the approached vessel is either of the same flag as the warship or is stateless, there is no other relevant basis for the warship engaged in counterproliferation operations to proceed to the Article 110 visit phase (scenarios involving WMD-wielding pirates notwithstanding). On the other hand, if the approach confirms the vessel's flag, the intercepting state could then request the flag state's consent to further enforcement actions, as paragraph 4.c of the Statement of Interdiction Principles contemplates.

The M/V *So San* incident demonstrates the efficacy—and limits—of the right of visit, as well as the central role of municipal laws against proliferation.[33] In response to U.S. and British intelligence, the Spanish frigates *Patino* and *Navarra,* operating in support of *Operation Enduring Freedom,* intercepted the M/V *So San* on the high seas, approximately 600 miles from the Horn of Africa.[34] No ship named *So San* appeared in any of the available vessel registries. The vessel was flying no flag at the time of the warships' approach and displayed no indication of its state of registry or home port. In fact, a North Korean flag on its funnel had been painted over, as were the Korean characters for *So San.* Because suspicions regarding the vessel's nationality "remained" at that point in the approach, the Spanish warship attempted to communicate with the *So San* by radiotelephone, a commonly used step in the exercise of the right of approach. The master of the vessel provided only cursory answers to radio questions from the *Navarra.* He indicated that his vessel was carrying a cargo of cement to Yemen. At the last minute, he also claimed that the ship was registered in Cambodia. Consistent with state practice, the MIO forces contacted the Cambodian government to confirm the claim. The government of Cambodia could only confirm that the ship matched the description of a vessel registered in Cambodia under a different name.[35] Concluding that the failure to fly a flag or display a name, together with the unverifiable claim of Cambodian registry, constituted reasonable grounds for suspecting that the ship was without a nationality (i.e., stateless), the *Navarra* chose to exercise the internationally recognized right of a warship to "visit" a vessel on the high seas.[36] Under such circumstances, Article 110(2) authorizes the warship send a boat (or a helicopter) under the command of an officer to board the ship and examine its

---

[33]The 2002 incident was foreshadowed by a similar incident involving two North Korean vessels transporting Scud missiles to Iran in 1992.

[34]The facts are taken primarily from U.S. DEP'T OF STATE, DIGEST OF UNITED STATES PRACTICE IN INTERNATIONAL LAW 2002, at 1052–57 (2003) [hereinafter "DIGEST OF U.S. PRACTICE IN INT'L LAW 2002"]. American and British intelligence satellites had been tracking the vessel since it left the North Korean port of Nampo in mid-November. Daniel H. Joyner, *The Proliferation Security Initiative: Nonproliferation, Counterproliferation, and International Law,* 30 YALE J. INT'L L. 507, 508 (2005).

[35]Although Cambodia could not verify the vessel's registration, it granted conditional consent to the boarding if the vessel was in fact registered in Cambodia.

[36]*See* LOS Convention, art. 110. *See also* Convention on the High Seas, Apr. 29, 1958, art. 22, 13 U.S.T. 2312, 450 U.N.T.S. 82.

documents.[37] If suspicion remains after the documents are checked, the visit detail may initiate a search of the vessel.

Up to this point, the *Navarra's* action cannot be characterized as an exercise of enforcement jurisdiction over the *So San.* It is noteworthy, however, that in light of the multiple conflicting nationality claims by the *So San,* the *Navarra* could have determined that the *So San* was a vessel that could be assimilated to statelessness under Article 92(2).[38] Had the *Navarra* made such a determination, the true flag state of the *So San* would no longer have primary jurisdiction over the vessel, and any other state with a valid basis for exercising jurisdiction could do so.[39] That development may not be as significant as it seems, however. Even if Spanish or U.S. warships had a basis under *international* law for asserting jurisdiction over activities on board the *So San,* any enforcement action would ultimately have to be based on a violation of the enforcing state's *municipal* laws.[40] As the discussion below explains, the only states that will likely have applicable laws under such circumstances are the vessel's flag state and the state from which the illicit cargo was exported. Neither Spain nor the United States fell within those categories.

Once aboard the *So San,* the Spanish boarding team uncovered 15 Scud surface-to-surface missiles[41] and conventional (high-explosive) warheads, along with parts to make eight more missiles and 85 drums of red fuming nitric acid (an oxidizer used in Scud fuel) buried beneath tons of bagged cement. The missiles, which had been sold by the government of North Korea to the government of Yemen, were not listed in the vessel's cargo manifest. Nevertheless, the legal analysts ultimately concluded that no applicable laws prohibited the sale or shipment of Scud missiles from

---

[37]In exercising a right-of-visit boarding, the enforcing vessel is no longer limited to sending boarding teams over by small boat. In contrast to Article 22 of the 1958 Convention on the High Seas, which spoke only of sending a boarding team by boat, Article 110 of the 1982 LOS Convention expressly extends the right of visit to military aircraft and any other duly authorized ships or aircraft clearly marked and identifiable as being on government service. *See* LOS Convention, art. 110(4) & (5).

[38]The LOS Convention does not prescribe procedures for "assimilating" a ship to stateless status. Accordingly, the issue continues to be governed by customary international law. *See* 3 UNCLOS 1982 COMMENTARY, at 127, ¶ 92.6(e).

[39]Under the holding of the *S.S. Lotus* case, the court will not presume a limit on a state's exercise of jurisdiction. Case of the S.S. *Lotus* (Fr. v. Turk.), 1927 P.C.I.J. (ser. A) No. 10, at p. 18 (Sept. 7).

[40]It is widely accepted that, as a policy choice, no state enforces the penal laws of another state. RESTATEMENT (SECOND) CONFLICTS OF LAW § 89 (1971); Banco Nacional de Cuba v. Sabbatino, 376 U.S. 398, 448 (1964) ("Our courts customarily refuse to enforce the revenue or penal laws of a foreign state, since no country has an obligation to further the governmental interests of a foreign state"). When assisting in the enforcement of flag state or coastal state law (as distinguished from the enforcing state's own municipal law), the assisting state will ordinarily limit any law enforcement actions to detaining the vessel and persons onboard on behalf of the flag or coastal state, along with actions necessary for boarding team safety or to prevent destruction of evidence. *See generally* U.S. Coast Guard, MARITIME LAW ENFORCEMENT MANUAL, para. 2.E.4.b, COMDTINST M16247.1C (2003) [hereinafter "COAST GUARD MLEM"].

[41]Scuds are capable of being fitted with conventional high explosive (HE) warheads or with chemical or nuclear warheads. The missiles on the *So San* reportedly had a designed range of roughly 300 kilometers, though some Scuds have a range of 700 kilometers.

North Korea to Yemen.[42] Accordingly, there was no legal basis for seizing the missiles, or taking further actions against the vessel or crew. At the urging of the U.S. Department of State, the *So San* was released and allowed to deliver its cargo to Yemen. The incident and the official positions taken by the involved governments are important developments in affirming the applicable principles of international law.[43]

STATELESS VESSELS

A stateless vessel or one that may, by its conduct, be "assimilated" to statelessness does not enjoy the navigation rights of properly registered vessels.[44] Accordingly, the warships and other properly marked enforcement vessels of any state may "interfere" with their navigation by intercepting and boarding them.[45] Some have argued for a more expansive stateless vessel doctrine under which the vessel's stateless status gives all states jurisdiction over it.[46] The short answer to such arguments is that a vessel's stateless status should not be confused with universal jurisdiction. The legal right to interfere with a vessel's navigation must be distinguished from questions regarding jurisdiction over the vessel. It would be more accurate to say that where a state has an independent basis in international law for exercising jurisdiction over a vessel that turns out to be stateless, there is no state possessed of primacy in the exercise of jurisdiction. Under those circumstances, a state that had a preexisting basis for exercising jurisdiction over the vessel would not be required to defer to the flag state's primary jurisdiction. Any such enforcement action must of course be based on an applicable municipal law that extended to the intercepted vessel or those on board the vessel.

THE PSI STATEMENT OF INTERDICTION PRINCIPLES AND THE LAW OF THE SEA

In the PSI Statement of Interdiction Principles, the participating states pledged to "take specific actions in support of interdiction efforts regarding cargoes of WMD,

---

[42] *Legal Maze over Scud Seizure*, BBC NEWS WORLD ED., Dec. 11, 2002, *available at* http://news.bbc.co.uk/2/hi/middle_east/2565905.stm.

[43] *See, e.g.*, Ari Fleischer, *White House Press Briefing*, Dec. 11, 2002 (reporting that "There is no provision under international law prohibiting Yemen from accepting delivery of missiles from North Korea. While there is authority to stop and search, in this instance there is no clear authority to seize the shipment of Scud missiles from North Korea to Yemen. And therefore, the merchant vessel is being released."), *available at* http://www.whitehouse.gov/news/releases/2002/12/20021211–5.html.

[44] It is unclear whether the legal fiction of "assimilation" strips the flag state of jurisdiction or merely negates the flag state's primacy over any other state with jurisdiction (i.e., it could not protest another state's exercise of jurisdiction). Whatever view one takes of the consequences of statelessness under international law, it does not obviate the need to identify an applicable municipal law basis for a state to take enforcement action.

[45] A true stateless vessel and its crew would appear to have no remedy for prompt release under Article 292 of the LOS Convention, there being no state with standing to bring such an action.

[46] *Soons*, at 311, n. 14.

their delivery systems, or related materials."[47] The "specific actions" are to include vessel boardings at sea and in port. All such boardings are to be conducted in compliance with applicable international and national laws.[48] For selected specific actions, this section examines the factors that must be considered in determining whether PSI activities conform to existing international law. The conclusion to be drawn from the analysis is that the existing legal regime will almost certainly prove inadequate to prevent the states and non-state actors of greatest proliferation concern from obtaining weapons of mass destruction and missile or UAV delivery systems, and that under existing geopolitical conditions, an adequate legal regime is unlikely to emerge in the immediate future. The remaining sections in the chapter turn to the possible alternatives: self-help countermeasures, self-defense, justification by necessity, and interdicting threatening shipments without claiming a legal right to do so.[49] The follow-on questions regarding the international law of state responsibility for acts in violation of international law are examined in Chapter 9.

THE ROLE AND REACH OF THE 1982 LOS CONVENTION

The touchstone for the legality of any maritime interception or enforcement action in offshore waters during peacetime is the conventional and customary law of the sea. Before beginning the analysis, it is important to address the criticism by some opponents of the 1982 LOS Convention who argue that the United States would be hindered in carrying out the PSI activities if it were to become party to the LOS Convention.[50] The argument is flawed, perhaps even intentionally misleading, in several important respects. The most serious flaw lies in the fact that the United States is already legally bound by virtually all of the relevant articles of the 1982 LOS Convention, either because they are part of the earlier 1958 Geneva Conventions on the Law of the Sea, to which the United States is party, or because they reflect existing customary law, to which the United States has announced it will adhere. Even while declining to sign the LOS Convention in 1982, President Reagan announced that the Convention's articles on navigation and other ocean's uses "generally confirm existing maritime law and practice and fairly balance the interests of all states."[51] Virtually every military and government

---

[47] *Statement of Interdiction Principles, infra* Appendix B, para. 1,

[48] *Ibid.* para. 4.

[49] Professor Byers refers to this as the "exceptional illegality" option; the rationale selected by several of the states that chose to intervene in the Kosovo crisis. Michael Byers, Comment, *Policing the High Seas: The Proliferation Security Initiative,* 98 AM. J. INT'L L. 526–45 (2004).

[50] *See* Bipartisan Security Group, *The Proliferation Security Initiative: The Legal Challenge,* at 2, Sept. 2003 ("The primary obstacle to interdicting North Korean shipments [of WMD] is the Law of the Sea Convention, which gives ships the rights of freedom of seas and innocent passage"), *available at* http://www.gsinstitute.org/gsi/pubs/09_03_psi_brief.pdf.

[51] Statement Accompanying Proclamation of Exclusive Economic Zone (Proclamation 5030, Mar. 10, 1983), 19 WEEKLY COMP. OF PRES. DOCS. 383 (1983) [hereinafter "Ocean Policy Statement"].

speaker who testified before the Senate Foreign Relations Committee concluded that the LOS Convention is consistent with the PSI Statement of Interdiction Principles.[52] It is also significant that every other PSI-participating state is a party to the 1982 LOS Convention, and there has been no suggestion that the United States, as the sole non-party, is by that reason legally permitted to take actions which the other states would be barred by the LOS Convention from taking.

The second flaw in the critics' attack on the LOS Convention is that it fails to recognize that the more important "defects" in the existing legal regime are not in the law of the sea but rather in the international and municipal laws governing proliferation. With rare exceptions, the LOS Convention does not prescribe crimes; it merely allocates jurisdiction and control competency for crimes created by other legal authorities. If the nonproliferation prescriptions are deficient in their scope or reach, applicability, or specificity, the law of the sea cannot be blamed for failing to provide an effective basis for interdicting shipments of WMD, their delivery systems, and related materials. The fact is, those shipments may well be just as legal under the manifestly imperfect nonproliferation regime as they are disquieting for states and members of the Security Council. As one commentator observed in analyzing the apparent "shortfall" in the reach of Article 110 for WMD shipments:

> The observation of the logic and jurisprudential correctness of having norms on substantive illegality precede norms on interdiction tends to support arguments for strengthening nonproliferation norms as a matter of great priority and shared emphasis with modern counterproliferation efforts, both in the context of nonproliferation regimes themselves and also as a foundation upon which to build counterproliferation programs.[53]

---

[52] *See* Senate Foreign Relations Committee, Report on the United Nations Convention on the Law of the Sea, S. Exec. Rep. No. 108–10 (Mar. 11, 2004) at 111, reporting the answer given by William H. Taft, IV, Department of State Legal Adviser, to a question by the committee chair, Sen. Richard Lugar, as to whether the terms of the LOS Convention were consistent with the PSI Statement of Principles. Mr. Taft noted that the Principles require that actions taken under the PSI be consistent with relevant international law, which will include the LOS Convention. Admiral Michael G. Mullen, Vice Chief of Naval Operations, added that the PSI Principles and the LOS Convention are "very consistent," and that "[c]learly, the uniformity of approach, both in PSI and what we typically do in our maritime interception operations, that consistency would be very beneficial." *Ibid.* at 112. *See also ibid.* at 49 (statement of Admiral Joseph Prueher, U.S. Navy (ret.), asserting U.S. accession to the LOS Convention will enhance PSI efforts), 64 (statement of Rear Admiral William L. Schachte Jr., JAGC, U.S. Navy (ret.), highlighting importance of LOS Convention Article 110 to maritime interception operations designed to interdict terrorists and WMD), 97 (statement of Mark T. Esper, Deputy Assistant Secretary for Negotiations Policy, Department of Defense). *See also* Congressional Research Service, *The Law of the Sea Convention and U.S. Policy,* CRS Issue Brief IB95010.

[53] Joyner, *The Proliferation Security Initiative,* at 543.

The 1982 LOS Convention is the latest in an ongoing constitutive approach to fashioning an international legal regime.[54] As "New Haven School" practitioner Professor William Burke counsels those who seek to understand the LOS Convention: over time, practice is what will determine the purport of the treaty.[55] State practice serves as an aid in determining the meaning of the treaty and as a potential source of new rules of customary international law.[56] The PSI is an important new source of state practice.

THE PSI STATEMENT OF INTERDICTION PRINCIPLES AND INTERNATIONAL LAW

The PSI is a political commitment, a cooperative framework, and a resource marshalling device. It is also a framework for further development of the national and international legal antiproliferation regime. The activities carried out under the PSI framework and the responses by other states in joining the PSI as a participating state, whether signaling their willingness to be a "supporting state," or protesting the legal right to engage in some PSI activities, together with pronouncements made by organs of the United Nations, the European Union, and the Group of Eight (G-8), are forming a substantial body of state practice regarding PSI operations. Indeed, some already argue that the PSI may lead to new rights under international law.[57]

Two components of the PSI Statement of Interdiction Principles are important in evaluating the effect of emerging state practice on customary law. First, the PSI participants have repeatedly emphasized that their activities will be consistent with international law frameworks, including the U.N. Security Council. Second, the participating states have committed to "work to strengthen when necessary relevant international law and frameworks in appropriate ways to support these commitments." The two commitments demonstrate an intent to respect, and work within, the international legal process without necessarily being satisfied with the existing legal regime. The fact that the United States took the further steps of negotiating bilateral ship boarding agreements with leading flag states while also working with the other members of the Security Council to craft a Chapter VII

---

[54]Harold D. Lasswell & Myres S. McDougal, Jurisprudence for a Free Society pt. IV, ch. 1 (1992) (describing the attributes of a constitutive process). A constitutive approach is particularly important when there is no effective legislative body at the international level to timely create new law to meet changing conditions.

[55]William T. Burke, *State Practice, New Ocean Uses, and Ocean Governance under UNCLOS,* in Ocean Governance: Strategies and Approaches for the 21st Century 222–23 (Thomas A. Mensah, ed., 1996).

[56]William T. Burke, *Threats to the Public Order of the Ocean,* in International Navigation: Rocks and Shoals Ahead? 384, 385 (Jon Van Dyke, et al., eds., 1988) (observing that "the premise that the Law of the Sea Convention was going to end the development of law by customary means was an illusion in the first place").

[57]*Byers,* at 528. Professor Byers does not, however, believe it will lead to a new rule justifying WMD boardings of foreign flag vessels on the high seas without the flag state's consent.

resolution to address some of the gaps in the existing international regime demonstrates its commitment to abide by the respect-but-improve principle embodied in the SIPs.

> ***SIP Chapeau:*** ***PSI participants are committed to the following interdiction principles to establish a more coordinated and effective basis through which to impede and stop shipments of WMD, delivery systems, and related materials flowing to and from states and non-state actors of proliferation concern, consistent with national legal authorities and relevant international law and frameworks, including the UN Security Council. They call on all states concerned with this threat to international peace and security to join in similarly committing to:***

The title of the "Interdiction Principles for the Proliferation Security Initiative" conveys the intent of the participating states to engage in future *interdictions.* The *chapeau* anticipates Resolution 1540 in the need to break the flow of WMD, delivery systems, and related materials to states and non-state actors of proliferation concern. It makes it clear that the participating states have committed to the principles that follow and calls upon other states that choose to support the PSI to also follow those principles. At the same time, it indicates that any actions taken within the PSI framework will be consistent with national legal authorities and relevant international law and frameworks, including the U.N. Security Council.

> ***SIP ¶ 1:*** ***Undertake effective measures, either alone or in concert with other states, for interdicting the transfer or transport of WMD, their delivery systems, and related materials to and from states and non-state actors of proliferation concern. "States or non-state actors of proliferation concern" generally refers to those countries or entities that the PSI participants involved establish should be subject to interdiction activities because they are engaged in proliferation through: (1) efforts to develop or acquire chemical, biological, or nuclear weapons and associated delivery systems; or (2) transfers (either selling, receiving, or facilitating) of WMD, their delivery systems, or related materials.***

The first operative paragraph following the *chapeau* acknowledges that PSI actions will be both unilateral and multilateral. Interdictions will target states and non-state actors of proliferation concern, which are loosely defined in the SIPs. It seems likely that class of non-state actors "of proliferation concern" at the very least includes all of the entities on the Security Council's consolidated list.[58] All states are already prohibited by binding Security Council resolutions from providing them with arms of any kind. Resolution 1540 extends that ban to WMD, their delivery systems, and related materials.

---

[58] *See* U.N. Security Council Resolution 1540, *infra* Appendix C, 8th preambular paragraph (expressly referring to non-state actors "such as those identified in the United Nations list established and maintained by the Committee established under Security Council resolution 1267 and those to whom resolution 1373 applies . . .").

Interdictions of WMD shipments to states "of proliferation concern" might give rise to several legal challenges. First, because the Security Council did not expressly refer to *states* of proliferation concern in Resolution 1540, the PSI-participating states will find only limited cover in the resolution.[59] A second problem concerns the practice of discriminating among states based on assessments about whether they present a "proliferation concern." *Prima facie,* all states enjoy the same rights and protections under international law. One state cannot curb the internationally protected rights of another state simply by labeling it a "rogue state." More specifically, the LOS Convention includes numerous nondiscrimination injunctions. Because the LOS Convention articles on innocent and transit passage include express nondiscrimination provisions, the nondiscrimination issues raised by PSI activities are discussed in the section on SIP ¶ 4.d, which addresses PSI activities in a coastal state's adjacent waters.

***SIP ¶ 2:** Adopt streamlined procedures for rapid exchange of relevant information concerning suspected proliferation activity, protecting the confidential character of classified information provided by other states as part of this initiative, dedicate appropriate resources and efforts to interdiction operations and capabilities, and maximize coordination among participants in interdiction efforts.*

Sharing relevant information presents no international law issues. It may, however, implicate the municipal laws of some states, such as the U.S., where intelligence sharing is restricted by constitutional and statutory measures.[60] Information sharing presents a practical problem as well, particularly if it may disclose the sources or methods for gathering intelligence, or it comes from a foreign intelligence source. A similar problem will arise when a state is asked to present the information that forms the "reasonable suspicion" for requesting consent to board or for proving the basis for a claim of necessity, self-help, or self-defense. Although some existing alliances, such as NATO, have in place procedures for intelligence sharing, there are no present plans to turn the PSI into a new intelligence sharing forum.

***SIP ¶ 4.** Take specific actions in support of interdiction efforts regarding cargoes of WMD, their delivery systems, or related materials, to the extent their national legal authorities permit and consistent with their obligations under international law and frameworks.*

Paragraph 4 of the SIPs establishes the central pillars of the PSI's political commitment to counter the growing threat of WMD proliferation. It calls on participating states to "take specific actions." The commitments contemplated by the SIPs include the following:

---

[59]Paragraphs 3(c) and 8 of the resolution are not limited to non-state actors.

[60]*See* Chapter 5.

***SIP ¶ 4.a.** Not to transport or assist in the transport of any such cargoes to or from states of non-state actors of proliferation concern, and not to allow any persons subject to their jurisdiction to do so.*

Paragraph 4.a of the SIPs largely echoes the duty of all flag states under Resolution 1540.[61] In fact, the resolution requires nothing less (at least with respect to transfers to non-state actors). To the extent that actions taken under Paragraph 4.a single out states of proliferation concern, such actions raise the same issues regarding nondiscrimination under the LOS Convention and WTO/GATT. Denying a nonnuclear weapon state access to some materials might also infringe on the target state's "inalienable right" under Article IV of the Nuclear Nonproliferation Treaty "to develop research, production and use of nuclear energy for peaceful purposes without discrimination."

Paragraph 4.a reaches beyond transportation or assistance by the state itself, by requiring the participating states to prohibit "persons subject to their jurisdiction" from transporting WMD cargoes to or from states of proliferation concern. For flag states, "persons subject to their jurisdiction" could include not only the master and crew of the vessel, but also the vessel owner and charterer. The fact that Paragraph 4.a extends the prohibitions to those who may "assist" in the transport of WMD cargoes makes it broad enough to reach shoreside brokers, freight forwarders, cargo handlers, and lenders or banks that facilitate the transaction.

***SIP ¶ 4.b.** At their own initiative, or at the request and good cause shown by another state, to take action to board and search any vessel flying their flag in their internal waters or territorial seas, or areas beyond the territorial seas of any other state, that is reasonably suspected of transporting such cargoes to or from states or non-state actors of proliferation concern, and to seize such cargoes that are identified.*

Paragraph 4.b addresses boardings by flag states in any waters outside the jurisdiction of another state. It affirms the flag state's obligation and its primacy in asserting jurisdiction and control over vessels flying its flag. Such boardings are consistent with the LOS Convention and the obligations imposed by other applicable international laws and Resolution 1540. It is well known, however, that not all states will be fully able or willing to carry out their obligations under this paragraph or Resolution 1540. States lacking the "ability" to conduct the necessary inspection and enforcement actions are encouraged by Paragraph 4.c (below) to seriously consider granting consent to another state to carry out the action. Liberia, the second-largest flag state, but which lacks a navy, was an early example of a state that chose the 4.c agreement path.

Paragraph 4.b, like several others, raises questions regarding the quantum of suspicion necessary to justify PSI actions. It can be seen that rules imposing a higher

[61]Actions carried out under this paragraph are consistent with U.N. Security Council Resolution 1540, paragraphs 3(c) and 10, at least with respect to non-state actors.

quantum give greater protection to the shared interest in freedom of navigation, while those with low standards would tend to increase the frequency of interference. The PSI Statement of Interdiction Principles uses two standards for triggering PSI actions: "good cause" in the first clause of paragraph 4.b, and "reasonable suspicion" in the penultimate 4.b clause and in paragraphs 4.d and 4.f.[62] Neither standard is defined in the SIPs, but analogues for those phrases can be found in the LOS Convention. The United States informally asserted that the test for "good cause" is a subjective one. The Department of State explains that in responding to requests for action under paragraph 4 of the Principles, "each state will decide for itself whether good cause has been shown; that is, each state will need to decide for itself whether the information provided by the requesting state warrants acceding to the request."[63] In assessing the quantum of suspicion necessary to support a finding of "reasonable suspicion," or "reasonable grounds for believing,"[64] it may be helpful to refer to Article 110 of the Law of the Sea Convention,[65] which uses similar language in setting out the right of visit under international law. Reasonable suspicion is tested by an objective standard. The reasonable suspicion standard must be distinguished from more stringent standards, such as the requirement for "clear grounds for believing" under Article 220(2) and "clear objective evidence" under Article 220(6).[66] Finally, it is important to bear in mind that if it is later determined that a state undertaking enforcement action lacked an adequate basis under international law for its actions, the state will likely bear international responsibility for any losses suffered.[67]

A final point raised above and in Chapter 5 concerns the practical and perhaps legal problems that might be triggered if the "good cause" or "reasonable suspicion" showing required disclosure of classified or otherwise sensitive intelligence. One can easily imagine situations in which a hostile state being asked to cooperate in a PSI interdiction would lodge endless demands for intelligence held by the requesting state under the pretext that the information is necessary for it to make an independent assessment as to whether the reasonable suspicion standard is satisfied. If forced to choose between disclosing intelligence that might reveal its sources or methods—particularly

---

[62] Statement of Interdiction Principles, *infra* Appendix A, para. 4. Reasonable suspicion is the same standard used in the bilateral boarding agreements between the United States and several flag states.

[63] U.S. Dep't of State, *PSI Frequently Asked Questions.*

[64] *Cf.* LOS Convention, art. 108 ("reasonable grounds for believing"). Article 111 of the LOS Convention, which codifies the right of hot pursuit, adopts a "good reason to believe" standard.

[65] *Ibid.* art. 110.

[66] *See generally* Robert C. F. Reuland, Note, *Interference with Non-National Ships on the High Seas: Peacetime Exceptions to the Exclusivity of Flag-State Jurisdiction,* 22 VAND. J. TRANSNAT'L L. 1161, 1172 n.26 (1989) (concluding that it is probably not possible or prudent to attempt to be precise in formulating the standard of suspicion).

[67] *See, e.g.,* LOS Convention, art. 110(3), which provides: "If the suspicions prove to be unfounded, and provided the ship boarded has not committed any act justifying them, it shall be compensated for any loss or damage that may have been sustained." *See also* LOS Convention, art. 111(8). This standard may be contrasted with the analogous remedy in Part XII of the LOS Convention, which imposes liability on states taking enforcement action against a foreign vessel where the measures were "unlawful or exceed those reasonably required in the light of available information." *Ibid.* art. 232.

if the source is another state's intelligence agencies or assets—or withholding the information, knowing that it will therefore be unable to discharge its burden of proof, most states will choose the latter course of action, particularly if it has reason to doubt that consent will be granted even if the additional information is provided.

SIP ¶ 4.c. ***To seriously consider providing consent under the appropriate circumstances to the boarding and searching of its own flag vessels by other states, and to the seizure of such WMD-related cargoes in such vessels that may be identified by such states.***

Subparagraphs 4(b) and 4(c) of the PSI Statement of Interdiction Principles provide a framework for participating and supporting states to grant their consent to boardings by other states. Such agreements provide a state that is willing but, for some reason, unable to exercise effective jurisdiction and control over its vessels with an option to call in help. The approach honors the flag state's primacy while guarding against the threat posed by vessels that would otherwise operate with impunity.

Although the common shorthand ascribes to vessels a freedom of navigation, properly speaking the navigation rights are possessed by the flag state, not the vessel. Any rights on the part of the vessel are derivative of the flag state. As a result, the flag state can waive the right. The flag state's waiver operates as consent to another state interfering with the vessel's navigation in a manner that would otherwise violate Article 110 of the Convention or the rights of innocent or transit passage. Moreover, at least in the United States, the vessel and its crew will likely be denied standing to independently allege a violation of the flag state's international rights as a defense to an enforcement action.[68] Boardings conducted with the consent of the flag state have a well-established pedigree, having been used in nineteenth-century efforts to interdict vessels engaged in the slave trade and later in the Prohibition Era in the United States. More recently, the flag state consent to stop-and-search operations approach is being applied in the counter-narcotics, illegal migrant smuggling, and high seas fisheries enforcement contexts.[69] Many of those agreements include similar "presumed consent" provisions, under which the flag state's consent may be inferred if it does not object in the time period established in the agreement.

Six flag states, Belize, Croatia, Cyprus, Panama, Liberia, and the Marshall Islands, collectively representing more than 60 percent of the world's shipping capacity by tonnage, have already entered into bilateral agreements with the United States that will allow the United States to conduct PSI boardings of vessels flagged in those states while in international waters. Like the bilateral counter-narcotics ship boarding agreements on which the PSI boarding agreements are modeled, the PSI agreements fall squarely within the language of Article 110 of the LOS Convention and are consistent with the obligations imposed by other applicable international laws and Resolution 1540. Interestingly, the bilateral ship boarding agreements entered into

---

[68] *See* United States v. Postal, 589 F.2d 873 (5th Cir.), *cert. denied,* 444 U.S. 832 (1979).

[69] The enforcing state must already have a basis for asserting concurrent jurisdiction with the consenting state, as is the case in many crimes subject to "prosecute or extradite" obligations.

by the United States so far take what might be characterized as a two-step approach. In the first step, the flag state expressly or tacitly consents to the other state "interfering" with the navigation rights of its vessels by conducting a boarding and search of the vessel.[70] In the second step, the flag state may choose to "waive" its "primary right to exercise jurisdiction" over the vessel and permit the boarding state to exercise its own jurisdiction.[71] As Chapter 7 highlighted, the fact that a flag state consents to a boarding does not in itself confer on the boarding state jurisdiction over the vessel. Nor will it always be clear what law should be applied if potential violations are discovered. As stated above, no state enforces the penal laws of another state. Accordingly, any enforcement action must be grounded in the enforcing state's municipal law, or the vessel and its cargo must be delivered to another state with jurisdiction and applicable municipal laws. It determining what municipal laws are applicable, it will be recalled from Chapter 7 that there is ample authority for the proposition that the flag state can consent to another state exercising jurisdiction over its vessels and applying its municipal law to them; however, the flag state's consent to a boarding does not necessarily carry with it the further consent to exercise jurisdiction to enforce the laws of the boarding state.

> ***SIP ¶ 4.d.* To take appropriate actions to (1) stop and/or search in their internal waters, territorial seas, or contiguous zones (when declared) vessels that are reasonably suspected of carrying such cargoes to or from states or non-state actors of proliferation concern and to seize such cargoes that are identified; and (2) to enforce conditions on vessels entering or leaving their ports, internal waters or territorial seas that are reasonably suspected of carrying such cargoes, such as requiring that such vessels be subject to boarding, search, and seizure of such cargoes prior to entry.**

Paragraph 4.d addresses boardings by coastal states in waters over which they exercise jurisdiction. Whether such boardings are consistent with the LOS Convention will turn on the vessel's location and the status of the vessel's passage. As suggested earlier, the flag state's consent to interference with a vessel's navigation or transit rights must be distinguished from the flag state's waiver of primacy in the exercise of jurisdiction over vessels flying its flag.[72] Where jurisdiction is concurrent with

---

[70] *See, e.g.*, Bilateral WMD Shipboarding Agreement, U.S.-Liberia, *infra* Appendix D, art. 4 (authority to board in international waters).

[71] *Ibid.* art. 5. The legal effect of flag state consent was raised in a contentious exchange in 1990 between the United States and Cuba after the United States attempted to board the Panamanian ship M/V *Hermann* on the high seas with the consent of the Panamanian government. The Cuban master and crew refused to submit to the boarding, apparently under instructions from the Cuban government. Cuba later protested the U.S. enforcement action to the U.N. Security Council. The U.S. replied that because Cuba was not the vessel's flag state it had no standing. U.S. DEP'T OF STATE, DIGEST OF UNITED STATES PRACTICE IN INTERNATIONAL LAW 1989–1990, at 452–56 (2003). The U.S. position is fully consistent with the ITLOS decision in the *M/V Saiga* case.

[72] In cases where jurisdiction is concurrent among two or more states and international law does not grant either primacy with respect to the other, any conflict must be resolved by application of comity or negotiation.

another state, the flag state (or the coastal state in whose waters the vessel is located) may elect to waive its jurisdictional primacy; however, such a waiver does not "transfer" to or otherwise confer jurisdiction on another state. Moreover, the enforcing state will almost certainly not be enforcing the laws of the flag state or any other state. Accordingly, any exercise of jurisdiction must be based on the state's own municipal laws and, at least in the eyes of the international community, on one of the accepted customary law bases.

Paragraph 4.d does not address the developing practice by which a coastal state grants consent to a state other than the flag state to take enforcement actions in the coastal state's territorial sea. The NATO states participating in *Operation Active Endeavor* have, in fact, been pursuing such authority from coastal states throughout the Mediterranean, and the United States is reportedly pursing similar agreements. The LOS Convention does not directly address whether a coastal state may authorize a third state to take actions in its waters; however, a U.S. circuit court decision has upheld such an arrangement.[73] Like other consensual arrangements, a coastal state's consent would not confer jurisdiction on the enforcing state to take action under its law. And, of course it is axiomatic that the coastal state cannot, by consent, grant what it does not possess. Thus if the coastal state would be barred from taking action against a vessel in innocent or transit passage, any consent to a third state taking such action would be ineffective.

PSI BOARDINGS AND THE RIGHT OF INNOCENT PASSAGE

Counterproliferation operations by a coastal state (or a third state to whom the coastal has granted consent to take enforcement) against a foreign vessel have the potential to come into a conflict with the vessel's right of innocent passage, unless the vessel's flag state has consented to the action. Article 25 of the LOS Convention recognizes that a coastal state may take the necessary steps in their territorial sea to prevent passage which is not innocent. As Chapter 7 points out, whether a vessel has a right of innocent passage turns on two inquiries. First, it must be determined whether the vessel is engaged in "passage" within the meaning of Article 18. If the vessel is in passage, the inquiry turns to the manner of that passage, in order to determine whether it is innocent under the test set out in Article 19. In the PSI context, the principal legal issues are likely to focus on the second, "innocence" prong of the test.

Article 19 contains two operative paragraphs. The first provides the general rule that passage is innocent "so long as it is not prejudicial to the peace, good order or security of the coastal State." The second paragraph then lists 12 activities that are presumed to be prejudicial to the coastal state's peace, good order or security, if engaged in by the passing vessel while in the coastal state's territorial sea. The United States and the former Soviet Union have taken the position that the list in the second

[73] *See* United States v. Conroy, 589 F.2d 1258, 1267–68 (5th Cir.) (upholding Coast Guard enforcement action in Haitian territorial sea with Haiti's consent), *cert. denied,* 444 U.S. 831 (1979).

paragraph is exhaustive; a transiting vessel that does not engage in any of the listed activities is in innocent passage.[74] However, nothing in that bilateral understanding suggests that either state considered the possibility that a transiting vessel might be engaged in an activity that has been condemned by the U.N. Security Council as a threat to international peace and security.

Application of Article 19 to PSI boardings raises at least two questions. The first is whether under Article 19(2)(a), the foreign vessel's passage must constitute a threat to the coastal state's own security to render the passage non-innocent. For example, could coastal state *A,* acting on intelligence that a foreign vessel is *en route* to state *B* with WMD, invoke Paragraph 2(a) of Article 19 and declare the vessel's passage non-innocent? Although some renowned commentators have reached a contrary conclusion,[75] the text of the article suggests the answer is no. To reach that conclusion, it is essential to give full effect to the *chapeau* in Paragraph 2 of Article 19 when construing subparagraph 2(a). The *chapeau* seems to make it clear that the list that follows sets out the activities that "shall be considered to be prejudicial to the peace, good order or security *of the coastal State."* None of the *travaux préparatoires* examined suggests that a threat to a third state was to be considered prejudicial to the coastal state.[76] However, the inquiry does not end there, because in the PSI context there is now a relevant declaration by the U.N. Security Council regarding the threat WMD proliferation poses to international peace, potentially including the peace and security of all nations.

The follow-on question, therefore, concerns whether a vessel transporting a cargo in contravention of Resolution 1540 threatens international peace and security, and is therefore not engaged in "innocent" passage, or the passage is not taking place in conformity with international law.[77] As to the effect of operating in violation of a prohibition contained in a Security Council resolution, as Professor Soons concludes with respect to Security Council embargoes "[i]t would seem beyond doubt that the coastal state would not be acting unlawfully if it took action against foreign ships violating [a Security Council embargo] while they are in innocent passage or in transit passage through an international strait."[78] Analysis of the "violation of international law" issue under Article 19(2) (and the parallel language in Article 39(1)(b) applicable to vessels in transit passage) is often muddied by the fact that Article 19

[74]*See* Chapter 7.

[75]Churchill & Lowe, at 85 (concluding that the text of Article 19(2)(a) "is wide enough to encompass threats directed against States other than the coastal State."). In reaching that conclusion, the authors do not analyze whether it is consistent with the law of neutrality.

[76]*See* 2 United Nations Convention on the Law of the Sea 1982: A Commentary 158–63 & 164–78 (Satya N. Nandan & Shabtai Rosenne, ed. 1993) [hereinafter "2 UNCLOS 1982 Commentary"].

[77]LOS Convention, art. 19(1). There is some question whether Security Council resolutions are a source of international law. The controversy is often sidestepped by grounding the "legal" argument on Article 25 of the Charter—clearly a source of law—which requires all states to comply with resolutions of the Council.

[78]*Soons,* at 323–24. Professor Soons notes that the issue was briefly discussed in the Second Committee during the Third U.N. Conference on the Law of the Sea. *Ibid.* at 324, n.53.

addresses activities by vessels that may or may not be public vessels. Arguments that a non-public vessel's conduct might violate "the principles of international law embodied in the Charter of the United Nations" must be careful to distinguish the rights and obligations of states under international law from those applicable to non-state actors and nonpublic vessels.

Even if a vessel is in innocent passage, the coastal state is not without legal authority to prescribe and enforce laws applicable to such vessels. Moreover, in the case of foreign vessels proceeding to internal waters or a port facility outside internal waters, the coastal state also has the right to take the necessary steps to prevent the breach of any applicable conditions of entry.[79] The conditions might include requirements for advance notice of arrival, advance transmission of a complete cargo manifest and crew list, carriage and operation of identifying electronic beacons, and even pre-arrival boardings and searches. There are, however, limits on the coastal state's jurisdiction over foreign vessels in innocent passage, particularly those not en route to the coastal state's ports or internal waters. Article 21, for example, imposes a number of limits on the coastal state's prescriptive jurisdiction with respect to foreign vessels in innocent passage. Those limits are somewhat extended, however, by the Article 23 provisions applicable to foreign ships carrying nuclear or other inherently dangerous or noxious substances. Nevertheless, Article 23 must be viewed as a recognition that vessels transporting nuclear or other inherently dangerous cargoes are not by that fact alone denied the right of innocent passage.[80]

Maritime counterproliferation operations in the territorial sea must also be mindful of the coastal state's duties under Article 24 and its rights under Article 25. It bears emphasizing that these two articles only apply to vessels engaged in innocent passage. The Article 24 prohibition against hampering a vessel's innocent passage protects the common interest in freedom of navigation. Coastal state practices barred by the article can be broken down into an "excessive requirements prong" and a "nondiscrimination prong." The nondiscrimination prong prohibits discrimination "in form or fact against the ship of any State or against ships carrying cargoes to, from or on behalf of any State."[81] The LOS Convention's nondiscrimination prong—also codified in the WTO/GATT agreements—gives effect to the principle of sovereign equality among states. As mentioned earlier, any interdiction that turns on the flag of the vessel or the origin or destination of the cargo (the pledge to stop and/or search in their territorial seas vessels that are reasonably suspected of carrying such cargoes "to or from states or non-state actors of proliferation concern") implicates the nondiscrimination principle. On the other hand, risk assessment necessarily must include an inquiry of the willingness of the state to use WMD. The port state

[79]LOS Convention, art. 25(2).

[80]CHURCHILL & LOWE, at 88–92. The authors do, however, report some discrepant state practice and objections by other states.

[81]Attempts by the coastal state to instead rely on its Article 25 power to temporarily suspend the innocent passage of such vessels on the ground that the suspension is "essential for the protection of its security" must similarly conform to the nondiscrimination principle in Article 25(3).

control regime implemented to enhance maritime safety and environmental protection has long operated on the principle of risk assessments that vary by the vessel's flag, type, owner, and cargo. To conform PSI boardings to existing "international law and frameworks" the PSI participating states must be prepared to demonstrate a principled, nondiscriminatory basis for applying the "proliferation concern" standard, much like the port state control regime did for maritime safety issues. "Proliferation concern" must focus not on perceptions of actual or potential hostility toward the interdicting state, but rather on the target state's adherence to and enforcement of generally accepted nonproliferation norms. Presumably, targeting states that are either not a party to widely accepted nonproliferation regimes or which are known to support or permit the transfer or transport of WMD and delivery systems to non-parties[82] or to non-state actors, or states in which proliferation networks operate with apparent impunity, would not violate the nondiscrimination standard.

Article 27 of the LOS Convention restricts the coastal state in its exercise of enforcement jurisdiction over persons on vessels in innocent passage through the territorial sea. It does not, however, limit the coastal state's jurisdiction over individuals who commit crimes while in state waters.[83] Operative paragraph 1 of Article 27 is cast in non-mandatory language, admonishing that the coastal state "should not" exercise criminal jurisdiction over an offense occurring on a foreign vessel during its innocent passage through the coastal state's territorial sea, unless the crime falls into one of the four enumerated categories. By contrast, operative paragraph 5 is cast in mandatory language, barring the coastal state from exercising jurisdiction over crimes that occurred before the vessel entered the territorial sea (unless the ship is leaving the coastal state's internal waters[84]). The International Law Commission explained the rationale and effect of the limitations on coastal state's criminal jurisdiction when it commented on what eventually became the parallel provision in the 1958 Convention on the Territorial Sea and Contiguous Zone:

> In such a case a conflict of interest occurs; on the one hand, there are the interests of shipping, which should suffer as little interference as possible; on the other hand, there are the interests of the coastal State, which wishes to enforce its criminal law throughout its territory. The coastal State's authority to bring the offenders before its courts (if it can arrest them) remains undiminished, but its power to arrest persons on board ships which are merely passing through the territorial sea is limited to the cases enumerated in this article.[85]

---

[82]*See, e.g.,* Nuclear Non Proliferation Treaty, art. III(2). Formulating a convincing nondiscriminatory test for missile transfers to states of proliferation concern will be particularly problematic because there is as yet no binding nonproliferation agreement on missile technology. A similar problem is likely to undermine attempts to formulate a standard applicable to dual-use materials.

[83]This includes crimes committed in the coastal state's internal waters, or violations of coastal state laws applicable in the contiguous zone, under Parts V or XII of the Convention. LOS Convention, art. 25(5).

[84]*See ibid.* art. 27(2).

[85]*Report of the International Law Commission Covering the Work of its Eight Session,* U.N. Doc. A/3159, article 20 Commentary, para. (1), 2 1956 Y.B. INT'L L. COMM'N 253, 275.

Operative paragraph 1 is unlikely to interpose an obstacle to a coastal state in its exercise of jurisdiction to enforce a criminal law proscribing the illicit transportation of WMD in the state's territorial sea. Security Council Resolution 1540 can reasonably be read as giving rise to a presumption that transporting illicit WMD poses a hazard to international peace and security, and therefore logically is also the kind of crime that disturbs the peace of the coastal state or the good order of the territorial sea. The more significant issue could be paragraph 5 of Article 27, which bars the coastal state from taking steps to board a foreign ship in innocent passage to arrest any person or conduct an investigation in connection with a crime that occurred before the vessel entered the territorial sea. In construing and applying that paragraph it will be important to distinguish completed crimes, such as unlawful sale or export, from ongoing or continuing crimes, such as possession or transporting of a contraband substance.[86] A crime that is ongoing while the vessel is transiting the territorial sea occurs in the territorial sea within the meaning assigned by Article 27.

PSI BOARDINGS AND THE RIGHT OF TRANSIT PASSAGE

Maritime counterproliferation operations against vessels engaged in transit passage through international straits, such as the Straits of Malacca, Dover, and Gibraltar, will face additional legal hurdles beyond those that apply to operations involving vessels in innocent passage. The coastal state's prescriptive jurisdiction over vessels in transit passage is more circumscribed than its jurisdiction over vessels in innocent passage.[87] There is, for example, no express coastal state regulatory authority with respect to vessels transporting nuclear or other inherently dangerous or noxious substances while in transit passage.[88] On the other hand, the coastal state may prescribe laws necessary to implement generally accepted international standards, such as SOLAS and the ISPS, INF, and IMDG Codes.

The coastal state's enforcement options when a transiting vessel violates coastal state laws prescribed in accordance with Article 42 of the LOS Convention or the prohibitions in Article 39 are also limited. Although nothing in the transit passage regime expressly limits the coastal state's enforcement jurisdiction,[89] as does Article 27 for vessels in innocent passage, one would expect that the more solicitous transit passage regime would not countenance a greater degree of interference than does the innocent passage regime. For that reason, scholars have read Articles 34 and 38 to incorporate into the transit passage regime the limits on the coastal state's exercise

[86] 2 UNCLOS 1982 COMMENTARY, at 237–43.
[87] *Compare* LOS Convention, arts. 21–25 *with* arts. 41–42
[88] Ships in transit passage must, however, comply with generally accepted international regulations for the safety at sea. *Ibid.* art. 39(2).
[89] Professors Churchill and Lowe conclude that the Convention's silence of the coastal state's enforcement jurisdiction over vessels in transit passage leads to the conclusion that the general territorial sea rules apply, under which enforcement should only be exercised where the good order of the territorial sea or coastal state is disturbed or the flag state or master requests assistance. CHURCHILL & LOWE, at 108–09.

of criminal enforcement jurisdiction set out in Article 27, applicable to vessels in innocent passage.[90]

If the vessel engages in any activity that is not an exercise of transit passage, it remains subject to the other applicable provisions of the Convention,[91] thus defaulting to the innocent passage regime.[92] Accordingly, if the nature of the vessel's activities renders its passage non-innocent, the coastal state is free to take the necessary steps to protect its interests.

PSI BOARDINGS IN THE CONTIGUOUS ZONE

Within the contiguous zone, the coastal state may exercise the control necessary to prevent or punish infringement of its customs, fiscal, immigration, and sanitary matters within its territory or territorial sea.[93] The requirement for vessels transporting nuclear or other inherently dangerous or noxious substances to carry documents, observe special precautionary measures established by international agreement, and confine their passage to designated sea lanes while in innocent passage could be classified as a customs measure, enforceable in the contiguous zone, if the vessel will pass through the state's territorial sea.[94] By extension of Article 25, the coastal state could also exercise control over a foreign vessel in the contiguous zone to prevent an infringement of a condition of entry for vessels bound for the internal waters or a port within the coastal state.[95] For foreign vessels not bound for the internal waters of the coastal state, Article 33 is otherwise not likely to add significantly to the coastal state's jurisdiction over vessels transporting WMD. Indeed, an aggressive use of the contiguous zone authority is likely to be criticized as an illegitimate attempt to extend the limited contiguous zone regime to coastal state security matters.

PSI PURSUITS INTO COASTAL STATE WATERS

A recurring issue raised in littoral regions is whether enforcement actions begun in international waters can be continued into the territorial sea of a third state. The conventional doctrine of hot pursuit expressly provides that pursuit must be terminated if the pursued vessel enters the territorial sea of its flag state or a third state,[96] at least

---

[90]Ivan A. Shearer, *The Development of International Law with Respect to the Law Enforcement Role of Navies and Coast Guards in Peacetime,* 71 U.S. Nav. War Coll., Int'l L. Studies 429, 432–33 (1998).

[91]LOS Convention, art. 38(3).

[92]Churchill & Lowe, at 107.

[93]LOS Convention, art. 33. As the PSI shipboarding agreements acknowledge, jurisdiction over vessels in a state's contiguous zone is concurrent at least between the coastal and flag state, and extends to third states in some circumstances. *See* U.S.-Liberia WMD Shipboarding Agreement, *infra* Appendix D, art. 5(2).

[94]LOS Convention, arts. 22(2) & 23. The argument is stronger as to the requirement to carry documents (which are akin to manifests) than the requirement to observe IMO or IAEA precautionary measures.

[95]*Ibid.* arts. 25 & 33. Those conditions might include carriage and operation of AIS or LRIT vessel identification and tracking equipment.

[96]*Ibid.* art. 111(3).

in the absence of consent by the coastal state. The U.S. Navy *Commander's Handbook on the Law of Naval Operations* posits a customary law right to pursue a fleeing pirate vessel into the territorial sea of a third state after first making "every effort" to obtain the consent of the coastal state.[97] The rationale for the putative right is the "international nature of the crime of piracy may allow continuation of pursuit if contact cannot be established in a timely manner with the coastal state to obtain its consent."[98] The *Handbook* adds that pursuit must be terminated immediately if the coastal state objects and that, in any event, the right to seize the pirate ship and prosecute the pirates devolves upon the coastal state. Finally, the *Handbook* asserts that warships may pursue pirate vessels through international straits overlapped by territorial seas or through archipelagic sea lanes with or without the consent of the coastal states, so long as the pursuit is expeditious and direct and the navigation rights of other vessels is not unreasonably constrained in the process.[99] The *Handbook* cites no authority (state practice or *opinio juris*) for its assertion,[100] and the claim is for that reason of doubtful validity.

SIP ¶ 4.f. ***If their ports, airfields, or other facilities are used as transshipment points for shipment of such cargoes to or from states or non-state actors of proliferation concern, to inspect vessels, aircraft, or other modes of transport reasonably suspected of carrying such cargoes, and to seize such cargoes that are identified***

Paragraph 4.f addresses port state boardings and inspections, an activity subject to virtually no limits under the LOS Convention—at least for vessels not entitled to sovereign immunity. In fact, for over a decade port state control boardings of foreign vessels to confirm compliance with international safety and environmental protection requirements have been aggressively employed. Such boardings do not impinge on navigation rights and can be conducted so as to minimize any impact on freight mobility. Port state boardings recognize that flag states have very little control over their vessels and their cargo operations while in foreign ports. Accordingly, to comply with its obligation under Resolution 1540, a flag state is virtually required to rely on port state enforcement of cargo-related laws and regulations.

All states have independent duties under Resolution 1540 to prevent proliferation of WMD, delivery systems, and related materials to non-state actors of proliferation concern. Port states may meet their obligation by effective enforcement of materials' safeguards and national and multilateral export control regimes. Effective enforcement with respect to dual-use materials will likely require export and transshipment states to engage in cooperative monitoring and enforcement measures with destination states to verify the legitimacy of the end-use and end-user.

---

[97] ANNOTATED SUPPLEMENT TO THE COMMANDER'S HANDBOOK OF THE LAW OF NAVAL OPERATIONS, at para. 3.5.3.2 (1997) [hereinafter "ANNOTATED COMMANDER'S HANDBOOK"].

[98] ANNOTATED COMMANDER'S HANDBOOK, at para. 3.5.3.2.

[99] *Ibid.*

[100] Even if there were such a rule at one time, it has likely lapsed through desuetude. *See* Michael J. Glennon, *How International Rules Die,* 96 GEO. L.J. 939, 941–42 (2005).

Port state boardings done in compliance with any applicable FCN treaty and GATT-WTO provisions will rarely present international law issues. Moreover, such inspections are subject to more liberal search and seizure standards under U.S. municipal laws. The U.S. Supreme Court has held, for example, that a warrantless, suspicionless search of a vehicle crossing the border does not violate the Fourth Amendment.[101] Robert Bonner, U.S. Customs and Border Protection Commissioner, said the decision, which expressly cited 19 U.S.C. § 1581(a), also applied to searches of cargo containers at ports. He hailed the decision as vital to the success of his bureau's mission to intercept terrorists.[102]

A JUSTIFICATION FOR SELF-HELP COUNTERMEASURES?

The contours and limits of a state's right to resort to countermeasures are subject to considerable debate; a debate that is likely to be even more contentious when those countermeasures touch on a matter over which the Security Council has announced that it remains seized. The customary law of countermeasures has so far not been extended to precautionary or preventative countermeasures prior to a breach, even if the breach may be said to be imminent. Moreover, under existing customary law, the predicate for countermeasures is a *state's* breach of its international law obligations. The orthodox view holds that unless the illicit WMD materials were being transported on a public vessel, or their transfer or transportation is otherwise "attributable" to a state, the legitimacy of any resort to the customary law of countermeasures is subject to serious doubt. However, given that the customary law of self-defense has now been extended to non-state actors, particularly international terrorist organizations, and that such organizations are the object of several Security Council resolutions, an argument can be made that self-help measures may also be taken against non-state actors, alone or in conjunction with self-defense and law enforcement measures. In fact, some argued for the role of self-help measures in counterproliferation strategies well before the September 11, 2001, attacks.[103]

In most cases likely to arise in the PSI context, the most likely basis for arguing "state action" will be the failure of the relevant state to discharge its international obligations as a flag state or under an applicable U.N. Security Council resolution. Neither is likely to trigger a right of self-help. The principal weakness in the argument that a flag state's breach of its obligation to exercise effective jurisdiction and control is that the LOS Convention prescribes procedures to be followed in such cases. The availability of those specific procedures militates against a concurrent right to exercise countermeasures to obtain relief. Those who suggest that a third-party state might, as a countermeasure, refuse to recognize the vessel's registration,

---

[101]United States v. Flores-Montano, 541 U.S. 149 (2004).

[102]Robert Motley, *Suspicionless Inspections,* AM. SHIPPER (May 2004), at 90.

[103]Guy B. Roberts, *The Counterproliferation Self-help Paradigm: A Legal Regime for Enforcing the Norm Prohibiting the Proliferation of Weapons of Mass Destruction,* 27 DENVER J. INT'L L. & POL'Y 483 (1999).

notwithstanding the clear purport of Article 92, in a manner roughly similar to "piercing" a corporate veil, face a nearly insurmountable burden of conventional law and tribunal decisions. Nevertheless, they might be aided by a movement that seeks to overcome flag state jurisdictional primacy impediments to non-flag state enforcement actions against high seas fishing scofflaws through a mixture of *lex lata* and *lex ferenda.*[104]

Attempts to rely on a generalized right to invoke self-help remedies against states in breach of a U.N. Security Council resolution would have to overcome three potential legal hurdles. First, any rights or powers conferred by the resolution must be set out in the text or fairly implied by that text. The text of Resolution 1540 neither requires flag states to grant consent to enforcement boardings by other states, nor does it grant non-flag states the authority to conduct such boardings without the flag state's consent. In fact, the record of the Security Council deliberations on Resolution 1540 confirms that at least one of the veto-wielding members of the Council opposed granting any new authority for maritime interdictions. Second, in most of the relevant resolutions, the Security Council remains seized of the matters addressed. In doing so, the Council arguably retains control over any questionable interpretations of the means and methods that may be used by any state acting under authority of that resolution. Finally, as even Professor Soons acknowledges in suggesting that a state might resort to countermeasures if a flag state refused consent to a boarding to enforce a Security Council measure (and thereby breached its international law obligation under the resolution), it is not necessarily the case that all states are empowered to enforce such resolutions.[105] States that are so empowered will find their authority in the resolution itself and the U.N. Charter, and need not rely on the controversial self-help rationale.

In assessing the potential role of the self-help doctrine, it is also important to distinguish the various justifications or defenses for a state's conduct that would otherwise be unlawful from the sources of the state's jurisdiction over a vessel, location, or activity. Even if an intercepting state was able to demonstrate that its actions in apparent violation of freedom of navigation and flag state primacy rules were legally justified, or that the actions fell within the ambit of lawful self-help or self-defense measures, that would not, in itself, confer jurisdiction over the foreign vessel or cargo. The most that could be said is that the justification precludes the apparent wrongfulness of the intercepting state's interference with the vessel's freedom of navigation or its exercise of an independent basis for concurrent jurisdiction, in apparent violation of the flag state's primacy.

---

[104] *See generally* Rosemary Gail Rayfuse, Non-Flag State Enforcement in High Seas Fisheries (2004) (arguing that a customary law exception to flag state primacy is emerging in the high seas fisheries context). In analyzing state practice it is important to distinguish enforcement actions taken under claim of a legal right to do so—evidence of an emerging rule of customary law—from a breach of existing law, based not on a claim of right but rather on principles of necessity or other exigent and compelling circumstances.

[105] *Soons,* at 317, n.33 & 318.

A JUSTIFICATION FOR SELF-DEFENSE MEASURES?

Although the question posed above is impossible to answer in the abstract, a serviceable answer is that reasonably foreseeable PSI activities will almost never fall within the customary law right of self-defense.[106] The reason does not directly lie in the divisive debate over whether the appropriate response to large-scale transnational terrorism should follow the law enforcement or self-defense paradigm. As nation-states lose their historical monopoly on the large-scale use of force, the line between police actions and self-defense measures blurs. It is true that the fact that Resolution 1540 calls on all states to prohibit the transport of WMD and enforce the prohibition through criminal or civil penalties argues in favor of a law enforcement approach. Congress has also expressed its "sense" that WMD proliferation calls for "enhanced" law enforcement efforts to identify and disrupt proliferation networks, activities and organizations.[107] At the same time, however, it is obvious to most that the destructive magnitude of terrorist attacks and their international character call for resources, intelligence capabilities, and extraterritorial operations that are beyond the capabilities of law enforcement agencies. Moreover, a law enforcement approach cannot reach the conduct of states that sponsor or support terrorism. The fact that acts of terrorism are crimes does not preclude a state from supplementing its law enforcement agencies with national intelligence and defense assets. The common goal of all public safety and defense forces is to provide a level of protection commensurate to the threat and to respond to terrorist attacks as necessary and proportional.

The principal difficulty in placing reliance on the inherent right of self-defense rationale would lie in trying to reach agreement on a working definition of the conditions that would be sufficient to invoke the right in response to a shipment of WMD materials.[108] It is not the mere existence of WMD and related materials aboard a vessel that presents a risk to a nation's security. It is the risk that those WMD materials might come into the possession of a rogue regime or terrorist organization. Possible PSI scenarios range from the shipment of dual-use components to a suspicious end-user who might combine those components with many others to construct a weapon, to an incoming vessel carrying a fully assembled nuclear device consigned to a notorious terrorist group. Frankly, a state's response to the second scenario is unlikely to be delayed or clouded by an extended discussion

---

[106]The potential use of government-owned vessels to transport WMD or missile delivery systems poses a legal and political risk that is fundamentally different from the risks associated with privately owned merchant vessels. Like warships, vessels owned or operated by the government and used only for government noncommercial service enjoy "complete immunity" wherever located. *See* LOS Convention, arts. 32 & 96; *see also* The Schooner *Exchange* v. McFadden, 11 U.S. (7 Cranch) 116 (1812). When in the territorial sea, such vessels may be directed to leave. *Cf.* LOS Convention, art. 30. On the other hand, actual involvement of public vessels directly involves the vessel's flag state and implicates possible self-help and self-defense remedies.

[107]Intelligence Reform and Terrorism Prevention Act of 2005, § 1022(e), codified at 50 U.S.C.A. § 404o-1 (West 2005).

[108]Some argue that if the right of self-defense extended this far it might be invoked, for example, by India against Pakistan, or Iran against Israel.

of legal rationales for interdicting and neutralizing the device.[109] It is just as unlikely that any state that respects, and benefits from, freedom of navigation and cargo mobility is going to contemplate any action under the first scenario without the consent of the flag state or, failing that, a port state when the vessel arrives to discharge the cargo.[110] The multitude of scenarios falling between those extremes will be the ones that challenge the existing international legal frameworks.

Ultimately, however, any discussion of whether PSI interdictions can be justified as an act of self-defense will likely be dismissed because it begs the question whether conducting a PSI interception boarding even constitutes a use of armed force against the territorial integrity or political independence of a state. Put another way, the analysis rushes to answer the Article 51 question without first determining whether the PSI boarding and interdiction constitutes a use of armed force under Article 2 (4) of the Charter.[111] For example, in an article appearing shortly after the PSI was launched, two London writers confidently opined that:

> If the US knew that a given North Korean ship or aircraft was carrying plutonium outside the country, it would simply stop it, justifying the action as self-defence under Article 51 of the UN charter. Since North Korea has recently threatened to export plutonium, since it has a history of exporting weaponry to nasty customers and since the US has been attacked by a terrorist organization that has a stated desire for nuclear weapons, the legal and political cases would be solid.[112]

It is submitted that the fallacy in the journalists' analysis is that it presumes that stopping a vessel's transport of plutonium constitutes the use of armed force under Article 2(4). The triggering event for a boarding is not an armed attack (actual or imminent), but rather suspicion of illicit activity. Any force used is not intended to vanquish an enemy, but rather to compel compliance with the exercise of law enforcement authority. Distinguished academic commentators distinguish the use of police force from armed force. Nothing in the decisions by the International Court of Justice in the *F/V Estai* case or by the International Tribunal for the Law

---

[109] *See National Defense Strategy of the United States of America* 9–10, Mar. 1, 2005, *available at* http://www.defenselink.mil/news/Mar2005/d20050318nds2.pdf:

> Under the most dangerous and compelling circumstances, prevention might require the use of force to disable or destroy [weapons of mass destruction] in the possession of terrorists or others or to strike targets (e.g., terrorists) that directly threaten the United states of U.S. friends or other interests.

[110] One key benefit of the PSI is that it provides a system for marshalling the legal and operational capabilities of a number of states, enabling the participants to identify the state or states with the necessary capabilities.

[111] The 9/11 Commission Report quipped that the "FBI and the Justice Department do not have cruise missiles. They declare war by indicting someone." *Final Report of the National Commission on Terrorist Attacks Upon the United States* 82 (2004).

[112] *See* Michael Levi & Michael O'Hanlon, *A Global Solution is Needed for Illicit Weapons,* FIN. TIMES, July 11, 2003.

of the Sea in the case of the *M/V Saiga* suggests the contrary is true, even if force is used to conduct the boarding.

AN OTHERWISE ILLEGAL INTERFERENCE JUSTIFIED BY NECESSITY?

The necessity "defense" to international responsibility has been derisively characterized as the last desperate grasp for cover by the leaders of a state that felt impelled to take action in almost certain violation of international law, and when no other justification for the action is available. The critics might be surprised at the arguments of President Thomas Jefferson, who argued that:

> A strict observance of the written laws is doubtless one of the high duties of a good citizen, but it is not the highest. The laws of necessity, of self-preservation, of saving our country when in danger, are of higher obligation. To lose our country by a scrupulous adherence to written law, would be to lose the law itself, with life, liberty, property and all those who are enjoying them with us; thus absurdly sacrificing the end to the means.[113]

As the materials in Chapter 9 explain, the International Court of Justice has not entirely ruled out a role for the necessity justification; however, the Court has set the bar for prevailing on the justification so high that any state bearing the burden of proof on the justification faces an almost insurmountable challenge.[114] The International Law Commission's Draft Articles on State Responsibility have similarly adopted a restrictive view of the necessity defense.[115] The International Tribunal on the Law of the Sea adopted the ILC Draft Articles definition of necessity in its decision in the *M/V Saiga* case.[116]

Some view the necessity justification as a natural supplement to the self-defense doctrine in the post–U.N. Charter era. In cases not involving an actual or imminent armed attack, but nevertheless posing a grave and imminent peril to the essential interests of a state, a proportional response to abate the threat would be seen as justified, thereby precluding a finding of state responsibility. While a tempting source of cover, the necessity justification comes at a cost. The first, discussed above in several other contexts, is the need to disclose the information or intelligence that gave rise to the claimed necessity. The second is the effect on customary law of even claiming that the state's actions were justified by necessity. Past tribunal and arbitral decisions and the ILC Commentary to the Draft Articles on State Responsibility give

---

[113]THOMAS JEFFERSON, THE WRITINGS OF THOMAS JEFFERSON 279 (Paul Ford, ed. 1898).
[114]*See* Gabčíkovo-Nagymaros Project (Hung. V. Slovk.), 1997 I.C.J. REP. 7, 40–41, paras. 51–52 (Sept. 25).
[115]*See* Draft Articles on State Responsibility, art. 25. *See also* International Covenant on Civil and Political Rights, art. 4(1) (adopting a "strictly required by the exigencies of the situation" test for derogation from certain human rights).
[116]*See* Chapter 9 for an examination of the ICJ and ITLOS decisions and the ILC Draft Articles.

little reason to believe that a necessity defense is likely to succeed. As a matter of state practice, asserting that otherwise illegal actions were justified by necessity is also likely to erode well-established principles regarding navigation freedoms and the role of flag states.

WHAT MIGHT THE 2005 PROTOCOL TO THE SUA CONVENTION ADD?

The provisions of the 2005 Protocol to the SUA Convention calling for states-parties to prohibit the transport of WMD by sea and to prosecute or extradite those who violate its provisions are discussed in Chapter 7. To facilitate enforcement of the new WMD maritime transport prohibitions, the Protocol also prescribes procedures for one party to the amended SUA Convention to follow in situations where it desires to board a ship flying the flag of another party.[117] A state-party that has reasonable grounds to suspect that a ship or a person on board the ship is, has been, or is about to be, involved in the commission of an offense under the SUA Convention, may request the cooperation of the flag state and authorization to board the vessel. The Protocol requires the flag state, if a party to the Protocol, to cooperate to the fullest extent possible and to respond to requests as expeditiously as possible. At the same time, it makes it clear that express authorization by the flag state is required before the requesting state may conduct such a boarding,[118] unless there exists some other legal authority to conduct the boarding, such as a right of visit.[119] Because the Protocol does not authorize boardings without the flag state's authorization, and the flag state is free under the Protocol to withhold authorization, the boarding scheme under the Protocol closely parallels the existing scheme under Article 108 of the LOS Convention for the interdiction vessels suspected of transporting illicit drugs.

The 2005 SUA Protocol includes two options that permit a flag state to modify the above described *ad hoc* consent procedure.[120] The first alternative provides that a party may, with respect to ships flying its flag, authorize a requesting state to board and search the ship, its cargo, and persons on board, in any case where the flag state has not responded to the request within four hours of acknowledgement of receipt of the request. Under the second alternative, the flag state authorizes, in advance, other parties to the Protocol to board and search its ship, their cargo, and persons on board, and to question the persons on board to determine if an offense under the SUA Convention has been, or is about to be, committed. The flag state is free to withdraw from either option at any time. It is too early to predict whether any flag states of interest are likely to adopt either option.

---

[117] 2005 Protocol to the SUA Convention, *infra* Appendix E, art. 8, para. 2 (adding Article 8*bis* to the SUA Convention).

[118] *Ibid.* art. 8*bis*, para 5(c).

[119] *Ibid.* art. 8*bis*, para. 11.

[120] *Ibid.* art. 8*bis*, para. 5(d). The alternatives are invoked by notifying the IMO Secretary-General.

Although the IMO member-states' action in adopting the Protocol is an important development in the evolving global proliferation security regime, the short answer to the question posed by the title of this section is that the likely effect of the 2005 SUA Protocol—should it enter into force—will likely be more notional than operational. A widely ratified treaty banning the transportation of illicit WMD materials will have a laudable norm-generating effect,[121] particularly if the instrument is seen as a logical and carefully crafted response to Security Council Resolution 1540. However, its operational relevance will be limited to those states that choose to sign it, ratify it, enact the necessary implementing laws, and discharge their obligations in good faith, in light of the Protocol's object and purpose. But the fact that the states of greatest proliferation concern will likely not be parties to the Protocol, and that the Protocol cannot be said to reflect customary law, will mean that shipments of the kind that top the world's worry list will be beyond the reach of the Protocol. The states involved in the *BBC China* interception discussed in Chapter 4 did not require a legally binding instrument to signal the responsible course of action to take in response to a common danger, and the states involved in the sale and transport of the missiles aboard the M/V *So San* are not likely to conclude that it is in their interest to ratify the SUA Protocol. Because a treaty binds only those states party to it (unless it reflects a codification of customary law),[122] the SUA Protocol could not be invoked by third-party states as a sufficient legal authority to conduct a boarding of a vessel flagged in a state that is not party to the Protocol.

POTENTIAL LIABILITY OF MASTER, CREW, AND OWNER OF VESSEL

When a boarding team discovers that a vessel is transporting WMD, their delivery systems, or related materials to a state or non-state actor of proliferation concern, the intercepting state must determine whether a seizure or arrest of the vessel and its crew is legally justified.[123] In assessing the potential civil or criminal liability of a vessel or its owner, master or crew, the sale or transfer of the illicit cargo must be distinguished from its transport. It is possible, indeed likely unless the governing legal standard imposes strict liability on transporters, that a vessel transporting what turns out to be WMD materials is not violating any applicable laws.[124] It is therefore significant

---

[121]*Cf.* North Sea Continental Shelf cases (F.R.G. v. Neth./F.R.G. v. Den.), 1969 I.C.J. Rep. 3, 69 (Feb. 20) (observing that a multilateral treaty may be seen as "reflecting, or as crystallizing, received or at least emergent rules of customary international law"). However, a state that persistently objected to the emerging rule would not be bound. *See* Anglo-Norwegian Fisheries case, 1951 I.C.J. Rep. 116, 131 (Dec. 18).

[122]Vienna Convention on the Law of Treaties (1969), arts. 34 & 38.

[123]Several related issues, including rights of foreign crew members under the International Covenant for Civil and Political Rights, the Vienna Convention on Consular Relations, potentially applicable bilateral consular treaties, and the applicability of national protections for privacy and due process rights, must be considered, but are beyond the scope of this project.

[124]In this section the "applicable laws" are those that apply to vessels, non-state entities, and individuals, not international laws applicable to states.

that the 2005 Protocol to the SUA Convention will, if it enters into force, limit its prohibition on the maritime transport of WMD to situations in which the person acted unlawfully and intentionally, "knowing" the illicit nature or intended use of those materials.[125]

If the boarding team determines there is probable cause to believe one or more of the persons aboard the vessel are engaged in criminal activity, the officials from the intercepting state generally have two options: arrest and prosecute the individuals for violating the laws of the intercepting state or, if requested, detain the individuals until they can be delivered to officials of another state with jurisdiction over the offense. The governing law applicable to the probable cause determination will be the municipal law of states with jurisdiction over the vessel and perhaps any state where the cargo is loaded or transshipped. Under U.S. law, a shipper or transporter could incur civil or criminal liability in cases involving smuggling goods into the United States or a foreign nation,[126] false oral, written, or documentary statements regarding the vessel's cargo,[127] bringing or possessing explosive or other dangerous weapons aboard a U.S. flag ship,[128] transferring or possessing chemical weapons,[129] or biological weapons,[130] transporting explosives without a license,[131] obstructing justice,[132] and conspiracies to violate the laws.[133] If the materials are destined for a terrorist organization, the transporter might also face prosecution under a variety of statutes prohibiting certain terrorist acts and providing support for terrorists.[134] Some civil and criminal statutes include provisions for seizure and/or *in rem* liability on the part of the vessel and the forfeiture of assets used in committing the violation.

It must be emphasized that the foregoing list of potentially applicable criminal laws is included only to suggest the range of possible offenses. Each of the criminal or civil offenses listed has elements, including jurisdictional requirements, which must be met. In nearly every case, some nexus with the United States is required, and application of those laws to a foreign vessel is likely to require close coordination among various agencies within the government.[135] Parties to a WMD materials transfer might also face prosecution for violating municipal laws restricting the export of such materials. It will also be recalled that in the United States, federal crimes are "solely creatures of statutes,"[136] (not common law, treaty, or customary

[125] 2005 SUA Protocol, *infra* Appendix E, art. 4 (adding Article 3*bis* to the SUA Convention).
[126] 18 U.S.C.A. §§ 545–546 (West 2005).
[127] *See, e.g.*, 18 U.S.C.A. § 1001 (West 2005); 19 U.S.C.A. §§ 1581(c), 1584 (West 2005).
[128] 18 U.S.C.A. § 2277 (West 2005).
[129] 18 U.S.C.A. § 229(a) (West 2005).
[130] 18 U.S.C.A. § 175 (West 2005).
[131] 18 U.S.C.A. § 842(3) (West 2005).
[132] 18 U.S.C.A. § 1505, 1510 (West 2005).
[133] 18 U.S.C.A. §§ 371–372 (West 2005).
[134] *See* 18 U.S.C.A. §§ 2331–2339C (West 2005).
[135] Within the United States, counterproliferation operations in the maritime domain will likely be coordinated in part by the National Counter Proliferation Center, perhaps in conjunction with the National Security Council, using procedures prescribed in the Maritime Operational Threat Response plan.
[136] United States v. Liparota, 471 U.S. 419, 423 (1985).

law) and that U.S. courts will ordinarily not enforce the penal laws[137] or revenue laws[138] of another state. Unless a universally enforceable ban on transportation of WMD materials and/or requirement for complete and accurate cargo manifests emerges, and states like the United States and its PSI partners enact those universal prohibitions into their municipal law, enforcement actions against vessels and their crews will likely be limited to flag states and port states.

DISPOSITION OF SEIZED VESSEL AND MATERIALS

The Proliferation Security Initiative Statement of Interdiction Principles do not directly address disposition of any materials discovered in the course of an interception. The U.S. Department of State has announced that if illicit materials are discovered in the course of a PSI operation the disposition of the materials will depend on the precise circumstances of the particular case.[139] In operations carried out pursuant to one of the bilateral shipboarding agreement, the agreement expressly addresses the disposition of the vessel and cargo.[140] Similarly, if and when the 2005 Protocol to the SUA Convention enters into force, it will provide for flag state primacy in jurisdiction over the vessel, cargo, and persons on board, even when the boarding is conducted by another state.[141] It is likely that similar provisions regarding seized cargo and vessels will apply to actions carried out under an *ad hoc* agreement with the flag state outside the SUA framework.

The cargo's legitimacy in this context turns on three issues: the nature of the cargo itself, its intended end-use, and its end-user. Some WMD and delivery systems are categorically martial, with no peaceful use. If such materials are destined for a state or non-state actor of proliferation concern, they clearly fall within the ambit of the SIPs. However, the majority of the materials likely to be encountered will fall into the dual-use category. Under such circumstances the intercepting state will have to consider both the nature of the materials and their intended end-use.[142] The U.S. Department of State has attempted to reassure those involved in the sale or transport of legitimate dual-use materials by explaining:

> The PSI seeks to halt efforts by states and non-state actors of proliferation concern to ship or receive WMD, their delivery systems, or related materials. If we have adequate information that a shipment is destined for an end-user of proliferation concern, we will

---

[137]The *Antelope,* 23 U.S. (10 Wheat.) 66, 123 (1825).

[138]Pasquantino v. United States, 544 U.S. 349 (2005).

[139]U.S. Dep't of State, *PSI Frequently Asked Questions.*

[140]*See, e.g.,* U.S.-Liberia WMD Shipboarding Agreement, *infra* Appendix D, arts. 8 & 12.

[141]2005 SUA Protocol, *infra* Appendix E, art. 8 (adding Article 8*bis*, para.8, to the SUA Convention). The Protocol further provides that "the flag State may, subject to its constitution and laws, consent to the exercise of jurisdiction by another state having jurisdiction under article 6."

[142]The end-use inquiry turns on two issues. First, the identity of the end-user must be considered to determine whether a dual-use cargo is legitimate or not. Second, the emerging global counterproliferation scheme targets WMD materials destined for states and non-state actors "of proliferation concern."

> work to stop that shipment, consistent with national legal authorities and international law and frameworks.
>
> PSI participants will not stop and inspect every shipment that might involve items that could be used in proliferation program. Our intent is to take action based on solid information regarding shipments that we believe are destined for states or non-state actors of proliferation concern. Legitimate dual-use commerce will very rarely be affected by PSI.[143]

Historically, in situations where diversion or detention is justified, vessels subject to interdiction by MIO forces have been diverted to a port chosen by the interdicting state.[144] It should be noted, however, that no enforcement action can be taken against the vessel in the port selected unless that state has jurisdiction over the offense. The mere presence of the vessel will not necessarily confer jurisdiction over WMD transfer or transport violations on the port state. The LOS Convention embraces the principle that in most cases a detained or arrested ship and crew must be promptly released upon the posting of adequate security. Although not directly applicable to PSI interdictions, it is noteworthy that Article 225 of the LOS Convention imposes a duty on states that detain a foreign vessel for marine pollution violations. Among other things, that article directs that the enforcing state shall not, in its enforcement action, endanger the safety of navigation or otherwise hazard the vessel, or bring it to an unsafe port or anchorage.[145] Similarly, Article 25 requires a coastal state in its exercise of criminal jurisdiction in the territorial sea to have due regard for the interests of navigation.[146] There is every reason to believe that those sound principles reflect a generally applicable rule of customary law. Moreover, those principles have been incorporated into the 2005 Protocol to the SUA Convention.[147] The detaining state's duties are discussed more fully in Chapter 7.

---

[143]U.S. Dep't of State, *PSI Frequently Asked Questions.*

[144]The measures that imposed sanctions on Iraq following its invasion of Kuwait required the maritime interception forces to report diversions and seizures to the U.N. Sanctions Committee; however, that committee did not control disposition of the vessels diverted or their cargoes.

[145]LOS Convention, art. 225. The enforcement articles for violations in the territorial sea or of marine living resources laws applicable in the EEZ contain no similar provision.

[146]*Ibid.* art. 25. *See also* 2 UNCLOS 1982 COMMENTARY, at 243, ¶ 27.8(e) ("This repeats one of the main themes of the Convention, that of ensuring the safety and freedom of navigation").

[147]2005 Protocol to the SUA Convention, *infra* Appendix E, art. 8, para. 2 (adding Article 8*bis* to the SUA Convention).

9

Compensating the Innocent: State Responsibility and Liability for Unjustified Boardings

The international law of state responsibility deals with the means and measure by which a state may enforce its rights when that state or one of its nationals is harmed by another state's violation of international law. The sources of law potentially applicable to substantive and procedural issues regarding state responsibility under international law, and to the liability of states under municipal laws, are almost as numerous as those governing the issues regarding the rights and obligations of port, coastal, flag, and interdicting state analyzed in the preceding chapters. This chapter provides an outline of relevant law, to alert policy makers and analysts to the responsibility and liability issues that must be considered in counterproliferation decisions.[1] Those called upon to make and execute counterproliferation decisions must be mindful of the potential magnitude of the commercial losses that could flow from various interception, boarding, diversion, and inspection scenarios. For example, a one-week delay of a large container ship loaded with cargo destined for consignees who rely on just-in-time deliveries from their supply chain is certain to carry a staggering price tag if all of the direct and indirect costs are included. The friction costs to the global trade and transportation system if such occurrences were anything more than isolated and exceptional would be far more damaging.

It is not difficult to imagine circumstances in which a state might feel so threatened by a WMD shipment that it believes it must act to interdict the shipment even if it is uncertain whether there is an adequate legal basis for doing so. Under such circumstances, the state would bear responsibility for the consequences of any conduct that

[1]For a more thorough review see MALCOLM N. SHAW, INTERNATIONAL LAW chs. 14 & 18–19 (2d ed. 2003) and ROBIN R. CHURCHILL & A. VAUGHAN LOWE, THE LAW OF THE SEA ch. 19 (3d ed. 1999).

proved to be internationally wrongful. This chapter takes the position that damages payable for counterproliferation actions that are found to have violated international law must be considered a cost of the interdicting states' strategic choices and must be promptly paid if the program is to be seen as legitimate. Moreover, states carrying out maritime counterproliferation activities must abide by established methods for resolving disputes and make reparations in appropriate circumstances. Accordingly, the measure of potential reparations that must be factored into any interception decision should never be overlooked.

State responsibility and liability are established by both conventional and customary sources, which developed against several background principles, including the widely followed but poorly defined doctrine of sovereign immunity. Under customary law, a state responsibility claim arises when an act or omission attributable to a state violates a duty owed under international law to another state and causes injury to the claimant state or one of its nationals.[2] The doctrine has no application to claims between a state and its own nationals or vessels. The 1982 LOS Convention includes a number of situation-specific provisions that impose responsibility on states for unwarranted or unreasonable enforcement actions.[3] On the state-to-state level, reparations for acts or omissions in violation of international law can be sought through a variety of processes, ranging from low-level diplomatic negotiations to formal adjudications before international tribunals. Alternatively, an injured shipowner or cargo shipper might seek compensation through national courts, an approach that often raises questions regarding sovereign immunity and perhaps the act of state doctrine.

STATE RESPONSIBILITY UNDER CUSTOMARY INTERNATIONAL LAW

The International Court of Justice articulated the principle of state responsibility in the 1928 *Chorzów Factory* case, in which the court explained that "it is a principle of international law, and even a general conception of law, than any breach of an engagement involves an obligation to make reparations," even if the underlying treaty does not expressly mention such a duty.[4] The court explained that reparation is "the indispensable complement of a failure to apply a convention."[5] For roughly five decades,

---

[2]*See generally* 8 MARJORIE M. WHITEMAN, DIGEST OF INTERNATIONAL LAW, ch. XXIV (1965).

[3]Other treaties, including, for example, those in the IMO and WTO-GATT families, as well as bilateral friendship, commerce, and navigation treaties, may impose international obligations the breach of which might implicate state responsibility.

[4]Factory at Chorzów, (Ger. v. Pol.) 1928 P.C.I.J. (ser. A) No. 17, at 29 (Sept. 13). The court held that "reparation must, as far as possible, wipe out all the consequences of the illegal act and reestablish the situation which would, in all probability, have existed if that act had not been committed." *Ibid.* at 47. *See also* The *Virginius* case (1873), reported in JOHN BASSETT MOORE, DIGEST OF INTERNATIONAL LAW, 1906, vol. 2, at 895 (claim concerning Spanish warship's interdiction of a U.S. flag vessel being used to transport arms to Spanish-held Cuba and the execution of 53 of its crew members).

[5]*Ibid.*

the International Law Commission (ILC) has been at work preparing what has come to be called the Draft Articles on State Responsibility.[6] The final version of the Draft Articles, which represents both codification of customary law and progressive development of that law, is founded on the principle that every internationally wrongful act of a state entails the international responsibility of that state.[7] An internationally wrongful act consists of an act or omission attributable to the state under international law that constitutes a breach of an international obligation of the state.[8] The ILC Draft devotes eight articles to attribution principles.[9] The obligations on which a state responsibility claim may be predicated may be owed to another state, a group of states, an international organization, or "to the international community as a whole"[10] (i.e., an *erga omnes* norm). Whether an act or omission is internationally wrongful is governed solely by international law.[11] Internationally wrongful acts can consist of a violation of customary international law, a treaty, the U.N. Charter, or even a mandatory resolution of the Security Council. However, a state's act or omission does not constitute a breach of an international obligation unless the state is bound by the obligation at the time the act or omission occurs.[12] The temporal element in that standard may implicate the circumstances under which a state may no longer be bound by a treaty due, for example, to a material breach by the other party, impossibility, or under the *rebus sic stantibus* doctrine.[13] A state's conduct will not give rise to responsibility where it was justified by consent,[14] self-defense,[15] *force majeure,*[16] distress,[17] or necessity.[18] In addition, countermeasures taken by a state in

---

[6]Draft Articles on Responsibility of States for Internationally Wrongful Acts, adopted by the International Law Commission at its Fifty-third session (2001), U.N. GAOR, 53d Sess., Supp. No. 10, U.N. Doc. A/56/10 (2001) [hereinafter "Draft Articles on State Responsibility"]. The Commentary to the Draft Articles is reproduced in THE INTERNATIONAL LAW COMMISSION'S ARTICLES ON STATE RESPONSIBILITY: INTRODUCTION, TEXT, AND COMMENTARIES (James Crawford, ed. 2002).

[7]Draft Articles on State Responsibility, art. 1.

[8]*Ibid.* art. 2.

[9]*Ibid.* arts. 4–11.

[10]*Ibid.* arts. 33, 42(b), 48.

[11]*Ibid.* art. 3. *See also ibid.* art. 32.

[12]*Ibid.* art. 13.

[13]*See* Vienna Convention on the Law of Treaties, arts. 60–62. *Rebus sic stantibus* refers to the principle that a fundamental change of circumstances may excuse a state from performance under a treaty. *Id.* art. 62.

[14]Draft Articles on State Responsibility, art. 20.

[15]*Ibid.* art. 21 ("The wrongfulness of an act of a State is precluded if the act constitutes a lawful measure of self-defense taken in conformity with the Charter of the United Nations."). The ILC did not address similar defenses that might be available to states participating in U.N. peacekeeping or peace enforcement operations.

[16]*Ibid.* art. 23. *Force majeure* is the occurrence of an irresistible force or of an unforeseen event, beyond the control of the state, making it materially impossible in the circumstances to perform the obligation.

[17]*Ibid.* art. 24. Article 24 of the Articles appears to limit distress to situations where human life is in danger. Arguably, distress under maritime law is broader, and the so-called "good Samaritan" doctrine is more forgiving. *See* LOS Convention, art. 98. *See also* 46 U.S.C.A. § 2302(c) (West 2005) (good Samaritan immunity).

[18]Draft Articles on State Responsibility, art. 25. *See also* IAN BROWNLIE, PRINCIPLES OF PUBLIC INTERNATIONAL LAW 447–49 (6th ed. 2003).

conformity with the Draft Articles are not wrongful.[19] The ILC omits from its treatment retorsions that do not constitute a violation of international law.[20]

The responsible state is under an obligation to make full reparation for the injury caused by the internationally wrongful act.[21] Reparation may include restitution, compensation, and satisfaction.[22] As the International Court of Justice explained most recently in *Case Concerning Armed Activities on the Territory of the Congo (Congo v. Uganda),* it is "well established in general international law that a State which bears responsibility for an internationally wrongful act is under an obligation to make full reparation for the injury caused by that act."[23] In cases where compensation is the appropriate form of reparation, it should cover any financially assessable damage, including lost profits and interest.[24] The Draft Articles adopt a form of comparative fault, providing that the amount of compensation will take into account the extent to which a negligent act or omission by the injured state, or a person or entity for whom reparation is sought, contributed to the injury.[25] Importantly, the Draft Articles do not apply where and to the extent that responsibility is governed by special rules of international law (*lex specialis*).[26] The 1982 LOS Convention includes such provisions.

STATE RESPONSIBILITY UNDER CONVENTIONAL INTERNATIONAL LAW

The 1982 U.N. Convention on the Law of the Sea codifies the requirement for a state to make reparations for an unjustified interference with foreign vessels. For example, Article 110, paragraph 3, of the LOS Convention provides that "[I]f the suspicions prove to be unfounded, and provided that the ship boarded has not committed any act justifying them, it shall be compensated for any loss or damage that may have been sustained." Similar provisions are contained in Articles 106 (liability for seizure of suspected pirate vessel without adequate grounds),

---

[19]Draft Articles on State Responsibility, art. 22. Countermeasures are addressed in articles 49–54.

[20]The ILC Draft Articles on countermeasures have been characterized as "one of the lightning rods of criticism and controversy for the articles" and are likely as much a product of progressive development as a codification effort. *See* David J. Bederman, *Counterintuiting Countermeasures,* 96 AM. J. INT'L L. 817, 817, 827–28 (2002). *See also* A. Vaughan Lowe, *Precluding Wrongfulness or Responsibility: A Plea for Excuses,* 10 EUR. J. INT'L L. 405 (1999).

[21]Draft Articles on State Responsibility, art. 31.

[22]*Ibid.* art. 34.

[23]I.C.J. REP. 2005, para. 259.

[24]Draft Articles on State Responsibility, arts. 36, 38. Compare this standard to the more restrictive "pecuniary" loss compensation standard in Article 12 of the Draft Convention on State Sovereign Immunity discussed below.

[25]*Ibid.* art. 39. It is not clear how this Article 39 comparative fault provision will apply in cases involving right of visit boardings where the "suspicions prove to be unfounded," within the meaning of Article 110 of the LOS Convention but the ship boarded "committed any act justifying" the boarding. Article 110 suggests an all-or-nothing approach.

[26]*Ibid.* art. 55. Plainly included here are the WTO agreements and the growing family of bilateral investment treaties.

111 (liability for unjustified stoppage or seizure in exercise of hot pursuit), and 232 (liability for unlawful or excessive pollution enforcement measures). In addition, numerous maritime conventions, including SOLAS,[27] STCW,[28] MARPOL,[29] and the 2005 SUA Protocol[30] require states to provide compensation for unwarranted enforcement actions.

The 1982 LOS Convention—*lex specialis* under the Draft Articles framework—sets out a number of specific state responsibility rules. Of principal relevance to maritime counterproliferation operations, the LOS Convention expressly addresses state responsibility and liability for enforcement actions that are unlawful or exceed those reasonably required in the light of available information.[31] At the same time, the Convention "saves" customary law rules regarding responsibility and liability for damage.[32] The LOS Convention also establishes the responsibility of certain international organizations,[33] such as the European Union. Against these background sources, each of the bilateral boarding agreements entered into so far by the United States for proliferation security boardings includes provisions establishing safeguards, limiting the use of force, and processes for presenting claims and resolving disputes between the parties.[34] Should it enter into force, the 2005 Protocol to the SUA Convention will provide additional protections.[35]

---

[27]SOLAS Convention, art. 19(f).

[28]Convention on Standards of Training, Certification and Watchstanding of Seafarers, Dec. 1, 1978, art. X (4), S. Exec. Doc. No. EE, 1361 U.N.T.S. 190 [hereinafter "STCW Convention"].

[29]International Convention for the Prevention of Pollution of the Sea by Vessels, Nov. 2, 1973, art. 7, T.I.A.S. 10561, 1340 U.N.T.S. 184, 12 I.L.M. 1319 (1973), as amended by, 1978 Tanker Safety and Pollution Prevention Protocol, June 1, 1978, 1340 U.N.T.S. 61, 17 I.L.M. 546 (1978).

[30]Draft 2005 SUA Protocol, *infra* Appendix E, art. 8, ¶ 8(b).

[31]*See, e.g.,* LOS Convention, art. 106 ("Where the seizure of a ship or aircraft on suspicion of piracy has been effected without adequate grounds, the State making the seizure shall be liable to the State the nationality of which is possessed of the ship or aircraft for any loss or damaged caused by the seizure"); art. 110(3) ("If the suspicions proved to be unfounded, and provided that the ship boarded has not committed any act justifying them, it shall be compensated for any loss or damage that may have been sustained"); art. 111(8) ("Where a ship has been stopped or arrested outside the territorial sea in circumstances which do not justify the exercise of hot pursuit, it shall be compensated for any loss or damage that may have been thereby sustained"); art. 232 ("States shall be liable for damage or loss attributable to them arising from measures taken [under Part XII] when such measures are unlawful or exceed those reasonably required in light of available information. States shall provide for recourse in their courts for actions in respect of such damage or loss").

[32]*Ibid.* art. 304; *see also* M/V "Saiga" (No. 2) (Saint Vincent and the Grenadines v. Guinea), paras. 169–173, 38 I.L.M. 1323 (judgment) (ITLOS 1999) [hereinafter "M/V Saiga case"] (applying *Chorzów Factory* standard under Article 304 of the LOS Convention).

[33]LOS Convention, Annex IX, arts. 1 & 6.

[34]*See, e.g.,* Agreement Between the Government of the United States of America and the Government of the Republic of Liberia Concerning Cooperation To Suppress the Proliferation of Weapons of Mass Destruction, Their Delivery Systems, and Related Materials By Sea, arts. 8, 9, 13, *available at* http://www.state.gov/t/np/trty/32403.htm.

[35]Draft 2005 SUA Protocol, *infra* Appendix E, art. 8 (adding Article 8*bis*, para.10(b) to the SUA Convention).

INTERNATIONAL FORA FOR ASSERTING STATE RESPONSIBILITY CLAIMS

To the extent that any disputes arising out of maritime counterproliferation operations will concern "the interpretation or application" of the LOS Convention,[36] a species of *lex specialis,* such disputes will fall within the compulsory dispute settlement procedures set out in Chapter XV of that convention. Under both the U.N. Charter and the LOS Convention, states have an obligation to settle their disputes peacefully.[37] Remedies for violations of international law may be pursued by the state injured, or whose national was injured, through an exercise of diplomatic protection. Only a state with standing may assert a claim for diplomatic protection.[38] In most cases, a state has standing to assert such a claim only on behalf of one its nationals (individuals, corporations, vessels, and aircraft). However, it is now accepted that a vessel's flag state may assert claims not only on behalf of the vessel but also on behalf of the vessel's crew and passengers, even if those individuals are not nationals of the flag state.[39]

Historically, disputes between states arising out of actions by or against vessels have been referred to a variety of settlement procedures, including independent inquiries (the USS *Maine* explosion in 1898), joint inquiries (the Dogger Bank incident of 1904; the *Red Crusader* incident of 1961), arbitration (the *I'm Alone* sinking in 1929) or adjudication (the *Corfu Channel* case and the *M/V Saiga* case).[40] Modernly, the LOS Convention preserves that flexibility by providing states-parties with the option of choosing, at the time of ratification or accession, among four dispute settlement procedure options: the International Court of Justice, the International Tribunal for the Law of the Sea (ITLOS), Annex VII "General" Arbitration, or Annex VIII "Special" Arbitration.[41]

Maritime interdiction actions under the multilateral PSI could implicate a number of treaty obligations other than the LOS Convention, including the General Agreement on Tariffs and Trade (GATT) or one of the many treaties of friendship, commerce, and navigation (FCN). Actions to remedy such violations might be brought within the WTO dispute settlement system or the tribunal named in the compromissory clause of the FCN treaty. Absent some other agreement by the parties, the ITLOS may exercise jurisdiction over actions for "provisional measures" under Article 290 or "prompt release" of a detained vessel and crew under

---

36 LOS Convention, art. 288.

37 Charter of the United Nations, arts. 2(3) & 33; LOS Convention, arts. 279–280.

38 *See* Draft Articles on State Responsibility, art. 42. A relevant exception is the provision in Article 292 of the LOS Convention permitting actions for the prompt release of detained vessels and their crews to be brought "by or on behalf of the flag state."

39 *See M/V Saiga* case, para. 106; RESTATEMENT FOREIGN RELATIONS LAW OF THE UNITED STATES § 502, comment *h* & § 902(2) (1987).

40 *See generally* J.G. MERILLS, INTERNATIONAL DISPUTE SETTLEMENT (4th ed. 2005).

41 LOS Convention, art. 297.

Article 292, even if the relevant parties have elected to have another forum resolve the underlying dispute.[42]

Whether the operations constitute "law enforcement" boardings or "military activities" can have an effect on dispute resolution options. Under the LOS Convention, a state may elect to exclude certain activities from the scope of the convention's compulsory dispute settlement procedures. Article 298(1) of the Convention permits states-parties to exclude the following from the CDS procedures:

> (b) disputes concerning military activities, including military activities by government vessels and aircraft engaged in non-commercial service, and disputes concerning law enforcement activities in regard to the exercise of sovereign rights or jurisdiction excluded from the jurisdiction of a court or tribunal under Article 297, paragraph 2 or 3;
>
> (c) disputes in respect of which the Security Council of the United Nations is exercising the functions assigned to it by the Charter of the United Nations, unless the Security Council decides to remove the matter from its agenda or calls upon the parties to settle it by the means provided for in this convention.[43]

The fact that disputes arising out of military or law enforcement activities may be excepted from compulsory dispute settlement obligations does not absolve the states concerned of their international responsibilities or the requirement to settle all disputes by peaceful means.

Under the Draft Understandings proposed by the Senate Foreign Relations Committee in its 2004 report on the LOS Convention, the committee recommended that the Senate's advice and consent to accession should be subject to a declaration by the United States that it does not accept any of the listed compulsory dispute settlement procedures for the above two categories of disputes (among others).[44] Moreover, the committee recommended that the Senate condition its assent on entry of an "understanding" that, under Article 298(1)(b) "each State Party has the exclusive right to determine whether its activities are or were 'military activities' and that such determinations are not subject to review."[45] Given the unanimity of the Foreign Relations

---

[42]Article 290 provides that any court or tribunal agreed upon the parties or, if they can not reach agreement within two weeks, the ITLOS, may hear applications for provisional measures pending the constitution of an arbitral tribunal. Article 292 provides a similar option, but the time for reaching agreement is only 10 days. *See also* LOS Convention, Annex VI (Statute of the ITLOS), art. 25 (provisional measures).

[43]LOS Convention, art. 298. *See* Continental Shelf Case (Tunisia v. Libyan Arab Jamahiriya), 1982 I.C.J. REP. 18, 230 (June 3) (Oda, J. dissenting) (predicting that disputes arising out of Article 73 enforcement activities will likely be excluded from the LOS Convention's compulsory dispute settlement provisions by virtue of Article 298 of the convention).

[44]*See* Senate Foreign Relations Committee, Report on the United Nations Convention on the Law of the Sea, S. EXEC. REP. NO. 108–10 (Mar. 11, 2004), at 16 (proposed Text of Resolution of Advice and Consent to Ratification, § 2, para. 2). *See also* Government of Canada, Declaration Made Upon Ratification, *reprinted in* LAW OF THE SEA BULL. No. 53 (2004), at 15 (rejecting compulsory jurisdiction procedures prescribed by part XV of the LOS Convention for disputes concerning, *inter alia,* military and law enforcement activities).

[45]*Senate Foreign Relations Committee Report,* at 16.

Committee's 2004 recommendation, there is every reason to expect that, when the Senate again takes up the question of U.S. accession to the LOS Convention, the earlier understandings will be carried forward.

ADMISSIBLE CLAIMS UNDER THE LOS CONVENTION

The basis for responsibility under the LOS Convention varies from article to article; however, a common theme that any interference with foreign vessels must be founded on a sufficient level of suspicion of wrongful activity runs throughout. The fact that no evidence or insufficient evidence of an actual violation of applicable law by the vessel, master, owner, or crew is discovered does not necessarily mean the boarding state's actions violated international law. It is important in each case to examine the basis for the boarding.[46] For example, if the vessel was boarded out of suspicion that it was engaged in piracy, Article 106 provides that the boarding state must compensate the vessel for any loss or damage caused by the seizure if the seizure was "effected without adequate ground."[47] By contrast, liability for a right-of-visit action attaches only if the "suspicions prove to be unfounded, and provided that the ship boarded has not committed any act justifying them."[48] When a ship has been stopped or arrested "in circumstances which do not justify the exercise of hot pursuit, it shall be compensated for any loss of damage that may have been thereby sustained."[49] Finally, where enforcement measures undertaken under Part XII of the LOS Convention to protect the marine environment are "unlawful or exceed those reasonably required in light of available information," the enforcing state is liable for any loss or damage attributable to the enforcement action.[50]

As with the customary law of state responsibility, under the LOS Convention an individual harmed in violation of the convention is normally required first to exhaust any local remedies in the state causing the harm before the injured individual's state of nationality may assert a diplomatic protection action.[51] The ITLOS has concluded, however, that exhaustion is not required before an Article 292 prompt release action may be brought before the tribunal.[52] It is not clear whether the tribunal's decision would extend to cases in which the detaining state has opted to exclude military and law enforcement disputes from the convention's dispute settlement procedures.

---

[46]The prudent commanding officer of any vessel conducting a boarding will articulate the legal basis for a boarding and the facts relied upon to reach that conclusion.

[47]LOS Convention, art. 106.

[48]*Ibid.* art. 110(3).

[49]*Ibid.* art. 111.

[50]*Ibid.* art. 232.

[51]*Ibid.* art. 295.

[52]The "Camouco"Case (Pn. v. Fr.) (Feb. 7) (ITLOS 2000), 39 I.L.M. 666 (2000) (rejecting France's argument that local remedies must be exhausted before an Article 292 prompt release action is admissible), *noted in* 94 AM. J. INT'L L. 713 (2000).

STATE RESPONSIBILITY FOR FAILURE TO ACT

Customary law recognizes that a breach of international law may consist of an affirmative act or the failure to act where international law imposes a duty to do so. The duty to exercise "active due diligence" to prevent injury to another state was recognized in the 1872 arbitral award ordering Great Britain to compensate the United States for the former's failure, as a neutral state, to exercise due diligence to prevent British shipbuilders from constructing vessels for use by the Confederacy to attack Union ships during the Civil War.[53] With regard to omissions by flag states, the *Restatement (Third) of Foreign Relations Law of the United States* has adopted the position that "[a]ny nation that has, or whose nationals have, suffered a loss as a result of the failure of a flag state to exercise proper jurisdiction and control may present an international claim for damages against the flag state."[54] Under the *Restatement* view, which is not widely shared, a state that fails to carry out its obligations under Article 94 of the LOS Convention would bear international responsibility for any harm suffered by the breach. Similar arguments might be made in cases involving the breach of a universal obligation imposed by a U.N. Security Council resolution that causes harm to another state. Efforts to obtain reparations for injuries caused by a flag state's failure to exercise due diligence in controlling its vessels may actually be frustrated by the LOS Convention, however, which provides a relatively weak and potentially time-consuming mechanism for other states to respond to the failure of a flag state to effectively carry out its obligation to exercise effective control and jurisdiction.[55]

DEFENSES TO STATE RESPONSIBILITY CLAIMS

A number of defenses might be raised in response to an admissible claim under the LOS Convention. Presumably, all of the defenses recognized in the Draft Articles on State Responsibility, including consent, self-defense, *force majeure,* distress or necessity, are available under the LOS Convention. In addition, Chapter 7 identified a number of articles in the LOS Convention that recognize situation-specific rights to employ self-help countermeasures. However, the ITLOS examined and ultimately rejected a "necessity" defense in the *M/V Saiga* case. The tribunal cited the ICJ's decision in the *Case Concerning the Gabcikovo-Nagymaros Project,*[56] before "endorsing" the conditions for invoking the necessity defense in the International Law

[53]*See* Alabama Claims Case (1871/2), in JOHN BASSETT MOORE, HISTORY AND DIGEST OF THE INTERNATIONAL ARBITRATIONS TO WHICH THE UNITED STATES HAS BEEN A PARTY, vol. I, at 653 (1898). The arbitrators ordered Great Britain to pay the United States $15.5 million.

[54]*See* RESTATEMENT § 502, comment *f* (citing Article 235 of the LOS Convention).

[55]LOS Convention, art. 94(6) provides: "A State which has clear grounds to believe that proper jurisdiction and control with respect to a ship have not been exercised may report the facts to the flag state. Upon receiving such a report, the flag State shall investigate the matter and, if appropriate, take action necessary to remedy the situation."

[56]The *M/V Saiga* case, paras. 132–136 (citing Gabčíkovo-Nagymaros Project (Hung. v. Slovk.), 1997 I.C.J. REP. 7 (Sept. 25)).

Commission's Draft Articles on State Responsibility.[57] Under that test, the party asserting the "state of necessity" justification for conduct that would otherwise be unlawful must establish the following:

> (a) the act was the only means of safeguarding an essential interest of the State against a grave and imminent peril; and
> (b) the act did not seriously impair an essential interest of the State towards which the obligation existed.[58]

Finding that Guinea, the state asserting the state of necessity justification, failed to produce evidence that its essential interests were in grave and imminent peril, the tribunal rejected the argument.[59]

REPARATIONS FOR BREACH OF INTERNATIONAL RESPONSIBILITY

The LOS Convention variously provides grounds for state responsibility,[60] liability,[61] and a duty to provide compensation,[62] but does not attempt to define their measure. In the *M/V Saiga* case, the ITLOS implicitly adopted the Draft Articles on State Responsibility in determining the measure of reparations.[63] The Draft Articles recognize a duty to cease conduct that violates international law and to make reparations for any injury caused by an internationally wrongful act by the state. The first obligation is always to cease the offending conduct.[64] The preferred remedy is restitution—reestablishing the conditions that existed before the wrongful act was committed.[65] To the extent that restitution is excused or does not make good the damages sustained, the responsible state is required to provide compensation.[66] Returning to the ITLOS decision in the *M/V Saiga* case, it is noteworthy that the tribunal, applying the ILC Draft Articles, held that the right to reparation extended to the damage suffered directly by the flag state, as well as for damage or other loss suffered by the vessel and all persons involved or interested in its operations, and that

---

[57] *Ibid.* para. 134. The Tribunal noted that the ICJ had earlier concluded that Article 33 of the ILC Draft Articles reflects customary law. *Ibid.*

[58] *Ibid.* para. 133 (citing ILC Draft Articles, art. 33).

[59] *Ibid.* art. 135. The Tribunal's opinion suggests that the burden of proof is on the state asserting the justification.

[60] *See, e.g.,* LOS Convention, art. 31.

[61] *Ibid.* arts. 106 & 232. *See also ibid.* art. 235.

[62] *Ibid.* arts. 110(3), 111(8).

[63] The *M/V Saiga* case, para. 171.

[64] Draft Articles on State Responsibility, art. 30.

[65] *Ibid.* art. 35. Restitution is not required where it is not materially possible or it involves a burden out of all proportion to its benefits.

[66] *Ibid.* art. 36. In the 1929 *I'm Alone* case, the arbitration commission denied compensation to the owners on the ground that they were U.S. nationals and the claim was asserted against the United States, but the arbitrators nevertheless ordered the United States to apologize and pay $25,000 in compensation to the United Kingdom for its insult to the U.K. flag.

the measure of damages included loss of profits and other economic losses.[67] It should also be noted that the provisions of the LOS Convention requiring prompt release of seized vessels and crews and compensation for delay are more specific than the Draft Articles.[68] Additionally, the LOS Convention provides a procedure for obtaining provisional relief where, for example, the state committing the wrongful conduct has failed to cease and discontinue that conduct.[69]

PRIVATE CLAIMS AGAINST STATES FOR DAMAGES

International law generally requires an individual to exhaust any available local remedies before that individual's flag state may espouse a claim on the individual's behalf.[70] Individual claims for damages caused by states might be filed in the defendant state's own courts, the courts of the injured party, or in the courts of a third state. Private suits against states for damages need not be based on a violation on international law. On the contrary, such suits nearly always turn on tort law principles.[71] Claimants suing governments in U.S. courts will likely face a number of potential defenses not available to nongovernment defendants, including sovereign immunity and the closely related act of state doctrine.[72] Despite ongoing attempts to establish uniform standards for state sovereign immunity and its exceptions, the standards continue to vary widely from state to state, giving claimants an incentive to forum shop. The draft U.N. Convention on Jurisdictional Immunities of States and Their Properties,[73] which would apply when a claim against a state is brought in the municipal courts of another state, would establish a presumption in favor of immunity in such cases. Article 5 of the Draft Convention provides that: "A state enjoys immunity, in respect of itself and its property, from the jurisdiction of the courts of another State subject to the provisions of the present Convention."

---

[67]The *M/V Saiga* case, para. 172. Compensation was awarded for injury to persons, unlawful arrest, detention, or other forms of ill-treatment and damage to or seizure of property. *Ibid.*

[68]*See, e.g.,* LOS Convention, arts. 73, 106, 110(3), 111(8), 232, 304.

[69]*Ibid.* art. 279. *See, e.g.,* Southern Bluefin Tuna Cases (N.Z. v. Japan; Austl. v. Japan) (ITLOS, Aug. 27, 1999), 38 I.L.M. 1624 (1999).

[70]The exhaustion requirement does not apply in "prompt release" actions before the International Tribunal for the Law of the Sea, or in cases where the flag state was directly injured.

[71]Potential "tort" theories include acts by government officers without, or in excess of, legal authority. *See, e.g.,* Canada v. Berhard, 2005 F.C.A. 267 (Can. Fed. Ct. App. 2005) (denying shipowner's claim for damages arising out of four month detention of M/V *Lantau Peak* by Canadian port state control authorities).

[72]The judicially created "act of state doctrine" bars, with some exceptions, a court from reviewing the legality of the conduct of a foreign state taken within that state's territory. *See* Banco Nacional de Cuba v. Sabbatino, 376 U.S. 398 (1964).

[73]*See* Draft U.N. Convention on Jurisdictional Immunities of States. The Draft Convention was prepared by the ILC and a working group authorized by UNGA Res. 46/55 (Dec. 9, 1991), 44 I.L.M. 803 (2005). The final text adopted by the General Assembly in 2004 is attached as an annex to UNGA Res. 59/38 (Dec. 2, 2004).

The Draft Convention then goes on to list a number of exceptions to the general rule,[74] including one addressed specifically to ships owned or operated by the state.[75]

The position taken by the Draft Convention can be characterized as the "restrictive view" of sovereign immunity, largely subjecting the commercial transactions of states and their instrumentalities to the same rules as transactions by other entities.[76] Claims arising out of the activities of warships and other public vessels not engaged in commercial activities are *not* included in the exception.[77] Accordingly, the Draft Convention is unlikely to aid private parties asserting claims for damages arising out of a maritime counterproliferation operation by a warship or other public vessel.

Depending on the location of the boarding and its outcome, the U.S. sovereign immunity waiver statutes might be less restrictive than the Draft Convention. The statutory scheme for claims against nation states in the United States draws a distinction between claims against the U.S. federal government[78] and those against the government of a foreign state. Suits in U.S. courts against foreign governments must generally fall within one of the exceptions set out in the Foreign Sovereign Immunities Act, which closely tracks the Draft Convention.[79] When the harm was caused by an agent of the U.S. federal government, relevant sovereign immunity waivers must be found in the Federal Tort Claims Act (FTCA),[80] the Suits in Admiralty Act (SIAA),[81] the Public Vessels Act (PVA),[82] or the Foreign Claims Act.[83] Additionally, the Tucker Act may provide a cause of action for just

---

[74]*See* Draft Convention on Jurisdictional Immunities, arts. 7–9 & pt. III.

[75]*Ibid.* art. 16.

[76]David P. Stewart, *The UN Convention on Jurisdictional Immunities of States and Their Property*, 99 Am. J. Int'l L. 194 (2005).

[77]Draft Convention on Jurisdictional Immunities, art. 16. The article preserves immunity of warships, naval auxiliaries, and other state-owned or state-operated vessels used only on government noncommercial service.

[78]Suits against individual states within the United States and related 11th Amendment issues are beyond the scope of this examination.

[79]28 U.S.C.A. § 1605 (West 2005). *See also* Restatement, ch. 5. The FSIA provides the sole basis for obtaining jurisdiction over foreign sovereigns; such claims may not be brought under the Alien Tort Statute, 28 U.S.C. § 1370. Argentine Republic v. Amerada Hess Shipping Corp., 488 U.S 428 (1989).

[80]The FTCA does not apply to claims "arising in a foreign country." *See* 28 U.S.C.A. § 2680(k); Sosa v. Alvarez-Machain, 542 U.S. 692 (2004) (rejecting claim based on "headquarters doctrine" exception to § 2680(k) for claim alleging mistreatment of a Mexican national in Mexico); Smith v. United States, 507 U.S. 197 (1993) (rejecting claim for damages arising out of a death in Antarctica).

[81]46 U.S.C.A. app. §§ 741–750 (West 2005).

[82]46 U.S.C.A. app. §§ 781–789 (West 2005); *see also* Koohi v. United States, 976 F.2d 1328 (9th Cir. 1992) (dismissing PVA claims arising out of incident in which USS *Vincennes* mistakenly shot down an Iranian airliner after court concluded that the FTCA's exception, in 28 U.S.C. § 2680(j), for "any claim arising out of combatant activities of the military or naval forces, or the Coast Guard, during time of war" also applies to PVA claims).

[83]10 U.S.C.A. § 2734 (West 2005). Claims arising out of combatant activities or for damage caused by naval vessels are generally not payable.

compensation in cases where the federal government took private property (such as a vessel or its cargo) within the meaning of the Fifth Amendment of the Constitution.[84]

Although the FTCA exempts the government from immunity actions arising from the detention of goods by customs or other law enforcement officers,[85] there is no similar exemption in the SIAA and PVA.[86]

[84] 28 U.S.C.A. § 1491 (West 2005). The extraterritorial application of the Fifth Amendment to non-nationals of the United States is beyond the scope of this analysis.

[85] 28 U.S.C.A. § 2680(c) (West 2005).

[86] *See* B & F Trawlers v. United States, 841 F.2d 626 (5th Cir. 1988) (declining to read the law enforcement exception into the SIAA/PVA).

10

Conclusion

Maritime counterproliferation operations are but one component in a far-reaching, yet still incomplete, proliferation security regime. Global efforts to halt and eventually reverse proliferation of the world's most dangerous weapons incorporate a range of antiproliferation measures, including bans on production or use of some WMD, with the long-term goal of disarmament, provisions for safeguarding materials in transport or storage, export controls in source states, information sharing, and interdictions. The global antiproliferation regime now includes landmark Chapter VII resolutions (1373 and 1540) by the UN Security Council that signal the first collective steps to remove the threats to international peace and security posed by terrorism and proliferation of WMD. The Security Council later extended its antiproliferation measures with additional resolutions directed at the proliferation threats posed by North Korea and Iran.

The Proliferation Security Initiative has the potential to add credibility to the nonproliferation regime while also enhancing compliance with a number of conventions and codes adopted under the auspices of the International Maritime Organization (IMO), the International Atomic Energy Agency (IAEA), and the World Customs Organization. These instruments, if effectively implemented, form a layered defense. In the layered defense approach to national and homeland security, the PSI offers a forward strategy that complements the more passive nonproliferation approach. Theoretically, a threat must successfully penetrate all of the layers to strike the objective. Stated another way, all of the layers must fail for the attack to be successful. States taking a "precautionary approach" to national security are apt to erect as many layers as practicable, consistent with other national goals.

The PSI adopts a fresh approach to collective action that combines flexibility and adaptability. It is best understood as a mechanism for marshalling legal authorities and resources. It is already bringing together national and homeland security personnel from around the world. They are practicing and promoting cooperation, information sharing, and interoperability. States that need assistance are getting it. By fusing the informational, diplomatic, and operational assets of the coalition, and by drawing on the combined legal authorities of all the participating states in their capacities as port states, coastal states, and flag states, the PSI has the potential to measurably enhance the effectiveness of the counterproliferation enforcement system. It might in fact prove to be one of the most successful multilateral partnerships of the early years new century.

The success of the PSI will in no way be undermined if the United States accedes to the 1982 LOS Convention. The law of the sea has long exhibited flexibility in adapting to new international concerns. The rapid emergence of the international prescriptions against unlicensed broadcasting from the high seas and its incorporation into the right of visit in Article 110 demonstrate that the law of the sea is able to evolve relatively quickly in response to coastal state interests much less compelling than the threat of WMD proliferation. Moreover, it is important to bear in mind that the LOS Convention was never intended to provide an exhaustive international code covering all aspects of maritime law. Rather, it provides an overarching framework, within which other international agreements provide more detailed provisions, which can be adapted to meet new or changed problems. For example, a number of states have entered into bilateral counter-narcotics boarding agreements that provide a basis for bilateral cooperation between "wiling" and "able" states. The United States has also entered into bilateral boarding agreements with six states specifically to implement the mutual undertakings set out in the PSI. The IMO member states amended the MARPOL Convention to address coastal state concerns over the pollution risks posed by single-hulled tankers following the T/V *Prestige* spill. If it enters into force, the 2005 Protocol to the SUA Convention could facilitate international cooperation in combating maritime trafficking in WMD and delivery systems, at least among those states that become parties to the Protocol. Each of these international agreements fits neatly into the framework established by the LOS Convention and provides a much needed basis and process for cooperation and coordination in maritime safety and security operations.

Even with the PSI, the global antiproliferation system is not without serious gaps. Perhaps such gaps are inevitable in a horizontal community of sovereign states, the collective security of which is the responsibility of an ideologically divided Security Council whose members display disparate attitudes toward risk, particularly when the risk is to an abstract and distant "international" peace and security rather than to their individual or regional security. Despite the system's shortcomings, recent developments give reason for hope. When the commitment and organizational accomplishments of the PSI participants is combined with norm-generating developments in the U.N. Security Council and General Assembly, the G-8, European Union, IMO, and IAEA, the pressure on those who refuse to close the gaps and effectively enforce the global security regime grows. It is too soon to predict whether these developments might one day lead to a new basis for a crime of universal jurisdiction or to progressive development of the right of visit under the law of the sea to include PSI-type boardings. In the meantime, while the Security Council monitors progress on the implementation of its terrorism and counterproliferation resolutions, nations participating in the PSI and those cooperating with them will move forward with a pragmatic and adaptive program to counter the growing threat posed by the conjunction of global terrorism and WMD proliferation. In doing so, they have pledged to both honor existing law and urge that it be adapted as necessary to meet those threats.

Appendix A

Interdiction Principles for the Proliferation Security Initiative[1]

PSI participants are committed to the following interdiction principles to establish a more coordinated and effective basis through which to impede and stop shipments of WMD, delivery systems, and related materials flowing to and from states and non-state actors of proliferation concern, consistent with national legal authorities and relevant international law and frameworks, including the UN Security Council. They call on all states concerned with this threat to international peace and security to join in similarly committing to:

1. Undertake effective measures, either alone or in concert with other states, for interdicting the transfer or transport of WMD, their delivery systems, and related materials to and from states and non-state actors of proliferation concern. "States or non-state actors of proliferation concern" generally refers to those countries or entities that the PSI participants involved establish should be subject to interdiction activities because they are engaged in proliferation through: (1) efforts to develop or acquire chemical, biological, or nuclear weapons and associated delivery systems; or (2) transfers (either selling, receiving, or facilitating) of WMD, their delivery systems, or related materials.
2. Adopt streamlined procedures for rapid exchange of relevant information concerning suspected proliferation activity, protecting the confidential character of classified information provided by other states as part of this initiative, dedicate appropriate resources and efforts to interdiction operations and capabilities, and maximize coordination among participants in interdiction efforts.
3. Review and work to strengthen their relevant national legal authorities where necessary to accomplish these objectives, and work to strengthen when necessary relevant international law and frameworks in appropriate ways to support these commitments.

[1] *Done* at Paris, Sept. 4, 2003, at http://www.state.gov/t/np/rls/fs/23764.htm. The Interdiction Principles complement those set out in the 2002 *G-8 Global Partnership Principles to Prevent Terrorists, or Those that Harbor Them, from Gaining Access to Weapons or Materials of Mass Destruction, at* http://www.G-8.gc.ca/2002Kananaskis/kananaskis/globpart-en.asp.

4. Take specific actions in support of interdiction efforts regarding cargoes of WMD, their delivery systems, or related materials, to the extent their national legal authorities permit and consistent with their obligations under international law and frameworks, to include:
   a. Not to transport or assist in the transport of any such cargoes to or from states or non-state actors of proliferation concern, and not to allow any persons subject to their jurisdiction to do so.
   b. At their own initiative, or at the request and good cause shown by another state, to take action to board and search any vessel flying their flag in their internal waters or territorial seas, or areas beyond the territorial seas of any other state, that is reasonably suspected of transporting such cargoes to or from states or non-state actors of proliferation concern, and to seize such cargoes that are identified.
   c. To seriously consider providing consent under the appropriate circumstances to the boarding and searching of its own flag vessels by other states, and to the seizure of such WMD-related cargoes in such vessels that may be identified by such states.
   d. To take appropriate actions to (1) stop and/or search in their internal waters, territorial seas, or contiguous zones (when declared) vessels that are reasonably suspected of carrying such cargoes to or from states or non-state actors of proliferation concern and to seize such cargoes that are identified; and (2) to enforce conditions on vessels entering or leaving their ports, internal waters or territorial seas that are reasonably suspected of carrying such cargoes, such as requiring that such vessels be subject to boarding, search, and seizure of such cargoes prior to entry.
   e. At their own initiative or upon the request and good cause shown by another state, to (a) require aircraft that are reasonably suspected of carrying such cargoes to or from states or non-state actors of proliferation concern and that are transiting their airspace to land for inspection and seize any such cargoes that are identified; and/or (b) deny aircraft reasonably suspected of carrying such cargoes transit rights through their airspace in advance of such flights.
   f. If their ports, airfields, or other facilities are used as transshipment points for shipment of such cargoes to or from states or non-state actors of proliferation concern, to inspect vessels, aircraft, or other modes of transport reasonably suspected of carrying such cargoes, and to seize such cargoes that are identified.

Appendix B

United Nations Security Council Resolution 1373 (2001)[1]

Security Council
4385th meeting (Sep. 28, 2001)

The Security Council,

Reaffirming its resolutions 1269 (1999) of 19 October 1999 and 1368 (2001) of 12 September 2001,

Reaffirming also its unequivocal condemnation of the terrorist attacks which took place in New York, Washington, D.C. and Pennsylvania on 11 September 2001, and expressing its determination to prevent all such acts,

Reaffirming further that such acts, like any act of international terrorism, constitute a threat to international peace and security,

Reaffirming the inherent right of individual or collective self-defence as recognized by the Charter of the United Nations as reiterated in resolution 1368 (2001),

Reaffirming the need to combat by all means, in accordance with the Charter of the United Nations, threats to international peace and security caused by terrorist acts,

Deeply concerned by the increase, in various regions of the world, of acts of terrorism motivated by intolerance or extremism,

Calling on States to work together urgently to prevent and suppress terrorist acts, including through increased cooperation and full implementation of the relevant international conventions relating to terrorism,

---

[1]U.N. Security Council Res. 1373, U.N. Doc. No. S/RES/1373 (2001). Reaffirmed and supplemented by U.N. Security Council Res. 1617, U.N. Doc. No. S/RES/1617 (2005).

Recognizing the need for States to complement international cooperation by taking additional measures to prevent and suppress, in their territories through all lawful means, the financing and preparation of any acts of terrorism,

Reaffirming the principle established by the General Assembly in its declaration of October 1970 (resolution 2625 (XXV)) and reiterated by the Security Council in its resolution 1189 (1998) of 13 August 1998, namely that every State has the duty to refrain from organizing, instigating, assisting or participating in terrorist acts in another State or acquiescing in organized activities within its territory directed towards the commission of such acts,

Acting under Chapter VII of the Charter of the United Nations,

1. *Decides* that all States shall:

   (a) Prevent and suppress the financing of terrorist acts;

   (b) Criminalize the wilful provision or collection, by any means, directly or indirectly, of funds by their nationals or in their territories with the intention that the funds should be used, or in the knowledge that they are to be used, in order to carry out terrorist acts;

   (c) Freeze without delay funds and other financial assets or economic resources of persons who commit, or attempt to commit, terrorist acts or participate in or facilitate the commission of terrorist acts; of entities owned or controlled directly or indirectly by such persons; and of persons and entities acting on behalf of, or at the direction of such persons and entities, including funds derived or generated from property owned or controlled directly or indirectly by such persons and associated persons and entities;

   (d) Prohibit their nationals or any persons and entities within their territories from making any funds, financial assets or economic resources or financial or other related services available, directly or indirectly, for the benefit of persons who commit or attempt to commit or facilitate or participate in the commission of terrorist acts, of entities owned or controlled, directly or indirectly, by such persons and of persons and entities acting on behalf of or at the direction of such persons;

2. *Decides also* that all States shall:

   (a) Refrain from providing any form of support, active or passive, to entities or persons involved in terrorist acts, including by suppressing recruitment of members of terrorist groups and eliminating the supply of weapons to terrorists;

   (b) Take the necessary steps to prevent the commission of terrorist acts, including by provision of early warning to other States by exchange of information;

   (c) Deny safe haven to those who finance, plan, support, or commit terrorist acts, or provide safe havens;

   (d) Prevent those who finance, plan, facilitate or commit terrorist acts from using their respective territories for those purposes against other States or their citizens;

   (e) Ensure that any person who participates in the financing, planning, preparation or perpetration of terrorist acts or in supporting terrorist acts is brought to justice and ensure that, in addition to any other measures against them, such terrorist acts are established as serious criminal offences in domestic laws and regulations and that the punishment duly reflects the seriousness of such terrorist acts;

(f) Afford one another the greatest measure of assistance in connection with criminal investigations or criminal proceedings relating to the financing or support of terrorist acts, including assistance in obtaining evidence in their possession necessary for the proceedings;

(g) Prevent the movement of terrorists or terrorist groups by effective border controls and controls on issuance of identity papers and travel documents, and through measures for preventing counterfeiting, forgery or fraudulent use of identity papers and travel documents;

3. *Calls* upon all States to:

(a) Find ways of intensifying and accelerating the exchange of operational information, especially regarding actions or movements of terrorist persons or networks; forged or falsified travel documents; traffic in arms, explosives or sensitive materials; use of communications technologies by terrorist groups; and the threat posed by the possession of weapons of mass destruction by terrorist groups;

(b) Exchange information in accordance with international and domestic law and cooperate on administrative and judicial matters to prevent the commission of terrorist acts;

(c) Cooperate, particularly through bilateral and multilateral arrangements and agreements, to prevent and suppress terrorist attacks and take action against perpetrators of such acts;

(d) Become parties as soon as possible to the relevant international conventions and protocols relating to terrorism, including the International Convention for the Suppression of the Financing of Terrorism of 9 December 1999;

(e) Increase cooperation and fully implement the relevant international conventions and protocols relating to terrorism and Security Council resolutions 1269 (1999) and 1368 (2001);

(f) Take appropriate measures in conformity with the relevant provisions of national and international law, including international standards of human rights, before granting refugee status, for the purpose of ensuring that the asylum-seeker has not planned, facilitated or participated in the commission of terrorist acts;

(g) Ensure, in conformity with international law, that refugee status is not abused by the perpetrators, organizers or facilitators of terrorist acts, and that claims of political motivation are not recognized as grounds for refusing requests for the extradition of alleged terrorists;

4. *Notes* with concern the close connection between international terrorism and transnational organized crime, illicit drugs, money-laundering, illegal arms trafficking, and illegal movement of nuclear, chemical, biological and other potentially deadly materials, and in this regard *emphasizes*the need to enhance coordination of efforts on national, subregional, regional and international levels in order to strengthen a global response to this serious challenge and threat to international security;

5. *Declares* that acts, methods, and practices of terrorism are contrary to the purposes and principles of the United Nations and that knowingly financing, planning and inciting terrorist acts are also contrary to the purposes and principles of the United Nations;
6. *Decides* to establish, in accordance with rule 28 of its provisional rules of procedure, a Committee of the Security Council, consisting of all the members of the Council, to monitor implementation of this resolution, with the assistance of appropriate expertise, and *calls upon* all States to report to the Committee, no later than 90 days from the date of adoption of this resolution and thereafter according to a timetable to be proposed by the Committee, on the steps they have taken to implement this resolution;
7. *Directs* the Committee to delineate its tasks, submit a work programme within 30 days of the adoption of this resolution, and to consider the support it requires, in consultation with the Secretary-General;
8. *Expresses* its determination to take all necessary steps in order to ensure the full implementation of this resolution, in accordance with its responsibilities under the Charter;
9. *Decides* to remain seized of this matter.

Appendix C

United Nations Security Council Resolution 1540 (2004)[1]

Security Council
4956th Meeting (PM) (Apr. 28, 2004)

The Security Council,

Affirming that proliferation of nuclear, chemical and biological weapons, as well as their means of delivery,* constitutes a threat to international peace and security,

Reaffirming in this context, the Statement of its President adopted at the Council's meeting at the level of Heads of State and Government on 31 January 1992 (S/23500), including the need for all Member States to fulfil their obligations in relation to arms control and disarmament and to prevent proliferation in all its aspects of all weapons of mass destruction,

Recalling also that the Statement underlined the need for all Member States to resolve peacefully in accordance with the Charter any problems in that context threatening or disrupting the maintenance of regional and global stability,

Affirming its resolve to take appropriate and effective actions against any threat to international peace and security caused by the proliferation of nuclear, chemical and biological weapons and their means of delivery, in conformity with its primary responsibilities, as provided for in the United Nations Charter,

Affirming its support for the multilateral treaties whose aim is to eliminate or prevent the proliferation of nuclear, chemical or biological weapons and the importance for all States parties to these treaties to implement them fully in order to promote international stability,

Welcoming efforts in this context by multilateral arrangements which contribute to non-proliferation,

---

[1]U.N. Security Council Res. 1540, U.N. Doc. No. S/RES/1540 (2004).

Affirming that prevention of proliferation of nuclear, chemical and biological weapons should not hamper international cooperation in materials, equipment and technology for peaceful purposes while goals of peaceful utilization should not be used as a cover for proliferation,

Gravely concerned by the threat of terrorism and the risk that non-State actors* such as those identified in the United Nations list established and maintained by the Committee established under Security Council resolution 1267 and those to whom resolution 1373 applies, may acquire, develop, traffic in or use nuclear, chemical and biological weapons and their means of delivery,

Gravely concerned by the threat of illicit trafficking in nuclear, chemical, or biological weapons and their means of delivery, and related materials,* which adds a new dimension to the issue of proliferation of such weapons and also poses a threat to international peace and security,

Recognizing the need to enhance coordination of efforts on national, subregional, regional and international levels in order to strengthen a global response to this serious challenge and threat to international security,

Recognizing that most States have undertaken binding legal obligations under treaties to which they are parties, or have made other commitments aimed at preventing the proliferation of nuclear, chemical or biological weapons, and have taken effective measures to account for, secure and physically protect sensitive materials, such as those required by the Convention on the Physical Protection of Nuclear Materials and those recommended by the IAEA Code of Conduct on the Safety and Security of Radioactive Sources,

Recognizing further the urgent need for all States to take additional effective measures to prevent the proliferation of nuclear, chemical or biological weapons and their means of delivery,

Encouraging all Member States to implement fully the disarmament treaties and agreements to which they are party,

Reaffirming the need to combat by all means, in accordance with the Charter of the United Nations, threats to international peace and security caused by terrorist acts,

Determined to facilitate henceforth an effective response to global threats in the area of non-proliferation,

Acting under Chapter VII of the Charter of the United Nations,

1. *Decides that* all States shall refrain from providing any form of support to non-State actors that attempt to develop, acquire, manufacture, possess, transport, transfer or use nuclear, chemical or biological weapons and their means of delivery;

2. *Decides also* that all States, in accordance with their national procedures, shall adopt and enforce appropriate effective laws which prohibit any non-State actor to manufacture, acquire, possess, develop, transport, transfer or use nuclear, chemical or biological weapons and their means of delivery, in particular for terrorist purposes, as well as attempts to engage in any of the foregoing activities, participate in them as an accomplice, assist or finance them;

3. *Decides also* that all States shall take and enforce effective measures to establish domestic controls to prevent the proliferation of nuclear, chemical, or biological weapons and their

means of delivery, including by establishing appropriate controls over related materials and to this end shall:

(a) Develop and maintain appropriate effective measures to account for and secure such items in production, use, storage or transport;

(b) Develop and maintain appropriate effective physical protection measures;

(c) Develop and maintain appropriate effective border controls and law enforcement efforts to detect, deter, prevent and combat, including through international cooperation when necessary.

4. *Decides* to establish, in accordance with rule 28 of its provisional rules of procedure, for a period of no longer than two years, a Committee of the Security Council, consisting of all members of the Council, which will, calling as appropriate on other expertise, report to the Security Council for its examination, on the implementation of this resolution, and to this end calls upon States to present a first report no later than six months from the adoption of this resolution to the Committee on steps they have taken or intend to take to implement this resolution;

5. *Decides* that none of the obligations set forth in this resolution shall be interpreted so as to conflict with or alter the rights and obligations of State Parties to the Nuclear Non-Proliferation Treaty, the Chemical Weapons Convention and the Biological and Toxin Weapons Convention or alter the responsibilities of the International Atomic Energy Agency or the Organization for the Prohibition of Chemical Weapons;

6. *Recognizes* the utility in implementing this resolution of effective national control lists and calls upon all Member States, when necessary, to pursue at the earliest opportunity the development of such lists;

7. *Recognizes* that some States may require assistance in implementing the provisions of this resolution within their territories and invites States in a position to do so to offer assistance as appropriate in response to specific requests to the States lacking the legal and regulatory infrastructure, implementation experience and/or resources for fulfilling the above provisions;

8. *Calls upon* all States:

(a) To promote the universal adoption and full implementation, and, where necessary, strengthening of multilateral treaties to which they are parties, whose aim is to prevent the proliferation of nuclear, biological or chemical weapons;

(b) To adopt national rules and regulations, where it has not yet been done, to ensure compliance with their commitments under the key multilateral non-proliferation treaties;

(c) To renew and fulfil their commitment to multilateral cooperation, in particular within the framework of the International Atomic Energy Agency, the Organization for the Prohibition of Chemical Weapons and the Biological and Toxin Weapons Convention, as important means of pursuing and achieving their common objectives in the area of non-proliferation and of promoting international cooperation for peaceful purposes;

(d) To develop appropriate ways to work with and inform industry and the public regarding their obligations under such laws;

9. *Calls upon* all States to promote dialogue and cooperation on non-proliferation so as to address the threat posed by proliferation of nuclear, chemical, or biological weapons, and their means of delivery;

10. Further to counter that threat, *calls upon* all States, in accordance with their national legal authorities and legislation and consistent with international law, to take cooperative action to prevent illicit trafficking in nuclear, chemical or biological weapons, their means of delivery, and related materials;

11. *Expresses* its intention to monitor closely the implementation of this resolution and, at the appropriate level, to take further decisions which may be required to this end;

12. *Decides* to remain seized of the matter.

* Definitions for the purpose of this resolution only:
Means of delivery: missiles, rockets and other unmanned systems capable of delivering nuclear, chemical, or biological weapons, that are specially designed for such use.
Non-State actor: individual or entity, not acting under the lawful authority of any State in conducting activities which come within the scope of this resolution.
Related materials: materials, equipment and technology covered by relevant multilateral treaties and arrangements, or included on national control lists, which could be used for the design, development, production or use of nuclear, chemical and biological weapons and their means of delivery.

Appendix D

AGREEMENT BETWEEN THE GOVERNMENT OF THE UNITED STATES OF AMERICA AND THE GOVERNMENT OF THE REPUBLIC OF LIBERIA CONCERNING COOPERATION TO SUPPRESS THE PROLIFERATION OF WEAPONS OF MASS DESTRUCTION, THEIR DELIVERY SYSTEMS, AND RELATED MATERIALS BY SEA

Signed February 11, 2004; provisionally applied from February 11, 2004.

The Government of the United States of America and the Government of the Republic of Liberia (hereinafter, "the Parties");

Deeply concerned about the proliferation of weapons of mass destruction (WMD), their delivery systems, and related materials, particularly by sea, as well as the risk that these may fall into the hands of terrorists;

Recalling the 31 January 1992 United Nations Security Council Presidential statement that proliferation of all WMD constitutes a threat to international peace and security, and underlines the need for Member States of the UN to prevent proliferation;

Further recalling the International Ship and Port Facility Security Code, adopted by the International Maritime Organization on 12 December 2002;

Mindful of the Convention on the Prohibition of the Development, Production, Stockpiling and Use of Chemical Weapons and on their Destruction, done at Paris 13 January 1993; the Treaty on Nonproliferation of Nuclear Weapons, done at Washington, London and Moscow 1 July 1968; and the Convention on the Prohibition of the Development, Production and

Stockpiling of Bacteriological (Biological) and Toxin Weapons and on their Destruction, done at Washington, London and Moscow 10 April 1972;

Acknowledging the widespread consensus that proliferation and terrorism seriously threaten international peace and security;

Convinced that trafficking in these items by States and non-state actors of proliferation concern must be stopped;

Inspired by the efforts of the International Maritime Organization to improve the effectiveness of the Convention for the Suppression of Unlawful Acts against the Safety of Maritime Navigation, done at Rome 10 March 1988;

Reaffirming the importance of customary international law of the sea, and mindful of the provisions in that respect of the 1982 United Nations Convention on the Law of the Sea;

Committed to cooperation to stop the flow by sea of WMD, their delivery systems, and related materials to or from States or non-state actors of proliferation concern;

Have agreed as follows:

ARTICLE 1
DEFINITIONS

In this Agreement, unless the context otherwise requires:

1. "Proliferation by sea" means the transportation by ship of weapons of mass destruction, their delivery systems, and related materials to or from States or non-state actors of proliferation concern.
2. "Weapons of mass destruction" (WMD) means nuclear, chemical, biological and radiological weapons.
3. "Related materials" means materials, equipment and technology, of whatever nature or type, that are related to and destined for use in the development, production, utilization or delivery of WMD.
4. "Items of proliferation concern" means WMD, their delivery systems, and related materials.
5. "States or non-state actors of proliferation concern" means those countries or entities that should be subject to interdiction activities because they are or are believed to be engaged in: (1) efforts to develop or acquire WMD or their delivery systems; or (2) trafficking (either selling, receiving, or facilitating) of WMD, their delivery systems, or related materials.
6. "Security Force Officials" means:
    a. for the United States, uniformed or otherwise clearly identifiable members of the United States Coast Guard and the United States Navy, who may be accompanied by clearly identifiable law enforcement officials of the Departments of Homeland Security and Justice, and other clearly identifiable officials duly authorized by the Government of the United States of America and notified to the Competent Authority of the Republic of Liberia; and

b. for Liberia, uniformed or otherwise clearly identifiable members of the armed forces or law enforcement authorities of Liberia, duly authorized by the Government of the Republic of Liberia and notified to the Competent Authority of the United States.

7. "Security Force vessels" means warships and other vessels of the Parties, or of third States as may be agreed upon by the Parties, on which Security Force Officials of either or both Parties may be embarked, clearly marked and identifiable as being on government service and authorized to that effect, including any vessel and aircraft embarked on or supporting such vessels.
8. "Suspect vessel" means a vessel used for commercial or private purposes in respect of which there are reasonable grounds to suspect it is engaged in proliferation by sea.
9. "International waters" means all parts of the sea not included in the territorial sea, internal waters and archipelagic waters of a State, consistent with international law.
10. "Competent Authority" means for the United States, the Commandant of the United States Coast Guard (including any officer designated by the Commandant to perform such functions), and for Liberia, the Agent of the Commissioner of Maritime Affairs appointed under section 13 of Title 21 (the Maritime Law) of the Laws of the Republic of Liberia.

ARTICLE 2
OBJECT AND PURPOSE OF AGREEMENT

1. The object and purpose of this Agreement is to promote cooperation between the Parties to enable them to prevent the transportation by vessel of items of proliferation concern.
2. The Parties shall carry out their obligations and responsibilities under this Agreement in a manner consistent with the principles of international law pertaining to the sovereign equality and territorial integrity of States.
3. The Parties shall cooperate to the fullest extent possible, subject to the availability of resources and in compliance with their respective laws.

ARTICLE 3
CASES OF SUSPECT VESSELS

Operations to suppress proliferation by sea pursuant to this Agreement shall be carried out only against suspect vessels, including suspect vessels without nationality, suspect vessels assimilated to vessels without nationality, and suspect vessels registered under the law of one of the Parties under a bareboat charter notwithstanding an underlying registration in another State not party to this Agreement, but not against a vessel registered under the law of one of the Parties while bareboat chartered in another State not party to this Agreement.

ARTICLE 4
OPERATIONS IN INTERNATIONAL WATERS

1. Authority to Board Suspect Vessels. Whenever the Security Force Officials of one Party ("the requesting Party") encounter a suspect vessel claiming nationality in the other Party ("the requested Party") located seaward of any State's territorial sea, the

requesting Party may request through the Competent Authority of the requested Party that it:

a. confirm the claim of nationality of the suspect vessel; and

b. such claim is confirmed:

i. authorize the boarding and search of the suspect vessel, cargo and the persons found on board by Security Force Officials of the requesting Party; and

ii. if evidence of proliferation is found, authorize the Security Force Officials of the requesting Party to detain the vessel, as well as items and persons on board, pending instructions conveyed through the Competent Authority of the requested Party as to the actions the requesting Party is permitted to take concerning such items, persons and vessels.

2. Contents of Requests. Each request should contain the name of the suspect vessel, the basis for the suspicion, the geographic position of the vessel, the IMO number if available, the homeport, the port of origin and destination.

3. Responding to Requests.

a. If the nationality is verified, the requested Party may:

i. decide to conduct the boarding and search with its own Security Force Officials;

ii. authorize the boarding and search by the Security Force Officials of the requesting Party;

iii. decide to conduct the boarding and search together with the requesting Party; or

iv. deny permission to board and search.

b. The requested Party shall answer through its Competent Authority requests made for the verification of nationality within two hours of its acknowledgment of the receipt of such requests.

c. If the nationality is not verified within the two hours, the requested Party may, through its Competent Authority:

i. nevertheless authorize the boarding and search by the Security Force Officials of the requesting Party; or

ii. refute the claim of the suspect vessel to its nationality.

d. If there is no response from the Competent Authority of the requested Party within two hours of its acknowledgment of receipt of the request, the requesting Party will be deemed to have been authorized to board the suspect vessel for the purpose of inspecting the vessel's documents, questioning the persons on board, and searching the vessel to determine if it is engaged in proliferation by sea.

4. Right of Visit. Notwithstanding the foregoing paragraphs of this Article, the Security Force Officials of one Party ("the first Party") are authorized to board suspect vessels claiming nationality in the other Party that are not flying the flag of the other Party, not displaying any marks of its registration or nationality, and claiming to have no documentation on board the vessel, for the purpose of locating and examining the vessel's documentation. If documentation or other physical evidence of nationality is located, the foregoing paragraphs of this Article apply. If no documentation or other physical evidence of nationality is available, the other Party will not object to the first Party assimilating the vessel to a ship without nationality consistent with international law.

5. Use of Force. The authorization to board, search and detain includes the authority to use force in accordance with Article 9 of this Agreement.
6. Shipboarding Otherwise in Accordance with International Law. This Agreement does not limit the right of either Party to conduct boardings of vessels or other activities consistent with international law whether based, *inter alia*, on the right of visit, the rendering of assistance to persons, vessels, and property in distress or peril, or an authorization from the Flag or Coastal State, or other appropriate bases in international law.

ARTICLE 5
EXERCISE OF JURISDICTION OVER DETAINED VESSELS, AS WELL AS ITEMS AND PERSONS ON BOARD

1. Jurisdiction of the Parties. In all cases covered by Article 4 concerning the vessels of a Party located seaward of any State's territorial sea, that Party shall have the primary right to exercise jurisdiction over a detained vessel, cargo or other items and persons on board (including seizure, forfeiture, arrest, and prosecution), provided, however, that the Party with the right to exercise primary jurisdiction may, subject to its Constitution and laws, waive its primary right to exercise jurisdiction and authorize the enforcement of the other Party's law against the vessel, cargo or other items and persons on board.
2. Jurisdiction in the contiguous zone of a Party. In all cases not covered by Article 4 involving the vessel of a Party that arise in the contiguous zone of a Party and in which both Parties have authority to board and to exercise jurisdiction to prosecute—
   a. except as provided in paragraph (b), the Party which conducts the boarding shall have the primary right to exercise jurisdiction;
   b. in cases involving suspect vessels fleeing from the territorial sea of a Party in which that Party has the authority to board and to exercise jurisdiction, that Party shall have the primary right to exercise jurisdiction.
3. Disposition Instructions. Consultations as to the exercise of jurisdiction pursuant to paragraphs 1 and 2 of this Article shall be undertaken without delay between the Competent Authorities.
4. Form of waiver. Where permitted by its Constitution and laws, waiver of jurisdiction may be granted verbally, but as soon as possible it shall be recorded in a written note from the Competent Authority and be processed through the appropriate diplomatic channel, without prejudice to the immediate exercise of jurisdiction over the suspect vessel by the other Party.

ARTICLE 6
EXCHANGE OF INFORMATION AND NOTIFICATION OF RESULTS OF ACTIONS OF THE SECURITY FORCES

1. Exchange of Operational Information. The Competent Authorities of both Parties shall endeavor to exchange operational information on the detection and location of suspect vessels and shall maintain communication with each other as necessary to carry out the purpose of this Agreement.

2. Notification of Results. A Party conducting a boarding and search pursuant to this Agreement shall promptly notify the other Party of the results thereof through their Competent Authorities.
3. Status Reports. The relevant Party, in compliance with its laws, shall timely report to the other Party, through their Competent Authorities, on the status of all investigations, prosecutions and judicial proceedings and other actions and processes, arising out of the application of this Agreement.

ARTICLE 7
CONDUCT OF SECURITY FORCE OFFICIALS

1. Compliance with Law and Practices. Each Party shall ensure that its Security Force Officials, when conducting boardings and searches pursuant to this Agreement, act in accordance with its applicable national laws and policies and consistent with international law and accepted international practices.
2. Boarding and Search Teams.
   a. Boardings and searches pursuant to this Agreement shall be carried out by Security ForceOfficials from Security Forcevessels and vessels and aircraft embarked on or otherwise supporting such Security Force vessels, as well as by vessels and aircraft of third States as agreed between the Parties.
   b. The boarding and search teams may operate from Security Forcevessels of the Parties and from such vessels of other States, according to arrangements between the Party conducting the operation and the State providing the vessel and notified to the other Party.
   c. The boarding and search teams may carry arms.

ARTICLE 8
SAFEGUARDS

1. Where a Party takes measures against a vessel in accordance with this Agreement, it shall:
   a. take due account of the need not to endanger the safety of life at sea;
   b. take due account of the security of the vessel and its cargo;
   c. not prejudice the commercial or legal interests of the Flag State;
   d. ensure within available means, that any measure taken with regard to the vessel is environmentally sound under the circumstances;
   e. ensure that persons on board are afforded the protections, rights and guarantees provided by international law and the boarding State's law and regulations;
   f. ensure the master of the vessel is, or has been, afforded the opportunity to contact the vessels' owner, manager or Flag State at the earliest opportunity.
2. Reasonable efforts shall be taken to avoid a vessel being unduly detained or delayed.

ARTICLE 9
USE OF FORCE

1. All uses of force pursuant to this Agreement shall be in strict accordance with the applicable laws and policies of the Party conducting the boarding and applicable international law.
2. Each Party shall avoid the use of force except when and to the degree necessary to ensure the safety of Security Force Officials and vessels or where Security Force Officials are obstructed in the execution of their duties.
3. Only that force reasonably necessary under the circumstances may be used.
4. Boarding and search teams and Security Force vessels have the inherent right to use all available means to apply that force reasonably necessary to defend themselves or others from physical harm.
5. Whenever any vessel subject to boarding under this Agreement does not stop on being ordered to do so, the Security Force vessel should give an auditory or visual signal to the suspect vessel to stop, using internationally recognized signals. If the suspect vessel does not stop upon being signaled, Security Force vessels may take other appropriate actions to stop the suspect vessel.

ARTICLE 10
EXCHANGE AND KNOWLEDGE OF LAWS AND POLICIES OF OTHER PARTY

1. Exchange of Information. To facilitate implementation of this Agreement, each Party shall take steps necessary to ensure the other Party is appropriately informed of its respective applicable laws and policies, particularly those pertaining to the use of force.
2. Knowledge. Each Party shall take steps necessary to ensure that its Security Force Officials are knowledgeable concerning the applicable laws and policies in accordance with this Agreement.

ARTICLE 11
POINTS OF CONTACT

1. Information. Each Party shall inform the other Party, and keep current, the points of contact for communication, decision and instructions under Articles 4 and 5, and notifications under Articles 6 and 10 of this Agreement. Such information shall be updated by and exchanged between the Competent Authorities.
2. Availability. The Parties shall ensure that the points of contact have the capability to receive, process and respond to requests and reports at any time.

ARTICLE 12
DISPOSITION OF SEIZED PROPERTY

1. Except as otherwise agreed by the Parties, cargo and other items seized in consequence of operations undertaken onboard vessels subject to the jurisdiction of a

Party pursuant to this Agreement, shall be disposed of by that Party in accordance with its laws.

2. The Party exercising jurisdiction may, in any case, transfer forfeited cargo and other items or proceeds of their sale to the other Party. Each transfer generally will reflect the contribution of the other Party to facilitating or effecting the forfeiture of such assets or proceeds.

ARTICLE 13
CLAIMS

1. Injury or Loss of Life. Any claim for injury to or loss of life of a Security Force Official of a Party while carrying out operations arising from this Agreement shall normally be resolved in accordance with the laws of that Party.
2. Other Claims. Any other claim submitted for damage, harm,injury, death or loss resulting from an operation carried out by a Party under this Agreement shall be resolved in accordance with the domestic law of that Party, and in a manner consistent with international law.
3. Consultation. If any loss, injury or death is suffered as a result of any action taken by the Security ForceOfficials of one Party in contravention of this Agreement, or any improper or unreasonable action is taken by a Party pursuant thereto, the Parties shall, without prejudice to any other legal rights which may be available, consult at the request of either Party to resolve the matter and decide any questions relating to compensation or payment.

ARTICLE 14
DISPUTES AND CONSULTATIONS

1. Disputes. Disputes arising from the interpretation or implementation of this Agreement shall be settled by mutual agreement of the Parties.
2. Evaluation of Implementation. The Parties agree to consult as necessary to evaluate the implementation of this Agreement and to consider enhancing its effectiveness. The evaluation shall be carried out at least once a year.
3. Resolving Difficulties. In case a difficulty arises concerning the operation of this Agreement, either Party may request, through the Competent Authorities, consultations with the other Party to resolve the matter.

ARTICLE 15
EFFECT ON RIGHTS, PRIVILEGES AND LEGAL POSITIONS

Nothing in this Agreement:

a. alters the rights and privileges due any person in any administrative or judicial proceeding conducted under the jurisdiction of either Party.
b. shall prejudice the position of either Party with regard to international law.

ARTICLE 16
COOPERATION AND ASSISTANCE

1. The Competent Authority of one Party may request, and the Competent Authority of the other Party may authorize, Security Force Officials to provide technical assistance, such as specialized assistance in the conduct of search of suspect vessels, for the boarding and search of suspect vessels located in the territory or waters of the requesting Party.
2. Nothing in this Agreement precludes a Party from authorizing the other Party to suppress proliferation in its territory, waters or airspace, or to take action involving suspect vessels or aircraft claiming its nationality, or from providing other forms of cooperation to suppress proliferation.

ARTICLE 17
ENTRY INTO FORCE AND DURATION

1. Entry into Force. This Agreement shall enter into force upon an exchange of notes indicating that the necessary internal procedures of each Party have been completed.
2. Provisional Application. Beginning on the date of signature of this Agreement, the Parties shall, to the extent permitted by their respective national laws and regulations, apply it provisionally. Either Party may discontinue provisional application at any time. Each Party shall notify the other Party immediately of any constraints or limitations on provisional application, of any changes to such constraints or limitations, and upon discontinuation of provisional application.
3. Termination. This Agreement may be terminated by either Party upon written notification of such termination to the other Party through the diplomatic channel, termination to be effective one year from the date of such notification.
4. Continuation of Actions Taken. This Agreement shall continue to apply after termination with respect to any administrative or judicial proceedings regarding actions that occurred during the time the Agreement was in force.

ARTICLE 18
RIGHTS FOR THIRD STATES

1. The Parties agree that the Government of the Republic of Liberia may extend, *mutatis mutandis*, all rights concerning suspect vessels claiming its nationality under the present Agreement to such third States as it may deem appropriate, on the understanding that such third States shall likewise comply with all conditions set forth in the present Agreement for the exercise of such rights, and subject to agreement by that Party and such third States on the designation of points of contact in accordance with Article 11.
2. Such third States shall enjoy rights and be subject to all conditions governing their exercise as set forth in paragraph 1 of this Article effective on the date of a notification by the third State to that Party that it will comply with the conditions for the exercise of those rights.

3. Such rights shall be revocable by that Party or the third State in writing. Such rights shall be revoked, and the conditions governing their exercise shall cease to apply, effective on the date of notification.
4. Such rights shall be subject to modification by mutual concurrence in writing of that Party and the third State. Upon establishment of such mutual written concurrence by that Party and the third State in question, such rights shall be modified effective on the date agreed between that Party and the third State.

IN WITNESS WHEREOF, the undersigned, being duly authorized by their respective Governments, have signed this Agreement.

DONE AT Washington, this eleventh day of February 2004, in duplicate, both texts being equally authentic.

FOR THE GOVERNMENT OF THE UNITED STATES OF AMERICA:

/s/ John S. Wolf

[JOHN S. WOLF, Assistant Secretary, Bureau of Nonproliferation]

FOR THE GOVERNMENT OF THE REPUBLIC OF LIBERIA:

/s/ T. Nimley

[THOMAS YAYA NIMLEY, Minister of Foreign Affairs]

Appendix E

CONSOLIDATED TEXT OF THE CONVENTION FOR THE SUPPRESSION OF UNLAWFUL ACTS AGAINST THE SAFETY OF MARITIME NAVIGATION ("SUA CONVENTION"), 1988 AND THE DRAFT PROPOSED PROTOCOL OF AMENDMENT, 2005

(Proposed new text is shown in **bold** type; 1988 Convention text proposed for deletion is shown ~~stricken through~~.)

ARTICLE 1

1. For purposes of this Convention, the term —

(a) "serious injury or damage" means (A) death, (B) serious bodily injury, (C) extensive destruction of a place of public use, State or government facility, infrastructure facility, or public transportation system, resulting in major economic loss, or (D) substantial damage to the environment, including the air, soil, water, fauna or flora;

(b) "precursor" means any chemical reactant which takes part at any stage in the production by whatever method of a toxic chemical. This includes any key component of a binary or multicomponent chemical system.

(c) "BCN Weapon" means:

(i) "biological weapons", which are:

(A) microbial or other biological agents, or toxins whatever their origin or method of production, of types and in quantities that have no justification for prophylactic, protective or other peaceful purposes; and

(B) weapons, equipment or means of delivery designed to use such agents or toxins for hostile purposes or in armed conflict.

(ii) "chemical weapons", which are, together or separately:

(A) toxic chemicals and their precursors, except where intended for:

(I) industrial, agricultural, research, medical, pharmaceutical or other peaceful purposes;

(II) protective purposes, namely those purposes directly related to protection against toxic chemicals and to protection against chemical weapons;

(III) military purposes not connected with the use of chemical weapons and not dependent on the use of the toxic properties of chemicals as a method of warfare; or

(IV) law enforcement including domestic riot control purposes; as long as the types and quantities are consistent with such purposes; and

(B) munitions and devices, specifically designed to cause death or other harm through the toxic properties of those toxic chemicals specified in subclause (A), which would be released as a result of the employment of such munitions and devices; and

(C) any equipment specifically designed for use directly in connection with the employment of munitions and devices specified in subclause (B).

(iii) nuclear weapons and other nuclear explosive devices.

(d) "ship" means a vessel of any type whatsoever not permanently attached to the sea-bed, including dynamically supported craft, submersibles, or any other floating craft.

(e) "toxic chemical" means any chemical which through its chemical action on life processes can cause death temporary incapacitation or permanent harm to humans or animals. This includes all such chemicals, regardless of their origin or of their method of production, and regardless of whether they are produced in facilities, in munitions or elsewhere.

(f) "transport" means to initiate[, arrange] or exercise effective control or decision-making authority over the movement of a person or item.

(g) "Organization" means the International Maritime Organization (IMO).

(h) "Secretary-General" means the Secretary-General of the Organization.

2. **For the purposes of this Convention,**

(a) the terms "place of public use," "State or government facility," "infrastructure facility," and "public transportation system" have the meaning given those terms in the International Convention for the Suppression of Terrorist Bombings, done at New York on 15 December 1997, and

(b) the terms "source material" and "special fissionable material" have the meaning given those terms in the International Atomic Energy Agency Statute, done at New York on 26 October 1956.

ARTICLE 2

1. This Convention does not apply to:

(a) a warship; or

(b) a ship owned or operated by a State when being used as a naval auxiliary or for customs or police purposes; or

(c) A ship which has been withdrawn from navigation or laid up.

2. Nothing in this Convention affects the immunities of warships and other government ships operated for non-commercial purposes.

ARTICLE 2*bis*

1. **Nothing in this Convention shall affect other rights, obligations and responsibilities of States and individuals under international law, in particular the purposes and principles of the Charter of the United Nations and international human rights, refugee and humanitarian law.**
2. **This Convention does not apply to the activities of armed forces during an armed conflict, as those terms are understood under international humanitarian law, which are governed by that law, and the activities undertaken by military forces of a State in the exercise of their official duties, inasmuch as they are governed by other rules of international law.**
3. **Nothing in this Convention shall affect the rights, obligations and responsibilities under the Treaty on the Non-Proliferation of Nuclear Weapons, done at Washington, London and Moscow on 1 July 1968, the Convention on the Prohibition of the Development, Production and Stockpiling of Bacteriological (Biological) and Toxin Weapons and on their Destruction, done at Washington, London and Moscow on 10 April 1972 or the Convention on the Prohibition of the Development, Production, Stockpiling and Use of Chemical Weapons and on their Destruction, done at Paris on 13 January 1993, of States Parties to such treaties.**
4. **Activities by State Parties to the Treaty on the Non-Proliferation of Nuclear Weapons that are within the scope of and are consistent with that treaty shall not constitute offences under this Convention.**
5. **The transport of any equipment, materials, software or related technology intended to be used in the delivery of a nuclear weapon or other nuclear explosive device, where such nuclear weapon or other nuclear explosive device is held by a State Party to the Treaty on the Non-Proliferation of Nuclear Weapons, consistent with its obligations under that treaty, shall not constitute an offence under this Convention.**

ARTICLE 3

1. Any person commits an offence **within the meaning of this Convention** if that person unlawfully and intentionally:

(a) seizes or exercises control over a ship by force or threat thereof or any other form of intimidation; or

(b) performs an act of violence against a person on board a ship if that act is likely to endanger the safe navigation of that ship; or

(c) destroys a ship or causes damage to a ship or to its cargo which is likely to endanger the safe navigation of that ship; or

(d) places or causes to be placed on a ship, by any means whatsoever, a device or substance which is likely to destroy that ship, or cause damage to that ship or its cargo which endangers or is likely to endanger the safe navigation of that ship; or

(e) destroys or seriously damages maritime navigational facilities or seriously interferes with their operation, if any such act is likely to endanger the safe navigation of a ship; or

(f) communicates information which he knows to be false, thereby endangering the safe navigation of a ship~~; or~~

~~(g) injures or kills any person, in connection with the commission or the attempted commission of any of the offences set forth in subparagraphs (a) to (f)~~.

2. Any person also commits an offence if that person~~:~~

~~(a) attempts to commit any of the offences set forth in paragraph 1;~~

~~(b) abets the commission of any of the offences set forth in paragraph 1 perpetrated by any person or is otherwise an accomplice of a person who commits such an offence; or~~

~~(c)~~ threatens, with or without a condition, as is provided for under national law, aimed at compelling a physical or juridical person to do or refrain from doing any act, to commit any of the offences set forth in paragraph 1, subparagraphs (b), (c) and (e), if that threat is likely to endanger the safe navigation of the ship in question.

ARTICLE 3*bis*

1. **Any person commits an offence within the meaning of this Convention if that person unlawfully and intentionally:**

(a) when the purpose of the act, by its nature or context, is to intimidate a population, or to compel a Government or an international organization to do or to abstain from doing any act:

(i) uses against or on a ship or discharges from a ship any explosive, radioactive material or BCN Weapon in a manner that causes or is likely to cause death or serious injury or damage; or

(ii) discharges, from a ship, oil, liquefied natural gas, or other hazardous or noxious substance, which is not covered by clause (i), in such quantity or concentration that causes or is likely to cause death or serious injury or damage; or

(iii) uses a ship in a manner that causes death or serious injury or damage; or

(iv) threatens, with or without a condition, as is provided for under national law, to commit an offence set forth in clause (i), (ii) or (iii); or

(b) transports on board a ship:

(i) any explosive or radioactive material, knowing that it is intended to be used to cause, or in a threat to cause, with or without a condition, as is

provided for under national law, death or serious injury or damage for the purpose of intimidating a population, or compelling a Government or an international organization to do or to abstain from doing any act; or

(ii) any BCN Weapon, knowing it to be a BCN Weapon as defined in Article 1; or

(iii) any source material, special fissionable material, or equipment or material especially designed or prepared for the processing, use or production of special fissionable material, knowing that it is intended to be used in a nuclear explosive activity or in any other nuclear activity not under safeguards pursuant to a comprehensive safeguards agreement; or

(iv) any equipment, materials or software or related technology that significantly contributes to the design, manufacture or delivery of a BCN Weapon, with the intention that it will be used for such purpose.

2. It shall not be an offence within the meaning of this Convention to transport an item or material covered by paragraph 1(b)(iii) or, insofar as it relates to a nuclear weapon or other nuclear explosive device, paragraph 1(b)(iv), if such item or material is transported to or from the territory of, or is otherwise transported under the control of, a State Party to the Treaty on the Non-Proliferation of Nuclear Weapons, where:

   (a) the resulting transfer or receipt (including internal to a State) of the item or material is not contrary to such State Party's obligations under the Treaty on the Non-Proliferation of Nuclear Weapons; and,

   (b) if the item or material is intended for the delivery system of a nuclear weapon or other nuclear explosive device of a State Party to the Treaty on the Non-Proliferation of Nuclear Weapons, the holding of such weapon or device is not contrary to that State Party's obligations under that Treaty.

ARTICLE 3*ter*

1. A person commits an offence within the meaning of this Convention if that person unlawfully and intentionally transports another person on board a ship knowing that the person has committed an act that constitutes an offence under Articles 3, 3*bis*, 3*quater* or an offence set forth in any treaty listed in the Annex, and intending to assist that person to evade criminal prosecution.
2. On depositing its instrument of ratification, acceptance, approval or accession, a State Party which is not a party to a treaty listed in the Annex may declare that, in the application of this Protocol to the State Party, the treaty shall be deemed not to be included in paragraph 1. The declaration shall cease to have effect as soon as the treaty enters into force for the State Party, which shall notify the Secretariat of this fact.
3. When a State Party ceases to be a party to a treaty listed in the Annex, it may make a declaration as provided for in this Article, with respect to that treaty.
4. On depositing its instrument of ratification, acceptance, approval or accession a State Party may declare that it will apply the provisions of paragraph 1 in

accordance with the principles of its criminal law concerning family exemptions of liability.

ARTICLE 3*quater*

Any person also commits an offence within the meaning of this Convention if that person:

1. **Unlawfully and intentionally injures or kills any person in connection with the commission of any of the offences set forth in Article 3, paragraph 1, Article 3*bis*, or Article 3*ter*; or**
2. **Attempts to commit an offence set forth in Article 3, paragraph 1, Article 3*bis*, paragraph 1, (a)(i), (ii) or (iii),or paragraph 1 of this Article; or**
3. **Participates as an accomplice in an offence set forth in Article 3, Article 3*bis*, Article 3*ter* or paragraph 1 or 2 of this Article; or**
4. **Organizes or directs others to commit an offence as set forth in Article 3, Article 3*bis*, Article 3*ter* or paragraph 1 or 2 of this Article; or**
5. **Contributes to the commission of one or more offences as set forth in Article 3, Article 3*bis*, Article 3*ter* or paragraph 1 or 2 of this Article by a group of persons acting with a common purpose, intentionally and either:**
   - **(a) with the aim of furthering the criminal activity or criminal purpose of the group, where such activity or purpose involves the commission of an offence as set forth in Article 3, Article 3*bis* or Article 3*ter*, or**
   - **(b) in the knowledge of the intention of the group to commit an offence as set forth in Article 3, Article 3*bis* or Article 3*ter*.**

ARTICLE 4

1. This Convention applies if the ship is navigating or is scheduled to navigate into, through or from waters beyond the outer limit of the territorial sea of a single State, or the lateral limits of its territorial sea with adjacent States.
2. In cases where the Convention does not apply pursuant to paragraph 1, it nevertheless applies when the offender or the alleged offender is found in the territory of a State Party other than the State referred to in paragraph 1.

ARTICLE 5

Each State Party shall make the offences set forth in Articles 3, ***3bis*, *3ter* and *3quater*** punishable by appropriate penalties which take into account the grave nature of those offences.

ARTICLE 5*bis*

1. **Each State Party, in accordance with its domestic legal principles, shall take the necessary measures to enable a legal entity located in its territory organized under its laws to be held liable when a person responsible for management or control of that legal entity has, in that capacity, committed an offence**

set forth in this Convention. Such liability may be criminal, civil or administrative.

2. **Such liability is incurred without prejudice to the criminal liability of individuals having committed the offences.**
3. **Each State Party shall ensure, in particular, that legal entities liable in accordance with paragraph 1 above are subject to effective, proportionate and dissuasive criminal, civil or administrative sanctions. Such sanctions may include monetary sanctions.**

ARTICLE 6

1. Each State Party shall take such measures as may be necessary to establish its jurisdiction over the offences set forth in Articles 3, ***3bis, 3ter*** **and** ***3quater*** when the offence is committed:
   (a) against or on board a ship flying the flag of the State at the time the offence is committed; or
   (b) in the territory of that State, including its territorial sea; or
   (c) by a national of that State.
2. A State Party may also establish its jurisdiction over any such offence when:
   (a) it is committed by a stateless person whose habitual residence is in that State; or
   (b) during its commission a national of that State is seized, threatened, injured or killed; or
   (c) it is committed in an attempt to compel that State to do or abstain from doing any act.
3. Any State Party which has established jurisdiction mentioned in paragraph 2 shall notify the Secretary-General~~ of the International Maritime Organization (hereinafter referred to as "the Secretary-General")~~. If such State Party subsequently rescinds that jurisdiction, it shall notify the Secretary-General.
4. Each State Party shall take such measures as may be necessary to establish its jurisdiction over the offences set forth in Articles 3, ***3bis, 3ter*** **and** ***3quater***in cases where the alleged offender is present in its territory and it does not extradite him to any of the States Parties which have established their jurisdiction in accordance with paragraphs 1 and 2 of this Article.
5. This Convention does not exclude any criminal jurisdiction exercised in accordance with national law.

ARTICLE 7

1. Upon being satisfied that the circumstances so warrant, any State Party in the territory of which the offender or the alleged offender is present shall, in accordance with its law, take him into custody or take other measures to ensure his presence for such time as is necessary to enable any criminal or extradition proceedings to be instituted.
2. Such State shall immediately make a preliminary inquiry into the facts, in accordance with its own legislation.

3. Any person regarding whom the measures referred to in paragraph 1 are being taken shall be entitled to:
   (a) communicate without delay with the nearest appropriate representative of the State of which he is a national or which is otherwise entitled to establish such communication or, if he is a stateless person, the State in the territory of which he has his habitual residence;
   (b) be visited by a representative of that State.
4. The rights referred to in paragraph 3 shall be exercised in conformity with the laws and regulations of the State in the territory of which the offender or the alleged offender is present, subject to the proviso that the said laws and regulations must enable full effect to be given to the purposes for which the rights accorded under paragraph 3 are intended.
5. When a State Party, pursuant to this Article, has taken a person into custody, it shall immediately notify the States which have established jurisdiction in accordance with Article 6, paragraph 1 and, if it considers it advisable, any other interested States, of the fact that such person is in custody and of the circumstances which warrant his detention. The State which makes the preliminary inquiry contemplated in paragraph 2 of this Article shall promptly report its findings to the said States and shall indicate whether it intends to exercise jurisdiction.

ARTICLE 8

1. The Master of a ship of a State Party (the "flag State") may deliver to the authorities of any other State Party (the "receiving State") any person who he has reasonable grounds to believe has committed one of the offences set forth in Articles 3, ***3bis, 3ter*** **or** ***3quater***.
2. The flag State shall ensure that the Master of its ship is obliged, whenever practicable, and if possible before entering the territorial sea of the receiving State carrying on board any person whom the Master intends to deliver in accordance with paragraph 1, to give notification to the authorities of the receiving State of his intention to deliver such person and the reasons therefor.
3. The receiving State shall accept the delivery, except where it has grounds to consider that the Convention is not applicable to the acts giving rise to the delivery, and shall proceed in accordance with the provisions of Article 1. Any refusal to accept a delivery shall be accompanied by a statement of the reasons for refusal.
4. The flag State shall ensure that the Master of its ship is obliged to furnish the authorities of the receiving State with the evidence in the Master's possession which pertains to the alleged offence.
5. A receiving State which has accepted the delivery of a person in accordance with paragraph 3 may, in turn, request the flag State to accept delivery of that person. The flag State shall consider any such request, and if it accedes to the request it shall proceed in accordance with Article 7. If the flag State declines a request, it shall furnish the receiving State with a statement of the reasons therefor.

ARTICLE 8*bis*

1. The States Parties shall co-operate to the fullest extent possible to prevent and suppress unlawful acts covered by this Convention, in conformity with international law, and shall respond to requests pursuant to this Article as expeditiously as possible.

   (a) Each request pursuant to this Article should, if possible, contain the name of the suspect ship, the IMO identification number, the port of registry, the ports of origin and destination, and any other relevant information. If a request is conveyed orally, the requesting Party shall confirm the request in writing as soon as possible. The requested Party shall acknowledge its receipt of any written or oral request immediately.

   (b) States Parties shall take into account the dangers and difficulties involved in boarding a ship at sea and searching its cargo, and give consideration to whether other appropriate measures agreed between the States concerned could be more safely taken in the next port of call or elsewhere.

2. A State Party that has reasonable grounds to suspect that an offence under Articles 3, 3*bis,* 3*ter* or 3*quater* is, has been or is about to be committed involving a ship flying its flag, may request the assistance of other States Parties in preventing or suppressing that offence. The States Parties so requested shall use their best endeavours to render such assistance within the means available to them.

3. Whenever law enforcement or other authorized officials of a State Party ("the requesting Party") encounter a ship flying the flag or displaying marks of registry of the first Party ("the first Party"), located seaward of any State's territorial sea, and the requesting Party has reasonable grounds to suspect that the ship or a person on board the ship is, has been or is about to be involved in, the commission of an offence under Articles 3, 3*bis,* 3*ter* or 3*quater* and the requesting Party desires to board,

   (a) it shall request, in accordance with paragraph 1, that the first Party confirm the claim of nationality, and,

   (b) if nationality is confirmed, the requesting Party shall ask the first Party (hereinafter, "the flag State") for authorization to board and to take appropriate measures with regard to that ship, which may include stopping, boarding and searching the ship, its cargo and persons on board, and questioning the persons on board in order to determine if an offence under Articles 3, 3*bis*, 3*ter*or 3*quater*has been, or is about to be, committed; and

   (c) the flag State shall either:

      (i) authorize the requesting Party to board and to take appropriate measures set out in subparagraph (b) of this paragraph, subject to any conditions it may impose in accordance with paragraph 5; or

      (ii) conduct the boarding and search with its own law enforcement or other officials; or

      (iii) conduct the boarding and search together with the requesting Party, subject to any conditions it may impose in accordance with paragraph 5; or

(iv) decline to authorize a boarding and search.

The requesting Party shall not board the ship or take measures set out in subparagraph (b) of this paragraph without the express authorization from the flag State.

[(d) If a requested State, which has not made a declaration in accordance with the subparagraphs 3(e) or (f) of this Article, does not comply with its obligation under paragraph 1 to this Article to respond to either of the requests pursuant to the subparagraphs 3(a) and 3(b) of the present Article, the requesting Party shall consider the need to warn other States Parties concerned.]

(e) On or after it deposits its instrument of ratification, acceptance, approval or accession, a State Party may notify the Secretary-General that, with respect to ships flying its flag or displaying its mark of registry the requesting Party is granted authorization to board and search the ship, its cargo and persons on board, and to question the persons on board in order to locate and examine documentation of its nationality and determine if an offence under Articles 3, 3*bis,* 3*ter* or 3*quater* has been, or is about to be, committed, if there is no response from the first Party within four hours of acknowledgement of receipt of a request to confirm nationality.

(f) On or after it deposits its instrument of ratification, acceptance, approval or accession, a State Party may notify the Secretary-General that, with respect to ships flying its flag or displaying its mark of registry, the requesting Party is authorized to board and search a ship, its cargo and persons on board, and to question the persons on board in order to determine if an offence under Articles 3, 3*bis*, 3*ter* or 3*quater* has been or is about to be, committed.

The notifications made pursuant to this paragraph can be withdrawn at any time.

4. When evidence of conduct described in Articles 3, 3*bis,* 3*ter* or 3*quater* is found as the result of any boarding conducted pursuant to this Article, the flag State may authorize the requesting Party to detain the ship, cargo and persons on board pending receipt of disposition instructions from the flag State. The requesting Party shall inform promptly the flag State of the results of a boarding, search, and detention conducted pursuant to this Article. The requesting Party shall also inform promptly the flag State of the discovery of evidence of illegal conduct that is not subject to this Convention.

5. A flag State, consistent with the other provisions of this Convention, may subject its authorization under paragraphs 3 or 4 to conditions, including obtaining additional information from the requesting Party, and conditions relating to responsibility for and the extent of measures to be taken. No additional measures may be taken without the express authorization of the flag State, except when necessary to relieve imminent danger to the lives of persons or those that derive from relevant bilateral or multilateral agreements.

6. For all boardings pursuant to this Article, the flag State has the right to exercise jurisdiction over a detained ship, cargo or other items and persons on board

(including seizure, forfeiture, arrest and prosecution); however, the flag State may, subject to its Constitution and laws, consent to the exercise of jurisdiction by another State having jurisdiction under Article 6.

7. **When carrying out the authorized actions under this Article, the use of force shall be avoided except when necessary to ensure the safety of its officials and persons on board, or where the officials are obstructed in the execution of the authorized actions. Any use of force pursuant to this Article shall not exceed the minimum degree of force which is necessary and reasonable in the circumstances.**

8. **Safeguards:**

   (a) Where a State Party takes measures against a ship in accordance with this Article, it shall:

   (i) take due account of the need not to endanger the safety of life at sea;

   (ii) ensure that all persons on board are treated in a manner which preserves their basic human dignity, and in compliance with the applicable provisions of international law, including international law of human rights;

   (iii) ensure that a boarding and search pursuant to this Article shall be conducted in accordance with applicable international law;

   (iv) take due account of the safety and security of the ship and its cargo;

   (v) take due account of the need not to prejudice the commercial or legal interests of the flag State;

   (vi) ensure, within available means, that any measure taken with regard to the ship or its cargo is environmentally sound under the circumstances;

   (vii) ensure that persons on board against whom proceedings may be commenced in connection with any of the offences set forth in Articles 3, 3*bis,* 3*ter* or 3*quater* are afforded the protections of Article 10(2), regardless of location;

   (viii) ensure that the Master of a ship is advised of its intention to board, and is, or has been, afforded the opportunity to contact the ship's owner and the flag State at the earliest opportunity; and

   (ix) take reasonable efforts to avoid a ship being unduly detained or delayed.

   (b) Provided that authorization to board by a flag State shall not per se give rise to its liability, States Parties shall be liable for damage, harm or loss attributable to them arising from measures taken pursuant to this Article when:

   (i) the grounds for such measures prove to be unfounded, provided that the ship has not committed any act justifying the measures taken; or

   (ii) such measures are unlawful or exceed that reasonably required in light of available information to implement the provisions of this Article.

   State Parties shall provide for effective recourse in respect of such damage, harm or loss.

   (c) Where a State Party takes measures against a ship in accordance with this Convention, it shall take due account of the need not to interfere with or to affect:

(i) the rights and obligations and the exercise of jurisdiction of coastal States in accordance with the international law of the sea; or

(ii) the authority of the flag State to exercise jurisdiction and control in administrative, technical and social matters involving the ship.

(d) Any measure taken pursuant to this Article shall be carried out by law enforcement or other authorized officials from warships or military aircraft, or from other ships or aircraft clearly marked and identifiable as being on government service and authorized to that effect and, notwithstanding Articles 2 and *2bis,* the provisions of this Article shall apply.

(e) For the purposes of this Article "law enforcement or other authorized officials" means uniformed or otherwise clearly identifiable members of law enforcement or other government authorities duly authorized by their government. For the specific purpose of law enforcement under this Convention, law enforcement or other authorized officials shall provide appropriate government-issued identification documents for examination by the Master of the ship upon boarding.

9. **This Article does not apply to or limit boarding of ships, conducted by any State Party in accordance with international law, seaward of any State's territorial sea, including boardings based upon the right of visit, the rendering of assistance to persons, ships and property in distress or peril, or an authorization from the flag State to take law enforcement or other action.**

10. **The States Parties are encouraged to develop standard operating procedures for joint operations pursuant to this Article and consult, as appropriate, with other States Parties with a view to harmonizing such standard operating procedures for the conduct of operations.**

11. **States Parties may conclude agreements or arrangements between them to facilitate law enforcement operations carried out in accordance with this Article.**

12. **Each State Party shall take appropriate measures to ensure that its law enforcement or other authorized officials, and law enforcement or other authorized officials of other States Parties acting on its behalf, are empowered to act pursuant to this Article.**

13. **On or after it deposits its instrument of ratification, acceptance, approval or accession, each State Party shall designate the authority, or, where necessary, authorities to receive and respond to requests for assistance, for confirmation of nationality, and for authorization to take appropriate measures. Such designation, including contact information, shall be notified to the Secretary-General within one month of becoming a Party, who shall inform all other States Parties within one month of the designation. Each State Party is responsible for providing prompt notice through the Secretary-General of any changes in the designation or contact information.**

ARTICLE 9

Nothing in this Convention shall affect in any way the rules of international law pertaining to the competence of States to exercise investigative or enforcement jurisdiction on board ships not flying their flag.

ARTICLE 10

1. The State Party in the territory of which the offender or the alleged offender is found shall, in cases to which Article 6 applies, if it does not extradite him, be obliged, without exception whatsoever and whether or not the offence was committed in its territory, to submit the case without delay to its competent authorities for the purpose of prosecution, through proceedings in accordance with the laws of that State. Those authorities shall take their decision in the same manner as in the case of any other offence of a grave nature under the law of that State.
2. Any person ~~regarding whom~~ **who is taken into custody or regarding whom any other measures are taken or** proceedings are being carried out ~~in connection with any offences set forth in Article 3~~ **pursuant to this Convention** shall be guaranteed fair treatment ~~at all stages of the proceedings~~, including enjoyment of all rights and guarantees ~~provided for such proceedings by~~ **in conformity with** the law of the State in the territory of which ~~he is present~~ **that person is present and applicable provisions of international law, including international human rights law.**

ARTICLE 11

1. The offences set forth in Articles 3, ***3bis, 3ter*** **and** ***3quater*** shall be deemed to be included as extraditable offences in any extradition treaty existing between any of the States Parties. States Parties undertake to include such offences as extraditable offences in every extradition treaty to be concluded between them.
2. If a State Party which makes extradition conditional on the existence of a treaty receives a request for extradition from another State Party with which it has no extradition treaty, the requested State Party may, at its option, consider this Convention as a legal basis for extradition in respect of the offences set forth in Articles 3, ***3bis, 3ter*** **and** ***3quater***. Extradition shall be subject to the other conditions provided by the law of the requested State Party.
3. States Parties which do not make extradition conditional on the existence of a treaty shall recognize the offences set forth in Articles 3, ***3bis, 3ter*** **and** ***3quater*** as extraditable offences between themselves, subject to the conditions provided by the law of the requested State.
4. If necessary, the offences set forth in Articles 3, ***3bis, 3ter*** **and** ***3quater*** shall be treated, for the purposes of extradition between States Parties, as if they had been committed not only in the place in which they occurred but also in a place within the jurisdiction of the State Party requesting extradition.
5. A State Party which receives more than one request for extradition from States which have established jurisdiction in accordance with Article 7 and which decides not to prosecute shall, in selecting the State to which the offender or alleged offender is to be extradited, pay due regard to the interests and responsibilities of the State Party whose flag the ship was flying at the time of the commission of the offence.
6. In considering a request for the extradition of an alleged offender pursuant to this Convention, the requested State shall pay due regard to whether his rights as set forth in Article 7, paragraph 3, can be effected in the requesting State.

7. With respect to the offences as defined in this Convention, the provisions of all extradition treaties and arrangements applicable between States Parties are modified as between States Parties to the extent that they are incompatible with this Convention.

ARTICLE 11*bis*

None of the offences set forth in Articles 3, *3bis, 3ter* or *3quater* shall be regarded for the purposes of extradition or mutual legal assistance as a political offence or as an offence connected with a political offence or as an offence inspired by political motives. Accordingly, a request for extradition or for mutual legal assistance based on such an offence may not be refused on the sole ground that it concerns a political offence or an offence connected with a political offence or an offence inspired by political motives.

ARTICLE 11*ter*

Nothing in this Convention shall be interpreted as imposing an obligation to extradite or to afford mutual legal assistance, if the requested State Party has substantial grounds for believing that the request for extradition for offences set forth in Articles 3, *3bis, 3ter* or *3quater* for mutual legal assistance with respect to such offences has been made for the purpose of prosecuting or punishing a person on account of that person's race, religion, nationality, ethnic origin or political opinion or that compliance with the request would cause prejudice to that person's position for any of these reasons.

ARTICLE 12

1. State Parties shall afford one another the greatest measure of assistance in connection with criminal proceedings brought in respect of the offences set forth in Articles 3, ***3bis, 3ter* and *3quater*.** including assistance in obtaining evidence at their disposal necessary for the proceedings.
2. States Parties shall carry out their obligations under paragraph 1 in conformity with any treaties on mutual assistance that may exist between them. In the absence of such treaties, States Parties shall afford each other assistance in accordance with their national law.

ARTICLE 12*bis*

1. **A person who is being detained or is serving a sentence in the territory of one State Party whose presence in another State Party is requested for purposes of identification, testimony or otherwise providing assistance in obtaining evidence for the investigation or prosecution of offences set forth in Articles 3, *3bis*, *3ter*or *3quater*may be transferred if the following conditions are met:**
   (a) The person freely gives his informed consent; and
   (b) The competent authorities of both States agree, subject to such conditions as those States may deem appropriate.

2. For the purposes of the present Article:

(a) The State to which the person is transferred shall have the authority and obligation to keep the person transferred in custody as long as necessary to effectuate the needs of paragraph 1, unless otherwise requested or authorized by the State from which the person was transferred;

(b) The State to which the person is transferred shall without delay implement its obligation to return the person to the custody of the State from which the person was transferred as agreed beforehand, or as otherwise agreed, by the competent authorities of both States;

(c) The State to which the person is transferred shall not require the State from which the person was transferred to initiate extradition proceedings for the return of the person;

(d) The person transferred shall receive credit for service of the sentence being served in the State from which he was transferred for time spent in the custody of the State to which he was transferred.

3. Unless the State Party from which a person is to be transferred in accordance with the present Article so agrees, that person, whatever his nationality, shall not be prosecuted or detained or subjected to any other restriction of his personal liberty in the territory of the State to which that person is transferred in respect of acts or convictions anterior to his departure from the territory of the State from which such person was transferred.

ARTICLE 13

1. States Parties shall co-operate in the prevention of the offences set forth in Articles 3, ***3bis, 3ter* and *3quater*** particularly by:

(a) taking all practicable measures to prevent preparations in their respective territories for the commission of those offences within or outside their territories;

(b) exchanging information in accordance with their national law, and co-ordinating administrative and other measures taken as appropriate to prevent the commission of offences set forth in Articles 3, ***3bis, 3ter* and *3quater*.**

2. When, due to the commission of an offence set forth in Articles 3, ***3bis, 3ter* or *3quater*,** the passage of a ship has been delayed or interrupted, any State Party in whose territory the ship or passengers or crew are present shall be bound to exercise all possible efforts to avoid a ship, its passengers, crew or cargo being unduly detained or delayed.

ARTICLE 14

Any State Party having reason to believe that an offence set forth in Articles 3, ***3bis, 3ter* or *3quater*** will be committed shall, in accordance with its national law, furnish as promptly as possible any relevant information in its possession to those States which it believes would be the States having established jurisdiction in accordance with Article 6.

ARTICLE 15

1. Each State Party shall, in accordance with its national law, provide to the Secretary-General, as promptly as possible, any relevant information in its possession concerning:
   (a) the circumstances of the offence;
   (b) the action taken pursuant to Article 13, paragraph 2;
   (c) the measures taken in relation to the offender or the alleged offender and, in particular, the results of any extradition proceedings or other legal proceedings.
2. The State Party where the alleged offender is prosecuted shall, in accordance with its national law, communicate the final outcome of the proceedings to the Secretary-General.
3. The information transmitted in accordance with paragraphs 1 and 2 shall be communicated by the Secretary-General to all States Parties, to Members of the **Organization** ~~International Maritime Organization (hereinafter referred to as "the Organization")~~, to the other States concerned, and to the appropriate international intergovernmental organizations.

ARTICLE 16

1. Any dispute between two or more States Parties concerning the interpretation or application of this Convention which cannot be settled through negotiation within a reasonable time shall, at the request of one of them, be submitted to arbitration. If, within six months from the date of the request for arbitration, the parties are unable to agree on the organization of the arbitration any one of those parties may refer the dispute to the International Court of Justice by request in conformity with the Statute of the Court.
2. Each State may at the time of signature or ratification, acceptance or approval of this Convention or accession thereto, declare that it does not consider itself bound by any or all of the provisions of paragraph 1. The other States Parties shall not be bound by those provisions with respect to any State Party which has made such a reservation.
3. Any State which has made a reservation in accordance with paragraph 2 may, at any time, withdraw that reservation by notification to the Secretary-General.

ARTICLE 20*bis*

1. **The Annex may be amended by the addition of relevant treaties that:**
   (a) Are open to the participation of all States;
   (b) Have entered into force; and
   (c) Have been ratified, accepted, approved or acceded to by at least [__] States Parties to this Protocol.
2. **After the entry into force of this Protocol, any State Party thereto may propose such an amendment to the Annex. Any proposal for an amendment shall be communicated to the Secretary-General in written form. The Secretary-General shall circulate any proposed amendment that meets the requirements of paragraph 1 to all**

members of the Organization and seek from the State Parties to this Protocol their consent to the adoption of the proposed amendment.

3. The proposed amendment to the Annex shall be deemed adopted after more than [____] of the States Parties to this Protocol consent to it by written notification.

4. The adopted amendment to the Annex shall enter into force [___] days after the deposit with the Secretary-General of the [___] instrument of ratification, acceptance or approval of such amendment for those States Parties to this Protocol that have deposited such an instrument. For each State Party to this Protocol ratifying, accepting or approving the amendment after the deposit of the [___] instrument with the Secretary-General, the amendment shall enter into force on the [___] day after deposit by such State Party of its instrument of ratification, acceptance or approval.

ANNEX

1. Convention for the Suppression of Unlawful Seizure of Aircraft, done at The Hague on 16 December 1970.
2. Convention for the Suppression of Unlawful Acts against the Safety of Civil Aviation, done at Montreal on 23 September 1971.
3. Convention on the Prevention and Punishment of Crimes against Internationally Protected Persons, including Diplomatic Agents, adopted by the General Assembly of the United Nations on 14 December 1973.
4. International Convention against the Taking of Hostages, adopted by the General Assembly of the United Nations on 17 December 1979.
5. Convention on the Physical Protection of Nuclear Material, adopted at Vienna on 26 October 1979.
6. Protocol for the Suppression of Unlawful Acts of Violence at Airports Serving International Civil Aviation, supplementary to the Convention for the Suppression of Unlawful Acts against the Safety of Civil Aviation, done at Montreal on 24 February 1988.
7. Protocol for the Suppression of Unlawful Acts against the Safety of Fixed Platforms Located on the Continental Shelf, done at Rome on 10 March 1988.
8. International Convention for the Suppression of Terrorist Bombings, adopted by the General Assembly of the United Nations on 15 December 1997.
9. International Convention for the Suppression of the Financing of Terrorism, adopted by the General Assembly of the United Nations on 9 December 1999.

Bibliography

BOOKS

Allison, Graham, *Nuclear Terrorism: The Ultimate Preventable Catastrophe* (2004)
Attard, David J., *The Exclusive Economic Zone in International Law* (1987)
Barnett, Roger W., *Asymmetrical Warfare: Today's Challenge to U.S. Military Power* (2003)
Brackett, D.W. *Holy Terror: Armageddon in Tokyo* (1996)
Bobbitt, Philip, *The Shield of Achilles: War, Peace, and the Course of History* (2002)
Boczek, Boleslaw A., *Flags of Convenience: An International Legal Study* (1960)
Brownlie, Ian, *Principles of Public International Law* (6th ed. 2003)
Carter Ashton B., & William J. Perry, *Preventive Defense: A New Security Strategy for America* (1999)
Churchill, Robin R. & A. Vaughan Lowe, *The Law of the Sea* (3d ed. 1999)
Claire, Rodger W., *Raid on the Sun: Inside Israel's Secret Campaign that Denied Saddam the Bomb* (2004)
Clark, Wesley, *Waging Modern War* (2001)
Clausewitz, Carl von, *On War* (Howard & Paret, transl. & eds., 1976, rev. 1984)
Cole, Leonard A., *The Anthrax Letters: A Medical Detective Story* (2003)
Colombos, C. John, *The International Law of the Sea* (6th rev. ed. 1967)
Creveld, Martin van, *The Rise and Decline of the State* (1999)
———, *The Transformation of War* (1991).
Dinstein, Yoram, War, *Aggression and Self-Defence* (2001)
Drucker, Peter F., *The Essential Drucker* (2001)
Ellis, Jason D. & Geoffrey D. Kiefer, *Combating Proliferation: Strategic Intelligence and Security Policy* (2004)

Ferguson, Charles D. & William C. Potter, *The Four Faces of Nuclear Terrorism* (Center for Nonproliferation Studies 2004)
Fukuyama, Francis, *State-Building: Governance and World Order in the 21st Century* (2004)
Gaddis, John Lewis, *Surprise, Security and the American Experience* (2004)
Grotius, Hugo, *The Freedom of the Seas or the Right Which Belongs to the Dutch to Take Part n the East Indian Trade* (James Brown Scott ed., Oxford Univ. Press 1916) (1608)
Haber, Ludwig F., *The Poisonous Cloud: Chemical Warfare in the First World War* (1986)
Huntington, Samuel P., *The Clash of Civilizations and the Remaking of World Order* (1996)
Ignatieff, Michael, *The Warrior's Honor* (1997)
Int'l Inst. Humanitarian Law, *San Remo Manual on International Law Applicable to Armed Conflicts at Sea* (Louise Doswald-Beck, ed. 1995)
Jayson, Lester S. & Robert Longstreth, *Handling Federal Tort Claims: Administrative and Judicial Remedies* (2001)
Jefferson, Thomas, *The Writings of Thomas Jefferson* (Paul Ford, ed. 1898)
Kasoulides, George C., *Port State Control and Jurisdiction: Evolution of the Port State Regime* (1993)
Keegan, John, *A History of Warfare* (1993)
———, *Intelligence in War: Knowledge of the Enemy from Napoleon to Al-Qaeda* (2003)
Kissinger, Henry M,. *Does America Need a Foreign Policy? Toward a Diplomacy for the 21st Century* (rev. 2002 ed.)
Lasswell, Harold D. & Myres S. McDougal, *Jurisprudence for a Free Society* (1992)
Lauterpacht, Hersch, *Oppenheim's International Law,* (Robert Jennings & Arthur Watts, eds., 9th ed. 1992)
Locke, John, *Second Treatise on Government* (1689)
Lowenthal, Mark A., *Intelligence: From Secrets to Policy* (2d ed. 2003)
Mead, Walter Russell, *Power, Terror, Peace, and War: America's Grand Strategy in a World at Risk* (2004)
Merills, J.G., *International Dispute Settlement* (4th ed. 2005)
Meyer, Stephen M., *The Dynamics of Nuclear Proliferation* (1984)
Moore, William, *Gas Attack! Chemical Warfare 1915–1918 and Afterward* (1987)
Murphy, John, *The United Nations and The Control of International Violence* (1982)
National Academy of Sciences, *Biotechnology Research in an Age of Terrorism* (2004)
Nye, Joseph S. Jr., *The Paradox of American Power: Why the World's Only Superpower Can't Go it Alone* (2002)
Posner, Richard A., *Catastrophe: Risk and Response* (2004)
———, *Preventing Surprise Attacks: Intelligence Reform in the Wake of 9/11* (2005)
Poulantzas, Nicolas M., The Right of Hot Pursuit in International Law (2d ed. 2002)
Rabkin, Jeremy A., *The Case for Sovereignty* (2004)
Rayfuse, Rosemary Gail, *Non-Flag State Enforcement in High Seas Fisheries* (2004)
Restatement (Third) Foreign Relations Law of the United States (1987)
Restatement (Second) Conflict of Laws (1971)
Roberts, Adam & Richard Guelff, *Documents on the Laws of War* (3d ed. 2000)
Shaw, Malcolm M., *International Law* (5th ed. 2003)
Simon, Steven & Dan Benjamin, *The Age of Sacred Terror* (2003)

Stern, Jessica, *Terror in the Name of God: Why Religious Militants Kill* (2003)
Stockholm International Peace Research Institute, *The Problems of Chemical and Biological Warfare: A Study of the Historical, Technical, Military, Legal and Political Aspects of CBW, and Possible Disarmament Measures* (1971–1975)
U.S. Dep't of State, *Digest of United States Practice in International Law 1975* (1976)
———, *Digest of United States Practice in International Law, 1981–88* (1994)
———, *Digest of United States Practice in International Law 1989–90* (2003)
———, *Digest of United States Practice in International Law 2001* (2002)
———, *Digest of United States Practice in International Law 2002* (2003)
———, *Digest of United States Practice in International Law 2003* (2004)
Waltz, Kenneth N., *Man, the State and War* (1959)
Whiteman, Marjorie M., *4 Digest of U.S. Practice in International Law* (1965)
———, *5 Digest of U.S. Practice in International Law* (1965)
———, *6 Digest of U.S. Practice in International Law* (1968)
———, *8 Digest of U.S. Practice in International Law* (1968)
———, *9 Digest of U.S. Practice in International Law* (1968)
———, *10 Digest of U.S. Practice in International Law* (1968)
———, *11 Digest of U.S. Practice in International Law* (1968)
———, *12 Digest of U.S. Practice in International Law* (1971)
———, *18 Digest of U.S. Practice in International Law* (1976)
Williams, Paul L., *Al Qaeda Connection: International Terrorism, Organized Crime, and the Coming Apocalypse* (2005)
Wilson, James Q. & Richard J. Herrnstein, *Crime and Human Nature* (1986)
Zakaria, Fareed, *The Future of Freedom* (2004)
———, *Combating Weapons of Mass Destruction: Avoiding the Abyss* (PSI, Barry R. Schneider & Jim A. Davis, eds. 2006)
———, *Documents of the United Nations Conference on International Organizations* (San Francisco 1945)
———, *Encyclopedia of Public International Law* (Rudolph Bernhardt, ed., 2000)
———, *League of Nations Conference for the Codification of International Law* (Shabtai Rosenne, ed., 1975)
———, *The International Law Commission's Articles on State Responsibility: introduction, Text, and Commentaries* (James Crawford, ed. 2002)
———, *United Nations Convention on the Law of the Sea 1982: A Commentary, vol. 2* (Satya N. Nandan & Shabtai Rosenne eds. 1993)
———, *United Nations Convention on the Law of the Sea 1982: A Commentary, vol. 3* (Satya N. Nandan & Shabtai Rosenne, ed. 1995)

INTERNATIONAL/NATIONAL GOVERNMENT REPORTS

United Nations

U.N. Office for Ocean Affairs and the Law of the Sea, *Navigation on the High Seas: Legislative History of Part VII, Section 1 (Articles 87, 89, 90–94, 96–98) of the United Nations Convention on the Law of the Sea,* U.N. Pub. No. E.89.V.2 (1989)

U.N. Division of Ocean Affairs and the Law of the Sea, *The Law of the Sea: Obligations of States Parties under the United Nations Law of the Sea and Complementary Instruments* (2004)

U.N., 2004 Report of the Secretary-General, Oceans and the Law of the Sea, U.N. Doc. A/59/62 (2004)

U.N., The United Nations' Secretary-General's High-Level Panel on Threats, Challenges and Change, Final Report:*A More Secure World: Our Shared Responsibility,* U.N. Doc. A/59/565, Dec. 1, 2004

United States

Report on the Commission on the Intelligence Capabilities of the United States Regarding Weapons of Mass Destruction (2005)

U.S. Congress, *Joint Inquiry into Intelligence Community Activities before and after the Terrorist Attacks of September 11, 2001,* S. Rep. No. 107–351, H. Rep. No. 107–792 (Dec. 2002)

U.S. Congress, Office of Technology Assessment, *North Korea's Nuclear Weapons: How Soon an Arsenal?* CRS Rep. RS21391 (updated Feb. 2, 2004)

———, *Proliferation of Weapons of Mass Destruction: Assessing the Risks,* Report No. OTA-ISC-559 (1993)

———, *Terrorist Motivations for Chemical and Biological Weapons Use: Placing the Threat in Context,* CRS Rep. RL31831 (Mar. 28, 2003)

———, *Technologies Underlying Weapons of Mass Destruction,* Report No. OTA-BP-ISC-115 (1993)

———, *Weapons of Mass Destruction: Trade Between North Korea and Pakistan,* CRS Report RL31900 (updated Mar. 11, 2004)

U.S. Congressional Research Service, *Intelligence and Law Enforcement: Countering Transnational Threats to the U.S.,* CRS Rep. No. RL 30252 (updated Dec. 3, 2001)

———, *Missile Technology Control Regime (MTCR) and International Code of Conduct Against Ballistic Missile Proliferation: Background and Issues for Congress,* CRS Rep. RL31848

———, *Nuclear, Biological, Chemical and Missile Proliferation Sanctions: Selected Current Law,* CRS Rep. RL31502

———, *Nuclear Terrorism: A Brief Review of Threats and Responses,* CRS Rep. RL32595 (Sept. 22, 2004)

———, *Port and Maritime Security: Background Issues for Congress,* updated May 27, 2005, CRS Rep. No. RL31733

———, *Proliferation Control Regimes: Background and Status,* CRS Rep. RL31559

———, *Proliferation Security Initiative,* CRS Rep. RS21881 (June 7, 2005)

———, *Radiological Dispersal Devices: Select Issues in Consequence Management,* CRS Rep. RS21766

———, *Terrorism, the Future and U.S. Foreign Policy,* Issue Brief 95112 (updated Apr. 11, 2003)

———, *Terrorist "Dirty Bombs": A Brief Primer,* CRS Rep. RS21528

———, *The Law of the Sea Convention and U.S. Policy,* CRS Issue Brief IB95010

U.S. General Accounting Office, *Nonproliferation: Improvements Needed for Controls on Exports of Cruise Missile and Unmanned Aerial Vehicle Technology,* GAO-04–493T (2004)

———, *Nonproliferation: Strategy Needed to Strengthen Multilateral Export Control Regimes,* GAO-03–43 (Oct. 25, 2002)

———, *Transportation Security, Post-September 11th Initiatives and Long-Term Challenges,* Apr. 1, 2003, GAO-03–616T

———, *Weapons of Mass Destruction: DOD's Actions to Combat Weapons Use Should Be More Integrated and Focused,* GAO NSIAD-00–97 (2000)

U.S., *Final Report of the National Commission on Terrorist Attacks Upon the United States* (2004)

U.S. *Report of the Interagency Commission on Crime and Security in U.S. Seaports* (2000)

U.S. Senate Foreign Relations Committee, *Report on the United Nations Convention on the Law of the Sea,* S. Exec. Rep. No. 108–10 (Mar. 11, 2004)

U.S. Senate, Select Committee on Intelligence, *Report on the U.S. Intelligence Community's Prewar Intelligence Assessments on Iraq,* S. Rep. No. 108–301 (2004)

ARTICLES

Abramowitz, David, *The President, the Congress, and the Use of Force: Legal and Political Considerations in Authorizing the Use of Force Against International Terrorism,* 43 HARV. INT'L L.J. 71 (2002)

Albright, Madeleine K., *A Testing of American Foreign Policy,* 77 FOREIGN AFFAIRS 50 (1998)

Allison, Graham, *How to Stop Nuclear Terror,* 83 FOREIGN AFFAIRS 64 (2004)

Anderson, Andrew W., *Jurisdiction Over Stateless Vessels on the High Seas: An Appraisal Under Domestic and International Law,* 13 J. MAR. L. & COM. 323 (1982)

Arend, Anthony Clark,*Do Legal Rules Matter? International Law and International Politics,* 38 VA. J. INT'L L. 107 (1998)

Beard, Jack M., *America's New War on Terror: The Case for Self-Defense under International Law,* 25 HARV. J. L. & PUB. Pol'y 559 (2002)

Beck, Michael E., *The Promise and Limits of the PSI,* THE MONITOR 16 (2004)

Bederman, David J., *Counterintuiting Countermeasures,* 96 AM. J. INT'L L. 817 (2002)

Betts, Richard K., *Analysis, War, and Decision: Why Intelligence Failures are Inevitable,"* in THE ART AND PRACTICE OF MILITARY STRATEGY (National Defense University 1984)

Byers, Michael, *Comment, Policing the High Seas: The Proliferation Security Initiative,* 98 AM. J. INT'L L. 543 (2004)

Blackwell, Robert D. & Ashton B. Carter, *The Role of Intelligence,* in NEW NUCLEAR NATIONS: CONSEQUENCES FOR U.S. POLICY 234 (Robert D. Blackwell & Albert Carnesale, ed. 1993)

Bradley, Curtis A., *Universal Jurisdiction and U.S. Law,* 2001 U. CHI. LEGAL FORUM 323

Brilmayer, Lea & Charles Norchi, *Federal Extraterritoriality and Fifth Amendment Due Process,* 105 HARV. L. REV. 1217 (1992)

Burke, William T., *Customary Law of the Sea: Advocacy or Disinterested Scholarship?,* 14 YALE J. INT'L L. 508 (1989)

———, *State Practice, New Ocean Uses, and Ocean Governance under UNCLOS,* in OCEAN GOVERNANCE: STRATEGIES AND APPROACHES FOR THE 21ST CENTURY 222 (Thomas A. Mensah, ed., 1996)

———, *Threats to the Public Order of the Ocean,* in INTERNATIONAL NAVIGATION: ROCKS AND SHOALS AHEAD? 384 (Jon Van Dyke, et al., eds., 1988)

Callard, James & Peter Faber, *An Emerging Synthesis for a New Way of War,* Geo. J. Int'l Affairs 61 (2002)

Canty, Rachel, *International Maritime Law: Limits of Coast Guard Authority to Board Foreign Flag Vessels on the High Seas,* 23 Mar. Law. 123 (1998)

Carlson, James, *Comment: Presidential Proclamation 7219: Extending the United States' Contiguous Zone—Didn't Someone Say This Had Something to Do with Pollution?*, 55 U. Miami L. Rev. 487 (2001)

Carter, Ashton B., *How to Counter WMD,* 83 Foreign Affairs 72 (2004)

Chase, Alison E., *Legal Mechanisms of the International Community and the United States Concerning State Sponsorship of Terrorism,* 45 Va. J. Int'l L. 41 (2004)

Christopher, Warren, *A New Consensus of the Americas,* 5 U.S. Dep't of State Dispatch 20 (1994)

Cirincione, Joseph, *Deadly Arsenals: Tracking Weapons of Mass Destruction* (Carnegie Endowment 2004)

Crook, John R., *Current Developments: The 2003 Judicial Activity of the International Court of Justice,* 98 Am. J. Int'l L. 308 (2004)

D'Amato, Anthony, *Israel's Air Strike Upon the Iraqi Nuclear Reactor,* 77 Am. J. Int'l L. 584 (1983)

Degan, Vladimir D., *Internal Waters,* 17 Neth. Y.B. Int'l L. 3, 44 (1986)

Damas, Philip & Eric Kulisch, *Nations Back WCO Security Rules,* Am. Shipper, Aug. 2005

Eisenstadt, Mike, *The Sword of the Arabs: Iraq's Strategic Weapons* 6 (Wash. Inst. Policy Papers No. 21)

Fallows, James, *Will Iran be Next?,* Atlantic Monthly (Dec. 2004)

Feinstein, Lee & Anne-Marie Slaughter, *A Duty to Prevent,* 83 Foreign Affairs 136 (2004)

Fidell, Eugene R., *Maritime Transport of Plutonium and Spent Nuclear Fuel,* 31 Int'l Lawyer 757 (1997)

Fielding, Lois E., Maritime Interception" Centerpiece of Economic Sanctions in the New World Order, 53 La. L. Rev. 1191 (1993)

Frowein, Jochen & Nico Kirsch, *Introduction to Chapter VII, in* The Charter of the United Nations: A Comment 701–716 (Bruno Simma, et al. eds. 2d ed. 2002)

Gaddis, John Lewis, *The Long Peace: Elements of Stability in the Postwar International System,* 10 Int'l Security 92–142 (1986)

Garrett, Laurie, *The Nightmare of Bioterrorism,* 80 Foreign Affairs 76 (2001)

Gladwell, Malcolm, *Connecting the Dots,* New Yorker, Mar. 10, 2003

Glennon, Michael J., *How International Rules Die,* 96 Geo. L.J. 939 (2005)

———, *Military Action Against Terrorists Under International Law: The Fog of Law: Self-Defense, Inherence and Incoherence in Article 51 of the United Nations Charter,* 25 Harv. J. L. & Pub. Pol'y 539 (2002)

———, *The Rise and Fall of the U.N. Charter's Use of Force Rules,* 27 Hastings Int'l & Comp. L. Rev. 497 (2004)

———,*Why the Security Council Failed,* Foreign Affairs (2003)

Guillaume, Gilbert, *Terrorism and International Law,* 53 Int'l & Comp. L. Q. 537 (2004)

Hammond, Matthew C., *Note, The Posse Comitatus Act: A Principle in Need of Renewal,* 75 Wash. U.L.Q. 953 (1997)

Happold, Matthew, *Security Council Resolution 1373 and the Constitution of the United Nations,* 16 LEIDEN J. INT'L L. 593 (2003)

Heinegg, Wolff Heintschel von, *The Proliferation Security Initiative: Security vs. Freedom of Navigation,* 35 ISRAEL Y.B. HUMAN RIGHTS 181 (2005)

———, *Naval Blockade,* 75 U.S. Nav. War Coll. INT'L L. STUDIES 203–230 (2000)

———, *Visit, Search, Diversion, and Capture in Naval Warfare, Pts. I & II,* 29 CAN. Y.B. INT'L L. 283 (1991) & 30 Can. Y.B. Int'l L. 89 (1992)

Hess, Berkhard, *The International Law Commission's Draft Convention on Jurisdictional Immunities of States and Their Property,* 4 EUROPEAN J. INT'L L. 269 (1993)

Holmes, James R. & Janne E. Nolan, *Weapons of Mass Destruction and the Proliferation Dilemma: Render unto Caesar: Bureaucracy and Nonproliferation after the Iraq War?,* 28 FLETCHER FORUM WORLD AFFAIRS 73 (2004)

Holmes, James R. & Andrew C. Winner, *WMD: Interdicting the Gravest Danger,* U.S. NAVAL INST. PROC. (Feb. 2005), at 72

Jesus, H.E. José Luis, *Protection of Foreign Ships against Piracy and Terrorism at Sea: Legal Aspects,* 18 INT'L J. MARINE & COASTAL L. 363 (2003)

Jinks, Derek, *State Responsibility for Sponsorship of Terrorist and Insurgent Groups,* 4 CHI. J. INT'L L. 83 (2003)

Joyner, Daniel H., *The Proliferation Security Initiative: Nonproliferation, Counterproliferation, and International Law,* 30 YALE J. INT'L L. 507 (2005)

Kellman, Barry, *Bridling the International Trade in Catastrophic Weapons,* 43 AM. U. L. REV. 755 (1994)

Kirgis, Frederick L., *Cruise Missile Strikes in Afghanistan and Sudan,* ASIL INSIGHTS, Aug. 1998

———, *North Korea's Withdrawal from the Nuclear Proliferation Treaty,* ASIL INSIGHTS, Jan. 2003

Kramek, Joseph E., *Bilateral Maritime Counter-Drug and Immigration Interdiction Agreements: Is this the World of the Future?,* 31 U. MIAMI INTER-AM. L. REV. 121, 133–34 (2000)

Kulisch, Erick, *U.S., EU Cooperate: Agreement Paves Way for Expanding Container Security Initiative,* AM. SHIPPER, June 2004, at 17

Lake, Anthony, *American Power and American Diplomacy,* 5 U.S. DEP'T OF STATE DISPATCH 46 (1994)

———, *Confronting Backlash States,* 73 FOREIGN AFFAIRS 45 (1994)

Lederer, Calvin M., *Developments Involving the Convention on the Suppression of Unlawful Acts Affecting Maritime Navigation,* 2004 Y.B. COMITÉ MARITIME INT'L 45

Lehman, John, *Our Enemy is Not Terrorism,* U.S. NAVAL INST. PROC. (May 2004), at 52

Lehrman, Thomas D., *Note: Enhancing the Proliferation Security Initiative: The Case for a Decentralized Nonproliferation Architecture,* 45 VA. J. INT'L L. 223 (2004)

Lillich, Richard B., *Forcible Self-Help Under International Law,* 62 U.S. Nav. War Coll. INT'L L. STUDIES 129 (1980)

Linnan, David, *Iran Air Flight 655 and Beyond: Mistaken Self-Defense and State Responsibility,* 16 YALE J. INT'L L. 245 (1991)

Logan, Samuel E., *The Proliferation Security Initiative: Navigating the Legal Challenges,* 14 J. TRANS. L. & POL'Y 253 (2005)

Lowe, A. Vaughan, *The Development and Concept of the Contiguous Zone,* 1981 BRIT. Y.B. INT'L L. 109 (1982)

———, *The Right of Entry into Maritime Ports in Customary Law,* 14 SAN DIEGO L. REV. 597 (1986)

Loy, James M. & Robert G. Ross, *Global Trade: America's Achilles' Heel,* 7 DEFENSE HORIZONS (Feb. 2002)

McDorman, Ted L., *Stateless Fishing Vessels, International Law and the U.N. High Seas Fisheries Conference,* 25 J. MAR. L. & COM. 531 (1994)

McDougal, Myres S., *Authority to Use Force on the High Seas,* 61 U.S. Nav. War Coll. INT'L L. STUDIES 551 (1979)

McHugh, James J., *Forcible Self-Help in International Law,* 62 U.S. Nav. War Coll. INT'L L. STUDIES 139 (1980)

Mobley, Richard, *The Beira Patrol,* 55 NAVAL WAR COLLEGE REV. 63 (2002)

Moran, Daniel, *The International Law of the Sea in a Globalized World,* in GLOBALIZATION AND MARITIME POWER (Sam J. Tangredi, ed., 2002)

Motley, Robert, *Suspicionless Inspections,* AM. SHIPPER (May 2004), at 90

Murray, Christopher F., *Note: Any Port in a Storm? The Right of Entry for Reasons of Force Majeure or Distress in the Wake of the* Erika *and the* Castor, 63 OHIO ST. L.J. 1465 (2002/2003)

Orlov, Vladimir A., *Illicit Nuclear Trafficking and the New Agency,* IAEA BULLETIN 46/1, at 55 (June 2004)

Oxman, Bernard, *The Regime of Warships Under the United Nations Convention on the Law of the Sea,* 24 VA. J. INT'L L. 813 (1984)

Pardo-Guerra, Juan Pablo, *Nanotechnology and the International Regime on Chemical and Biological Weapons,* 2 NANOTECHNOLOGY, LAW & BUS. NO. 1 (2005)

Perry, William J., *Preparing for the Next Attack,* 80 FOREIGN AFFAIRS 31 (2001)

Porterfield, Richard B., *Naval Intelligence: Transforming to Meet the Threat,* U.S. NAV. INST. PROC. (SEPT. 2005), at 13

Powell, Colin L., *A Strategy of Partnerships,* 83 FOREIGN AFFAIRS 22 (2004)

Reisman, W. Michael, *Why Regime Changes Are (Almost Always) Wrong,* Hudson Medal Lecture to the 98th Annual Meeting of the American Society of International Law, Apr. 2, 2004, 98 AM J. INT'L L. 516 (2004)

Reuland, Robert C.F., *Note, Interference with Non-National Ships on the High Seas: Peacetime Exceptions to the Exclusivity of Flag-State Jurisdiction,* 22 VAND. J. TRANSNAT'L L. 1161 (1989)

Roach, J. Ash, *Container and Port Security,* 18 INT'L J. MARINE & COASTAL L. (Sept. 2003)

Roberts, Guy, *The Counterproliferation Self Help Paradigm: A Legal Regime for Enforcing the Norm Prohibiting the Proliferation of Weapons of Mass Destruction,* 27 DENV. J. INT'L L. & POL'Y 483 (1999)

Robertson, Horace B., *Interdiction of Iraqi Maritime Commerce in the 1990–1991 Persian Gulf Conflict,* 22 OCEAN DEV. & INT'L L. 289 (1992)

Rogoff, Kenneth, *The Cost of Living Dangerously: Can the Global Economy Absorb the Expenses of Fighting Terrorism?,* FOREIGN POL'Y 70 (Nov./Dec. 2004)

Rosand, Eric, *Current Developments, Security Council Resolution 1373, the Counter-Terrorism Committee, and the Fight Against Terrorism,* 97 AM. J. INT'L L. 333 (2003)

Schachte, William L. Jr. & J. Peter A. Bernhardt, *International Straits and Navigational Freedoms,* 33 VA. J. INT'L L. 527 (1993)

Schmitt, Michael N., *Preemptive Strategies in International Law,* 24 MICH. J. INT'L L. 513 (2003)

Shearer, Ivan A., *The Development of International Law with Respect to the Law Enforcement Role of Navies and Coast Guards in Peacetime,* 71 U.S. Nav. War Coll. INT'L L. STUDIES 429 (1998)

Sloss, David. *Forcible Arms Control: Preemption Attacks on Nuclear Facilities,* 4 CHI. J. INT'L L. 39 (2003)

Sofaer, Abraham D., *Terrorism, The Law, and The National Defense,* 126 MIL. L. REV. 89 (1989)

———, *Terrorism and the Law,* 64 FOREIGN AFFAIRS 901 (1986)

Sohn, Louis, *Peacetime Use of Force on the High Seas,* 64 U.S. Nav. War Coll. INT'L L. STUDIES 38 (1991)

Soons, Alfred H.A., *Enforcing the Economic Embargo at Sea,* in UNITED NATIONS SANCTIONS AND INTERNATIONAL LAW 307–24 (W. Gowlland-Debbas, ed., 2001)

———, *Reflections on the Practice of International Law* (T.D. Gill & W.P. Heere, eds. 2000)

Stern, Jessica, *The Protean Enemy,* 82 FOREIGN AFFAIRS 27 (2003)

Stewart, David P., *The UN Convention on Jurisdictional Immunities of States and Their Property,* 99 AM. J. INT'L L. 194 (2005)

Stossel, Scott, *North Korea: The War Game,* ATLANTIC MONTHLY 97 (July/Aug. 2005)

Szasz, Paul C., *The Security Council Starts Legislating,* 96 AM. J. INT'L L. 901 (2002)

Treves, Tullio, *Flags of Convenience Before the Law of the Sea Tribunal,* 6 SAN DIEGO INT'L L. J. 179 (2004)

Trimble, Phillip R., *The Supreme Court and International Law: The Demise of Restatement Section 403,* 89 AM. J. INT'L L. 53 (1995)

Weisburd, A. Mark. *Due Process Limits on Federal Extraterritorial Legislation?,* 35 COLUM. J. TRANSNAT'L L. 379 (1997)

Williams, Malcolm J., *Bilateral Maritime Agreements Enhancing International Cooperation in Suppression of Illicit Maritime Narcotics Trafficking,* in OCEANS POLICY: NEW INSTITUTIONS, CHALLENGES AND OPPORTUNITIES (Myron H. Nordquist & John Norton Moore, ed. 1999)

Winner, Andrew C., *The Proliferation Security Initiative: The New Face of Interdiction,* 28 WASH. QTRLY. 129 (Spring 2005)

Ye Ru'an & Zhao Qinghai, *The PSI: Chinese Thinking and Concerns,* THE MONITOR 22 (Spring 2004)

Zeigler, Richard, *Ubi Sumus? Quo Vadimus? Charting the Course of Maritime Interception Operations,* 43 NAVAL L. REV. 1 (1996)

———, *Al Qaeda, Amorphous But Alive,* THE ECONOMIST, June 5, 2004

———, *Criminal Liability for Transportation of Explosives and Other Dangerous Articles under 18 U.S.C.A. §§ 831–835,* 8 ALR FED. 938

———, *Nuclear Weapons: An Exchange,* 54 Naval War Coll. Rev. 13–46 (2001)

———, *North Korea: Playing With Plutonium,* THE ECONOMIST, Jan. 24, 2004, at 36–37

———, *North Korea's Nuclear Taunts: Don't be Panicked,* THE ECONOMIST, Jan. 24, 2004, at 15

———, *Perils on the Sea,* THE ECONOMIST, Oct. 2, 2003

———, *Proliferating Worries,* THE ECONOMIST, Mar. 1, 2004

———, *Special Report on Proliferation,* THE ECONOMIST, Feb. 28, 2004, at 27
———, *The Nation-State is Dead. Long Live the Nation-State,* THE ECONOMIST, Dec. 23, 1995, at 15–18
———, *Weapons of Mass Destruction: If You Push I'll Shove,* THE ECONOMIST, July 10, 2004, at 40–41

Index

About the Author

CRAIG H. ALLEN is the Judson Falknor Professor of Law at the University of Washington in Seattle. He joined the university faculty in 1996, following his retirement from the U.S. Coast Guard. He is a licensed master mariner and serves on the U.S. Navigation Safety Council. He is also on the board of editors of *Ocean Development and International Law* and is the author of *Farwell's Rules of the Nautical Road* (Naval Institute Press, 2004). For the 2006–2007 academic year he served as the Charles H. Stockton Chair in International Law at the U.S. Naval War College.